Test by Fire

THE EVOLVING AMERICAN PRESIDENCY SERIES

Series Foreword:

The American Presidency touches virtually every aspect of American and world politics. And the presidency has become, for better or worse, the vital center of the American and global political systems. The Framers of the American government would be dismayed at such a result. As invented at the Philadelphia Constitutional Convention in 1787, the Presidency was to have been a part of a government with shared and overlapping powers, embedded within a separation-of-powers system. If there was a vital center, it was the Congress; the Presidency was to be a part, but by no means, the centerpiece of that system.

Over time, the presidency has evolved and grown in power, expectations, responsibilities, and authority. Wars, crises, depressions, industrialization, all served to add to the power of the presidency. And as the United States grew into a world power, presidential power also grew. As the United States became the world's leading superpower, the presidency rose in prominence and power, not only in the U.S., but on the world stage.

It is the clash between the presidency as invented and the presidency as it has developed that inspired this series. And it is the importance and power of the modern American presidency that makes understanding the office so vital. Like it or not, the American Presidency stands at the vortex of power both within the United States and across the globe.

This Palgrave series recognizes that the Presidency is and has been an evolving institution, going from the original constitutional design as a Chief Clerk, to today where the president is the center of the American political constellation. This has caused several key dilemmas in our political system, not the least of which is that presidents face high expectations with limited constitutional resources. This causes presidents to find extra-constitutional means of governing. Thus, presidents must find ways to bridge the expectations/power gap while operating within the confines of a separation-of-powers system designed to limit presidential authority. How presidents resolve these challenges and paradoxes is the central issue in modern governance. It is also the central theme of this book series.

Michael A. Genovese
Loyola Chair of Leadership
Loyola Marymount University
Palgrave's **The Evolving American Presidency**, Series Editor

The Second Term of George W. Bush
>edited by Robert Maranto, Douglas M. Brattebo, and Tom Lansford

The Presidency and the Challenge of Democracy
>edited by Michael A. Genovese and Lori Cox Han

Religion and the American Presidency
>edited by Mark J. Rozell and Gleaves Whitney

Religion and the Bush Presidency
>edited by Mark J. Rozell and Gleaves Whitney

Test by Fire: The War Presidency of George W. Bush
>by Robert Swansbrough

Test by Fire

The War Presidency of George W. Bush

Robert Swansbrough

palgrave
macmillan

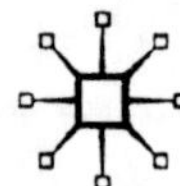

TEST BY FIRE
Copyright © Robert Swansbrough, 2008.

First published in 2008 by
PALGRAVE MACMILLAN™
175 Fifth Avenue, New York, N.Y. 10010 and
Houndmills, Basingstoke, Hampshire, England RG21 6XS
Companies and representatives throughout the world.

PALGRAVE MACMILLAN is the global academic imprint of the Palgrave Macmillan division of St. Martin's Press, LLC and of Palgrave Macmillan Ltd. Macmillan® is a registered trademark in the United States, United Kingdom and other countries. Palgrave is a registered trademark in the European Union and other countries.

ISBN-13: 978–0–230–60100–0 paperback
ISBN-10: 0–230–60100–6 paperback
ISBN-13: 978–0–230–60099–7 hardback
ISBN-10: 0–230–60099–9 hardback

Library of Congress Cataloging-in-Publication Data

Swansbrough, Robert H.
　　　Test by fire : the war presidency of George W. Bush / by Robert Swansbrough.
　　　　　p. cm.—(The evolving American presidency series)
　　　Includes bibliographical references and index.
　　　ISBN 0–230–60099–9—ISBN 0–230–60100–6
　　　　1. United States—Foreign relations—2001– 2. United States—Military policy.
　　3. War on Terrorism, 2001– 4. Afghan War, 2001– 5. Iraq War, 2003–
　　6. Bush, George W. (George Walker), 1946– I. Title. II. Series.
JZ1480.S93 2008
973.931—dc22　　　　　　　　　　　　　　　　　　　　　　　　　2007045898

A catalogue record for this book is available from the British Library.

Design by Newgen Imaging Systems (P) Ltd., Chennai, India.

First edition: May 2008

10 9 8 7 6 5 4 3 2 1

Printed in the United States of America.

I dedicate this book to the American men and women who serve or have served in Afghanistan and Iraq since the 9/11 attacks. As a former Navy officer from the Vietnam era, I respectfully salute their courage, sacrifice, and patriotism.

Contents

Acknowledgments   xi

Foreword   xiii

Preface   xvii

Introduction

One   **A War President's Decisions: Seeking Insights**   3
     The War President   3
     Changing Personas   5
     Three Analytical Lenses   11
     Critical Choices   14
     An Ambitious Agenda   17

Part I   Path to the White House

Two   **The Fortunate Son: Star-Spangled Eyes**   23
     Looking Up to Dad   23
     The Family Business   29
     Deep Pockets, Empty Wells   31
     The Loyalty Thermometer   32
     Political Home Run   34

Three   **Lone Star Challenger: A Taste of Power**   37
     Karl Rove, the Architect   37
     Changing the Texas Landscape   39
     Challenging an Icon   44
     Lone Star Governor   48
     Launching a Second Term   51

Four   **White House Quest: Selling the Son**   53
     Crafting the Plan   53
     Bumps in the Road   55
     The Image Battles   61
     Debate Face-Off   64
     Nose-to-Nose Finish   65

Part II   A War President Emerges

Five   **The Early Months: Clear-Eyed Realism**   71
     A Seasoned Team   71

Strategic Ambiguity or Confusion?   78
Missile Defense, Not Terrorism   81
Rejecting Clinton's Diplomacy   84
A Unilateralist Course?   85

Six   Ignored Warnings: A Call to Destiny   89
A Zigzag Return   90
Taking Charge   91
Opportunity Costs   95
A Flawed Process   97
Personality and Politics   101

Seven   New Kind of War: Breaking the Rules   105
The "Quaint" Geneva Conventions   106
Walk on the Dark Side   108
Hidden from View   111
Big Brother is Listening   113
Creating a New Paradigm   117

Eight   March to War: Vision or Vengeance?   123
Victory or Unfinished Business?   123
The Neoconservatives' Moment   125
Next Step in War on Terror   128
Words of War   130
Decision-Making in the Shadows   136

Nine   Bush's War: Break It…and It's Yours   139
Shock, Awe, and Chaos   139
Viceroy in Combat Boots   144
A Bloody Cakewalk   147
A Futile Search   149
The Blame Game   152

Part III   Pursuing a Vision

Ten   Axis of Evil: An Inverted Threat Matrix   159
Friends to Bitter Foes   160
Rejecting Engagement   162
A Diplomatic Agreement   168
A Visceral Enemy   170
A Revised Approach   174

Eleven   Ending Tyranny: Bush's Democracy Agenda   177
Controlled Path to Democracy   178
Israel in His Heart   182
Democracy Boomerangs   186
The Hezbollah Challenge   189
Clashing Goals   191

Conclusion

Twelve **Tested by Fire: Mixed Legacy**   **197**
    Progress or Morass?   198
    The Decider   202
    A Last Hurrah   205
    Assessment of the War President   209
    Hallowed Pantheon   212

Notes   215

Bibliography   255

Index   280

Acknowledgments

I deeply appreciate the helpful comments of a number of colleagues who reviewed various chapters in the manuscript. Professors Loch Johnson, Fouad Moughrabi, and David Brodsky made substantive and stylistic suggestions that proved quite significant. Dr. Spiro Macris also applied his keen eye to review several chapters. Of course, any errors are my responsibility.

Most importantly, I would like to acknowledge the insightful observations and corrections of my son Jimmy Swansbrough, who employed his fine Davidson College education in English to thoughtfully critique my presentation in many of the chapters. As both a writing teacher and a writer, his comments proved extremely valuable.

Karen Adsit, my computer guru for those mysterious problems that arise in software, patiently helped me resolve those technical issues. She and Charles Hart of the Grayson Walker Teaching Resource Center at the University of Tennessee at Chattanooga provided assistance when I encountered difficulties.

I would also like to thank the UTC Library staff for their long-term and patient cooperation in helping me obtain reference materials and obtain inter-library loan journal articles, documents, and books. The Reference staff guided me through the bewildering array of Internet search engines to find materials that used to take many hours of browsing in the library stacks and card catalogue.

A UTC sabbatical afforded me a semester to concentrate on the manuscript, without worrying about teaching or administrative responsibilities. Dean Herbert Burhenn provided additional time so I could meet the deadline for the manuscript. The dean's staff, Terry Zimmer and Marge Fergason, extended their support while I worked on the book.

Toby Wahl at Palgrave McMillan bestowed the essential editor's encouragement and friendly nudges to complete the project on schedule, aided by his editorial assistant Emily Hue.

My daughter Christy also offered encouragement throughout this long process.

And last, but not least, I appreciate my wife Mary's patience, particularly as the manuscript submission deadline approached and I hovered over my computer on weekends to complete the final editing. Yes, you will get your husband back!

Foreword

Robert Swansbrough, a scholar of the presidency, has always shown great breadth in his understanding of America's premier political office. I have followed his career as a political scientist and university administrator for almost forty years. What has struck me most about his work, other than the consistently clear style of writing, is his holistic approach to research. He is remarkably sensitive to the interplay among the three levels of analysis—international, domestic, and individual—that preoccupies students of the presidency.

All too often studies of various presidents and their administrations limit their examination to how well the United States coped with foreign crises. Or, more commonly, scholars will probe the successes and failures of presidents at home, as they face the inevitable buffeting of domestic politics that push against administrations from all sides. Sometimes, too, although this is more rare, political scientists will attempt to tell us something about the president as an individual, delving into the idiosyncrasies of personalities in the White House and the question of psychological affects on public policy. Professor Swansbrough knows that none of these influences can be overlooked, and that they interact in myriad ways to shape the contours of an administration. His forte lies in tracing these often-subtle relationships.

He brings other strengths to his study of the George W. Bush administration. He understands the importance of theory and elsewhere has crafted sophisticated, lucid models of presidential behavior; but most of his writing, and certainly this book, concentrates on dissecting the interwoven stories of history and politics that are the warp and woof of every administration. Swansbrough's work reminds us that history without a sense of politics, or politics without a sense of history, are exercises in taxidermy. Only when the two are brought together does the subject come alive. Swansbrough's ability to explore the second Bush administration on all three levels of analysis, while bringing to the story the richly textured history and politics of this era, make this book an extraordinarily good read as well as a mother lode of scholarly insight into the rocky ride George W. Bush has given the nation.

The definitive analysis of this administration will not come for another 50 years, when key classified documents and sealed private papers are finally released to the public. In the meantime, Swansbrough's study provides us with as reliable and perceptive a look into these recent years as one is apt to find. Certainly his choice of a topic could hardly be more riveting or significant. While President Bush's tenure started off in a mundane fashion, with the president headed down the road to obscurity and a legacy comparable to that of Millard Fillmore or Franklin Pierce, the terrorist attacks of 9/11 and the subsequent wars in Afghanistan and Iraq have guaranteed this presidency will not be soon forgotten.

Especially controversial has been the manner in which the Bush administration responded to the terrorist attacks of September 11, 2001. At first stunned by the boldness and the horror of the attacks, the administration soon had in its crosshairs the group responsible: al Qaeda, along with the Taliban regime in Afghanistan that had provided a haven for the terrorists. Thanks largely to a contingency plan against Al Qaeda that the Central Intelligence Agency (CIA) had been working on since 1998, the administration was able to retaliate rapidly, forcefully, and successfully against the Taliban regime, overthrowing its grip on Afghanistan through a coordinated combination of CIA covert action, Special Forces operations, B-52 bombing, and able assistance from anti-Taliban factions inside Afghanistan known as the Northern Alliance (residing in the northern region of the nation).

The administration failed, however, to close the noose on the Al Qaeda leadership, which managed to flee to mountainous redoubts along the Afghan-Pakistani border. Otherwise, the military and intelligence operations were a textbook success, with the Taliban government smashed and Al Qaeda in disarray. The CIA has never had a finer hour since its establishment in 1947; and the skill with which U.S. spies and soldiers worked together was striking. Then, as Professor Swansbrough chronicles so well in this book, things began to fall apart.

The most fateful decision made by the Bush administration after this initial success against the 9/11 terrorists was to shift the nation's attention and resources away from finishing the job. Instead, the White House turned toward another adversary: Saddam Hussein of Iraq. How could this have happened? Much of this book offers answers to this complicated question, which is bound up in the views of so-called neoconservatives toward the world and above all their goal of enhancing the safety of Israel. The neoconservatives held influential positions in the administration, such as Paul Wolfowitz, the second-in-command at the Department of Defense. They managed to persuade the president and Vice President Dick Cheney to adopt a radical new approach toward the conduct of American foreign policy: coercive democracy. It was not enough to declare one's support for democratic regimes around the world, in the spirit of Woodrow Wilson, John F. Kennedy, and Ronald Reagan; one had to use the unmatched military might of the United States to overthrow dictators around the globe and install in their place democratic regimes—starting with Saddam.

Moreover, as advisors in the administration underscored for the president, the remaining Al Qaeda and Taliban targets in Afghanistan were ghost-like, hiding in deep caves that made B-52 bombing raids irrelevant. In contrast, Iraq offered a target-rich environment. More important still, Saddam was arguably the major long-term threat to Israel in the Middle East. Further, he had attempted to assassinate the president's mother and father, Barbara and George H.W. Bush, when they toured Kuwait after the 1991 war against Iraq. This was personal. Also, conveniently, the CIA and most of its companion intelligence agencies feared that Saddam might have developed weapons of mass destruction (WMDs). Here was a plausible public reason for going to war, even if the intelligence was more ambiguous than the White House wanted to believe (or the director of Central Intelligence communicated to the president), and even though the supposed presence of WMDs could have been determined within a few months, had not the administration rushed to war for its other purposes.

So off to battle the nation went in March of 2003, joined by what the president referred to as a "coalition of the willing," but which included only the United Kingdom and a rag-tag group of half-hearted supporters (several of whom were bought off by promises of increased U.S. foreign aid). Accompanying the war in Iraq and the wider global struggle against Islamic extremists came a series of overreactions: the torture of detainees at the Abu Ghraib prison in Baghdad; their imprisonment without counsel or trial at Guantánamo, secret CIA prisons in Albania (among other places), "extraordinary renditions" that had the CIA kidnapping terrorist suspects in Europe and flying them to brutal prisons in Cairo and elsewhere. As news of these activities seeped out to the world, the standing of the United States plummeted—even in places such as Australia and Scandinavia, where America had been held in high regard.

The myths surrounding the war were profoundly misleading and fed by the administration's spin-doctors. The war would be paid for with Iraqi oil money. American troops would be greeted as liberators and handed flowers by the Iraqis, just like U.S. soldiers along the Champs-Elysées in 1945. A small and nimble U.S. force could get the job done, topple Saddam, and come home, easy as pie. The initial invasion did go well, but then Iraq quickly turned into another Vietnam: costly in blood and treasure, with no victory in sight, a quagmire. President Bush, egged on by his vice president and the neocons, had rolled the dice down the table in the name of democracy and, by 2007, History had called out "snake eyes." President Bush, no longer a Fillmore or Pierce, had taken on the attributes of a Lyndon Johnson—a failed presidency stained irreparably by a failed war.

This is the story that lies before the reader in this book, told better here than anywhere else—a story of tragic dimensions that will continue to haunt the United States for decades. It is a story that holds important lessons for those who study it closely. May these lessons be learned and remembered by all of us who seek a United States that is, as John Quincy Adams so wisely advised in his Inaugural Address, "the friend of all the liberties in the world, [but] the guardian of only her own."

Loch K. Johnson
Author of *Seven Sins of American
Foreign Policy*

Preface

*I'm a war president. I make decisions here in the Oval Office
in foreign-policy matters with war on my mind.*

After his January 1993 inauguration, America's forty-first president—George H.W. Bush—proudly escorted friends on personal tours of the historic White House. The former vice president would pause reflectively before his favorite painting, George Healy's "The Peacemakers," portraying President Abraham Lincoln with his Civil War generals. "He was tested by fire," Bush would tell his old friends, thus demonstrating his greatness.[1]

The elder President Bush, a decorated World War II Navy torpedo plane pilot and seasoned Cold War warrior, also spoke candidly with top White House aides about his belief that only presidents victorious in war became truly great American presidents.

The elder President Bush soon faced his major test by fire—wartime leadership—when he masterly forged in 1991 a broad international diplomatic and military alliance that forced Iraqi dictator Saddam Hussein to withdraw his occupying troops from Kuwait after a blatant act of aggression. American-led coalition forces wracked great destruction upon Iraq's armed forces and armor, compelling Saddam Hussein to order battered troops to retreat under fearsome firepower.

However, despite the stunning battlefield victory, the brutal dictator retained power in Baghdad. Saddam Hussein's subsequent bloody repression of uprisings by Iraqi Shiites and Kurds generated criticism in the United States about the premature conclusion of the Gulf War, contributing to the failure of George Bush to attain the coveted status of a great American president. Indeed, despite the impressive victory of the senior Bush as a War President, albeit in a "limited war," George H.W. Bush lost his reelection bid for a second White House term, which embittered his admiring namesake son, George W. Bush.

A decade later George W. Bush, only the second president to enter the White House after his father, would likewise face the leadership test of fire after the horrendous September 11, 2001, al Qaeda terrorist attacks on the World Trade Center and Pentagon. President George W. Bush confronted that challenge by proclaiming a war on terror, attacking al Qaeda and Taliban forces in Afghanistan and then invading Iraq to remove Saddam Hussein from power. But will history evaluate the twenty-first century's first War President as having successfully passed the test by fire to achieve a place in the hallowed Pantheon of great American presidents? That represents the underlying theme in this book and analysis of President Bush's war on terrorism.

In attempting to analyze George W. Bush as a War President, one quickly discovers the wisdom embodied in John Godfrey Saxe's poem "The Blind Men and the Elephant," based upon an old tale from India. The first blind man touches the large animal's sturdy side and describes the Elephant as like a wall. A second feels a tusk and describes the Elephant as smooth and sharp, like a spear. The next blind man grasps the squirming trunk and pictures the Elephant like a snake. The fourth reaches out and touches a mighty leg, describing it as like a tree. The next one rubs the ear and compares it to a fan. The sixth blind man seizes the swinging tail and declares the Elephant is like a rope. The lesson of the parable: "Though each was partly in the right, And all were in the wrong!"[2]

The White House of President George W. Bush established an opaque cloak of secrecy to purposely blind observers from internal deliberations over policy issues. David Gergen, adviser to four presidents (both Republican and Democrat), observed on a CNN program: "This administration has engaged in secrecy at a level we have not seen in over 30 years."[3] Early in the administration, Vice President Dick Cheney stood firm against releasing information about his energy task force's meeting with major oil company executives to the Government Accountability Office. [4] Cheney asserted—supported by President Bush—that since Watergate too much information has been made public, impairing White House decision-making and undermining presidential authority.

White House press secretary Ari Fleischer criticized Congress for "fishing expeditions and endless investigations," as the Legislative Branch sought to exercise its oversight responsibilities.[5] On national security issues the Bush administration advanced a similar claim vis-à-vis congressional oversight committees seeking information that could justify the commander-in-chief's authorization of the National Security Agency's (NSA) surveillance over American citizens' communications without court approval.[6]

The White House emphasis on secrecy and "message discipline" prevented leaks about internal disputes. Bush officials placed questionable team players either in the "ice box," as Powell called the exclusion from key decision-making, or ousted them from their posts.[7] However, the isolated White House appeared tone-deaf to warnings from congressional Republicans, unaware of the growing opposition to the war in Iraq and insensitive to worries about homeland security, such as when the Bush administration approved a Dubai company to run six American ports.[8]

After President Bush's job approval rating plunged to 31 percent in May 2006, the newly appointed Chief of Staff Joshua B. Bolten tried to bring greater transparency and different viewpoints into the insular Bush White House in a concerted effort to bolster the president's standing with Congress and the public.[9] As one Republican close to the administration described the change, "There is more openness, there is more real discussion about the challenges that are faced. People aren't trying to gloss over bad news."[10]

No wonder Congress, the press, and the public—though not blind—could not penetrate the Bush administration's barrier of secrecy. Outsiders could not understand how the War President established his goals, strategies, and political objectives—or determine whether contrary or even cautious voices received any attention.

Furthermore, public opinion polls revealed a yawning chasm of partisan polarization, unmatched in prior administrations for the level of intensity separating Republican and Democrat attitudes toward President George W. Bush. The Gallup Poll found a 64-point gap between the Republican and Democrat job ratings of Bush in May 2006, greater than the widest partisan divisions for Presidents

Reagan, Bill Clinton, Bush senior, or Jimmy Carter.[11] In his book *A Divider, Not a Uniter,* Gary C. Jacobson concluded that George W. Bush was "the most divisive occupant of the White House in at least 50 years."[12]

Therefore, as in the parable about the blind men and the Elephant, most Republicans pictured President Bush and his tough-minded foreign policy as a wall, a resolute bulwark against terrorists. In sharp contrast, many Democrats depicted Bush as a dangerous snake; his ill-advised policies cost American lives overseas, antagonized the world against the United States, and deflected resources from pressing problems at home. But like the fable, other Americans perceived the nature of the Elephant differently. Neoconservatives, buoyed by the Bush administration's post-9/11 aggressiveness, described the Elephant as a spear, with Bush rightly asserting America's dominant role over global affairs as the sole superpower.

On the other hand, a growing number of congressmen felt that the White House represented a rope that constricted their constitutional role in the foreign policy-making process, tightened through mushrooming claims of presidential war powers. And Born-Again white fundamentalists perceived the president as a sturdy tree, firmly rooted with staunch Christian beliefs, standing tall against the howling winds of terrorists, abortionists, and gays. As Saxe concluded his fable: "Though each was partly in the right, And all were in the wrong!"

Introduction

Chapter One

A War President's Decisions: Seeking Insights

If I could give you the job description, it would be "decision-maker."
I have to make a lot of decisions.

President George W. Bush's evolution into a War President, triggered by the 9/11 terrorist attacks, involved a series of decisions on how to respond to the bloody assault upon American soil that led to his global campaign against terrorism. Probing the factors that influenced President Bush's important decisions in his war against terror reveals how the 43rd president perceived the challenges, weighed different viewpoints, and responded with orders to mobilize the tremendous resources of the U.S. government.

President Bush did not make those decisions in a vacuum. He had to evaluate information flowing from many sources, select among the competing bureaucratic policy recommendations, and bolster public, congressional, and international confidence in his leadership ability—untested at that point in time. Bush's MBA training, political personas, and limited experience in international affairs all played a role in his response to the 9/11 horror.

The War President

President George W. Bush delivered his first State of the Union address on January 29, 2002, shortly after U.S. armed forces had overthrown the Taliban regime in Afghanistan and destroyed al Qaeda's terrorist training bases in that country. He spoke to the nation as a triumphant War President, radiating the confidence emanating from a halo of astronomical job approval ratings. The president rallied both Republicans and Democrats after the 9/11 terrorist attacks to back his military actions against the Taliban and the al Qaeda terrorist plotters. Other nations flocked to America's banner after the airliners hijacked by al Qaeda zealots struck the U.S. World Trade Center, killing almost 3,000 innocent people. Indeed, an editorial in the liberal French newspaper Le Monde declared, "Today we are all Americans."[1]

In the address a resolute President Bush sounded an alarm to awaken the shell-shocked American people about the looming menace of an "axis of evil" consisting of three dangerous states: Iraq, Iran, and North Korea.[2] The production of weapons of mass destruction by those rogue states, Bush direly warned, could provide terrorist groups such as al Qaeda with deadly tools to attack the United States, its allies, and friends. Identifying Iraq as the most pressing menace, President Bush planted the seeds that he hoped would grow into broad support for a military campaign against the Iraqi dictator Saddam Hussein in the coming months—the second step in his war on terror.

A year later President Bush marshaled his State of the Union rhetoric to highlight—on the eve of the Iraq war—the vast quantity of weapons of mass destruction in Saddam Hussein's arsenal and the regime's ties to al Qaeda terrorists. But at the time of the January 2003 speech, Bush's ratings had fallen drastically as the international community, congressional opponents, and the general public expressed reservations over the administration's relentless drive for a preemptive war with Iraq.

President Bush cited a 1999 UN report and intelligence sources to bolster his contention that Iraq possessed huge stores of weapons of mass destruction (WMD). Bush employed a worst-case scenario to dramatize a danger that seamlessly blended the public's terrifying memories of 9/11 with a deep fear of chemical and biological weapons in the hands of the demonic Saddam Hussein: "Imagine those 19 hijackers with other weapons and other plans—this time armed by Saddam Hussein. *It would take one vial, one canister, one crate slipped into this country to bring a day of horror like none we have ever known*" (author's emphasis).[3]

President Bush revealed that his well-respected Secretary of State Colin Powell would present classified U.S. intelligence to the UN Security Council on February 5 to prove America's charges against Iraq.

President Bush announced the start of the war against Iraq on March 19, 2003. After an intense precision bombing and missile campaign, a strategy labeled "Shock and Awe" by the Pentagon, coalition forces invaded Iraq and commenced a swift, successful drive toward Baghdad.[4] On May 1 President Bush, donning a flight suit reminiscent of the popular movie "Top Gun," landed on the deck of the aircraft carrier *USS Abraham Lincoln* near the coast of San Diego, California. A huge "Mission Accomplished" banner—supplied by the White House—provided the backdrop for this photo opportunity that symbolized Bush's second military victory as the nation's War President.

However, the increasingly costly occupation of Iraq by U.S. forces, rising violence by insurgents, bloody suicide attacks by Islamic *jihadists* (Muslim warriors in a holy war), and limited international participation in the administration's "coalition of the willing" combined in 2004 to almost evenly divide the public on President Bush's handling of the situation in Iraq. The inability of American armed forces to check the growing violence in Iraq, with mounting American casualties, impaired Bush's reputation as a successful War President.

The president's political advisers decided to unofficially kick-off Bush's 2004 reelection campaign by utilizing the State of the Union address to frame his reelection message. President Bush's formal address in the majestic House chamber sought to spotlight his image as the nation's steadfast commander-in-chief, boldly leading the Afghanistan and Iraq military operations in the worldwide war on terror—while simultaneously countering terrorist threats at home.

Presidential aides sought to boost Bush's political stature by scheduling a February 8 interview in the Oval Office on NBC's "Meet the Press" with Tim Russert. A Bush campaign adviser explained that the Russert interview would highlight President George W. Bush as more human and humble. "I think that will make him a little less vulnerable to charges of arrogance and hardheadedness."[5]

Early in the TV program Tim Russert asked President Bush why the newly appointed commission investigating U.S. intelligence on WMD would report five months after the presidential election. The president's lengthy answer stressed several times, "We still have a dangerous world." Then he suddenly exclaimed: *"I'm a war president.* I make decisions here in the Oval Office in foreign-policy matters with war on my mind" (author's emphasis).[6]

One observer got to the heart of Bush's interview with Russert—President Bush's idealized image of an American leader. Anne Applebaum wrote, "The overall impression is one of a man striving to live up to his own preconceived notions of what a 'leader' should be: tough, decisive, a man with rapid-fire answers, never wrong about anything, never making a mistake."[7] In essence, President Bush and his advisers sought to cast the 43rd president as embodying the perceived leadership strengths of the Republican Party's modern icon—President Ronald Reagan—rather than Bush's father.

George W. Bush's vaunted standard for leadership—especially by a War President—guided his administration after the 9/11 terrorist attacks. Bush's national security team analyzed all threats through the prism of this heroic model to create, sustain, and defend the image of a stalwart War President. Therefore, President Bush could not acknowledge strategic misjudgments, admit policy mistakes, or hold key subordinates accountable for errors.

However, fulfilling the requirements of such an assertive, bold, and unyielding posture became a double-bladed sword for Bush as War President. One edge of the sharp sword blade could slice opponents of George W. Bush's aggressive foreign policies as weak, vacillating, or unpatriotic. But the opposite edge of the president's war sword could cut Bush himself for his brash, arrogant, and risky approach toward global challenges. *Test by Fire* examines how President George W. Bush—as the self-proclaimed War President—handled that double-edged sword in leading America in the war on terror, dealing with the axis of evil states and pursuing his vision of a democratic Middle East.

Changing Personas

The White House prefers to portray George W. Bush as a simple man, embracing Christian values stemming from his mid-life Born Again experience, while leading the nation with a courageous, consistent, and uncompromising policy course. But Bush represents an elusive, complex target to fully understand since George W.'s beliefs, aspirations, and behavior shifted throughout the course of his life. George W. Bush's different personas can be analyzed through three distinct styles and behaviors: the Bombastic Bushkin, Machiavellian Politico, and Righteous Hawk.

Bombastic Bushkin

The earliest and most persistent persona is the "Bombastic Bushkin," as his Midland (Texas) friends called him. During his prep school years, Bush's tart-tongued quips won him the admiring moniker of "The Lip." Although not a gifted Andover athlete or student like his father, George W. used his wit, gregariousness, and rough-edged humor to gain attention and applause from his teenage peers. When the younger Bush attended Yale he displayed his affability, memory for names, and boisterousness to know many fellow students and become president of his fraternity. An average student, George W. Bush employed his bantering, hard-drinking, and family clown antics to deflect attention away from an inability to match his father's notable accomplishments in the classroom or on the baseball field.

Despite his frustrations as an underachieving first-born and namesake son, after graduating from Yale George W. doggedly followed his father's deep and impressive footsteps. He sought his fortune in the Lone Star State's oil patch, attempted to enter the "family business" with a precipitous jump into a congressional race and trained as a pilot in the Texas Air National Guard during the Vietnam War.

Bush finally meshed his personal attributes of likeability, an ability to attract attention and down-to-earth humor in 1989 when he became managing copartner of the Texas Rangers baseball team. His main tasks entailed enhancing the profile of the team and increasing the value of the franchise. The new responsibilities also allowed George W. to build name recognition for a later entry into Texas politics through handing out his personal baseball cards, appearing frequently in the media to promote the Rangers, and assuming a good ol' boy image by his willingness to have people see him as just another fan, "eating the same popcorn, peeing in the same urinal."[8]

When George W. Bush ran for governor of Texas in 1994, he proved a surprisingly effective campaigner against a formidable Democratic incumbent. His Bombastic Bushkin persona proved popular among grassroots voters, while Grand Old Party (GOP, the Republican Party) heavyweights appreciated the potential of his family name and fund-raising prowess. George W's down-home manner, ready quips, and energy made him an attractive candidate in the retail arena of grip-and-grin politics.

Despite his prior tendency to "feist out" at critics of his father, Bush learned to manage his temper and stay on message under Karl Rove's tutelage. However, at unscripted moments, the tough, bawdy language of his Bombastic Bushkin persona reappeared. For example, an open microphone recorded the president's discussion on Israel's 2006 war against Lebanon's Hezbollah militia with British Prime Minister Tony Blair during a G-8 summit break: "What they need to do is get Syria to get Hezbollah to stop doing this shit and it's over."[9]

Bush applied his personal charm, replete with teasing and assigning nicknames, to woo the reporters covering him. George W.'s propensity to give people nicknames carried on into the White House, but sometimes the nicknames took a more caustic tone when individuals criticized him or displayed less than absolute loyalty. Treasury Secretary Paul O'Neill found his nickname sarcastically changed from "Pablo" to "Big O" for speaking too candidly with the press.[10] Likewise, Bush's renowned "needling" of reporters sometimes got him into trouble, as when the president later had to apologize to *Los Angeles Times* reporter Peter Wallsten after kidding him about wearing sunglasses at a sunny Rose Garden press conference. The reporter had Stargardt's disease, a degenerative condition that caused blindness, which became aggravated by sunlight.[11]

Machiavellian Politico

Bush's second persona appeared during his 1994 race for governor, although the Machiavellian Politico style reflected political lessons accrued over many years through campaigning for his father, working in the Senate campaigns of several family friends, and his early bid for a congressional seat. Two political consultants played key mentoring and advisory roles in developing George W. Bush's appreciation of the potency of aggressive campaign tactics, pursuit of high-risk policies, and exercise of raw political power: Lee Atwater and Karl Rove. Atwater served as Vice President Bush's campaign manager in the victorious 1988 presidential race and Karl Rove, a Texas consultant, stayed at George W.'s side during his ascent to the presidency—and in the White House.

George W. worked intimately with Atwater for one and a half years during his father's 1988 presidential campaign, while serving as the Bush family's "loyalty thermometer." Bush admired Atwater's strategic acumen, successful "spinning" of the media, and jugular approach to campaign tactics. George W. closely observed Atwater's mastery of the art of negative TV ads that exploited the voters' emotional response to "wedge issues." Indeed, George W. helped Atwater convince his father to "go negative" in 1988—warning he would lose if the campaign failed to air negative TV ads. The infamous Willie Horton TV ad, renounced by Atwater on his deathbed, epitomized the campaign's low-road appeal to visceral racial fears.

Atwater loved to quote from Niccolò Machiavelli's *The Prince* and Sun Tzu's *The Art of War.* He bragged to one reporter that he read *The Prince* 21 times, while boasting to friends he reread Machiavelli every year.[12] The senior Bush rewarded Atwater for guiding his successful presidential campaign by appointing him chairman of the Republican National Committee (RNC). As RNC chairman Atwater traveled around the country with an assistant carrying a case containing copies of Machiavelli's *The Prince* and Sun-Tzu's *The Art of War.*[13] The two books symbolized Atwater's approach to politics as total warfare.

Atwater played a key role in Karl Rove's election as chairman of the College Republican National Committee in 1973, mustering support for Rove in the South. The election became controversial when a *Washington Post* story revealed that Rove had taught College Republicans in GOP-sponsored workshops in 1971 and 1972 about political espionage and dirty tricks. Like Atwater, Karl Rove "was a great reader of Machiavelli."[14]

Karl Rove first met George W. Bush in Washington, D.C. while the younger Bush was a graduate student at Harvard. The elder Bush assigned Rove the task of handing George W. the family car keys when he visited Washington. Rove remembered his initial impression of the younger Bush: easygoing, indifferent, wearing a leather flight jacket and chewing gum. Rove admiringly recalled: "He was...*cool.*"[15] Karl Rove decided early in his career that George W. afforded him the opportunity to attain national prominence by guiding Bush on a path to the White House. In his campaign biography, George W. Bush touted Karl Rove as "the Lee Atwater of Texas politics."[16]

Like Atwater, Rove ruthlessly fought to win every election—by any means and at any price. His fundamental strategy mirrored Atwater's intensely aggressive political approach: "attack, attack and attack," as Rove recommended in a 1986 campaign memorandum.[17] He became the conservative trustee over computerized lists of Texas GOP big donors, using that financial clout to bludgeon Texas Democrats who stood in the way of his master plan for George W. Bush's future presidential bid. Chuck McDonald, a Democratic consultant, underscored Karl

Rove's cold-blooded approach to politics: "I always knew where I stood with Karl. I knew he was trying to kill me....He approaches everything as life or death."[18]

Lee Atwater had demonstrated to George W. Bush the effectiveness of negative TV ads and divisive tactics in his father's 1988 victory. Rove employed similar harsh techniques, with George W.'s approval, to put Bush into the Texas governor's mansion and then the White House. George W. Bush, recognizing the power and explosiveness of these tactics, prudently followed Machiavelli's dictum that "princes ought to have others carry out unpopular tasks and keep pleasing ones for themselves."[19] For example, after Senator John McCain's stunning 18-point victory over Bush in the 2000 New Hampshire primary, a supporter during the critical South Carolina GOP primary asked George W. when he would attack McCain's soft spots. Bush replied that his campaign would hit hard, but (we're) "not going to do it on TV."[20] Soon push polls slandered Senator McCain with telephone allegations that he had a black child and his wife had a drug problem.[21] Bush defeated McCain in South Carolina by 11 points.

Early in President Bush's first term Karl Rove described how his concept of political capital meant that success in the war against Afghanistan's Taliban regime and the al Qaeda terrorist organization "will create political capital that can be used to expand on other things whether international or domestic." Rove stressed the short life of political capital: "If you don't spend it...it is perishable."[22] Rove convinced the president to expend his political capital in Bush's successful late 2002 campaign blitz to reverse the historic losses of a president's party in mid-term congressional elections.

After his 2004 reelection President Bush told reporters: "I earned capital in the campaign, political capital, and now I intend to spend it. It is my style."[23] Such thinking contributed to the president's announcement of his administration's ambitious call for democracy throughout the world and a radical reform of the popular Social Security program. However, Bush pragmatically refused to squander his political capital on passing the controversial ban on gay marriage constitutional amendment, which his campaign brandished to drive conservative religious voters to the polls in November 2004.[24] But the bold initiatives of pushing democracy in the world and reforming Social Security conflicted with Machiavelli's caveat that "there is nothing more difficult to manage, or more doubtful of success, or more dangerous to handle than to take the lead in introducing a new order of things."[25]

Righteous Hawk

George W. Bush's third persona did not fully reveal itself until after the deadly 9/11 terrorist attacks. In the close 2000 election evangelical voters had demonstrated their faith in his Born Again beliefs, overwhelmingly voting for Bush. George W.'s campaign biography credited a 1985 walk with internationally renowned evangelist Billy Graham on a Kennebunkport beach as fostering his spiritual awakening. But a year prior evangelist Arthur Blessitt knelt down with Bush and an oilman friend to recite "The Sinners Prayer," confessing the need for forgiveness and salvation through Jesus Christ.[26] After a booze-filled celebration of his fortieth birthday with friends in July 1986, Bush announced to his wife Laura he would quit drinking.

After listening to a 1999 sermon by his Methodist minister in Midland about the reluctance of Moses to become a leader, Bush decided to run for the White House. He told James Robison, a prominent Texas evangelical minister: "I've heard the call. *I believe God wants me to run for president*" (author's emphasis).[27] Doug Wead, an evangelical liaison for Bush's father during the 1988 race, secretly recorded conversations with George W. as Bush prepared for his 2000 presidential campaign. Bush acknowledged the need to use "code words" with Christian conservatives. He tested his lines with Wead before meeting with influential evangelicals in 1999: "I'm going to tell them the five turning points in my life.…Accepting Christ. Marrying my wife. Having children. Running for governor. And listening to my mother."[28]

Admitting that he did not always "walk-the-talk," Bush received advice from Robison to admit that "I've sinned and I've learned" when talking with Christian conservatives. During a December 1999 Iowa Republican Primary debate, then Governor Bush replied to a question about which political philosopher had influenced him the most: "Jesus Christ…because he changed my heart."[29] He added that "when you accept Christ as the Savior, it changes your heart. It changes your life. And that's what happened to me." President Bush underscored his religious commitment in an interview with Brit Hume in September 2003: "Well, I pray daily, and I pray in all kinds of places. I mean, I pray in bed, I pray in the Oval Office. I pray a lot … as the Spirit moves me. And faith is an integral part of my life."[30]

The shock and horror the nation felt as the hijacked airliners struck the World Trade Center reverberated even more potently within the untested president. Although President Bush appeared disoriented the first day, his performance over the subsequent days and weeks reassured the country. When President Bush addressed the nation on September 20, he projected confidence, determination, and strength, a leader poised to swing the sword of retribution at al Qaeda and its Taliban hosts in Afghanistan. Bush's job ratings soared to 90 percent approval in Gallup's September 21–22 survey, the highest assessment any president has ever received.[31]

Three days after the terrorist attacks, President George W. Bush in his Righteous Hawk persona declared in a National Cathedral speech that America's responsibility after the attacks was to "rid the world of evil."[32] Bob Woodward observed in *Bush at War*: "The president was casting his mission and that of the country in the grand vision of God's master plan."[33] President Bush invoked God in his September 20 address to the nation: "Freedom and fear, justice and cruelty…we know that God is not neutral between them."[34] The president described the terrorist hijackers as instruments of evil at a Pentagon memorial: "And in the terrorists, evil has found a willing servant."[35]

David Domke observed in his book, *God Willing?*, that Bush employed his political fundamentalism in the war on terror. He found after 9/11 the Bush administration chose "language and communication approaches that were structurally grounded in a conservative religious outlook but were political in content and applications."[36] What made George W. Bush different from other presidents, Domke maintained, was how Bush talked as though he knew what God wants for America: "He speaks as if he's a prophet of God."[37] Domke cited Bush's statement in the third presidential debate in 2004: "I believe that God wants everybody to be free…and that's been part of my foreign policy." Bush also used the religious term "called," as in summoned by God, when addressing Christian evangelicals: "We're called to fight terrorism around the world."[38]

President Reagan's speechwriter Peggy Noonan described President Bush's 2005 second Inaugural address as "rather heavenish. It was a God-drenched speech."[39] Noonan considered Bush's idealistic pledge to "end tyranny in the world" as "over the top." That ambitious Bush administration goal, while popular in abstract terms, would increasingly confront the complex realities of Middle East politics and stir resentment among key nondemocratic allies in the war on terror.

George W. Bush's aggressive Righteous Hawk persona also reflected the 43rd president's reliance on his gut instincts. During Woodward's interview with Bush about his reactions to 9/11 and the war in Afghanistan, the president mentioned about a dozen times that his instincts played a pivotal role in his foreign policy decision-making. Woodward concluded: "His instincts are almost his second religion."[40] As the nation's first president holding a Masters in Business Administration degree (Harvard 1975), but with little knowledge of foreign affairs, President Bush appointed a highly experienced national security team. But he told an interviewer that although those seasoned advisers had their say after the 9/11 attacks, "my instincts were part of this."[41] Bush flatly rejected any suggestion that he received advice from his experienced father: "I have no outside advice."

Administration aides defended the display of Bush's "unvarnished instincts" as he prepared the nation for war in Afghanistan, such as the president's reference that Osama bin Laden belonged on an Old West "Wanted: Dead or Alive" poster. They argued that those blunt words demonstrated President Bush's tough Western roots, steely determination, and *macho* demeanor toward the al Qaeda terrorists. One flattering *Time* portrait of Bush concluded, "What he lacks in experience, he has made up in instinct."[42] The president further disclosed to Woodward: "I just think it's instinctive. I'm not a textbook player. I'm a gut player."[43]

The praise President Bush received for his post-9/11 toppling of the Taliban and disruption of al Qaeda's operations in Afghanistan only reinforced Bush's instincts that favored bold action, contributing to the subsequent decision to invade Iraq.[44] Highly placed neoconservatives in the Bush administration encouraged Bush's tendency to favor risky, aggressive actions in the war on terror.

Of course, if President Bush had not acted militarily against al Qaeda's stronghold in Afghanistan the American public would have reacted angrily. Gary Jacobson observed: "With nearly 90 percent of the public favoring military action against the terrorists, anything less might have actually cost him public support."[45] Bush's decision to employ U.S. armed forces and airpower against the Taliban essentially boiled down to questions of *how* and *when*—not *whether* to order military action.

President George W. Bush's reliance on instinct and gut feelings impacted upon his personal approach to diplomacy, at times alarming traditional Republican realists. After his first face-to-face meeting with Russia's President Vladimir Putin in Slovenia, lasting less than two hours, Bush told reporters: "*I looked the man in the eye…I was able to get a sense of his soul*" (author's emphasis).[46] The U.S. president concluded that he and the Russian president shared values, such as love for their families. Bush glossed over Putin's KGB career and spying several years in Germany when making this gut, eyeball-to-eyeball appraisal.

In June 2006, hoping to boost sagging job ratings, President Bush secretly flew to Baghdad to meet Prime Minister Nouri al-Maliki after he announced the final members of his cabinet. Bush told the Iraqi prime minister, who was notified of Bush's personal visit only minutes before they met, that he'd come "to look you in the eye."[47] Bush later told American troops in a palace meeting that he had traveled to Baghdad "to look at Prime Minister Maliki in the eyes and determine whether or not he is as dedicated to a free Iraq as you are." He assured the soldiers: "And I believe he is."

In summary, George W. Bush displayed all three personas in his personal development, political battles, and evolution into a War President. The three personas reflected the personal qualities of George W. Bush as a leader. At different points after the horrific 9/11 events the president had to make—or approve—decisions that critically impacted upon the course of his proclaimed war on terror. The values, outlook, and style embodied in each Bush persona helped shape those policy choices.

Three Analytical Lenses

On a general level, the three decision-making "lenses" Graham Allison developed to analyze the 1962 Cuban Missile Crisis—embodying the rational actor model, organizational procedures, and the bureaucratic context of vital decisions— provide a helpful framework for insights into critical Bush administration decisions in the war against terror.[48] In particular, the conceptual models explore the policy goals, procedures and recommendations, as well as the internal political battles, that influenced Bush's key choices as he confronted his test by fire after the 9/11 terrorist attacks.

First, the application of Allison's Rational Actor model to Bush's war on terror decisions focused upon the 9/11 bloody attack that clearly represented a strategic threat from a non-state terrorist organization. *Test by Fire* examined how Bush and his war cabinet established national goals in response to the danger, weighed U.S. policy alternatives and assessed each option's perceived costs and benefits.

In many ways George W. Bush should have been more comfortable with the Rational Actor perspective than other presidents, since his Harvard MBA education employed case study analyses of rational (value-maximizing) business decisions. A former Harvard MBA faculty member, who attended the program at the same time as George W. Bush, recalled: "The job of the executive is to weigh probabilities in evaluating imperfect information; to assess the costs and benefits of acting or not acting; and to construct scenarios around the various possible time frames for taking action...."[49]

President George W. Bush wisely compensated for his lack of experience and knowledge of foreign affairs by appointing a highly experienced national security team. In contrast, the elder Bush arrived in the Oval Office with a full resume of foreign policy experience: UN ambassador, special envoy to China, CIA director and vice president.

George W. learned from his father's aversion to "that vision thing," which led to criticism of the elder Bush's lack of overall goals, the importance of offering a leadership vision—like President Reagan. He proclaimed inspiring visions as governor of Texas and as president of the United States. Nevertheless, the 43rd president also defined himself in terms of decision-making: "If I could give you the job description, it would be 'decision-maker.' I have to make a lot of decisions."[50]

A full study of the context of a situation reveals both threats and opportunities, with the decision-maker selecting the policy option "that best advances his interests."[51] The Rational Actor decisional model assumes the accurate transmission of all available information to the president without concern for his policy preferences, providing the key U.S. foreign policy-maker with a full range of choices with the risks of each action clearly delineated. The creation of the National Security Council (NSC) in 1947 established the role of the NSC adviser to coordinate for the president the often conflicting policy recommendations from agencies, manage interagency groups, and provide advice.[52]

A president's attitude toward risk constitutes a central ingredient in making rational decisions among policy options in the midst of uncertainty. George W. Bush's preference for bold action, often relying upon his instincts, thus could significantly impact upon policy recommendations and the president's policy choices.[53]

Second, Allison's Government Organization Model examined policy actions from the perspective of organizational outputs influenced by a bureaucracy's standard operating procedures and organizational culture. In international affairs governmental organizations deal with uncertainties by creating various scenarios that become the basis for contingency planning. Of course, when no contingency plan exists because of the bureaucracy's reluctance to consider such a possibility, the policy-making process becomes more harried in a crisis situation. Organizations also tend to emphasize objectives "most congruent to their special capacities" and their organization's culture, which traditionally leads the State Department to emphasize diplomatic options and the Defense Department to suggest military solutions.[54] But not always.

For example, President Reagan's Secretary of State George Schultz favored military strikes on Hezbollah terrorist bases in the 1980s, while Defense Secretary Casper Weinberger urged a diplomatic approach. Weinberger, in a January 8, 1985 address to the National Press Club listed six criteria for the deployment of U.S. military forces into combat situations: vital U.S. or key allies' national interests at risk, wholehearted intent to win, precise political and military objectives with enough resources to accomplish them, assurance of congressional and public support, utilization of military force as a last resort, and continuing reassessments as events unfolded.[55]

General Colin Powell, then-serving as chairman of the Joint Chiefs of Staff, added a proviso calling for the application of "overwhelming force" to achieve the military objective. This later became the Powell Doctrine. Both Weinberger and Powell echoed Karl von Clauswitz, the famed strategist who wrote *On War* in 1832, stressing the centrality of political objectives: "War is merely the continuation of policy by other means."

Governmental organizations produce information for key decision-makers, generate action options, and implement the chosen policy alternative. Allison recognized that government departments often manifest an imperial attitude, seeking to enhance their budget, personnel, and areas of action—and defend their turf from incursions. Bureaucratic battles may occur within one organization, such as Pentagon struggles between the Rumsfeld civilian management team and top Army generals. Rumsfeld set up an Office of Special Plans in the Pentagon to rummage through raw intelligence and forward the most threatening information about Iraq to the Office of the Vice President (OVP)—ignoring the Pentagon's own Defense Intelligence Agency.[56]

The influence of a governmental organization may increase or diminish as a result of events. For example, the Central Intelligence Agency (CIA) reputation suffered from its failure to predict the 9/11 attacks. President Bush's loyal defense of CIA Director George Tenet generated internal pressures to produce intelligence supporting the policy viewpoints favored by the White House.[57]

Third, Allison proposed a Governmental Politics lens that viewed decisions and actions as the result of conflict, bargaining, and compromise among the government's key figures. This approach examines which key actors participated in the decision, since their values and preferences shape the policy choices. The model explores the perceptions of key participants, their stand on the issue, and preferred course of action. It also investigates the "action channel," the selected process for reaching a decision that could omit key players from the most critical decision-making.

Staffers and ad hoc participants from key congressional committees, interest groups, and friendly governments may play an important role in framing, informing, and tilting the decision-making toward particular choices. For example, White House aides believed that President Bush's meeting with three Iraqi exiles several months before the invasion deeply impacted upon his decisions on war with Iraq—especially their assurances that American troops would be enthusiastically greeted and democracy would spring forth with little effort.[58]

Allison emphasized that the "hard core of the governmental politics mix is personality."[59] Therefore, an application of the Governmental Politics lens must scrutinize the personal tensions between Secretary of Defense Rumsfeld and Secretary of State Powell in the planning and execution of the war on terror. Such Pentagon-Foggy Bottom rivalries appear in most administrations. However, in the Bush administration—largely through a close "cabal" between Rumsfeld and Cheney—the Pentagon received almost *carte blanche* (unrestricted authority) to run both the military offensive and postwar occupation operations in Iraq, the latter normally managed by experienced diplomats.[60]

In the first Bush term, although NSC Adviser Condoleezza Rice enjoyed President Bush's friendship and full confidence, she lacked the high-level experience, administration allies, and *gravitas* to balance the conflicting views of Secretaries Rumsfeld and Powell. Rumsfeld's recommendations usually prevailed, bolstered by Cheney's behind-the-scenes maneuvering, as they conformed more to President Bush's tendency to favor more "forward-leaning" proposals that projected a bold, tough approach to fighting terrorism.

President Bush never developed a close personal relationship with Secretary of State Powell, who had considered running for the GOP presidential nomination in 2000. Powell enjoyed greater popularity than Bush at home and abroad throughout his first term, an irritation for the proud president. White House aides sought to reduce Powell's tall profile within the administration, sometimes publicly embarrassing the secretary of state.

And significantly, unlike prior administrations, Vice President Cheney assumed unprecedented power in the U.S. foreign policy-making process. Cheney assembled a large staff of foreign policy specialists who shared his dark, threatening view of the world. Indeed, the vice president's staff rivaled the president's National Security Council staff. Furthermore, Cheney's close ties to Rumsfeld and neoconservative hard-liners throughout the administration provided special access, consistent support, and extraordinary vice presidential influence upon President Bush's policies.

Treasury Secretary Paul O'Neill described Cheney's technique of shaping policy, which he had observed when both he and Cheney served under other presidents, as a puppeteer who manipulated with strings and suggestions behind the scenes—leaving no fingerprints.[61] Indeed, the CIA's internal nickname for Cheney was Edgar, recalling the role of Edgar Bergen who manipulated the real puppet, Charlie McCarthy.[62]

Undoubtedly, this initial exploration of George W. Bush's key decisions, after assuming the tasks of War President, will benefit from the future declassification or disclosure of sensitive documents, candid interviews with key participants, and publication of the memoirs of administration insiders. As noted earlier, the Bush administration manifested a great penchant for secrecy. Therefore, this study offers important early findings into how President Bush made critical decisions in the global war on terror based upon what we know about his foreign policies at the time this manuscript was completed for publication in September 2007.

Critical Choices

Due to the shock of 9/11, partisan politics proved less constricting than normal in the early months of the war on terror. Congressional Democrats eagerly exhibited patriotic bipartisanship in the first days after the World Trade Center and Pentagon attacks, providing President Bush with a virtually unanimous resolution on September 14, 2001, authorizing the president to "use all necessary and appropriate force" against the people planning the 9/11 attacks or harboring such terrorists.[63] Congress also granted unprecedented law enforcement tools to the Executive in the Patriot Act in October, although 66 members expressed reservations in the House. The Senate passed the measure 98–1.[64]

However, as the Bush administration pounded the war drums against Iraq in 2002, partisan divisions began to reappear, emboldened by falling presidential job approval numbers, doubts about a war with Iraq, and the forthcoming congressional elections. More surprising, during summer 2002 key Republican realists from the senior Bush's national security team began to question the wisdom of rushing into a war with Iraq, warning that an invasion of Iraq would impair the progress of the war on terror.

Responding to 9/11

President George W. Bush's first critical decision in the war on terror occurred in September 2001 in the turbulent wake of the shocking attacks on the World Trade Center and Pentagon. Bob Woodward, who was granted extraordinary access to President Bush, war cabinet officials, and relevant documents, described those early policy deliberations between Bush and his national security principles. Although Woodward received criticism that his favored treatment presented a pro-administration viewpoint of the early planning, *Bush at War* contained important insights and previously classified information about the pressure-filled first 100 days after the 9/11 attacks.[65] However, readers should remember that with the administration's vaunted "message discipline," Bush officials sought to bolster President Bush's image as an informed, reflective, and bold leader—especially after his weak performance on the day of the terrorist attacks.

One Government Organization Model finding that emerges in chapter 6 from those initial War Cabinet meetings was the lack of a Pentagon "off-the-shelf" contingency plan for an invasion or major strike (with boots on the ground) against al Qaeda's bases in Afghanistan. Despite escalating al Qaeda violence against U.S. targets—beginning with the 1996 attack on American forces in Saudi Arabia's Khobar Towers—the Pentagon generals avoided drafting a contingency plan that might repeat the mistake of the Soviet Union by becoming deeply embroiled in a bloody land war in mountainous Afghanistan.

Testimony during the 9/11 Commission hearings disclosed that national security officials in both the Clinton and Bush administrations had concluded that prior to the September 11 terrorist attacks the American people would not back a major military ground assault upon Osama bin Laden's bases in Afghanistan. Therefore, in response to al Qaeda's attacks on U.S. embassies in Kenya and Tanzania, President Clinton ordered 60 Tomahawk missiles to strike Afghan terrorist bases in August 1998. Clinton also stationed submarines armed with Tomahawk missiles in the Arabian Gulf for a year waiting for "actionable intelligence" to locate and then target bin Laden.[66]

On the other hand, President Bush rejected costly missile attacks against primitively constructed training camps as "pinpricks." However, Bush's NSC Adviser Condoleezza Rice admitted to the 9/11 Commission: "I am not going to tell you that we were looking to invade Afghanistan during that seven months. We were not."[67]

Thus the Pentagon could not give President Bush an immediate, robust plan to attack Osama bin Laden and the Taliban government that harbored al Qaeda with U.S. air and ground forces. Instead, the CIA presented a proposal that won presidential approval after a graphic presentation by the CIA's counterterrorism chief Cofer Black. Black assured the president: "When we're through with them, they will have flies walking across their eyeballs."[68]

The Pentagon ended up playing an unaccustomed secondary role in a conflict with Special Forces units and bombers supporting the CIA teams working with Northern Alliance Afghan warlords to topple the Taliban regime. Rumsfeld fumed at the subordinate role of his organization in meeting the al Qaeda terrorist threat: "I never again want our army to arrive somewhere and meet the CIA on the ground."[69]

Abandoning the Geneva Convention on Prisoners

In his full-court offensive against terrorists, President George W. Bush decided in February 2002 to waive the Geneva Convention's safeguards on the treatment of prisoners of war to permit harsh interrogations to uncover any future plots. Although some in the administration probably considered this only a tactical move in the war on terror, the international reaction to this policy change involved significant costs for the United States, as chapter 7 explains.

Vice President Cheney helped lower the moral and operational standard in fighting the war on terror. Suskind described Cheney's lowered standard as suspicion, rather than evidence, as justifying action under a new "One Percent Doctrine."[70] This reduced threshold for proof impacted upon decisions about the interrogation of prisoners, since vital information might be extracted by employing torture to counter potential terrorist threats.

President Bush decided to ignore the Geneva Convention's restrictions, a policy shift that later contributed to the notorious abuse of Iraqi prisoners held at the Abu Ghraib prison outside of Baghdad. Internet photos of the degrading, humiliating, and harsh treatment of Iraqi prisoners by U.S. forces contaminated international feelings toward America's conduct of the war on terror, costing the United States critical support throughout the outraged Middle East.

The decision to abandon the Geneva Convention's standards for the treatment of prisoners of war sparked a major clash within the Bush administration out of the glare of the press. Vice President Cheney, Defense Secretary Rumsfeld, and CIA Director Tenet favored expeditious harsh tactics, regardless of international conventions, to obtain operational intelligence from suspected terrorists.

Secretary of State Powell cautioned about how allied governments and world opinion would react to the rejection of Geneva Convention restrictions. The Pentagon's Judge Advocate Generals' (JAG) top military lawyers all vigorously opposed this dramatic shift, which they felt would endanger U.S. troops operating abroad. Cheney's staff, working closely with White House Counsel Alberto Gonzales, increasingly excluded opponents of the policy change from the "action channel" discussions.

Several important questions arise about this controversial torture policy decision. President Bush risked international condemnation that undermined his widely trumpeted goals of promoting democracy and liberty. Why did Cheney's One Percent Doctrine win such persistent approval from President Bush, despite vigorous dissent from his secretary of state, Pentagon lawyers, and domestic as well as allied critics—until rejected by the Supreme Court on June 29, 2006 in the *Hamdan v. Rumsfeld* case?[71]

Iraq Too Soon?

Another critical decision in the war on terror occurred on November 21, 2001. While American bombers, Special Forces units, and CIA teams still fought Taliban and al Qaeda forces in Afghanistan, President Bush authorized Defense Secretary Rumsfeld to begin secret, operational planning for a war against Iraq.[72] That raised the question of whether Bush prematurely decided to topple Saddam Hussein before destroying the al Qaeda terrorist organization that had sparked the war on terror after the vicious 9/11 attacks.

Chapter 8 examines how the new focus on Iraq diverted CIA analysts, Special Forces units, and Arab translators from what many considered America's major threat—the destruction of the al Qaeda terrorist network. At one point the White House weighed the Americanizing of the Afghanistan war by deploying 50,000 U.S. troops as a worst-case scenario.[73] The decision to shift key units to planning the invasion of Iraq, in the minds of many observers, contributed to the failure to capture or kill Osama bin Laden and his top aides during the December 2001 Tora Bora offensive against al Qaeda terrorists.

The fight around the Tora Bora cave and tunnel complex relied upon U.S. precision air strikes, ill-equipped Afghanistan tribal forces whose warlords were paid by the CIA with crisp new $100 bills, and an onsite presence of only two dozen Special Forces troops. Gary Bernsten, head of the CIA's Jawbreaker team, requested through the CIA in early December that CENTCOM drop a battalion of U.S. Army Rangers (800 men) behind al Qaeda lines to block their escape to Pakistan.

General Tommy Franks denied the request, later asserting that the Afghan warlords and Pakistanis could block Osama bin Laden's flight to safety. Ironically, a more skeptical General Tommy Franks had told the NSC on November 2: "I don't place any confidence in the [National Alliance] opposition."[74]

Killing the head of the snake may not have ended the threat of Islamic terrorism, but many argued that wiping out al Qaeda's top leaders would have certainly impaired its future operations and clearly demonstrated the price for such a ruthless attack on America. Also, at that point in the war on terror most of the world cheered for the United States in its campaign against al Qaeda terrorists and Osama bin Laden, who had the 9/11 blood of innocents upon their hands.

Why did President Bush view the toppling of the Iraqi dictator as such a pressing threat—before the completion of the vital first step in the war on terror? At a visceral level for George W. Bush, Saddam Hussein had tried to "kill my dad" in a 1993 assassination plot.[75] Removing Saddam Hussein from power had surfaced as a major goal of the administration as early as the first NSC meeting with President Bush on January 30, 2001.[76]

Demobilizing and De-Baathification.

Two other major decisions occurred during the occupation phase when Ambassador Bremer ordered the "de-Baathification" of Iraqi society and the demobilization of the Iraqi army in May 2003. Chapter 9 analyzes these controversial actions that placed security in occupied Iraq squarely on the backs of American GIs and coalition allies. Bremer later told his CPA aides that the "White House, DOD, and State all signed off on this."[77] However, according to a New York Times account: "Neither Condoleezza Rice…nor the Joint Chiefs were consulted about the decision."[78] Why had the administration's "action channel" bypassed Rice, the Joint Chiefs, and CIA who should have been included in such a far-reaching decision?

Iraqi exiles such as Ahmed Chalabi, with close ties to Vice President Cheney, Deputy Secretary of Defense Paul Wolfowitz, and influential Washington neoconservatives, played a backstage role in pushing for rapid de-Baathification. These exile figures, lacking solid support within Iraq, hoped to benefit from the creation of a political void after the fall of Saddam Hussein. In April 2003 the Pentagon transported Chalabi and 570 of his Iraqi National Congress (INC) "fighters" to Iraq during the invasion—without informing the NSC, State Department, or CIA.

Furthermore, the administration demonstrated little understanding of the historic ethnic and sectarian schisms within Iraq, which potentially could undermine Bush plans for a secular, pluralistic democratic government in Iraq. Unstated assumptions held by the Pentagon's civilian leaders appeared to back an agenda favoring the pro-America Iraqi exile leader Ahmed Chalabi becoming the next ruler of Iraq. Since the Bush administration opposed nation-building, a smaller deployment of forces could accomplish the task of regime change before turning over power to Chalabi and going home soon afterward.

An Ambitious Agenda

President Bush's 2002 State of the Union Address warned Americans and other nations about the threat of rogue states possessing weapons of mass destruction.

Bush flagged the danger posed by an "axis of evil" comprising Iraq, Iran, and North Korea.[79] The speech launched the president's campaign to topple Saddam Hussein, with the Iraqi dictator clearly in the bull's-eye of Bush's military planning.

However, the president had also delivered notice to Iran's revolutionary Islamic regime and the reclusive, dangerous North Korean communist dictator regarding the administration's hostility toward their plans to develop nuclear weaponry. Soon he emphasized that only the advance of democracy in the Middle East could avoid the dangers posed by Islamic extremism.

Controlling North Korea and Iran

President Clinton, recognizing the danger emanating from North Korea's nuclear energy development and test-firing of missiles, expended considerable diplomatic efforts to achieve the Agreed Framework in 1994. The Pyongyang regime would freeze operations and halt construction of nuclear reactors; Washington suspected that these reactors could secretly supply plutonium to North Korea's covert nuclear weapons program. In return, North Korea would receive two less dangerous light-water nuclear power reactors and heavy fuel oil to produce electricity. Kim Jung Il agreed not to develop nuclear weaponry.

When newly confirmed Secretary of State Powell announced the administration's intent to build upon the Clinton administration's negotiations, the Bush White House publicly rebuked him and embarrassed South Korean President Kim Dae Jung. Bush administration hawks felt Clinton had made too many concessions to the brutal North Korean ruler. They proposed leveraging Kim Jong Il's desperate economic plight into a situation where the communist ruler would be forced to make major concessions or even lose power.

Chapter 10 examines how President Bush's actions toward the two axis of evil states reflected Rational Actor thinking, despite the administration's bellicose rhetoric. The costs of a U.S. attack upon each of these evil rogue nations could be estimated, despite gaps in the human intelligence. North Korea clearly possessed a sizeable arsenal of rockets and over 800 ballistic missiles—stationed within range of South Korea's capital Seoul. The stationing of 35,000 Marines in Korea near the demilitarized zone dividing the Korean peninsula would immediately entangle U.S. troops in any conflict. Therefore, the possibility of a second Korean War could immediately become very hazardous for the United States.

Iran, with a larger population than Iraq, also posed a military threat with its ability to respond to U.S. military moves by ordering Hezbollah terrorists to attack U.S. interests in the region. Since the 1979 fall of the Shah and the crisis over revolutionary Iran's seizure of American diplomats as hostages, the United States lacked solid intelligence about Iran, particularly on the progress and locations of its nuclear facilities. Furthermore, as a major exporter of oil on the world market, Iran could disrupt the flow of oil to further boost the price of a barrel of crude oil. Since U.S. troops became enmeshed in the Iraqi insurgency and civil war, the American forces could readily become the targets for Iranian terrorist attacks in retaliation for air strikes on Iran.

Ironically, among the three despised rogue regimes Bush highlighted in the axis of evil, Saddam Hussein emerged as the *least dangerous* to American forces. The 1991 Gulf War and UN-imposed sanctions had weakened Iraq forces until they appeared like an overripe plum waiting to be plucked. Coalition forces during the 1991 Persian Gulf War had destroyed much of Iraq's armor and UN sanctions denied the dictator Iraqi oil revenues to rebuild his military forces.

Therefore, an inverse threat matrix existed between the level of actual threat each of the axis of evil states represented and the anticipated costs for decisively halting their respective progress to acquire nuclear weapons. Instead of hitting Iran or North Korea with preemptive military attacks, President Bush opted for indirect diplomatic initiatives to deal with these threatening states. Although Bush spokesmen may have employed hot rhetoric toward Iran and North Korea—with neoconservatives aching for another demonstration of America's military prowess—the realist principle of "prudence" won a grudging nod from President George W. Bush.

But from a Rational Actor perspective, why did President Bush decide to include Iran and North Korea in his 2002 State of the Union address as part of an axis of evil? If the cost of military action against those two rogue states was so great, why bluster when military steps appeared so dangerous?

Ending Tyranny in the World

President George W. Bush proclaimed in his 2005 Inaugural Address the administration's "ultimate goal of ending tyranny in our world."[80] The president's declaration of this ambitious objective reflected a significant journey since the 2000 presidential campaign when Bush described himself as a "clear-eyed realist," promising a "humble" foreign policy. The expansive rhetoric echoed the idealism of President Woodrow Wilson.

The announcement of this visionary goal reflected some of the thinking of neoconservatives on how America should employ its preeminent military power to encourage democratic governments, particularly in the oil-rich Middle East, thus bolstering the security of Israel's democratic government. However, in the president's drive for war against Iraq, the administration advanced the following three core arguments: the fearful prospect of Saddam Hussein building nuclear weapons, Iraq's lethal links to al Qaeda terrorists, and cleverly implied hints of Saddam Hussein's involvement in the treacherous 9/11 attacks on America.

Promoting democracy in Iraq did not emerge as a major rationale for the preemptive war until after the CIA failed to find weapons of mass destruction in U.S.-occupied Iraq, as explored in chapter 11. However, the shadow of such a policy appeared in President Bush's February 26, 2003, address to the American Enterprise Institute: "The nation of Iraq...is fully capable of moving toward democracy and living in freedom."[81] Then the president framed the broader ideological goal: "The world has a clear interest in the spread of democratic values, because stable and free nations do not breed the ideologies of murder." But Bush stressed the promotion of democracy in Iraq after toppling Saddam Hussein as an *ex post facto* justification for the invasion, angering many key allies in the war on terror.

Traditional GOP realists strongly objected to such an idealistic declaration. For realists, the Rational Actor model would discourage such an ambitious and imprudent goal, since many of America's allies around the world in the fight against terrorism were not democratic regimes.

Critics of Bush's democracy vision for the Middle East considered their reservations validated when the Bush administration refused to delay a January 2006

Palestinian legislative election. Despite warnings by the Israeli Prime Minister and the Palestinian Authority president, Hamas won the parliamentary election, subsequently seizing control over the Gaza Strip. Since Hamas opposed a peace settlement with Israel—and refused to end its attacks against the Jewish state—Bush's democratic vision had complicated the goal of achieving a comprehensive Middle East peace settlement between Israel and the Palestinian Authority.

Furthermore, the summer 2006 war between Israel and Hezbollah, when Israeli planes conducted heavy bombing raids on Beirut and its Shiite-controlled environs, failed to crush Hezbollah. Secretary of State Rice prevented the UN Security Council from imposing an immediate cease-fire. But the Bush administration's perceived one-sided support of the Israel action, despite the initial provocation by Hezbollah, angered many Muslims in the region, generating even more anti-American sentiment.

President Bush ignored the Lebanon prime minister's pleas to halt the destruction by Israeli warplanes, even though Bush backed the democratic government. The Hezbollah guerrillas' disciplined stand against the Israel Defense Forces (IDF), holding it to a standstill while firing rockets into Israel, enhanced the group's status in Lebanon, threatening the ruling democratic coalition. Most importantly, Iran's influence in the region appeared bolstered through the conflict, since it was the major financial and military supporter of Hezbollah.

Because of its border with Afghanistan, Pakistan became a critical strategic ally early in the war on terror. But Pakistan's military ruler, President Pervez Musharraf, faced opposition within the intelligence service against taking strong action vis-à-vis the Taliban. Nevertheless, Musharraf bravely joined the United States to help destroy al Qaeda. However, when al Qaeda and Taliban forces fled to Pakistan's remote tribal areas, Musharraf hesitated on ordering military actions that could provoke Islamic protests. Furthermore, President Musharraf's efforts to retain the presidency, while remaining Army chief of staff, aroused popular opposition. President Bush confronted a clash between the war on terror goals and his democracy agenda.

Was President Bush's propensity for bold ambitious goals the deciding factor behind the Wilsonian-type declaration? Were George W. Bush's fundamentalist beliefs in the struggle between good and evil the critical influence? Or did President Bush simply acquiesce to neoconservative calls for the vigorous application of American power in the Middle East?

In summary, the challenges and frustrations George W. Bush faced in his first 40 years developed certain personal characteristics and behaviors that proved very successful when he became comanaging partner of the Texas Rangers, governor of Texas, and then, as president, confronting the horrifying 9/11 attacks on America. At times, however, the personas George W. Bush manifested in facing unprecedented challenges seemed less than a perfect fit for the complex situations he faced. The core question examined in the book focuses on whether his pursuit of the war on terror as a War President thus fulfilled the test by fire demanded of America's great presidents.

Part I

Path to the White House

Chapter Two

The Fortunate Son: Star-Spangled Eyes[1]

I want to be a fighter pilot because my father was.

George W. Bush began life as the fortunate, privileged son of an ambitious young World War II hero, determined to make his fortune early in life. The subsequent success of his father, George Bush, in the highly competitive oil industry, followed by high executive positions in two Republican administrations, public service as the nation's vice president and then election as president, set incredibly high expectations for George W., the oldest son who bore the proud name of his prominent father.

George W. Bush proved unable to achieve the academic, athletic, or business success of his father, leading to frustration and the emergence of boisterous and sometimes belligerent behavior patterns that diverted attention from his perceived inadequacies or failures. However, George W.'s gregarious personality and interpersonal skills finally led to success in his forties, ironically through baseball, the sport in which his father excelled. George W.'s comanager role with the Texas Rangers baseball team allowed him to follow the path of the great man in his life—his father, George Bush.[2]

Looking Up to Dad

As a toddler, George W. Bush spent his earliest days hanging around a ball field— the Yale baseball diamond. His mother, Barbara Pierce Bush, loyally attended all the Yale baseball games to watch her athletic, graceful, and enthusiastic husband captain the Yale team for a second Eastern Championship. Born on July 6, 1946, the eldest son of George and Barbara Bush started his life in New Haven, Connecticut, not far from the Greenwich home of his grandparents, Connecticut's U.S. Senator Prescott Bush and his wife Dorothy. Life was hectic for George W.'s mother, with her Navy veteran husband striving to obtain a Yale economics degree in two and a half years, while playing baseball and caring for his responsibilities as a husband and new father.

When George told his young wife of his decision to pursue postgraduation oil industry opportunities in West Texas with Ideco, as Dresser Industries' only trainee, she sardonically exclaimed: "I've *always wanted* to live in Odessa, Texas."[3] Barbara and two-year-old George W. loyally packed up and followed George's dream, arriving in Odessa by a propeller plane in spring 1948, one week after George Bush drove their new red Studebaker to West Texas.

Life in Odessa starkly contrasted from what both George and Barbara knew in the East. "Odessa was the hardscrabble, hard-drinking, honky-tonk underbelly of West Texas."[4] In spring 1949 Dresser transferred George Bush to California, where the family moved up and down the coast as he sold oil-drilling rigs. In December 1949 their second child Robin (Pauline Robinson) Bush was born. Shortly afterward, Ideco sent George and his family to Midland, Texas.

In 1950 the fast-track oriented George Bush formed Bush-Overbey Oil Development Company, Inc. with a neighbor, beginning an arduous and time-consuming scramble to make an early fortune in the Texas oil patch. Their second son Jeb (John Ellis) Bush was born in February 1953. George traveled extensively to build his new company: "I was gone all the time...busy with my job. It was Barbara who really raised him [George W.]."[5]

The October 1953 death of his three-year-old sister, Robin, deeply impacted upon seven-year-old George W. Bush. Diagnosed with an advanced case of leukemia, Robin was taken to cancer specialists in Midland and New York, hoping to prolong her young life. For six months George W.'s parents were often absent from home as they took Robin to hospitals to find treatments for her disease. Barbara and George decided not to tell their son his sister was dying. Barbara explained that "we felt it would have been too big a burden for such a little fellow."[6]

The death of his little sister hit George W. hard, even at his young age. A number of family members and friends viewed Little George's reaction to the loss of his sister and his mother's depression as the spur for him to assume a clownish, entertainer role within the family. His antics sought to cheer up his grieving mother after the painful loss. His cousin Elsie Walker felt close to George W. because of their shared experiences, since she had also lost a sister. "We're both clowns. I think kids who lose a sibling often try and find ways to, you know make things easier in the family."[7] Family members recalled that his antics often made his parents laugh. His sister Doro (Dorothy Walker Bush) later described the times with young George W. as always fun, wild, and daring. "He was always on the edge."[8]

George W. attended Midland's Sam Houston Elementary School from first to sixth grade. Midland became for George W. Bush the ideal place to grow up as a child, "a small town, with small town values."[9] His brother Neil Mallon Bush was born in 1955, then Marvin Pierce Bush in 1956, and sister Doro Bush in 1959. In the seventh grade George W. attended San Jacinto Junior High for one year, where he was elected class president. As the oldest son, he helped Barbara Bush raise his siblings while his father traveled on business. George W. was the first to notice his brother Neil's reading problem, diagnosed later as dyslexia. As Barbara recalled those difficult days after the loss of Robin—raising her young children with her husband often out of town—she wondered how she could have ever made it without her oldest son George W. "He was my Rock of Gibraltar...and because of that, we have a very special relationship."[10]

As chief executive officer (CEO) of Zapata Off-Shore, George Bush began spending more and more time traveling to Houston on business. The family decided to move to the larger city in 1959, when George W. finished the seventh grade. George Bush continued his travel to New York for meetings with investors and flew overseas to explore oil-drilling opportunities. As Jeb Bush recalled, "Even when we were growing up in Houston, Dad wasn't at home at night to play catch.... Mom was always the one to hand out the goodies and the discipline. In a sense, it was a matriarchal family."[11]

After attending Houston's private Kinkaid School for two years, George W. left Texas at age 15 to attend the elite boarding school Andover—like his father. He immediately confronted the senior George Bush's impressive student accomplishments at Andover, quickly realizing that his name carried a burden of very high expectations. At Benner House a large photograph of his father in his Andover baseball uniform hung on the wall. George W. lettered in baseball, junior varsity football and basketball, but did not excel in athletics like his father. Instead, he sought the limelight and campus popularity by organizing an informal stickball league, dubbing himself the "High Commissioner" or "Tweeds," for Boss Tweed. George W. also became the varsity football team's "chief cheerleader," organizing special skits for pregame pep rallies that made him the center of attention.

Bush received the nickname "The Lip" from his fellow Andover students, frankly confessing: "I was quick with a one-liner."[12] His dorm-mate James Lockart III pointed out that at Andover, such quips gained peer respect, since the "Andover atmosphere of sarcasm was sort of the language we spoke."[13] Fellow student Tory Peterson remembered George W.'s antics: "He sort of liked to be a little bit of a showman. He liked being liked, or getting people to like him, and it was one of those things where everybody in the whole school would know who you are."[14] Student peers considered him a prankster, mischievous and quick with the sarcastic comment. Most importantly, George W. learned at Andover: "I could make friends, and make my way, no matter where I found myself in life."[15]

Bush's cousin Elsie Walker Kilbourne felt that at Andover, when George W. first encountered the formidable legacy of his father—and discovered he could not achieve the elder Bush's academic or athletic accomplishments—he developed a mechanism to protect himself from family pressures. "George really saw the value of lowering expectations.... He became a master at it. The whole family clown thing was as much about lowering expectations so he wouldn't disappoint than anything."[16]

George W. struggled in his Andover classes, at one point worrying about flunking out of the elite school and embarrassing his family. He admitted, "Andover was hard, and I was behind."[17] Bush, worried about his mediocre grades, applied to the University of Texas as a fallback to Yale. But since Bush's great-great grandfather, his grandfather, his father, and seven uncles had attended Yale—and Senator Prescott Bush and great uncle Herby Walker served on Yale's board of directors— George W. received a Yale letter of acceptance.[18] His grandfather Senator Prescott Bush solemnly advised him: "George, Yale is not a choice; it is a commitment."[19]

Following the footsteps of his father and grandfather, George W. enrolled at Yale where again he failed to stand out academically or athletically. Both his grandfather and father graduated Phi Beta Kappa and were key players on Yale's winning baseball teams. First baseman and captain George Bush even met the New York Yankees slugger, Babe Ruth. *The New Yorker* published a copy of George W. Bush's Yale transcript that showed he was a C student. "Not once in his undergraduate career did he earn an A—but then he didn't flunk any courses, either."[20] George W. pitched on Yale's freshman baseball team, but later switched to rugby and intramural activities.

As a freshman George W. introduced himself to Yale's Chaplain Reverend William Sloan Coffin, a Skull and Bones member like his father. George W., who placed his idealized father on a pedestal, appeared stunned when Coffin said: "I knew your father, and your father lost to a better man," referring to George Bush's 1964 defeat by liberal Texas Senator Ralph Yarborough. That insensitive remark permanently scarred George W.'s memories of Yale, highlighting what he later called the "intellectual snobbery" of the East Coast establishment.[21]

Graduates in his 1968 class faced the prospect of an immediate draft for military service in Vietnam, because President Lyndon B. Johnson had just abolished college deferments. Protests against the Vietnam War and debates over options to avoid the draft rocked the campus. At George W.'s Yale graduation, 312 of the 955 graduating seniors signed an antiwar petition—but not Bush. A fellow Bonesman, Jordanian Muhammed Saleh, noted that George W. "was not obsessed by anything, or a cause. He didn't have any agenda, a timetable, a program."[22] Despite the turmoil and demonstrations in the 1960s, George W. Bush later reflected on those troubled times: "I don't remember any kind of heaviness ruining my time at Yale."[23] Neither he nor his friends protested the war: "I don't think we spent a lot of time debating it."[24]

In his fraternity Delta Kappa Epsilon (Deke), George W. Bush was always at the center of drinking, activities, and pranks. He later became president of the fraternity. Friends noted that George W. primarily studied the people around him at Yale. Robert McCallum, a member of Skull and Bones, recalled: "More than anything, George was a student of people, not subjects....He decided pretty early on to be people smart, not book smart."[25] Roland Betts, a close Yale friend and later a vital investor in the Texas Rangers, estimated that George W. probably knew 1,000 of the 4,000 undergraduates at Yale, far more than known by most of his peers. But that familiarity with people did not translate into perceived leadership ability. Fellow Bonesman Robert Birge observed: "If I had to go through my class, and pick five people who were going to run for president, it would never have occurred to me he would ever run....He did not carry himself like a statesman."[26]

The exclusive Skull and Bones Society tapped George W. for membership in the second semester of his junior year—like his grandfather and father. When George W. heard the traditional Tap Night knock on his door, he opened the door to find his father, then-Congressman Bush, standing outside to ask him to become a good man by joining Skull and Bones.[27] Several Bonesmen recalled that during the secret society's meetings, George W. often talked about his father in "almost God-like" terms.[28] His first cousin John Ellis described George W.'s relations with his mother Barbara as joshing comradeship. In contrast, "With his father, awe never left the equation."[29]

George W. Bush, like many other young men of his generation, grew anxious at the prospect of losing his college deferment when he graduated in June 1968. While he held mixed feelings about President Lyndon Johnson's execution of the Vietnam War, he embraced his father's position in supporting the war. George W. thus faced the dilemma of deciding how to avoid embarrassing his father, a decorated World War II hero, yet still avert being sent to fight in Vietnam. His Deke friend Roland Betts recalled, "He felt that in order not to derail his father's political career he had to be in military service of some kind."[30]

In spring 1968 George W. Bush's name leaped to the top of a waiting list of 500 men hoping to enter the Texas Air National Guard. Houston businessman Sidney Adger, a close friend of the Bush family, placed a call to Texas Speaker Ben Barnes to request his help in placing George W. in a pilot's spot in the Guard. Barnes in turn phoned Brigadier General James Rose, who was the assistant adjutant general for the Texas Air National Guard, according to a sworn deposition in a civil lawsuit.[31] When the commander of the Houston 147 Fighter Group, Lieutenant Colonel Walter "Buck" Staudt, asked George W. Bush why he wanted to join the Air National Guard, the congressman's eldest son replied: "I want to be a fighter pilot because my father was."[32]

George W. Bush scored 95 percent on the "officer quality" portion of the application questionnaire, but only 25 percent on the "pilot aptitude test," the lowest acceptable score.[33] On the question asking whether he wanted to go overseas, George W. Bush checked the box, "Do not volunteer." Joining the National Guard offered a safe way to sidestep combat in Vietnam, a path taken by the sons of two other Texas political elites, then-Congressman Lloyd M. Bensten and Senator John Tower.[34] *The New York Times* later calculated that only 15,000 of the total 1,040,000 National Guard and reservists were sent to Vietnam (1.4 percent). Furthermore, George W. received a direct commission and acceptance into the Texas Air National Guard's pilot training program. Normally, direct commissions went to men "who had college ROTC courses or prior Air Force experience. Bush had neither."[35]

Second Lieutenant Bush received six weeks of basic training at Lackland Air Force Base in Texas and then took an eight-week leave, beginning on September 5, 1968, to work in the Florida Senate campaign of Edward Gurney, a friend of his father. Afterward, Bush reported to Moody Air Force Base in Valdosta, Georgia, where he trained to fly the F-102 Delta Dagger. Even though he was the only National Guard trainee, he made friends and soon assigned his fellow trainees nicknames. In December 1969, Congressman Bush pinned on Second Lieutenant George W. Bush's wings at Houston's Ellington Air Force Base.

George W. requested a 1972 transfer to the Alabama Air National Guard, while he worked as a paid campaign director for Winton "Red" Blount, an old family friend and GOP challenger of Alabama's Democratic Senator John Sparkman. However, whether Lieutenant Bush served his required National Guard time in Alabama between May 1972 and May 1973 remains a mystery. Indeed, Bush's orders told him to report to Lt. Col. William Turnipseed of the Alabama Air National Guard. However, Turnipseed stated in May 2000: "To my knowledge, he never showed up."[36] Turnipseed noted that he had completed his own flight training in Texas. "If we had had a first lieutenant from Texas, I would have remembered."[37]

In response to a Freedom of Information request by *The New York Times* and other news organizations, the Pentagon on June 25, 2004, announced that some of Lieutenant George W. Bush's National Guard records had been inadvertently destroyed. Then, on July 23 the Pentagon found the missing records, which they could not locate earlier because of "incorrect accession numbers."[38] The released records showed that Lt. Bush did not perform required duties in the Alabama Air National Guard between July and September 1972, which the White House had acknowledged. But the records still left unclear, "how and where Mr. Bush performed his prescribed military service between May 1972 and May 1973."

The records noted that Lt. Bush was suspended from flying on August 1, 1972, for "failure to accomplish annual medical exam." Bush did not fly in the final 18 months of his Air National Guard service in 1972 and 1973. He was honorably discharged eight months early in October 1973, before completing his six-year National Guard obligation, to enroll in Harvard's Masters in Business Administration program. But Lieutenant George W. Bush's discharge papers "include no evidence of any duty between May 1972 and October 1973, when he left the Guard."[39]

Afterward, George W. went through his "irresponsible youth" stage, as he labeled it during the 1994 gubernatorial race. His heavy drinking and partying led his Texas friends to nickname George W. the "Bombastic Bushkin." After a Christmas 1972 drunken challenge to his father to go *mano a mano*, the senior Bush arranged for George W. to work with a Houston inner-city program (PULL) until he left to attend the Masters in Business Administration (MBA) degree program at Harvard in fall 1973. His mother Barbara later declared that George W.'s Harvard MBA degree gave "structure" to his life.

George W. exhibited at an early age a weak self-esteem and self-confidence, particularly because he bore the name of George Bush, a man he placed on a "pedestal (that) kept getting taller," as his close friend Joe O'Neill described the dilemma.[40] Since George W. could not excel in the classroom or on the athletic field like his father, he acted in boisterous ways to win attention, praise, affection, and love, particularly from his eminent and busy father. At home he played the role of "family clown," to use his brother Marvin's description of George W.'s behavior into his thirties.[41]

At Andover and Yale, Bush had sought notice through his pranks and outrageous behavior, assigning nicknames to his peers as a token of a special friendship. George W.'s academic, athletic, and military service fell woefully short of the achievements of George Bush. The inability to live up to his father's accomplishments must have bothered him immensely, considering his idealized devotion of his father. Therefore, George W. attempted to deflect attention from his mediocre performance in his youth through his clownish actions to lower expectations for the namesake of George Bush. This frustration probably contributed to the excessive drinking and partying during his college and his postgraduate "nomadic years," as George W. called them. It will be noted later that George W. Bush's political success in Texas and Washington was facilitated by opponents holding low expectations of him as a candidate.

His mother Barbara played the key role in the youthful development of his self-esteem, which centered on his gregariousness and quick repartee. Barbara would scream and discipline the children, as the tough parent. But if George would scold them or say, "I'm disappointed in you," the children "would almost faint" since they craved his love and attention.[42]

Since George Bush traveled a lot after the death of his daughter Robin, George W. and Barbara Bush developed a bantering relationship, very distinct from the awe toward his foreboding father. George W.'s description of Barbara Bush's sharp tongue could also describe his own sudden anger and barbed words: "My mother's always been a very outspoken person who vents very well—she'll just let it rip if she's got something on her mind. Once it's over, you know exactly where you stand and that's it."[43] His irreverence, bluntness, quick banter, and "in your face" attitude, according to relatives, appeared to have been acquired from his mother Bar (Barbara).[44] George W. also seemed to inherit Barbara's political instincts about people and a more folksy interpersonal style.

First cousin John Ellis insisted that the "whole key to understanding George W. is his relationship with his father."[45] George W., as the oldest son bearing his father's name, particularly bore the brunt of high expectations. As Elsie Walker Kilbourne pointed out, "The Bushes and the Walkers place a big emphasis on the oldest-son bit."[46] George W.'s continuing search for attention, applause, and friendship through humor, sarcasm, and spotlight-seeking antics, thus developed as a mechanism to overcome what George W. perceived as an inability to live up to the hopes of his high-achiever father.

The Family Business

In the five years after graduating from Yale, George W. served in the National Guard, worked for an agricultural business with a friend of his father's, campaigned for George Bush during his 1970 Senate bid and worked for two GOP Senate candidates. He had lived in Texas, Florida, Georgia, and Alabama during this "nomadic period" in his life. George W. Bush's 1970 application for admission to the University of Texas law school as an in-state resident had been rejected based upon his mediocre Yale grades. In September 1973 George W. began Harvard's MBA program in Cambridge, Massachusetts, which he felt would provide a new direction for his life. His family did not know he had applied to Harvard until the acceptance letter arrived. He bluntly told them: "I just wanted to let you know I could get into it."[47] Harvard's business graduate program thus represented a chance to start anew to prove himself to his father and the Bush-Walker family.

During George W.'s time in Cambridge, his father headed the Republican National Committee, taking a leading role in the defense of President Richard Nixon against the Watergate and impeachment charges. George W. Bush attended classes wearing his Air National Guard bomber jacket, chewing Copenhagen tobacco during class with a paper cup at his feet. He particularly enjoyed visiting the Hillbilly Ranch, a local bar that played country music. George W. came to dislike the arrogance on the Harvard campus, later describing the experience as "claustrophobic, intellectually and physically."[48] He often escaped on weekends to visit his aunt Nancy Ellis in Boston and relatives in New York. He also continued to enjoy his four Bs, as he called them—beer, bourbon, and Benedictine & Brandy liqueur (B&B). During this time his family noticed that his heavy drinking was turning into a problem. His Uncle Pres observed: "George was becoming a real boozer."[49]

With his prestigious Harvard MBA, George W. returned to Texas rather than accepting a Wall Street position with his uncle Jonathan Bush. His uncle understood his nephew's desire to pursue a path similar to his father in the oil industry. "If your family has kind of carved out a path in a certain area, it isn't too hard for you to imagine yourself in the same thing—and it's not hard for other people to imagine you in the same area."[50] Jonathan Bush also felt that Harvard, with George W.'s interactions with other ambitious and bright young men and women, had replaced his adolescent "swagger" with a more realist, intelligent, and confident approach to life.[51]

That summer George W. joined his parents and three of his siblings in China, where his father served as head of the U.S. Liaison Office. In June 1975 George W. drove his 1970 Oldsmobile Cutlass to Midland, fortified with $20,000 from his trust fund to serve as seed money for his dream of striking it big in the Texas oil patch. George W. began learning the oil business by working as a land man, earning $100 for researching titles and mineral rights for independent and large oil companies. He lived frugally, associated with some of the older oil men who knew his father, and socialized with old friends from his Midland youth. In June 1977 George W. Bush incorporated his own company, Arbusto Energy (*Arbusto* translated as Bush in Spanish) and began to raise money from family and friends. However, Security and Exchange Commission records indicate that Arbusto Energy did not start active operations until March 1979, after he lost a 1978 bid for a seat in Congress.[52]

In July 1977, when long-term Congressman George Mahon announced his retirement, George W. decided to run for the open Nineteenth Congressional District seat. Although back in Texas only two years, George W. told family-friend Jimmy Allison he would "take a shot at the family business."[53] When George W. phoned his father, then living in Houston planning a 1980 White House race, George Bush indicated support and pleasure that his oldest son was entering the political arena like himself and his grandfather. As the ever-competitive George Bush later told an historian: "You can't win unless you run."[54]

George W. Bush announced his candidacy for the Nineteenth Congressional District seat in July 1977. Several weeks later he met Laura Welch at a back-yard barbeque hosted by his old Midland friends, Jan and Joe O'Neill. After a whirlwind courtship, the couple became engaged five weeks later and married on November 6, 1977. Instead of a honeymoon, the newlyweds hit the campaign trail.

Thirty-two-year-old George W. Bush faced a serious opponent in the Republican primary, the former mayor of Odessa, Jim Reese. Reese had supported California Governor Ronald Reagan's 1976 campaign for president against President Gerald Ford; in June 1978 Reagan reciprocated by endorsing Reese. The senior Bush bitterly complained to the media: "I am surprised about what he [Reagan] is doing here, in my state.... They are making a real effort to defeat George."[55] Reagan's endorsement of Reese also manifested early jockeying for the 1980 GOP presidential nomination by Reagan and the elder Bush.

Reese blasted George W. Bush for misleading Texas voters about being born a Yankee in New Haven, Connecticut. Bush's brochure had stated: "Born July 6, 1946 and raised in Midland, Texas." Reese accused Bush of belonging to the Eastern Rockefeller wing of the Republican party. An observer commented that George W. enjoyed being the focus of attention and worked the crowds very effectively for a political neophyte.[56] George W. won the GOP primary, with 6,787 votes to 5,350 for Reese.

But the Bush team faced a tougher challenge when George W. faced the Democratic nominee, State Senator Kent Hance. A skilled campaigner, Hance adopted a strategy that painted George W. Bush as an "outsider," a carpetbagger with Eastern, privileged roots. Senator Hance drawled to crowds: "My daddy and granddaddy were farmers," so they didn't make the mess in Washington that Bush's father had helped create.[57] Hance mocked George W. for attending Andover, while he graduated from Dimmitt High School; for going to Yale University while Hance went to Texas Tech. Bush's opponents also circulated a rumor that his father was a member of Rockefeller's Trilateral Commission, which they charged promoted a world government.

The Hance campaign capitalized at the end of the hard-fought campaign on the Bush campaign's sponsorship of a Bush Bash featuring free beer for students at Texas Tech University. Senator Hance sent out a letter describing the event to over 4,000 members of the dry Church of Christ residing in the Nineteenth Congressional District. Kent Hance won the 1978 House race with 53 percent of the vote, with Bush receiving an impressive 47 percent as a political newcomer. Moreover, Bush family ties had allowed George W. Bush to raise $406,000, spending a third more than the Hance campaign. Federal Election Commission reports showed that 64 percent of his contributions came from outside of the district, with most of Bush's money coming from outside the state rather than from within Texas.[58] While his father did not campaign for George W. in the district, he held four fundraisers for him in Washington, Dallas, Houston, and Midland.

Deep Pockets, Empty Wells

George W. concentrated on his newly organized Arbusto Energy after his election defeat, beginning operations in March 1979. He set up a small office in Midland's Petroleum Building—the same building where his father began his oil business. He raised almost $5 million from 50 investors, including about $180,000 from family members.[59] George W. acknowledged that the investors "were mainly friends of my uncle," stockbroker Jonathan Bush. Charlie Younger, one of George W.'s close friends, recalled: "He could get into doors with his name that you and I couldn't—with oil people."[60]

George W. also hung out at the Petroleum Club with the older oilmen who knew his dad; "they appreciated the fact that good-humored Bush chewed tobacco, told jokes, drank, and cursed harder than a grease-stained roustabout."[61] Arbusto drilled about 10 wells a year, with about half of the wells hitting oil or natural gas. Although expenditures exceeded revenues, generous federal tax write-offs kept investors from getting too upset about their losses. Securities records revealed that by the end of 1984, Bush's limited partners had invested $4.6 million but received only $1.54 million in cash distributions—plus a generous $3.9 million in federal tax deductions. Geologist Paul Rea explained, "There's a lot of luck and a lot of science to oil drilling....He didn't have the luck."

After friends began calling the unsuccessful company Ar-BUST-o, George W. changed the name to Bush Exploration. George W. then attempted to sell stock in Bush Exploration on the stock market at a time of falling oil prices. He later admitted: "Going public was a mistake."[62] He had hoped to raise $6 million, but received only $1,141,000. At the end of 1983, Bush Exploration ranked 993rd in the production of Texas oil. One investor, Phillip Uzielli who lost almost $1 million recalled: "The good Lord just didn't put any oil out there."

Bush's struggling company escaped bankruptcy in February 1984 when it merged with Spectrum 7. George W. became the chief executive officer and received 1.1 million shares in the parent company. Rea, who helped arrange the merger, recalled that the Bush name was "definitely a drawing card."[63] But when oil prices tumbled to $10 per barrel in 1986, the vice president's son lamented: "I'm all name and no money."

Harken Energy purchased Spectrum 7 in April 1986. George W. received $600,000 of Harken stock for his 14.9 percent holding in Spectrum.[64] Phil Kendrick, the founder of Harken who still held stock in the firm, observed: "It's obvious why they kept George Bush [on the Harken board of directors]....He's worth $200,000 a year to them just for [instant credibility]...It helps...to be the son of a president."

George W. Bush served on the eight-person Harken board of directors and received a consulting fee up to $120,000 while working full time in 1987 and 1988 on his father's presidential campaign. The *Wall Street Journal* explored links between Bush's involvement with Harken and the rogue Bank of Credit and Commerce International (BCCI). The report concluded: "But the number of BCCI-connected people who had dealings with Harken—all since George W. Bush came on board—likewise raises the question of whether they mask an effort to cozy up to a presidential son."[65] George W. also sat on Harken's exploration advisory board. Questions arose when the Persian Gulf nation of Bahrain granted Harken international off-shore drilling rights. Not only had Harken never drilled overseas, it had never drilled an oil well at sea.[66] Some viewed the contract as Bahrain's attempt to gain White House favor, since the president's son sat on Harken's board of directors.

George W. Bush sold his 212,140 shares of Harken stock on June 22, 1990, for $835,307 at $4 per share. However, eight days later the sharp fall of the price of Harken's stock brought charges of insider trading, triggering an investigation by the Securities Exchange Commission. "Eight days after Bush's stock sale, Harken wound up its second quarter with operating losses from day-to-day activities of $6.7 million, almost three times the losses it reported for the second quarter of 1989."[67] Bush sat on Harken's three-person audit committee, which had met on June 11, 1990, with auditors from the accounting firm of Arthur Andersen & Co. But George W. had obtained clearance from Harken's attorney to sell his stock. He planned to use the profits from his sale of Harken stock for his share of the investment in the Texas Rangers.

An April 1991 SEC investigation found Bush had failed to file a notice of actual sale of stock until eight months after the deadline. Three weeks before Bush announced he was running for governor of Texas, the SEC sent him a letter dated an October 18, 1993, that said "the investigation has been terminated as to the conduct of Mr. Bush, and that, at this time, no enforcement action is contemplated with respect to him." Although George W. claimed this letter "exonerated" him in the Harken sale, the SEC associate director for enforcement, Bruce Hiler, declared that the statement "must in no way be construed as indicating that the party has been exonerated or that no action may result from the staff's investigation."

The Loyalty Thermometer

After the November 1984 re-election victory of the Reagan-Bush ticket, Bush family members met five months later at Camp David with Lee Atwater about running

Vice President Bush's 1988 presidential campaign. George W. probed Atwater about the depth of his loyalty to George Bush. George W. emphasized what the Bush family's loyalty test required, "If there's a hand grenade rolling around George Bush, we want you diving on it first."[68] Atwater responded that if George W. doubted his loyalty, he or another family member should work in the campaign headquarters to oversee his actions. George W. accepted the task, commuting to Washington DC while living in Midland, serving on the Harken board, and consulting for the energy company. In May 1987, the family moved to Washington until after the November 1988 election. George W. proudly told a *Time* reporter that in the 1988 presidential campaign: "I was the loyalty thermometer."[69]

George W. and Atwater soon became friends, sharing a cynical view of Washington insiders and tendencies toward rebellious antics. Lee Atwater and other staffers called him "Junior," but as George W. conceded, "In a presidential campaign two people named George Bush can be really confusing. You just have to swallow your pride a little."[70] Atwater often used George W. to sell his hard-hitting campaign tactics and negative TV ads to his father, like the tax "straddle" ad against Senator Robert Dole in the New Hampshire GOP primary and the general election negative wedge issue ads crafted to drive up Governor Michael Dukakis's personal negatives. Referring to the Willie Horton TV ad's appeal to racial prejudices, Atwater boasted: "If I can make Willie Horton a household name, we'll win the election."[71] George W. helped raise the necessary money and locate "sponsors" for the more controversial ads.[72] Atwater also used George W. to defuse a rumor about an affair between George Bush and a former vice presidential aide, Jennifer Fitzgerald. George W. told a *Newsweek* reporter: "The answer to the Big A question is N.O."[73]

Bush verbally assailed reporters who wrote unflattering stories about his father, describing his rage as "feisting out." One observer described George W. as the "Roman candle" of the Bush family because of his quick temper, profanity, and abusive language. Needless to say, George W. put a different spin on his 1988 behavior with the media and campaign staffers: "I was a pretty straightforward person....Many people in Washington are used to double-talk."[74] The shrewd South Carolina strategist Lee Atwater introduced George W. to the effectiveness of Machiavellian low-road tactics—including the explosive race card—to win elections. Although it did not show at the time, Atwater impressed upon George W. the importance of wooing the press.

Dough Wead, another member of the 1988 campaign staff, also influenced George W.'s political thinking. Wead helped sensitize George W. to the important language nuances and appeals needed to attract evangelicals to his father's campaign. Wead recalled that George W. demonstrated no interest in politics for himself: "He didn't give a rip about publicity or attention. He wanted to help his dad get elected and then get out of town. He was very decisive, very energetic."[75]

Wead found that George W. seemed more understanding and receptive to the evangelicals than his father, based upon the younger Bush's personal experiences in the last few years. Even though Bush denied he was "clinically an alcoholic," his heavy drinking had become a deep concern to his wife Laura and the Bush family in the 1980s.[76] Shellie Bush Jansing stated: "It was embarrassing to the family and Laura certainly didn't like it."[77] For example, in April 1986 an inebriated George W. cussed out a *Wall Street Journal* reporter in a restaurant in front of the man's wife and four-year-old son.[78] Cousin John Ellis remembered, "There was the feeling that he had become an embarrassment to the family, there had simply been too many incidents." His close friend Don Evans recalled: "Once he got started, he couldn't, didn't shut it off....He didn't have the discipline."[79] Elsie Walker Kilbourne viewed George W.'s heavy drinking as a form of self-medication to mask his frustrations over failing to meet the family's expectations for George Bush's eldest son.

George W. Bush later admitted his drinking caused problems: "I realized that alcohol was beginning to crowd out my energies and could crowd, eventually, my affections for other people."[80] In July 1986 he and Laura Bush went with several other couples to the Broadmoor Hotel in Colorado Springs to celebrate fortieth birthdays. The morning after the partying, George W. announced to Laura he had decided to stop drinking. His friend Joe O'Neill explained: "He looked in the mirror and said, 'Someday, I might embarrass my father. It might get my dad in trouble.' And boy, that was it. That's how high a priority it was.... And he never took another drink."[81] George W. later said: "I'm not really the type to wander off and sit down and go through deep wrestling with my soul...I just quit drinking."[82]

George W's second life-changing experience concerned his religious awakening. In his campaign biography, written by loyal media advisor Karen Hughes, Bush claimed the "seeds" for his decision to give up drinking had been planted by the internationally known evangelist Billy Graham in summer 1985 at the Bush family complex in Kennebunkport, Maine. But in November 2004, Rev. Graham told ABC's Brian Williams: "I cannot say that. I was with him and I used to teach the Bible at Kennebunkport to the Bush family when he was a younger man. But I never feel that I, in any way, turned his life around."[83]

However, the public relations oriented biography ignored the fact that over a year earlier, on April 3, 1984, George W. had privately met with the less-known Baptist evangelist Arthur Blessitt at Midland's Holiday Inn, a meeting arranged by oilman Jim Sale. Blessitt asked Bush: "If you died this moment, do you have the assurance you would go to heaven?"[84] Blessitt, Bush, and Sale then kneeled together and recited "The Sinners Prayer," which confessed the need for salvation through Jesus Christ, a request for forgiveness, and acceptance of Christ's salvation.[85] George W.'s decision to give up drinking and his new fundamentalist religious beliefs helped Bush reach out to evangelical leaders on his father's behalf. Doug Wead observed: "When G.W. meets with evangelical Christians, they know within minutes that he's one of theirs."[86]

Political Home Run

In October 1988 George W. Bush heard that Fort Worth oil baron Eddie Chiles wanted to sell the Texas Rangers baseball team, which had not enjoyed a winning season in 25 years. Baseball Commissioner Peter Ueberroth insisted that whoever bought the franchise must have significant local investment. George W. moved his family to Dallas in December 1988, after his father's presidential victory. Guided by Karl Rove, he began to increase his Texas media exposure for a possible 1990 gubernatorial race. Simultaneously he phoned possible investors for a deal to buy the Texas Rangers baseball franchise. Roland Betts, his New York Deke frater-nity brother, ultimately invested $3.6 million and his partner $2.4 million in the Rangers deal.

Commissioner Ueberroth, still insisting upon sizeable local investment in the Rangers, flew to Texas to encourage billionaire Richard Rainwater to put together a group of Texas investors; Rainwater had already turned down George W. Bush's proposal. Rainwater later told reporters: "I put the entire financing together. I structured everything. I put in place the management team."[87] The management team would consist of millionaire Edward "Rusty" Rose III and George W. Bush, who were named general partners and had to agree on all decisions. Rose would handle the Rangers' financial matters, while George W. Bush, who received a $200,000 salary, would handle media relations. In April 1989, 70 investors bought the Texas Rangers for $89 million. George W. Bush invested only $606,302 in the Rangers purchase, giving him 1.8 percent ownership of the team. However, his percentage would increase to 11.8 percent after the partners recouped their invest-ment with interest when the team was sold.

Baseball Commissioner Peter Ueberroth later described his version of the Rangers purchase. Ueberroth stated that he had asked Rainwater and Rose to include George W. Bush in the deal. "He was an asset because his father's career was going up and reaching the top. We just brought the young man over some-what out of respect for his father."[88]

Needless to say, George W. Bush's campaign biography described his key role in bringing the Texas Rangers investors together, which enhanced his political resume. "I was also the person that aggressively sought the deal. I was a pit bull on the pant leg of opportunity. I wouldn't let go."[89] George W. knew that his unsuc-cessful record in the oil industry failed to exemplify his leadership ability.

Immediately after the 1988 election, Bush had asked a high-ranking Republican Texas operative to check on his acceptability among big-money GOP contributors for a 1990 run for governor. She reported back: "George, everybody likes you, but you haven't done anything.... You're a Bush and that's all."[90] George W. admitted to his friend Roland Betts: "I could run for governor but I'm basically a media cre-ation. I've never done anything."[91] Thus, the Rangers purchase offered George W. Bush a springboard to pursue his future political aspirations. His brother Marvin observed, "This is a real opportunity for him to be George W. Bush and not George Bush Jr."[92]

However, George W.'s travels in spring 1989 to test the Texas political waters for a 1990 governor's campaign led to public and private warnings from two people close to him. His mother Barbara, concerned that his political agenda might undermine the Rangers project, told reporters: "George is a man on his own...and I'd rather he ran in eight years, four years, whatever."[93] Likewise, his close friend Roland Betts balked at investing in the Rangers if George W. ran for governor two years later. Even though a Mason-Dixon poll of Republican voters showed him leading the field of likely GOP candidates, George W. told an August 1, 1989, lawyers association meeting in Dallas that he would not run for governor the following year.

George W. Bush played an important role in negotiating an October 1990 agree-ment with Arlington Mayor Richard Greene to raise the local sales tax a half-cent to build a new $135 million ballpark dedicated to the Rangers. As the Texas Rangers' spokesman, Bush campaigned extensively to get Arlington voters to approve the resolution, which passed in January 1991 with 65 percent support. He then helped win the approval of the Texas legislature in April 1991 to create the Arlington Sports Facility Development Authority through exercising the power of eminent domain, which claimed 13 acres of private property for the new ballpark.[94]

In 1996 the Rangers won the American League West, going to the playoffs for the first time in the franchise's history. Bush would later use the Ballpark at Arlington as a campaign symbol to highlight his ability to "dream big dreams" and get things done. "And when all those people in Austin say, 'He ain't never done anything,' well, this is it."[95] But just as significantly, when Tom Hicks bought the Rangers for $250 million in 1998, George W. Bush became a multimillionaire, earning $14.9 million on an initial investment of $606,302. Bush's "Great Liberator," the gusher that would make him independently wealthy, had finally arrived.

In conclusion, George W. Bush's early years manifested a weak self-esteem stemming from his inability to meet the family's expectations for the namesake and eldest son of George Bush. This led George W. from an early age to seek attention, approval, and love through clowning antics to lower expectations and adult "over the edge" behavior, underscored by his Midland friends. George W. placed his very active, often absent, and highly idealized father, whose career kept rising to new heights—ultimately the presidency—on a tall pedestal. In turn, George W.'s personal sense of failure left him with feelings of inadequacy, disappointment, and bitterness, often drowned out through overindulgence in his favored four Bs.

George W. Bush's frustrations over his inability to even partially match his father's achievements at Andover and Yale, in the military, or in the Texas oil patch resulted in boisterous actions, heavy drinking, and "feisting out" at reporters. Bush's "feisting" represented a disproportionate reaction to incidents, a lack of empathy toward an offending objective reporter and a vindictive reaction toward those journalists or critics of the senior George Bush. He blasted them for failing to share George W.'s exalted love, loyalty, and respect for his idealized father.

George W. Bush represents the classic "late bloomer," not achieving a self-validating success until his mid-40s—when he quit drinking, formed deep religious beliefs, and emerged as the public face of the Texas Rangers baseball team. George W's comanagement of the Rangers allowed him to develop a unique Texas persona, kept him in the media limelight, and, most importantly, provided a very public symbol of what his vision and leadership could build—the Ballpark at Arlington. Prior to the Rangers, George W. Bush could not point to a single personal success to bolster his image as a promising, accomplished leader. Thanks to the Rangers, George W. at last stood tall on his own merits—no longer in the sizeable shadow of his father, George Bush.

Chapter Three

Lone Star Challenger: A Taste of Power

Texans appreciate bold leadership. I had earned political capital by spending it.

George W. Bush's selection of competent, loyal, and dedicated advisers to help achieve his political ambition represented an important factor in his rise to power. But Karl Rove emerged as the primary person contributing to George W. Bush's electoral success, a man who embodied the characteristics, strategic thinking, and tactical ruthlessness Bush deemed critical to succeed in national politics. Karl Rove became the omnipresent figure in George W. Bush's political career, fanning the fires of Bush's early political ambition. Rove became the first individual, both inside and outside of the Bush family, to recognize and appreciate that George W.'s engaging personality, valuable family legacy, and political instincts (with guidance) could lead to the White House.

However, Rove could not help George W. too much during his initial 1978 congressional race, since he still worked for the elder Bush in his 1980 bid for the presidency. But afterward one finds Karl Rove's patient hand planning, guiding, and maneuvering several steps ahead of Bush on the carefully plotted path to the Oval Office. The titles of two books about the influence of Karl Rove upon George W., *Bush's Brain* and *Boy Genius*, attest to the widely perceived pivotal role Bush's counselor and consultant played over many decades. George W. Bush, on his part, taunted and goaded Rove with early nicknames such as "Turd Blossom" and "Boy Genius," typical of his Bombastic Bushkin persona. But Rove's long-term strategic planning, tactical amorality, and crafty advice played a key part in Bush's climb to the political peak of the American presidency.

Karl Rove, the Architect

Karl Rove was born in Denver, Colorado, on December 25, 1950, grew up in Nevada, and moved to Salt Lake City, Utah, when he began high school. He displayed from an early age a fascination with politics despite his parents' lack of interest in political affairs. Young Rove developed into a focused student, self-described "complete nerd," and an excellent high school debater, often winning through a measure of deception and intimidation.[1] He enthusiastically embraced the Republican Party, particularly Richard Nixon's presidential campaign in 1968, even protesting outside the Mormon Tabernacle as Vice President Hubert Humphrey addressed a crowd.

Rove attended the University of Utah after high school, where he became president of the College Republicans. Rove's intense involvement in Republican politics led to the College Republican organization assigning him in 1970 to organize Illinois campuses on behalf of U.S. Senator Ralph Smith. He never returned to the University of Utah to complete his education. Although Rove attended classes at four other colleges—and later taught at the University of Texas—he lacked 12 credits to receive his B.A. degree.

The 19-year-old Rove engineered in 1970 what he later depicted as a "youthful prank" against Alan Dixon, the Democratic candidate for the Illinois state treasurer post. Rove posed as a Dixon supporter to get into his Chicago headquarters where he stole Dixon's stationary. Using the letterhead Rove drafted a fake invitation to Dixon's headquarters opening, maliciously promising: "Free beer, free food, girls, and a good time for nothing." Then he distributed 1,000 copies of the bogus flyer to a hippy commune, soup kitchen, and drunks in a rough section of Chicago that brought a raucous crowd to the Dixon opening.

Karl Rove's intelligence, cleverness, and energy led Joe Abate, the College Republican chairman, to hire Rove in 1971 as the organization's national executive director. In this position Rove organized 15 regional conferences to instruct College Republicans on campaign organization and candidate message—but added tips on political espionage and dirty tricks. At an August 1972 College Republican conference in Lexington, Kentucky, Rove described to the eager young GOP audience his dirty trick against Dixon. However, Rove and his colleague Bernie Robinson cautioned, "It's better off if you don't get caught."[2] That became the motif distinguishing Rove's surreptitious attacks in future campaigns: Leave no fingerprints.

In 1973 Karl Rove decided to run for chairman of the College Republican National Committee, enlisting South Carolinian Lee Atwater to help him capture delegate votes throughout the South. During the heated battle, ultimately adjudicated by then-national GOP chairman George H.W. Bush, Rove's foes leaked to the *Washington Post* the story (later with tapes and affidavits) of how Karl Rove had taught dirty tricks and political espionage at College Republican seminars, leading to an unflattering story during the Watergate scandal turmoil.[3] But the senior Bush ruled that Rove won the election and the new College Republicans chairman named Atwater as his executive director.

Several months later George Bush hired Rove as assistant to the chairman of the Republican National Committee, the beginning of his long-term relationship with the Bush family's political fortunes. In 1977 Rove moved to Houston to coordinate George H.W. Bush's political action committee, The Fund for Limited Government, for Bush's 1980 presidential bid. Rove traveled extensively over the next 18 months.

In 1978 Karl Rove became an independent political consultant for the Texas gubernatorial campaign of Republican Bill Clements; he also continued working for the elder Bush's political action committee (PAC). Clements benefited from Rove's mobilization of evangelical voters against the Democratic attorney general, John Hill, contributing to Clements' election as the first GOP governor since Reconstruction. This GOP victory created new opportunities for an ambitious political operative such as Rove, since at that point Democrats dominated the Lone Star State's elective offices: Republicans held 1 U.S. Senate seat, 2 of Texas' 18 House seats, 3 of 31 state senate seats, and only 18 of 140 Texas' lower house seats.

Governor Bill Clements became the first Republican to win one of the statewide posts in Texas.[4] Most important for the newly minted consultant, Rove's direct mail operations raised $1 million for Clements—and a list of 44,000 contributors interested in Republican victories. Ultimately, Karl Rove's ever-expanding mailing list became "a road map of Republican mega-money guys," a critical source of clients and influence for Rove.[5]

In 1980 Rove accepted the position of Governor Clements's deputy chief of staff, but with the understanding he would soon start his own business. That dream materialized with the 1981 establishment of Karl Rove + Company in Austin, with Clements as the only client. Rove directed Clements's reelection direct-mail campaign. However, the 1982 election had rejuvenated the Democratic Party, which defeated Clements as the Democrats regained their dominance of the Texas political landscape. The 1982 Democratic sweep included victories by Gary Mauro for land commissioner, Jim Hightower as commissioner of agriculture, and Ann Richards the new state treasurer. All would become Karl Rove targets in subsequent years.

Changing the Texas Landscape

Karl Rove's reputation as a GOP consultant rose steadily as he demonstrated an ability to raise campaign funds for Republican conservative candidates. His preferred approach involved either preempting opponents from entering a race through providing his client a huge financial advantage or overwhelming adversaries by a massive, well-funded ad campaign, a strategy that paid great dividends. As a political consultant, Karl Rove often resorted to ruthless tactics against both Democratic and Republican foes that embodied Machiavelli's amoral advice, "He who abandons what is done for what ought to be done learns his ruin rather than his preservation."[6] Victory at all costs became Rove's goal, justifying a disturbing pattern of vicious attack politics by push polls, whisper campaigns, anonymous flyers, and press leaks.

By 1985 Rove + Company handled 18 clients.[7] In the lean early business years, Rove augmented his income through direct-mail fund-raising campaigns for museums. In 1984 Rove provided direct-mail assistance in the election of another Texas Republican to the U.S. Senate, former Democratic congressman Phil Gramm, who joined GOP Senator John Tower. He also conducted direct-mail operations on behalf of the 1984 Reagan-Bush ticket.[8]

Bill Clements's 1986 drive to regain the governorship became a personal challenge for Rove. He drafted a strategy to defeat Democrat Mark White, the incumbent Texas governor who had defeated Clements in 1982. "Anti-White messages are more important than positive Clements messages," Rove counseled in a 1985 memo to Clements.[9] Rove underscored the imperative of an aggressive stance: "Attack. Attack. Attack." When Rove advised Clements to back a teachers' pay raise, he pointed out the key benefit of reassuring critical suburban voters with children; winning the votes of teachers was not the true goal. This early "Arabesque" technique, making one move while really trying to please another group, became one of Rove's tactical trademarks that he later brought into the Bush White House.[10]

The White campaign began to narrow Clements's lead toward the end of the race. Just a day before an early October 1986 gubernatorial debate that observers expected Governor White to win, Rove announced an electronic bug had been found in his office, disrupting the dynamics of the race. Two security experts hired by Rove found the bug behind his desk in a picture. At a press conference Rove charged that the only ones "who could have benefited from this detailed, sensitive information would have been the political opposition"—the Mark White campaign.[11]

However, the *Dallas Morning News* obtained through the Freedom of Information Act FBI memos that indicated Rove's private investigators probably planted the bug.[12] The Travis County District Attorney's office also felt the security experts Rove hired had placed the bug. Indeed, the owner of the surveillance firm refused to take a polygraph exam, making many people skeptical about Rove's claim. Nevertheless, the intense news coverage of the bugging incident a month before the election overshadowed White's debate performance and reversed the poll numbers. Clements emerged triumphant in his second election bout with White.

Texas reporters Moore and Slater acknowledged Rove's "exquisite sense of timing," always choosing the best moment to attack his opponent to inflict maximum political damage.[13] They concluded that with Rove's tactics, "there is no crime, just a victim." The necessity of a Clements victory, to unleash a GOP tsunami in Texas, appeared to justify the dubious bugging claim while enhancing Rove's reputation as a win-at-all-costs Republican consultant.

Democrat Gary Mauro, elected land commissioner in 1982, had previously worked for Texas controller Bob Bullock as his senior deputy. One day Bullock came to Mauro's office and warned him that Karl Rove had formed an alliance with FBI agent Greg Rampton, who Rove met during the bugging investigation. Bullock told Mauro: "Their sole job right now, their mission in life, is to figure out a way to indict you, me, Jim Mattox, Jim Hightower, and Ann Richards."[14] Indeed, Bullock's warning came to life in June 1984 when a reporter called with leaked information to ask about a FBI subpoena for land commission records, delivered only a half hour earlier.

Mauro recalled: "On the day of the Democratic state convention (he was speaking that day), I got a subpoena for every document you could possibly imagine," totaling 70,000 land office documents.[15] Mauro was never indicted and no charges were filed, but the FBI did not clear Mauro when it suspended the investigation. However, the reputation-damaging headlines resulting from the Rampton visit—with Karl Rove the likely source of the press leak about the FBI search for documents—sharply curbed Mauro's gubernatorial aspirations. As he caustically recalled: "I was no longer the Boy Wonder."

Rove's working relationship with FBI agent Greg Rampton led to other FBI investigations of Democratic office holders, often timed with the final stages of campaigns. If one applied the criteria Rove advanced to allege blame in the bugging incident, quite clearly Rove's clients benefited the most from the leaks about FBI investigations.

Texas Agriculture Commissioner Jim Hightower stood out as a prime target for the conservative Rove. Hightower had angered the Bush family, Texas Republicans, and Washington GOP insiders with his 1988 Democratic National Convention keynote speech zinger: "George Bush is the kind of guy who wakes up on third base and thinks he hit a triple."[16] On October 31, 1989, a story appeared in the *Dallas Morning News* revealing questionable credit card charges by Hightower and his top staff. Rove had a role in leaking the story, following up with other facts and angles for reporters. An *Austin American-Statesman* reporter, while acknowledging the agriculture story was driven by many sources, pointed out that he dealt with Rove "a whole, whole lot, several times a week."[17]

Several reporters received leaks about subpoenas even before they were delivered to witnesses; many reporters crediting Rove with sharing the privileged information he obtained from FBI agent Rampton. But a December 1989 state audit report cleared Hightower of wrongdoing. Nevertheless, that was only Rove's first barrage against Hightower's office. Rove continued to harass, intimidate, and smear Hightower's integrity in order to politically weaken him. On December 18, 1989, Rampton delivered a federal grand jury subpoena for an agriculture commission consultant to Hightower on the day Hightower planned to announce his reelection candidacy, clearly timing the orchestrated subpoena to raise doubts about Hightower's integrity in the news stories covering his bid for reelection.

Rove had recruited Rick Perry, a Democratic state representative, to switch to the Republican Party and challenge Hightower's 1990 reelection for agriculture commissioner. Then he maneuvered six Democrats to run against Hightower in the March Democratic primary, trying to force the incumbent into a runoff election. The besieged Hightower still won the primary election battle. At a summer fundraiser in Washington, DC, Rove announced that Hightower was under investigation, with indictments pending. Of course, the U.S. Department of Justice had not made such an announcement. Rove raised over $3 million for the Perry campaign.

Then in September Rove's favorite FBI agent Rampton visited the Texas secretary of state office to request copies of campaign contributions received by Hightower and Democrat Bob Bullock, then running for lieutenant governor. In the end, Rove's persistent guerrilla warfare against Hightower succeeded—fueled by FBI investigations and press leaks—contributing to his client Rick Perry's victory over the incumbent by about 50,000 votes. After the election, federal indictments were issued to four agriculture department officials, with three going to prison in 1993. However, Hightower was never charged with committing an offense. Indeed, politics in Texas had become a contact sport.

When Governor Clements nominated Karl Rove in 1991 for a seat on the East Texas State University's board of directors, the Democrats on the Texas Senate's Nominations Committee finally had the opportunity to directly question Rove—under oath—about his political machinations. When a senator asked how long he had known FBI agent Greg Rampton, Rove coyly replied: "Ah, Senator, it depends. Would you define 'know' for me?"[18] The questioning compelled Rove to admit that he leaked the FBI's investigation of the Texas Department of Agriculture in summer 1990: "I talked to a member of the press." He also acknowledged he spoke with Rampton in June or July 1990, October 1990, and early 1991—during the investigation of Hightower.

After Democrat Ann Richards won the governorship in 1990, her first major appointment placed State Representative Lena Guerrero on the Texas Railroad Commission to fill an unexpired term. Guerrero was viewed as a politically talented, likeable, and competent new face in Texas politics. The appointment highlighted Richards as a governor who promoted women and talented Latinos—while earning points with those key voting blocs. When Guerrero ran for the railroad commission post in 1992, Rove's client in the race was a little known Republican named Barry Williamson. Since the more colorful Guerrero led Williamson in the polls and fundraising, Rove looked for ammunition to undermine her candidacy and any support she might provide for Ann Richards—who would face George W. Bush two years later. Rove later admitted: "We needed to do something to cut off her money."[19]

Rove maneuvered to obtain Guerrero's confidential college transcript that disproved her education claims: Lena Guerrero had never graduated from the University of Texas, was not a member of Phi Beta Kappa, and had received low grades even in a course on Texas government. Rove employed his deadly sense of timing for a mortal blow, waiting until after the Democratic primary to feed reporters questions about misrepresentations of her education. Guerrero lost by 13 points, even trailing in the heavy Hispanic area of South Texas. A Texas political consultant emphasized how Rove held Guerrero's transcript "until the right moment. The perfect moment. Then he screwed her."[20]

Governor Clements appointed Republican Tom Phillips to become chief justice of the Texas Supreme Court in 1987 to fill an open position. Democrats had dominated the Supreme Court previously, but those statewide elections were not hotly contested. Karl Rove quickly signed on to run Phillips's 1988 campaign to win the position, as well as help the business-backed "Clean Slate '88" conservative drive to place six Republicans on the state's highest court. Five of the six Republican candidates won the 1988 race and by 1998 Republicans held all nine Texas Supreme Court seats.

Rove's 1988 strategic memo to Phillips suggested he adopt a populist posture. "No Republican has won by running as an establishment candidate. Our party's candidates have won by appearing as champions of the little man and not the big boys."[21] Rove's overarching goal envisioned business financial support for Republican candidates, rather than for conservative Democrats. He told business contributors that a GOP Supreme Court would be more likely to impose limits on compensation for injured workers and caps on jury awards against businesses. Most importantly, the pseudo-populist strategy served to curtail the political clout of trial lawyers, a major source of funding for Democratic candidates such as Ann Richards.

Karl Rove's success in electing Republicans to the Texas Supreme Court encouraged the Business Council of Alabama to retain Rove in 1994 to elect a slate of GOP candidates to the Alabama Supreme Court. No Republican had served on the Alabama high court in the prior century. Rove resorted to vicious tactics in several Alabama judicial races, including slanderous whisper campaigns.

One of Rove's foes was Supreme Court Justice Mark Kennedy. Rove often favored the approach, repeated in many races, of attacking an opponent's strongest asset, in this case Kennedy's reputation for helping children. Judge Kennedy had served many years as a juvenile and family court judge. Since the early 1980s he helped abused children through the creation of the Children's Trust Fund of Alabama. A former Rove staffer admitted to starting a whisper campaign that Kennedy was a pedophile to counter a Kennedy ad showing him with children. "It was our standard practice to use the University of Alabama Law School to disseminate whisper-campaign information."[22] Although Kennedy beat Rove's client by less than 1 percent of the vote, he decided not to run for reelection at the end of his new term.

In a 1996 fight against an incumbent Alabama Supreme Court justice by Republican candidate Harold See, Rove printed anonymous flyers attacking See and his family to generate a backlash of support from blue-collar, lower middle-class voters. A Rove worker was told: "Do not hand it to anybody, do not tell anybody who you're with, and if you can, borrow a car that doesn't have your tags."[23] Rove's client See won the post.

Rove also displayed his vicious and vindictive traits against Republicans who challenged his influence. He often appeared to embrace Machiavelli's dictum that "men must either be caressed or else destroyed."[24] Rove engaged in a running battle with Paul Pauken, who became chairman of the Texas Republican Party despite Rove's maneuvers. During the 1994 party convention, newly mobilized evangelical Christians flexed their GOP muscles after becoming active in support of TV evangelist Pat Robertson in the 1988 presidential race.

Always the Bush family loyalist, Rove as well as George W. never forgave the conservative Pauken for backing Senator Bob Dole in 1988 over George H.W. Bush. When the evangelicals joined with Pauken's supporters—many of them former Reagan activists—their numbers overwhelmed Rove's candidate, so he avoided a final floor fight. The pragmatic Rove, much like Bush senior, never fully shared the evangelical Christians' social agenda. Pauken, the newly elected Texas Republican Party chairman, promptly fired Rove as the state GOP's political consultant.

Rove, never one to meekly accept defeat, proceeded to contact major Republican donors to cut off their contributions to the GOP Texas state party while Pauken was at the helm. In 1977 Pauken sought the Republican nomination for state attorney general. Soon two other GOP candidates entered the primary, with Rove advising their well-financed races. Pauken lost the primary. The conservative Republican leader later disputed the depiction of Rove as a "right-winger." Instead, Pauken described Rove as a Cardinal Richelieu figure obsessed with political power, embracing "scorched earth" tactics to win battles. Pauken warned: "Rove will use conservatives when necessary but only as a means of consolidating and maintaining power for the establishment wing of the Republican Party."[25]

In 1992 Karl Rove was fired from President George H.W. Bush's reelection campaign after he leaked a story to the columnist Robert Novak that disparaged the leadership ability of the Bush campaign manager, Robert Mosbacher Jr.; Rove had met Novak in the 1980s and they often dined together when the columnist visited Austin. Novak's insider story claimed Mosbacher's campaign management was a "bust" and Bush faced serious trouble among Texas voters.

The dispute actually arose over the division of a $1 million contract for the elder Bush's direct-mail operations. Mosbacher told *The Houston Chronicle* in 2003: "I thought another firm was better.…I gave Rove a contract for $250,000 and $750,000 to the other firm."[26] John Weaver ran the other firm, a Republican competitor, who Rove would face in the 2000 presidential primaries when Weaver directed the campaign of Senator John McCain. Rove vindictively leaked the story to Novak to get even with Mosbacher. Mosbacher promptly fired Rove and gave his $250,000 contract to Weaver as well. A *New York Times* reporter resurrected the 1992 leak to Novak when examining how Rove may have similarly leaked the name of CIA agent Valerie Plame to Novak that appeared in a very damaging 2003 column.

George W. Bush forced his longtime consultant to sell Rove + Company in 1999 so Rove would devote all his time and talents to Bush's 2000 presidential race. Rove had worked for 75 candidates in 24 states, in many cases only handling direct-mail operations.[27] But according to one estimate, Rove's career record in races that he had run for statewide, national, or congressional offices achieved 34 victories to 7 losses.[28] When Rove left Texas to work inside the Bush White House in 2001,

Republicans held all 29 statewide Texas offices, many of the GOP victors former clients of Rove + Company.[29] An admiring Mark McKinnon, who switched from the Democratic Party to handle George W. Bush's media campaign, speculated that Karl Rove probably escalated the Republican take-over of Texas politics by about a decade.

Challenging an Icon

Karl Rove played a central strategic role in George W. Bush's gubernatorial campaign. The wily political consultant employed his contacts in summer 1993 to introduce Bush to key political players in Texas. Ironically, President George Bush's painful 1992 reelection loss to then-Arkansas Governor Bill Clinton had cleared away obstacles to George W. running for office, dissolving any fears of embarrassing the elder Bush. George W. could now stand for office as his own man. Moreover, he could tap into the extensive national network of campaign contributors, political talent, and contacts carefully nurtured by George and Barbara Bush over many decades in the oil business and public service. Nevertheless, George W. remained acutely aware that both Republican and Democratic foes would attack his candidacy as a bid to create a Bush dynasty.

Family friend Chase Untermeyer also recalled: "I think the major word to describe George W. circa 1993 and the governorship was competitiveness."[30] The fact that his younger brother Jeb Bush planned to run for governor of Florida in 1994, with the Bush family convinced Jeb would win, stoked George W.'s competitiveness as his father's namesake. In his biography, Bush resentfully acknowledged: "He (Jeb) was the brother who was supposed to have won in November of 1994."[31] Nevertheless, George W. ignored the Bush family's low expectations of him and his buffoon image. Barbara Bush advised George W. that his gubernatorial bid represented an ill-advised, ill-fated idea.[32] She warned that his prospect of winning appeared less likely than the likelihood of his brother Jeb becoming governor of Florida, prompting George W. to arrogantly reply: "Jeb might win. I *will* win."[33]

The 70 percent approval rating of the incumbent Texas governor, Democrat Ann Richards, failed to dissuade George W. from confronting her, since his strong ambition drove the quest to win this high-profile office, a stepping-stone to the White House. George W. appeared encouraged, liberated, and validated by his recent success in the business world with the Texas Rangers. In addition, the rankling echo of Richards's belittling words toward his father at the 1992 Democratic convention also goaded him to topple the incumbent. A rising Democratic star, keynoter Richards mocked George H.W. Bush's Eastern background and garbled speaking style: "(H)e was born with a silver foot in his mouth."[34] Nevertheless, the ever-pragmatic former president advised his sons George W. and Jeb in a 1994 letter to pursue their own political agendas without worrying about painful comparisons to him: "Chart your own course, not just on the issues but on defining yourself."[35]

During the 1988 presidential campaign George W. battled as his "father's staunchest defender" against media critics and political rivals. In his campaign biography Bush admitted: "I would run through a brick wall for my dad. And I was feisty about it."[36] George W. praised his father's politeness, mild manner, thoughtful behavior, and conflict avoidance. However, he starkly contrasted

George Bush's political style to his own brash, less diffident approach, positively explaining the differences in terms of their childhoods: "I went to Sam Houston Elementary School, and he went to Greenwich Country Day School."[37]

This assertion cleverly allowed George W. to present himself as a true Texan, distancing himself from the Bush family's Eastern establishment roots, disparaged in the Lone Star State. Obviously, such a claim ignored that George W. Bush was born in Connecticut and educated at some of the Eastern establishment's most exclusive schools: Andover, Yale, and Harvard. Bush had painfully learned the potency of populist attacks against his family background from his 1978 congressional opponent Kent Hance. Undoubtedly Karl Rove, who witnessed the corrosive impact of Hance's populist attacks, tutored Bush in redefining himself as emerging from the more boisterous mold of West Texas, rather than the East like the senior Bush. Unlike his father, George W. did not need to eat pork rinds and pitch horseshoes to establish his Texas credentials.

However, George W. Bush required an extreme makeover after his 1988 incendiary comments on the national political stage while defending his father; one writer described George W. as the Bush family's "Roman candle."[38] But George W.'s nicknames throughout his youth and adult years also reflected his persistent raucous behavior, biting comments and emotional outbursts: "the Lip" at Andover, the "family clown" at home, the "Bombastic Bushkin" among longtime Midland friends, and "Bush Boy" to grizzled oilmen who knew his father. George W. even called himself the "black sheep" of the Bush family.[39] Peter and Rochelle Schweizer interpreted this behavior as stemming from the pressures upon him. "George W. Bush is fundamentally, at his core, a rebel," who revolted against his father and the Bush family's expectations placed on him as the first son.[40] To deal with this candidate vulnerability and image problem, Rove arranged training sessions with George W. before the governor's race to curb his tendency to angrily "feist out." He hired consultant Don Sipple to coach Bush to respond more carefully to provocations and to make TV ads.[41]

George W. Bush had acquired valuable insights into "media seduction" from watching and listening to Lee Atwater during the 1988 presidential race. Indeed, Bush convinced investors in his deal to purchase the Texas Rangers: "I know how to handle the press."[42] As comanaging partner, Bush's duties excluded financial management or managing the team. His partners counted upon George W. to act as the public face of the Texas Rangers, the PR man, the glad-hander. Bush relished the importance of his role as the team's salesman: "Baseball is a marketing business. It's a business of being able to relate to fans and convince fans to come out."[43] George W. confessed he never considered becoming a kingmaker behind the Bush family, instead of the king. "I guess it doesn't fit my personality. When your name is George Bush, with the kind of personality I have, which is a very engaging personality, at least outgoing, in which my job is to sell tickets to baseball games, you're a public person."[44]

Although George W.'s behavior manifested a stylistic rebellion within the Bush family, he dutifully followed his father's path to Andover, Yale, and the Texas oil patch. But as one observer noted: "He became the *real* Texan in the family—chewing tobacco, using barnyard humor, settling in the state's western corner."[45] As the front man for the Texas Rangers, Bush sat behind their dugout where fans could see him and shrewdly distributed baseball cards with his name and picture on them. "I want the folks to see me sitting in the same kind of seat they sit in... eating the same popcorn, peeing in the same urinal."[46] Karl Rove highlighted how Bush's earthiness appealed to Texas voters: "He understands Bubba because there is more Bubba in him. He is clearly the wild son."[47]

George W. also discovered an important lesson from his father's 1992 defeat: "message matters." His father's failure to communicate to the public his concern about domestic policy contributed to the reelection loss. Bush regretfully observed: "He got defined by the opposition." But George W. partly blamed his father for the communication breakdown, because "the messenger was unable to carry the message."[48]

Since the lack of message discipline contributed to his father's loss, Bush and his advisers recognized the imperative of a clear agenda for Texas voters. His friend Don Evans described George W.'s gubernatorial strategy: "I'm going to get four issues, and I'm going to hammer on them, I'm going to hammer on them, I'm going to hammer on them."[49] The four issues became tort reform, crime, education, and welfare reform. His father's pollster Bob Teeter diplomatically observed: "He's been very good at learning a lot of things from his father to do—but I think he's also been very good at learning a lot of things from his father to do differently."[50]

George W. Bush confidently entered the Texas political fray, despite the reservations of his family. George W. had run for Congress in 1978, winning the primary, and campaigned for Senate candidates in Florida and Alabama. In addition, his extensive high-level involvement at Lee Atwater's side in George Bush's 1988 presidential bid had honed George W.'s political instincts: "I'm a political animal."[51] The younger Bush had obtained on-the-job training in the employment of campaign knowledge, tactical flexibility, and poll-guided persuasiveness. Although influenced by the high standards of public service exemplified by his grandfather, Connecticut Senator Prescott Bush, and his father, President George H.W. Bush, George W. viewed politics as "theater, but the play was about character. That was the essentialism in politics."[52] Bill Clinton, whose affair with a White House intern manifested his flawed character, animated George W. to restore respect for the presidency as exemplified in his father's years in the Oval Office.

Although George W. acknowledged the importance of issues and debates, he emphasized that "campaigning is really just a matter of getting the message out to the voters and getting the voters to the polls. It's not complicated." His years promoting the Texas Rangers and getting fans to buy tickets bolstered Bush's confidence that he knew how to engage, charm, and win the support of voters. Bush's consultant Karl Rove agreed: "His strengths are his ability to read the political environment and sense the best way to articulate a vision so that it comes across."[53]

California Governor Jesse Unruh once declared: "Money is the mother's milk of politics." George W. raised so much money for his gubernatorial bid that by August 1993 potential GOP candidates prudently decided against challenging Bush for the nomination. At the end of 1993 Bush had received $2 million in contributions, giving him the resources and flexibility to focus all of his attention on the Democratic incumbent—without a costly primary.[54]

In 1994 both George W. and Jeb Bush attempted to deflect criticism that they were only running on their father's name. George W. adopted and personalized the response Jeb Bush crafted for Florida voters by mentioning his twin daughters, Jenna and Barbara: "I am not running for governor because I am George Bush's son; I am running because I am Jenna and Barbara's father."[55] Both brothers kept their parents off the campaign trail for three months to demonstrate their independence. In March 1994 George and Barbara Bush attended two expensive fund-raising events in Texas that garnered $1.6 million for George W., whose campaign contributions trailed those of Governor Richards.

The core strategy of the Bush campaign involved repetition of the four agenda issues, presenting Bush as a likeable and successful man, and avoiding the appearance of a negative, reactive campaign. George W. knew he must shrug off the anticipated attacks by Richards, crafted to inflame his well-known thin skin, feistiness, and sharp tongue. During the course of the bitter race Governor Richards hurt herself by calling George W. indirectly and directly a "jerk" and "Shrub" Bush. One of her negative ads targeted Bush's claim that he was a successful businessman. The announcer's voice declared: "But official records show that every other Bush business venture has lost money, big money, net losses of $371 million....But can we afford the business experience of George W. Bush?"[56]

In his campaign biography Bush stated he learned from the 1978 House campaign that you always had to respond to attacks, a lesson he applied in 1994 and thereafter. His first TV ad featured images of a woman being robbed at gunpoint and a dead young boy's body covered with a sheet by police. Bush pledged in the spot: "I will end early release of criminals and end parole altogether for rapists and child molesters."[57] The Richards campaign charged that Bush had embraced the inflammatory technique Lee Atwater exploited in the infamous 1988 Willie Horton TV ads for the elder Bush.

Richards immediately responded to the Bush campaign's negative attacks, "I'm not one of those shy violets who's going to sit back and be taking it across the head and not respond."[58] Bush's communication strategy emphasized Richards's ties to President Bill Clinton, who in a 1994 Texas poll received a 40 percent unfavorable rating, with only 23 percent viewing the Democratic president favorably. Texas businessman Ross Perot, who ran against his father in his 1992 reelection race, came out in support of Ann Richards toward the end of the race, ridiculing George W.'s baseball experience: "(R)unning this state is a big business, not a sport."[59]

The Bush campaign also resorted to push polling and a whisper campaign to imply that Ann Richards supported lesbians or might even be a lesbian herself. Push poll interviewers called Texas voters to ask whether they would be more or less likely to vote for Governor Richards if they knew that lesbians dominated on her staff. The East Texas campaign chairman for Bush told reporters for the *Houston Post* that Richards's appointment of homosexuals could cost her East Texas. State Senator Bill Ratliff declared: "It is simply part of their culture...that (homosexuality) is not something we encourage, reward, or acknowledge as an acceptable situation."[60] That statement elevated the rumors from the gutter to the front page of all the Texas newspapers. Based on his low-road tactics in other campaigns, many observers attributed the vicious rumor and push poll calls to Karl Rove.

Bush ignored Richards's call to release his 1989 and 1990 income tax returns that would provide insights into the sale of his Harken Energy stock. When the *Houston Chronicle* asked George W. about illegal drug use, he replied: "Maybe I did, maybe I didn't. What's the relevance...? How I behaved as an irresponsible youth is irrelevant to this campaign."[61] Bush repeated the same vague answer to questions along the campaign trail about his prior heavy drinking and partying: "When I was young and irresponsible, I sometimes behaved young and irresponsibly."[62] He artfully dodged follow-up "gotcha" questions, as he shrewdly labeled them.

When the ballots were counted, George W. Bush won the governorship with 53.5 percent of the vote to 45.9 percent for Ann Richards. Karl Rove attributed Bush's victory partly to the failure of the Richards's campaign to articulate a program for a second term, lack of a central message, dissension within her campaign organization, and Richards's preoccupation with her opponent. Rove also underscored Richards's major mistakes: "She both simultaneously underestimated him and treated him with contempt."[63] Underestimating George W. Bush's political skills would prove the undoing of future rivals as well.

For the Bush family the 1994 election results proved less gratifying in Florida, where Jeb Bush encountered defeat. Former President George Bush commented about the mixed results: "The joy is in Texas, but our hearts are in Florida."[64] On election night Bush's Aunt Nancy Ellis stood near George W. while he talked with his father after Ann Richards conceded the Texas race. His aunt heard George W. say to his father, who was distraught about Jeb's loss: "Why do you feel bad about Jeb? Why don't you feel good about me?"[65] George Bush evidently could not understand why his son Jeb, who had diligently worked his way up the political ladder in Florida, had lost. Nor could the elder Bush grasp how George W. had won a significant statewide victory in Texas, a feat that had escaped him in his 1964 and 1970 Senate campaigns. George W.—for so many years the family clown, rebel, and boozer—absolutely stunned the extended Bush-Walker clan with his victory, handily surpassing their low expectations of him.

Lone Star Governor

Although President George Bush dismissed "the vision thing," Governor Bush highlighted in his first address the importance of a leader's vision for the future: "The history of our special land tells us this: that what Texans can dream, Texans can do."[66] Just as he had pointed to the Texas Rangers' Ballpark in the recent campaign as an example of his successful pursuit of a vision, George W. sought to portray his four-point reform program as a vision to improve the lives of Texans.

In organizing his staff to fit his personality and needs, George W. wanted to avoid the difficulty President George Bush encountered when autocratic John Sununu, his White House chief of staff, sharply restricted access to the president. George W. had to fire Sununu on behalf of his nonconfrontational father. Instead, Bush organized his Austin staff with a flat organizational chart, rather than a strong chief of staff who limited access to the governor. "I wanted the senior manager of different divisions in my office to report directly to me....I like to get information from a lot of different people, plus I knew that high-powered people would be frustrated unless they had direct access to the boss."[67] Even though he studied hierarchical corporate structures at Harvard's Business School, Bush's administrative schema reflected his experience in Washington, the Bush family's emphasis on loyalty, and his own political antennae.

He selected Clay Johnson, his roommate at Andover and Yale, to serve as his appointments director. Bush recalled: "I could trust him, absolutely. He was financially independent, and thus would not be looking to curry favor or line up a job for the future. He had no agenda, other than serving the state and helping me."[68] Johnson thus fulfilled the Bush family's criteria of unstinting loyalty, totally devoting himself to advancing George W.'s interests. Since Governor Bush's "laid-back" management style involved "sweeping" delegation to his principle staff and appointees, he placed great importance upon their competence and loyalty.[69]

George W. Bush had often railed against the maneuverings he witnessed within his father's White House staff, particularly as the president's popularity dropped and political appointees scouted out their next career step, rather than protecting the president. Bush named his campaign manager Joe Allbaugh as chief of staff and Karen Hughes as communications director. Karl Rove, who maintained his consulting business, continued to serve as Bush's major political adviser, phoning him sometimes 20 times a day, according to a member of the staff.[70]

George W. Bush promoted teamwork among his key aides, emphasizing they should respectfully answer each other's phone calls first. The new governor encouraged people to express their opinions, even dissenting views—when done privately. Bush noted: "Whether in a policy or appointments or legal briefing, I'll frequently stop, go around the room, and ask different individuals what they think and why."[71] Bush read his memos, but preferred quizzing staff directly about issues. Karen Hughes explained that George W. "explores, prods, then carefully watches how someone reacts to his pointed question.... He wants to find out if you are willing to stand up to him, willing to argue for your point of view."[72]

In Bush's presidential campaign biography *A Charge to Keep*, written by Bush's image-maker Hughes, George W. described his exercise of the governor's "bully pulpit" to push his message, agenda, and vision. "A *strong* person can make a powerful difference" (author's emphasis).[73] But since the 1876 Texas constitution limited the powers of a governor, Bush quickly recognized the pivotal role the state's lieutenant governor played in the passage of legislation.[74]

Five weeks before the 1994 election, Bush made a quiet courtesy visit to Bob Bullock, the powerful Texas lieutenant governor, then recovering from open-heart surgery. Bullock admitted his disappointment in Ann Richards, warning Bush: "If you're going to be that kind of pussyfooting, headline-grabbing, television grab-bing governor, forget it."[75] The foundation for a solid working relationship and eventual friendship evolved from that meeting. Five years later on his deathbed, Bullock requested George W. Bush to deliver the eulogy at his 1999 funeral.

Governor Bush's initial policy successes largely resulted from his persistent wooing of the top Democratic legislative leaders, Bullock in the Senate and House Speaker Pete Laney. The new governor and his advisers recognized that Bush required their support to attain his legislative agenda, which he could then tout as evidence of his leadership skills when running for president. Governor Bush began meeting once a week with "Bully" (George W.'s private nickname for Bullock) and Laney when the legislature was in session (140 days every 2 years). Bush listened respectfully to the crafty lieutenant governor and the speaker from West Texas.

Although policy differences emerged in the meetings, the three leaders kept their discussions confidential. However, Bullock and Laney were more conserva-tive than the Democratic leaders that Bush would later encounter in Congress, so the partisan and ideological chasm was not as wide. Speaker Laney told Bush at their first meeting, "We can make you a good governor—if you let us."[76] A pragmatic, working alliance between the new Republican governor and the two powerful Democratic leaders became essential, since Democrats controlled the House (89 to 61) and the Senate (17 to 14).

Governor Bush also mingled and met with individual legislators, joking with them and lobbying on the floor. And importantly, the GOP governor shared the credit with key Democratic chairmen when bills became law. In 1996 Bush did not campaign against Democratic incumbents who supported his agenda, despite the urging of GOP leaders, which enhanced his standing among Democratic legislators.[77]

Bush modestly portrayed his dealings with legislators as "an observer, a listener, and a learner."[78] However, a reporter more aptly described him as a "world-class schmoozer."[79] Bush bragged: "I knew how to sell the case."[80] George W. acknowledged that in the legislative process, a governor must build bipartisan alliances and "push and shove and maybe twist an arm or two, regardless of the party."[81] Indeed, Bush often compromised and accepted the Democratic legislature's changes to his bills, while claiming a victory for his program. Tom Pauken, the conservative Texas Republican Party chairman who fired Karl Rove as the party's consultant, charged: "Bush got credit in the media for the Bullock-approved 'reform' bills in areas ranging from education and welfare to the tort and criminal justice systems."[82]

Governor Bush succeeded in the seventy-fourth Legislative Session in passing his four agenda items, with the bipartisan support of Bullock and Laney who endorsed welfare cuts, granting more control to local school districts, stiffer penalties for juvenile offenders, and tort reform to reduce personal injury lawsuits. Texas reporter Minutaglio observed: "For most Democrats and many moderates, it was a pro-business but relatively benign agenda."[83] After his first legislative session, Governor Bush's job approval ratings rose, with one poll revealing that 59 percent of the Texas respondents thought it would be "fun to have him over for dinner."[84]

Buoyed by his initial success, Governor Bush announced to reporters in November 1996 that his major goal in the next legislative session aimed at a major revision of the state budget to reduce local school property taxes by $3 billion over two years. This stunning announcement, without any consultation with Bullock or Laney, reflected George W. Bush's plan to project his image as a bold, strong leader. Bush explained to Republican State Senator David Sibley: "I've got this political capital. If you're not going to do something with it, there's no sense having it."[85]

Bush aides later told a *Wall Street Journal* reporter that Bush formulated the concept of using political capital based upon his father's White House experience. The elder President Bush had failed to wield the tremendous political capital accrued after the Persian Gulf War victory to push through the Democrat-controlled Congress his program of domestic reforms and plans to jump-start the struggling U.S. economy.[86] Others attribute Bush's embrace of the idea of political capital to consultant Karl Rove, who knew it would appeal to George W.'s rebellious streak to go against popular wisdom, thus portraying Bush as a courageous and strong leader, unafraid of political risks.

The Republican governor admitted that he did not discuss the tax reform with the two Democratic legislative leaders: "I didn't feel like they were going to be supportive of it."[87] Bush added that the two Democratic leaders sought to safeguard the legislative prerogative over the state's budget: "And I was the executive branch, laying claim to part of it." Lieutenant Governor Bullock, who disliked surprises, coldly told reporters that the governor put "the cart before the horse," since he first heard about the plan from Bush's press conference. Privately Bullock warned Bush's senior staff members that the proposal could defeat him.

Governor Bush traveled two months around Texas promoting his tax reform, but the administration's budget plan failed to generate much legislative support. Indeed, Republican legislators, business, and professional groups—normally Bush stalwarts—all fought the proposal to reduce property tax by increasing business and sales taxes, particularly a new partnership tax on professionals. Bush also sought approval from the Clinton administration to privatize the state's administration of health care, housing, and other programs for the elderly and the poor. Under pressure from the state's unions and the American Federation of Labor and Congress of Industrial Organizations (AFL-CIO), the White House denied the request.

In the end, the Texas legislature approved a more modest property tax cut based upon the state's projected billion-dollar surplus, scaled back privatization, and reduced welfare spending. Failing in the battle to revamp the state's school financing system, Bush agreed to a compromise plan that simply took the anticipated $1 billion Texas budget surplus to "sweeten taxpayers' homestead exemption from property taxes."[88] He later claimed victory for both the tax cut and educational reform.

The lessons for the Bush team from this bold exercise of political capital were as follows: "Stick to simpler messages, less complex themes, and issues; stay attuned to more modest goals."[89] Bush recalled he personally discovered from the debacle: "First, it's hard to win votes for massive reform unless there is a crisis."[90] However, Bush also expressed a more dubious conclusion after the policy clash: "Texans appreciate bold leadership. I had earned political capital by spending it."

Launching a Second Term

In August 1997 before his reelection, Governor Bush addressed the GOP Midwestern Leadership Conference along with other 2000 Republican presidential hopefuls. He defined himself as a compassionate conservative who enacted a $1 billion property tax cut. Bush's speech failed to impress the national media or excite the Republican leaders. George W. then decided to follow his father's counsel that he should concentrate on a hefty second-term victory—making inroads into the traditional Democratic-leaning Hispanic and African-American vote—before publicly pursuing his presidential aspirations.

The 1998 reelection race against Democrat Garry Mauro focused upon "packaging him as a more palatable, caring candidate to Hispanic voters, women, and baby boomers," an image he wanted to project in the impending presidential campaign.[91] Also, George W.'s campaign strategists sought to elect his brother Jeb governor of Florida, since that critical Electoral College state played a vital role in their 2000 presidential plans (more critical than they realized). The famed Bush network filled Governor Bush's reelection coffer with over $17 million, while Mauro raised only $5 million despite assistance from President Clinton and Vice President Gore. As a sign of George W. Bush's growing potential as a GOP presidential candidate, his 1998 campaign received three times the amount of contributions from outside of Texas than his 1994 campaign.[92]

On Election Day the Texas governor won an impressive reelection with 67 percent of the cast ballots. Most importantly, his support among women voters rose from 50 percent to 65 percent, half of Hispanics now supported Bush (up from 40 percent) and his votes from African-Americans almost doubled from 17 percent to 31 percent. Bush received 98 percent of the Republican votes, as well as 75 percent of Independents and 31 percent of Democrats. His long coattails brought Republican Rick Perry into office as lieutenant governor.

Governor Bush's 1998 election night speech debuted themes he would voice in the 2000 presidential race: "Tonight's resounding victory says my compassionate, conservative philosophy is making Texas a better place." Bush added, aiming his words at GOP national kingmakers, that his Texas landslide proved that "a leader who is compassionate and conservative can erase the gender gap, can open the doors of the Republican Party to new faces and new voices."[93] The argument raised an attractive selling point in 1998, when the national Republican Party's fortunes had ebbed in the off-year election.

The public's negative reaction to the Gingrich "Revolution," harsh GOP House TV ads about Clinton's affair with intern Monica Lewinsky, and the looming Clinton impeachment proceedings angered many voters. Nationally, the Republican Party lost five House seats, made no gains in the Senate, and dropped from GOP control of 32 governorships to 31, including California, the state with the most votes in the Electoral College. Several days after the 1998 off-year election, Speaker Newt Gingrich resigned his Republican leadership post and seat in the House.

In summary, Bush's knowledgeable, shrewd, and often vicious political adviser Karl Rove played a key role in guiding Bush into the Texas governorship. Rove had cleared the path for Bush by defeating or weakening many Democratic foes, raising significant campaign contributions to deter other Republicans from entering the race, and smoothing the trail to the governor's mansion by dramatically wounding the Democratic Party. Over a number of years the Republican consultant had cut into the Democratic Party's financial base, shrunk the number of statewide Democratic officeholders, and built a financial network among conservative Texas contributors. Rove guided Republicans to attain and maintain power in the Lone Star State. He also tapped the Bush family's network of supporters to further bolster George W.'s financial advantages.

During the 1994 battle with incumbent governor Ann Richards, George W. Bush took the high road—surprising many by keeping his temper in check—but allowed Rove to employ a scandalous whisper campaign against Richards. Some of Bush's negative TV ads reflected the harsh lessons he learned from Lee Atwater, a strong believer in Machiavellian methods.

As governor of Texas, Bush prudently recognized that he needed the assistance of the state's Democratic lieutenant governor and House speaker to realize his "compassionate conservative" agenda. Governor Bush stoically accepted the Democrat-controlled legislature's changes to his bills, but declared that the enacted laws symbolized the success of his bipartisan leadership style. However, Bush stumbled in his second legislative session by calling for a tax reform without the support of the Democratic leaders. But even in defeat Bush brashly asserted that his proposal had demonstrated bold, strong leadership. Nevertheless, Bush's tax reform initiative had unwisely ignored the perils of instituting major changes without a looming crisis.

Governor Bush's 1998 reelection victory—with significant increased support among women, Hispanics, and African-Americans—allowed Bush's advisers to market him nationally as a GOP large-state governor with a broad voter appeal. The election results set the stage for his White House race.

Chapter Four

White House Quest: Selling the Son

I'm a uniter, not a divider.

George W. Bush sharpened his political skills through his unique political experiences: high-level work in two Senate campaigns, his 1978 try for a House seat, and his father's 1988 presidential campaign, when he worked closely with political consultant Lee Atwater. The Bush team carefully crafted the image of a strong, successful governor, enacting his "compassionate conservative" agenda through a Democrat-dominated Texas legislature. His impressive 1998 reelection in Texas featured sizeable gains among women and minorities, voter groups that often shunned GOP candidates.

Bush said he responded to situations with his political instincts, but adviser Karl Rove helped him plan his overall strategy after extensive polling, quantitative analyses of voting trends, and assessments of targeted voter blocs. But George W. also benefited from good fortune in his 2000 White House quest, as the Gingrich Revolution of 1994 had sizzled and burned by 1998. Traditional Republicans wanted to restore their political influence, apprehensive about the growing sway of the religious Right and social conservatives on GOP policies.

The key element in Rove's plan to realize George W.'s presidential aspiration involved wooing the corporate and country club Republicans craving the return of their power—without alienating the religious Right and hard-line conservatives who never fully trusted his father. Bush's *fortuna* of birth endowed him with the well-known name of the Republican president serving before the "crass" interruption of the Clinton years. The Bush family ties brought a network of major campaign contributors, political experts, and ambitious politicos into the camp of the relatively unknown Texas governor. George W. and his advisers confronted the challenge of creating a political image for Bush that reassured his father's traditional GOP supporters, attracted new voters to the party's standard, and avoided antagonizing the religious Right and social conservatives.

Crafting the Plan

Karl Rove hung a picture of George W. Bush in his office years before the 2000 presidential race, gratefully inscribed by the governor: "To Karl, the man with the plan."[1] Rove's long-range strategy had already attained its initial steps of portraying Bush with a desired positive image for the presidential campaign: partisan giant killer (Bush's upset victory over Governor Ann Richards); bipartisan problem solver (successful enactment of conservative bills in the Democrat-controlled Texas legislature); a Republican with broad appeal (Governor Bush's 1998 attraction among Hispanics, women, and African-Americans); and solid financial backers (mobilization of President Bush's national fundraising network). Governor Bush would proclaim during the presidential race: "I've learned to lead."[2]

Since the second-term governor lacked the requisite domestic and foreign policy knowledge to adeptly respond to probing questions from the national press corps, Karl Rove shrewdly turned that weakness into strength. Rove devised a "yellow rose garden" strategy at the Texas governor's mansion. For a history buff such as Rove, the tactic evoked memories of Republican William McKinley's front porch campaign of 1896. Immediately after Bush's 1998 victory, prominent Republican leaders such as Mississippi's former GOP Chairman Haley Barbour trekked to Austin for publicized visits to highlight George W.'s electoral attraction—before Bush formally announced his presidential candidacy. Ultimately, 114 congressmen, 14 U.S. Senators, and over a majority of his fellow-Republican governors traveled to Austin to endorse Bush, generating the desired media perception of a Draft Bush movement.[3]

Rove "home-schooled" Governor Bush by arranging sessions with experienced domestic and international policy experts and some foreign leaders to enhance his understanding of issues—simultaneously projecting the image of a thoughtful man who listened and learned from their advice.[4] Bush hosted over 15 policy sessions in the governor's mansion in winter 1998 and spring 1999.[5] President Ronald Reagan's Secretary of State George P. Shultz downplayed Bush's lack of experience on international affairs: "Nobody knows everything about what goes on in the world, so you've got to find out."[6]

Indianapolis Mayor Stephen Goldsmith chaired the domestic policy meetings and Stanford University Provost Condoleezza Rice presided over foreign and military affairs. These visits ultimately led to a "policy factory" where the Bush campaign established a large policy staff and committed many outside policy advisers to serve on committees that met regularly.[7] Rove excluded many Republicans who were closely aligned with Bush's father to make George W. appear more forward-looking, thus not antagonizing conservatives critical of the former president's pragmatic policies.[8] Many of the experts came from the conservative Hoover Institution, also a not-so-subtle message to GOP stalwarts.

However, the linchpin in Rove's scheme to portray George W. Bush as a new kind of Republican—not the stereotypical harsh, uncaring conservative—involved the concept of "compassionate conservatism." Even though other Republicans had used the term, like Senator Robert Dole in 1988, the Bush campaign applied it as a central organizing principle—until the potent challenge by Senator John McCain forced them to temporarily place it on the shelf.

In April 1999 Rove sketched out his master plan for Bush's presidential campaign to media consultant Stuart Stevens, underscoring the pivotal role compassionate conservatism would play in cutting the Gordian knot that limited GOP voter gains among women, minorities, and poorer Americans. Compassionate conservatism turned into a shorthand catchphrase that "would signal to the world that Bush was different" from other Republican conservatives: George W. expressed concern about education, cared about the poor and working class, and explored new policy solutions for these important issues.[9]

Governor Bush unveiled how his administration would apply compassionate conservatism in policy-making in a July 1999 address, declaring that his administration "will be government that both knows its limits and shows its heart."[10] He stated that the American dream should touch every willing heart and leave no one behind. Bush called for churches, synagogues, mosques, and community groups to fight for children and neighborhoods. The Texas governor emphasized his religious belief in the "transforming power of faith" and the hope of "redemption," arguing that government should welcome faith-based organizations as partners, not rivals. George W. Bush also rejected the extreme conservative view that attacked government as the enemy.

In September 1999 George W. Bush drew attention to his compassionate conservative beliefs by publicly criticizing a Republican congressional budget plan that would have delayed Federal tax breaks for 20 million working-class Americans. Bush declared: "I don't think they ought to balance their budget on the backs of the poor."[11] The conservative House majority whip, Texas Republican Tom DeLay, tartly responded: "He obviously doesn't understand how Congress works."

Governor Bush's carefully crafted statement succeeded in focusing the media spotlight on his compassionate conservative views. Calling himself a compassionate conservative sharply differentiated George W. Bush's philosophy from the cold, budget-cutting approach of hard-line House Republicans, who had dwindled in numbers as the Gingrich Revolution lost its appeal. One writer noted that by early 1997, "it was clear that the rowdy, ultraconservative members of Congress and their backers among the Christian right, the National Rifle Association, and militant, hard-right small businessmen had overreached."[12] Bush's criticism of the Republican congressional leaders reminded many observers of then-Governor Bill Clinton's June 1992 attack on African-American rapper Sister Souljah. That tactical move signaled Clinton's independence from extremist views within the black community, thus positioning Clinton as a centrist.

Most importantly, George W. Bush stood out among the other 2000 Republican presidential aspirants through his application of the concept of compassionate conservatism to symbolize his political beliefs and policies. The concept allowed the Bush campaign to feature George W. as a bold visionary, a caring man who could attract new voters to the GOP standard, and a strong leader who had enacted his beliefs into law, despite facing a Democrat-controlled Texas legislature. The compassionate conservative label also allowed Bush to underscore his born-again Christian religious beliefs.

Bumps in the Road

A Harris Poll conducted prior to Governor George W. Bush's 1998 reelection found that Republicans favored Colin Powell (24 percent) over "George Bush Jr." (20 percent) for the GOP presidential nomination.[13] But when the poll excluded Powell—the popular African-American retired general and chairman of the Joint Chiefs of Staff during the 1991 Gulf War—Bush led the early hopefuls with 27 percent of the respondents, followed by Elizabeth Dole at 13 percent. But Governor Bush's spectacular reelection results and escalating national media exposure boosted Bush's standing.

A Republican Leadership Council poll seven months later disclosed that Bush led the GOP primary pack with 40 percent of likely Republican voters, followed by Elizabeth Dole at 27 percent.[14] Dan Quayle garnered the backing of 9 percent of the polled Republicans, Steve Forbes 6 percent, and John McCain drew only 3 percent support. In August 1999 an ABC News Poll asked GOP respondents which candidate they would back in a primary or caucus for president.[15] George W. Bush led with 56 percent support, trailed by Elizabeth Dole at 14 percent, her numbers representing a decline of 11 points since a March ABC News Poll. Forbes and McCain tied at only 6 percent in the GOP survey.

But despite Governor Bush's early lead over other Republican hopefuls, a June 1999 *Newsweek* Poll found that 65 percent of voters said they knew little or nothing about Bush's career, yet he led the pack (47 percent), with Dole in second place at 16 percent. In the *Newsweek* Poll, a solid majority considered Bush a "moderate Republican," with almost half feeling he "cares about minorities," both findings indicating Governor Bush's compassionate conservative message had reached voters.[16] And, bolstering Rove's strategy to position George W. Bush as the candidate who could recapture the White House, the *Newsweek* Poll respondents indicated that Bush at that time would defeat Vice President Al Gore, the likely Democratic nominee by 16 points. The Bush "paint-by-numbers" campaign, as one reporter dubbed it, appeared on track, guided by the Rove master plan.[17]

The Bush campaign strategy counted upon a huge campaign war chest, filled through contributions from the Bush family's network of contributors and the major conservative donors that direct-mail consultant Karl Rove had tapped over years. Such a display of financial prowess would stifle the fund-raising efforts of other presidential hopefuls and attract the attention of the national media as a bellwether sign of Bush's strength. In addition, according to Rove's master plan, Bush's financial dominance would manifest the inevitability of his nomination and ultimate November victory.

Bush raised $36 million in the first six months and entered the GOP primaries in 2000 with $70 million in contributions.[18] The teeming campaign coffer permitted Governor Bush to reject Federal Election Commission (FEC) matching funds, allowing his campaign to ignore FEC spending limits in hotly contested states such as New Hampshire and South Carolina. Only billionaire Steve Forbes, by writing personal checks, could match Bush's financial clout in the nomination process. As Rove wryly confessed, "The only thing we haven't done well...is to lower expectations."[19]

On the early campaign trail, the confident Texas governor ignored his GOP rivals, focusing his attacks on Vice President Gore and the Clinton administration as though he had already won his party's nomination. The August 14, 1999, Iowa GOP straw poll in Ames represented the first test of Bush's strength. Twelve Republican presidential hopefuls were listed on the GOP ballot. The Iowa Republican Party designed the straw poll as a fund-raising event, with each vote costing $25—most often paid by the candidates—but it had evolved into an early media test of the candidates' electability. Arizona Senator John McCain chose to skip the Iowa contest calling it a "sham," preferring to campaign extensively in New Hampshire. In Governor Bush's 10-minute address to the Ames attendees, he stressed: *"I'm a uniter, not a divider"* (author's emphasis). Bush also reiterated his religion-tinged compassionate conservative message: "Prosperity must have a greater purpose."[20]

Everyone expected that George W. Bush, consistently leading in the national polls and far ahead of the other candidates in collecting campaign monies, would emerge the overwhelming GOP winner. However, his 31 percent victory in the Iowa GOP straw poll revealed that Bush enjoyed weaker support than anticipated. Publisher Steve Forbes, who also rejected FEC matching funds—with the FEC's spending limits in each state—came in second with 21 percent of the Iowa straw ballots, followed by Elizabeth Dole with 14 percent support. Forbes spent about $2 million to influence the Iowa straw poll, while Karen Hughes admitted that the Bush campaign exceeded its budgeted $750,000 to buy additional tickets for supporters (total of $825,000).

Although touted as the front-runner, Bush's modest win with Forbes nipping at his heels only 10 points behind, encouraged a Forbes spokesman to exult: "The wind is out of the sails of inevitability."[21] From the beginning, Karl Rove had worried mostly about billionaire Steve Forbes, who enjoyed the ability to write big checks that negated Bush's financial advantage. Indeed, Forbes ultimately "loaned" his campaign $42.3 million in the 2000 race.[22] Bush's longtime consultant did not assess Senator McCain as a serious threat to Bush's nomination, a perception that seemed validated in the early poll numbers.

The early Iowa event winnowed the field of GOP candidates. Shortly after the Ames straw poll, conservative commentator Pat Buchanan left the GOP to seek the Reform Party's nomination (and $12.6 million in Federal funds) and Lamar Alexander, who had served as Tennessee's governor and George Bush's Secretary of Education, abandoned the race. Former Vice President Dan Quayle's supporters began to jump ship, with his South Carolina advisers joining the McCain campaign. Quayle formally pulled out of the presidential race on September 27.[23]

Elizabeth Dole, President Reagan's secretary of transportation and the elder Bush's secretary of labor, withdrew from the presidential contest on October 20, after charging that in the current presidential election process, "the bottom line remains money."[24] Dole pointed to Forbes's unlimited resources and Governor Bush's substantial campaign war chest, raised through "a pre-existing network of political supporters." Dole admitted she could not compete against an 80 to 1 cash advantage.

The New Hampshire GOP primary stood out as the next step in the nomination process, traditionally a key early test for candidates of both parties because of extensive national media coverage. Bush continued to campaign above the Republican fray, committing the tactical error of dodging the first New Hampshire debate among the GOP candidates. The Bush team pragmatically concluded that the October 28 debate would only provide media exposure for his opponents and provide an opportunity to gang up on Bush as the front-runner. Bush media consultant Stuart Stevens admitted subsequently that the "dynamic in New Hampshire started to go sour" after Bush declined to participate in the Manchester debate, the only GOP candidate refusing the invitation.[25] The stated reason for turning down the debate was George W.'s commitment to attend a Southern Methodist University ceremony honoring his wife Laura, an alumnus.

Senator McCain spent two or three times the amount of time seeking New Hampshire votes as Governor Bush. A *Boston Herald* poll released the day before the first debate found McCain's favorable/unfavorable ratio (67 to 12 percent) ahead of Bush's (64 to 19 percent), although Bush remained ahead of McCain (44 percent to 26 percent) in a trial matchup.[26] In a 2001 postelection forum, Karl Rove confessed that the decision to skip the first New Hampshire debate represented a serious error: "We may have won New Hampshire if we had showed up."[27]

After that blunder, Bush prepared hard for the December 2 debate in New Hampshire, while Rove and Hughes attempted to lower expectations about Bush's debate performance, describing McCain as an experienced debater after serving many years in Congress.[28] In late December CNN's Larry King interviewed George W. Bush, asking about critics who pegged him as a "puny thinker." Governor Bush replied, in a rare public acknowledgment of his elite Eastern education: "They ignored the fact that I went to Yale and Harvard."[29]

When John McCain began campaigning in New Hampshire he stood at only 2 percent in the national presidential polls. But Senator McCain enjoyed a remarkable life story as a heroic warrior who spent five and a half years as a prisoner of war in Hanoi after an enemy missile downed his carrier-based A4E "Skyhawk" attack plane. McCain's real-life narrative thus directly challenged the strong-leader image Rove sought to fashion for George W. Bush, which sidestepped the young Bush's politically arranged entry into the Texas Air National Guard's "Champagne Squadron," spotty attendance record in the Guard, avoidance of combat duty in Vietnam, and early discharge.

In 1981 Captain John McCain retired from the Navy after 22 years of service, having been awarded the Silver Star, Bronze Star, Legion of Merit, Purple Heart, and Distinguished Flying Cross. John McCain's best-seller autobiography, *Faith of My Fathers,* acknowledged McCain's modest academic attainments at Annapolis (graduating 894 out of 899), depicted the harsh treatment and torture he and other POWs received from their North Vietnamese captors, candidly dealt with McCain's first failed marriage, and confessed to other personal flaws.

Senator McCain cleverly campaigned throughout New Hampshire in a bus named "Straight Talk Express," freely answering reporters' questions, thus winning their favor through his candor and willingness to tackle tough issues. Although the Arizona senator's central campaign message focused upon campaign finance reform, he staked out positions on other issues. McCain criticized President Clinton's air war in Kosovo, advocating the unpopular introduction of American ground forces: "No army has ever surrendered to an airplane."[30] He also questioned Clinton's friendly policy toward China.

Mark Salter, initially McCain's Senate foreign policy adviser and then chief of staff, helped write the Arizona senator's autobiography. Senator McCain informally listened to a small group of policy advisers, but often McCain simply bounced his ideas off them. The small size of the informal McCain brain trust stood in stark contrast to the Bush campaign. Since McCain had served in the House and Senate, including the Senate Armed Services Committee, he appeared more knowledgeable and comfortable discussing national and foreign policy issues than Governor Bush.

George W. Bush's huge loss in the February 1 New Hampshire primary, at the hands of party maverick John McCain, sent shockwaves through the Bush campaign organization and the Republican Party. McCain crushed the perceived front-runner with 48.5 percent of New Hampshire's votes to 30.4 percent for Bush.[31] Rove attempted to downplay the loss, claiming that front-runners inevitably encounter "a bump along the way." But the jarring New Hampshire loss, as Hughes subsequently confessed, "felt more like an avalanche than a bump."[32] The proclaimed inevitability of Bush's nomination suffered a severe blow from the lop-sided McCain victory. Likewise, polls showed McCain beating Gore in trail heats, undermining the Bush team's assertion that only he could recapture the White House for the GOP.[33] Bush's Boy Genius had committed the cardinal sin of warfare and politics, as both Sun Tsu and Machiavelli cautioned: "Never underestimate your opponent."

To George W. Bush's credit, he remained calm after the disaster and loyally refused to fire any campaign advisers as a result of the stunning New Hampshire defeat. Karl Rove, spinning the disheartening campaign moment, envisioned a silver lining in the disaster: "If the big rap against him is that he's never been tested, this will be a test. We'll come out of this better off than if we had won New Hampshire and cruised to the nomination."[34] However, that favorable outcome required a significant victory over Senator McCain in the South Carolina primary.

The Bush team decided upon three major tactical shifts in its campaign. First, Bush would reestablish himself as the only proven reformer in the race, rather than accept McCain's campaign finance proposals as proof of his reformer status. Karen Hughes designed the new slogan, "Reformer with Results," to highlight Bush's success in implementing change in Texas. Bush "welcomed the contrast and was frustrated that McCain had stolen the Outsider/Reformer label."[35]

Second, Bush set aside his compassionate conservative theme to outflank Senator McCain on the far Right. The Bush campaign targeted South Carolina's evangelical Christians and very conservative GOP voters. Bush's December 13, 2000, Des Moines debate response to a moderator's question, asking which political philosopher or thinker could he most identify with and why, aimed at attracting the Palmetto State's religious voters: "Christ, because he changed my heart."[36] When the Iowa local TV anchor asked Bush to elaborate, he gave a personal testimonial: "When you turn your heart and your life over to Christ, when you accept Christ as the Savior, it changes your heart. It changes your life. And that's what happened to me." George W. Bush's February 2 address at conservative Bob Jones University in Greenville sparked charges of pandering to extreme right-wing elements, since the Christian school had a reputation for racist and anti-Catholic policies.

The third decision launched an aggressive negative attack upon McCain in speeches, debates, TV, and radio ads—and more surreptitious communications. Milbank observed that Bush discovered the right formula, "tough, harsh attacks that expose weakness in policy and character."[37] The cunning Rove followed the pattern he had established in directing previous campaigns: he attacked a serious opponent's greatest strength. To meet the threat posed by John McCain, Rove set out to undermine the former POW's heroic image, divert the anticipated support of veterans from the decorated Navy POW, and raise disturbing questions about the conservative Arizona senator's character and beliefs.

Unidentified callers notified Republicans that McCain divorced his first wife, flyers attacked McCain's second wife Cindy for her addiction to painkiller drugs a decade prior, and a sympathetic Bob Jones professor e-mailed people that McCain had an illegitimate child.[38] An angry mother stood up in a McCain auditorium function to lash out at a "push poll" phone call to her home that labeled McCain "a cheat and a liar and a fraud."[39] Another telephone "push poll" asked South Carolina voters whether they would be more or less likely to vote for McCain if they knew he had fathered a black illegitimate child.[40] The smear ignored the fact that the McCains had adopted a Bangladeshi girl after Cindy McCain had visited Mother Theresa's orphanage.

When Rove taught a course at the University of Texas, he emphasized how negative campaign tactics can quickly alter a race. Rove pointed out that radio and direct mailing provided good channels for negative attacks since they were largely immune from press coverage. Rove emphasized: "It's better to narrowcast" powerful messages targeted at small groups, without stirring up the larger public.[41] Push polls, using Rove's terminology and logic, represented the most potent form of narrow casting aimed at specific blocs of voters that avoided alarming the opposition, arousing media coverage, or stirring public outrage.

Bush supporters spread rumors that the North Vietnamese possibly brainwashed McCain while imprisoned as a POW, making him unstable.[42] In Rove's unbridled determination to stop McCain, the Bush campaign played Lee Atwater's infamous brand of hardball politics. However, Rove carefully distanced the Bush campaign from the more unscrupulous tactics and avoided leaving his fingerprints on the below-the-belt blows. Bush had to smash McCain in South Carolina at all costs in order to end his burgeoning insurgency. A compelling Bush primary victory in the Palmetto State would halt McCain's momentum. Bush's other presidential rivals, Steve Forbes and Gary Bauer, also blamed the Bush campaign for the scurrilous attacks on Senator McCain. Texas observers noted that the vicious tactics mirrored Bush's 1994 whisper campaign in East Texas against Governor Ann Richards's tolerance for lesbians.[43]

Senator McCain fought back on the air and in speeches. However, when he compared George W. to Bill Clinton, a focus group of Republican voters felt he had crossed the line with an unfair comparison.[44] McCain's negative ads responding to Bush's attacks allowed the Bush campaign to muddy the water over who was running a dirty campaign, undercutting Senator McCain's reputation for fair play.

Bush achieved his goal of sabotaging support for McCain, a decorated Vietnam POW, with the charge that he ignored the needs of veterans when he went to Washington. The heavy purchase of Bush TV ads during the two weeks after the New Hampshire loss, employing his hefty financial advantage over the Arizona senator, depicted McCain as less supportive of tax cuts than the Texas governor and painted him as a dreaded liberal.

On February 19 Bush convincingly won the South Carolina primary, defeating McCain 53.4 percent to 41.9 percent. Nevertheless, three days later Senator McCain rallied to win Michigan and his home state of Arizona. But McCain turned off many Virginia GOP voters by charging that Christian conservative Pat Robertson exerted an "evil influence" on the Republican Party; Bush won the Virginia primary with 52.8 percent of the vote.

After the March 7 Super Tuesday primaries in 13 states, Bush's overwhelming delegate count led Senator McCain to "suspend" his presidential campaign two days later. However, the desperate fight against McCain's insurgency in the race to the White House had cost Bush his financial advantage, leaving only $10 million in his campaign war chest. The anxious Bush campaign had abandoned its positive message of compassionate conservatism to tread the hazardous trail of negative attacks in a calculated maneuver to attract right-wing votes in the bitter fight with McCain. One Bush advisor lamented the shift: "Somehow...we lost our mojo."[45]

The Image Battles

Vice President Al Gore, like Governor Bush, held all the aces in his party's nomination contest. He enjoyed a flush treasury as the Democratic heir apparent to President Clinton, fielded a large, campaign-experienced organization, and led in the early polls over his challenger, retired New Jersey Senator Bill Bradley, a former National Basketball Association star player. Gore came out early campaigning vigorously for the nomination, announcing the endorsements of Democratic officials and calling activists in New Hampshire.

During the early days he campaigned against George W. Bush as though the general election was the next hurdle. At the January 24 Iowa caucus Vice President Gore whipped Bradley by 28 points. But in New Hampshire Bradley built up a new head of steam and charged the net to produce an unexpectedly close primary, which Gore won 49.7 percent to 45.6 percent.[46] Traditional Democratic groups stood side-by-side with Gore, loyally respecting President Clinton's endorsement of Gore. Then the front-loaded primaries in early 2000 helped Gore defeat Bradley, particularly Gore's big wins in delegate-rich California and New York. Vice President Gore had visited California 44 times since 1993 to lock up that vital state.[47]

During the Democratic primaries Gore tried to alter his image as an unemotional, robotic candidate and policy wonk, establishing an advisory board of "real people." The Gore campaign scheduled "reverse town-hall meetings" for Gore to appear more relaxed and personable—while demonstrating his command over public policy issues. A reporter observed, "Real people are part of a broader effort to turn Analytical Al into Gregarious Gore."[48] The vice president sought to divorce himself from the taint of Clinton's infidelity scandal and the attempted GOP impeachment. However, the vice president's efforts to gain credit for the Clinton administration's enviable record on economic prosperity failed to gain much traction on the political track.

After winning their respective party nominations, contrasting views of the two candidates surfaced in national surveys. Governor Bush appeared ahead in the battle of images, perceived as a strong leader on national security issues. In the June 8–11, 2000, ABC News/*Washington Post* Poll respondents picked Bush (65 percent) over Gore (48 percent) as "a strong leader."[49] Bush's muscular stand on national defense and criticism of the Clinton administration's changing foreign policies led prospective voters to appraise Bush as closer to their views on defense matters than Gore. Respondents felt Bush had the more appealing personality, but that Gore was more intelligent. At that point in the campaign, respondents saw Bush as more likely to exaggerate his accomplishments than Gore.

Bush maintained up to a 17-point lead over Gore throughout the summer. Therefore, the media objectives of each campaign differed in stage-managing their party's convention. Since Bush coasted ahead of Gore, his handlers decided to reenergize his compassionate conservative image around the convention theme, "Renewing America's Purpose: Together." Republican convention keynote speakers such as Condoleezza Rice and General Colin Powell symbolized the GOP's inclusiveness, even though only 8 percent of the delegates were minorities.[50]

More controversial and extreme GOP figures were not given prime-time speaking slots in a conscious effort to avoid the elder Bush's mistake at the 1992 Republican convention. Bush's spokesman Ari Fleischer acknowledged: "We've changed the tone."[51] Nevertheless, Bush's choice for vice president, his father's Secretary of Defense Dick Cheney, played the traditional vice presidential hatchet-man role by attacking Clinton-Gore policies, followed by the refrain: "It's time for them to go."

Governor George W. Bush went through 18 drafts of his acceptance speech, fine-tuned by Rove and Hughes, diligently practicing to deliver a forceful address.[52] In his convention speech Governor Bush asserted what he viewed as the key lesson of the Vietnam War: "When America uses force in the world, the cause must be just, the goal must be clear, and the victory must be overwhelming," an echo of Reagan Defense Secretary Casper Weinberger's guidelines for the post-Vietnam deployment of U.S. armed forces.[53]

Governor Bush dramatized the reduced readiness of the American military under the Clinton administration's budget cuts, claiming that if called to report to active duty, "two entire divisions of the Army would have to report, 'Not ready for duty, sir.'" But the harsh accusation went over the top, angering Army officials. The Pentagon's critical reaction to the charge embarrassed Bush, forcing him to back away from the potent attack line. The GOP convention provided the anticipated "bounce" for the Bush/Cheney ticket, with Bush charging forth with a 16-point lead over Gore.[54]

The Gore team's strategy for the August 13–16 Democratic convention concentrated on capturing the lead in the presidential race by generating a postconvention bounce, achieved through hard-hitting Democratic attacks on Bush and keynote speeches that portrayed Gore as caring, religious, and personable. Al Gore's selection of Connecticut Senator Joe Lieberman, a very religious Orthodox Jew who had publicly chastised Bill Clinton on his infidelity, received accolades. Lieberman emerged as a key campaigner in Gore's plan to garner the overwhelming support of Jewish voters in the swing state of Florida. Trailing in the polls, the Democratic convention speeches were "more self-consciously mean and nasty."[55]

Tipper Gore introduced her husband before he accepted the Democratic Party nomination. When he walked on the stage the normally reserved Al Gore embraced and gave his wife a long passionate kiss to the delight of the delegates. "The Kiss" helped boost Gore's appeal among women and undercut his stiff, wooden image. The Gore/Lieberman ticket gained an eight-point bounce after the Democratic convention, finally pulling slightly ahead of Bush after the August 18–19 poll (47 percent to 46 percent). Gore remained slightly ahead of Bush throughout most of September.

Women voters became a key target group for both campaigns. Gore benefited from a Democratic-leaning 11-point "gender gap" in the September 9–11 *New York Times*/CBS News Poll. However, married women favored Bush over Gore, while unmarried women staunchly backed the Democrat Gore.[56] Bush's message of compassionate conservatism and education reform elicited applause from married women, whereas Gore's proposals addressed the economic anxieties of unmarried women.

The gender gap first arose in the 1980 election when Governor Ronald Reagan's strong support of the military, welfare reform proposals, and antiabortion stands frightened many women who began to shift to the Democratic standard bearer. George W. Bush's traditional GOP call for a stronger military assertion of U.S. power abroad, opposition to gun control, and as governor, approval of the ongoing execution of murderers in Texas, drew support among white male voters. Under normal circumstances, such *macho* characteristics appealed more to male than female American voters. The Rove solution to the dilemma counted upon compassionate conservatism to leverage Bush's support for education and moderate stands on other social issues to attract female votes.

The hunt for female votes brought both Al Gore and George W. Bush into the TV studio for separate interviews with the popular Oprah Winfrey, who drew an impressive audience of 22 million viewers—three-fourths female.[57] Oprah hoped to "break the political wall" to reveal what Gore and Bush were really like as people.[58] Thus, Gore admitted to Oprah on September 11, responding to her question about his alleged stiffness: "I know myself well enough to know there is actually some truth to it." He acknowledged that he did not fit the mold of a backslapping politician: "I'm a little bit more of a private person."

When Oprah asked about the big kiss he gave Tipper at the convention, Gore's answer won applause from the studio audience filled largely with women: "This has been a partnership and she is my soul mate." Clearly, Gore wanted to distance himself from Clinton's unfaithful behavior, underscoring his own devotion to "family values." The *Newsweek* poll released on September 16, after Gore appeared on Oprah's show and David Letterman's "Late Show," disclosed that Gore enjoyed a 12-point advantage over Bush.

Lagging in the polls, Governor Bush found himself forced to abandon his more controlled and scripted campaigning primarily among Republican loyalists. Bush also turned to the TV talk shows, sipping coffee on Regis Philbin's morning show and talking with Oprah Winfrey on September 19, a week after Gore's appearance. Bush responded to Oprah's question about public misconceptions of him by rebutting the belief he was "running on my daddy's name" or seeking to avenge his father 1992 defeat. "Revenge is such a negative thought. I'm running for positive reasons."[59] When she asked about his giving up drinking at age 40, Bush replied: "Alcohol was beginning to compete for my affections...for my wife and family. It was beginning to crowd out my energy and I decided to quit."

The Texas governor also defended himself against the perception that he was not intelligent. Recalling his anxieties when competing at the Andover prep school against smarter kids: "Eventually, I realized smarts are not only whether or not you can write well or whether or not you can do calculus, but *smarts also is instinct and judgment and competence,*" pointing to his education and experience (author's emphasis). Tears swelled up in the governor's eyes—although he normally sought to project a *macho* image—when he described how his wife Laura became toxemic when carrying their twins.[60] Bush also one-upped Gore by kissing Oprah on the cheek at the end of the show. By October 6 Governor Bush had regained a seven-point lead over Gore, but the margin narrowed or tied by the end of the campaign.[61]

Debate Face-Off

The three October presidential debates symbolized a high hurdle for George W. Bush to jump, since most observers considered him not very articulate or well informed on national issues. Of course, the Bush campaign encouraged such low expectations of the governor's performance over the experienced, hard-hitting debater Al Gore. The Bush team relied on the 500-page Republican National Committee's analysis of Gore's previous debate and public forum performances—including during the 1988, 1992, 1996, and 2000 elections—to prepare Governor Bush for the widely viewed televised face-off.[62] Consultant Stuart concluded Gore's debate prowess "was way overrated," though he recognized that Gore always scored painful blows. In preparing for the debates, Karen Hughes recalled: "Governor Bush doesn't like commotion before big events. He likes order, familiar people, a familiar routine," with no last-minute cramming or staff discussion of what he should say.[63]

Even though the initial October 4 debate in Boston featured domestic issues, Governor Bush used the podium to hit Clinton's policy toward Kosovo. Bush declared it "would be a wonderful time for the president of Russia to step into the Balkans" to convince Serbian President Slobodan Milosevic to leave office.[64] Gore quickly responded that it could endanger U.S. interests in the region if America invited the Russians to mediate the conflict. But when the moderator asked whether Bush would deploy U.S. forces to get Serbian leader Milosevic out of office, the governor prudently admitted he would not use force, only diplomatic initiatives.

Governor Bush cautioned: "I don't think we can be all things to all people in the world," expressing opposition to President Clinton's deployment of U.S. troops as nation builders. He disclaimed any desire "to be the world's policeman," arguing his proposed missile system could protect both America and its allies from becoming blackmailed or held hostage by rogue nations.

The second presidential debate centered on foreign policy. Governor Bush declared that how a president projected American power would impact upon the world's assessment of the United States. "If we're an arrogant nation, they'll resent us. If we're a humble nation, but strong, they'll welcome us."[65] Bush pledged: "We've got to be humble and yet project strength."

Bush charged that the Clinton administration's Iraq policy had failed since there were no longer UN weapons inspectors on Iraqi soil, the coalition forged by his father had fallen apart, and Saddam Hussein could again fish in the Middle East's "troubled waters." But Bush mistakenly urged "our European friends (to) become the peacekeepers in Bosnia and in the Balkans" with troops on the ground. As critics and America's allies quickly noted, the NATO countries already had 68,000 troops on the ground in Bosnia and Kosovo, compared with only 12,000 American troops.[66]

Bush saved his gunpowder for Clinton's ill-fated interventions in Somalia and Haiti, which he blasted as nation-building exercises. However, he agreed with Clinton's "right decision" not to send American forces to Rwanda to stop the 1994 genocide. Governor Bush stated that the deployment of the U.S. military abroad must serve a vital interest, establish a clear mission, and include an obvious exit strategy (the Powell Doctrine). Presenting himself as a reluctant warrior,

Governor Bush maintained: "I'm not so sure the role of the United States is to go around the world and say this is the way it's got to be." In the final debate, which covered many of the same topics, Bush advocated using America's technological advantage "to make our military lighter, harder to find, more lethal."[67]

Neither candidate scored a knockout blow in the debates, with both misspeaking a number of times. In the immediate reaction to the first debate performances, an ABC News Poll found 42 percent of the respondents declared Al Gore the winner, while 39 percent felt George W. Bush won.[68] However, after several days of media comments about Gore's inaccuracies, exaggerations, and criticism on his rude sighs and encroachment upon Bush's stage space, the numbers turned to favor Bush. Governor Bush began attacking "Gore's pattern of exaggerations," while Karen Hughes dubbed Gore a "serial exaggerator."[69]

Vice President Gore approached the second debate far more reserved. Viewers of the second debate on foreign policy, which should have been the experienced vice president's strongest topic, concluded that Bush clobbered Gore, with even a plurality of women picking Bush as the winner.[70] Gore became more aggressive in the third matchup, tying Bush at 41 percent. Gore won the nod from women, while men favored Bush's performance.[71]

After the third debate a national poll appraised the public impression of the characteristics and qualities of the two major candidates. Gore's aggressive debate demeanor resulted in viewers judging Bush the more likeable; respondents also considered the Texas governor more believable.[72] The media's scrutiny of Gore's exaggerations, reinforced by Bush attacks on his "white lies," had produced a credibility gap about the vice president's veracity. After the three rounds of debate, a poll found that Bush had surged ahead of Gore (51 percent to 40 percent), with the Reform Party's Pat Buchanan at 1 percent and the Green Party's Ralph Nader at 4 percent.[73]

Nose-to-Nose Finish

The campaigns intensified broadsides against their opponent after the debates, each trying to gain an edge in the competition for the White House. The Bush campaign ran its more positive ads while the Republican National Committee aired the negative spots, attempting to distance the GOP candidate from the harsh attacks in the eyes of voters. Democratic organizations acted similarly for the vice president. Unfortunately for Gore, the focus on character and ethics diverted public attention from the robust state of the economy under the eight years of the Democratic administration. Both campaigns stage-managed their communication by concentrating on an issue of the week to enhance media coverage of their message. Bush spokesman Ari Fleischer explained: "Voters are busy. You want to repeat. Just because you said it on Monday doesn't mean voters heard it on Monday."[74]

Governor Bush's slight lead disappeared as the candidates approached the November 7 Election Day finish line. Despite the tightness of the race, Rove confidently predicted Bush would win the race with about 320 Electoral College votes and a six-point advantage in the popular vote.[75] Then five days before the election, a news story broke revealing that when Bush was 30 years old, he had pleaded guilty to a 1976 drunk-driving arrest in Maine. The Bush camp and their candidate cried foul. However, the big question became why George W. attempted to cover up the DUI conviction, not revealing it earlier in the race to immunize himself against the fallout. Bush tried to convince reporters he kept silent only to protect his twin daughters. But Texas journalist Wayne Slater recalled when Governor Bush categorically told him he had never been arrested, other than as a result of a college prank.[76]

Karen Hughes later admitted she knew previously about the 1976 DUI conviction: "The governor had told me and a few others because he didn't want us blindsided or put in a position of lying about it."[77] After the 2000 election Karl Rove claimed that the DUI story cost the campaign its momentum and Maine's electoral votes, contributing to the nose-to-nose finish.[78] Nevertheless, Rove acknowledged he participated in the decision not to disclose the DUI arrest and still felt it represented the correct course of action.

The closeness of the final Election Day tally (a virtual tie), with networks reversing their pronouncements on who won in Florida, created confusion, anger, and legal maneuvering in the state of Florida. Controversy over a butterfly ballot, overseas military ballots, "pregnant" and "hanging chads" led to a prolonged Florida vote count. The U.S. Supreme Court intervened on December 12, 2000. The nation's high court decision in *Bush v. Gore* (divided 5–4 along partisan lines) stopped the Florida recount, thus awarding George W. Bush the White House prize.

When the political dust settled, Vice President Al Gore had won the national popular vote by about a 540,000 vote margin. However, the capture of Florida's 25 electoral votes gave Governor Bush a slight majority (271) of the Electoral College votes, compared with Gore's 266 electoral vote count. If Gore had won his home state of Tennessee (11 electoral votes), he would have been inaugurated President.[79] Rove admitted that he missed a "whole series of little tactical miscues" about the close Florida race, which might have produced a more intense ground game.[80] Vice President Gore gracefully respected the Supreme Court decision: "Tonight, for the sake of our unity of the people and the strength of our democracy, I offer my concession."

Democrats bitterly lambasted Ralph Nader's decision to stay in the race, since his tiny 1 percent of the popular vote would have likely gone to Gore, allowing the Democratic nominee to win the close contests in Florida and New Hampshire. The postelection aftermath featured a lot of strategic and tactical "What ifs" among Democratic and Republican strategists.

The Voter News Service's November 7 Exit Poll, funded by a consortium of news organizations, revealed the persistence of the gender gap. Gore received 11 points more support among women, while Bush garnered an 11-point spread among men; working women overwhelmingly favored Gore.[81] Bush received the votes of 60 percent of white men. Governor Bush's compassionate conservative message failed to sway many minorities, with only 8 percent of blacks and 35 percent of Latinos backing the Bush ticket. Independents, a critical swing group for both camps, divided their ballots fairly equally between Bush and Gore. Self-identified moderates (half of all voters) went to Al Gore. Moderates represented another key target group that Governor Bush hoped to attract by marketing himself as a compassionate conservative.

Religion played a role in the 2000 General Election with Protestants favoring Bush, Jews overwhelmingly picking Gore, and Catholics by a narrow three-point margin choosing Gore. But among respondents who considered themselves in the Religious Right, Bush amassed 80 percent of their ballots. Attendance in church also impacted upon candidate choices, with Bush's well-publicized religious views winning the support of people who attended church more than weekly or weekly, while Gore drew more support from people who never or seldom went to church.

Gore won over a majority of voters who identified the economy/jobs, education, and social security as the most important issues influencing their presidential ballot. World affairs ranked fifth in a list of issues impacting upon a respondent's candidate choice, but a majority of these individuals voted for Bush. Almost half of the voters agreed with Governor Bush that in the past eight years the U.S. military had become weaker.

Vice President Gore's dilemma on whether to warmly embrace Clinton's domestic policy success was reflected in two findings. A hefty 57 percent of all respondents approved of President Clinton's job performance, but at the same time 60 percent expressed an unfavorable opinion of Bill Clinton as a person. Almost two-thirds of the respondents felt the country was moving in the right direction, with Gore winning 61 percent of these voters.

When voters assessed candidate qualities that they had considered important when casting their ballots, Governor Bush's supporters identified honesty and a strong leader as the qualities they most admired in him. Individuals voting for Vice President Gore selected experience, understands issues, and cares about people as the qualities they particularly liked about Gore. When asked to rate each candidate, two-thirds of all respondents acknowledged that Gore had the knowledge to serve as president, compared with a majority saying Bush had the requisite knowledge for the high post.

In a February 2001 postelection forum, Karl Rove argued that the Gore campaign failed to exploit the eight years of prosperity and peace during the Clinton administration. He maintained, perhaps mocking his opponents: "We should have gotten our brains beat" in November.[82] But Gore's pollster Stan Greenberg disclosed: "Anything we tried to take credit for just did not work." Bob Shrum, one of the vice president's top strategists, observed: "If there had been no so-called scandals...does anyone doubt who would be sitting in the Oval Office today?"

In summary, George W. Bush won the close 2000 presidential race by successfully focusing the campaign on character and ethical questions, thereby diverting voter attention from the thriving U.S. economy. Bush promoted the concept of compassionate conservatism to broaden his appeal, at the same time selling himself as a tough, strong leader who would make America stand tall in the world again—like Ronald Reagan. He cleverly presented himself as a cautious warrior in the presidential debates to avoid upsetting female voters. Nevertheless, the Texas governor's deliberate attacks on Clinton's defense spending cuts, opposition to *rapprochement* with China, and promotion of a missile defense system shaped the emerging image of George W. Bush—if elected president—as a strong, assertive commander-in-chief.

President Clinton's accomplishments helped the Democratic nominee Al Gore, especially on the economy, healthcare, and social security issues. However,

Clinton's personal flaws cast a pall over the entire Gore campaign. The shadow of Bill Clinton's moral transgression with a White House intern created a potent issue for the Bush campaign to exploit.

Governor Bush had established a Texas legislative record and developed campaign skills built upon his easygoing, affable personality to successfully challenge the experienced vice president. Bush's carefully honed political style, message disciple, and successful strategic plan allowed George W. Bush to exceed expectations about his capabilities as a leader. The first U.S. president of the twenty-first century headed to the White House—this time successfully following his father's footsteps.

Part II

A War President Emerges

Chapter Five

The Early Months:
Clear-Eyed Realism

I'm interested in solving problems.... That's what a leader does.

The election of George W. Bush as the forty-third president of the United States raised questions about the direction of America's foreign policy with his hand at the helm. While Bush expressed some of his views during the October 2000 presidential debates, a carefully timed series of interviews and speeches earlier in the campaign had sketched out the course his administration would pursue in the international arena. In particular, the ideas of his father's former National Security Council (NSC) staff member Condoleezza Rice and tutorials with major foreign policy officials from the Reagan and first Bush administration provided the core concepts and ideas that George W. Bush then embraced.

President George W. Bush entered the White House with foreign policies developed from his advisers' Cold War experiences, traditional realist concepts, and Republican reactions to the alleged vacillation and weakness of President Bill Clinton's policies abroad. Neoconservative beliefs, while held by some individuals close to Bush, failed to appear in the campaign rhetoric of Governor Bush, who positioned himself in the mainstream of the GOP internationalist, strong defense, and free-trade approach to foreign policy-making.

Since President Bush lacked foreign policy credentials, he surrounded himself with seasoned men and women to reassure domestic and foreign observers about America's new leader. Many of these people had served in George W. Bush's "Vulcans" group of foreign policy mentors during the campaign before accepting positions in the NSC, Department of State, and Pentagon.[1] Secretary of Defense Donald Rumsfeld epitomized the overall Bush approach to national security issues by subsequently calling the administration's foreign policy as "forward-leaning." That term highlighted a new bold, ambitious, and aggressive approach to protecting and advancing America's national interests in the world.

A Seasoned Team

The Bush campaign team recognized from the beginning that George W. Bush's woeful lack of knowledge on national security topics represented a serious vulnerability in the presidential race, particularly against the experienced vice president. Stanford's Condoleezza Rice led the early Vulcan tutorial sessions with the Texas governor to familiarize him with challenges from abroad. In April 1999 conservative New York Times columnist William Safire conducted an early interview of Governor Bush to assess whether Bush had the "right stuff" on national defense issues. Deflecting criticism that he lacked a background in international affairs, Bush assured Safire thus: "I am surrounding myself with good, smart people who understand my principles and with whom I am going to become more knowledgeable."[2]

Four months later in a *National Journal* interview, Governor Bush once again elaborated upon his decision-making style and approach to U.S. foreign policy: "I'm interested in solving problems.... That's what a leader does."[3] He appeared to embrace the pragmatic, problem-solver approach of his father.[4] Bush described himself as a decisive person, a good listener, someone who reads summaries and then asks questions. However, Bush also acknowledged: "I rely upon the judgment of people a lot." The Texas governor emphasized: "I am smart enough to know what I don't know, and I have good judgment about who will either be telling me the truth, or has some agenda."

The well-seasoned national security team the new president put together represented many years of public service at high levels in the Ford, Reagan, and Bush administrations, but also under Democratic presidents. Although the new advisors appeared to validate the foreign policy course of the new administration, the prestigious appointments concealed clashing ideologies, personal enmity, and conflicting policy-making styles within the Bush national security team. These differences would create major problems as the strong-willed advisers wrestled to influence the inexperienced president, who lacked well-developed foreign policy views.

The vice presidential choice of Dick Cheney, former secretary of defense in his father's administration during the Gulf War, helped George W. Bush to project a White House image of experience, ability, and toughness. Dick Cheney had begun his public service during the Nixon administration. When Gerald Ford became president after Nixon's resignation, Cheney rose to become Ford's White House deputy chief of staff under Donald Rumsfeld and then chief of staff when Rumsfeld switched jobs to head the Pentagon. In 1978 Cheney was elected to represent Wyoming in Congress. He served five terms in the House of Representatives, winning three Republican House leadership positions, including minority whip. George H.W. Bush appointed Cheney his secretary of defense in 1988. After the elder Bush's defeat, Cheney became the chief executive officer of Halliburton, a large energy corporation, until George W. tapped him as his running mate in 2000.

From the beginning Vice President Cheney played a very powerful role in the administration's discussions on energy, national security, and, after 9/11, terrorism. He also exerted considerable sway over the appointment of people to high positions in the new Bush administration. Although not formally considered a neoconservative, Cheney's tough foreign policy approach resulted in close relations with many of the neoconservative hard-liners in the Bush administration.

When President Bush named Colin Powell his secretary of state, the retired African-American four-star general, the move won applause around the world and from Democrats and minorities, who respected Powell for his integrity, moderation, and career achievements. Polls showed Colin Powell "was the most popular political figure in the United States."[5] Powell, the son of Jamaican immigrants, had attended the City College of New York, where he joined the Army Reserve Officer Training Corps (ROTC). After graduation the Army sent him as a junior officer to Vietnam, where he served two tours, earning the Bronze Star, Legion of Merit, Soldier's Medal, and Purple Heart. Powell won a White House Fellowship and from that experience drew the admiring attention of prominent figures in both Democratic and Republican administrations.

During President Carter's administration Powell worked as assistant to the Deputy Secretary of Defense Frank Carlucci. In the Reagan years General Powell became the senior military assistant to Defense Secretary Casper Weinberger, with Reagan later selecting him as his National Security Adviser. President George H.W. Bush ignored 15 more senior generals to name Powell as chairman of the Joint Chiefs of Staff in 1991. General Powell served in that important role during the Desert Storm operation that expelled Iraqi forces from occupied Kuwait.

After retirement General Powell joined former President Carter and Senator Sam Nunn on a peace-making trip to Haiti to end military rule, avoid a full-scale U.S. troop invasion, and reinstitute the democratically elected Haitian government. Powell published a popular 1995 autobiography, *My American Journey*, and chaired a national nonprofit organization, America's Promise—The Alliance for Youth, until becoming Bush's secretary of state.

During the 2000 campaign Colin Powell did not participate in the Vulcan foreign policy discussions or on the missile defense group. At the 2000 GOP convention Powell delivered one of the keynote addresses, implicitly appealing for minority votes on behalf of compassionate conservative George W. Bush. At the end of the race General Powell campaigned at Bush's side to help attract minorities, moderates, and veterans to the GOP banner. Governor Bush hinted that Powell would be his choice for secretary of state to boost Bush's appeal among the same groups.[6]

Besides the anticipated appointment of Powell as secretary of state, announced shortly after the 5–4 Supreme Court's decision in *Bush v. Gore*, few were surprised when president-elect Bush tapped Rice as his NSC adviser. Condoleezza Rice lacked the extensive experience, Washington network, or insider influence of Powell or Rumsfeld, but more importantly, she enjoyed the confidence and friendship of George W. Bush. As Bush stated during the campaign, Rice was one of the few people who "can explain foreign policy matters in a way that I can understand."[7]

Dr. Rice had taught political science at Stanford University as a Soviet scholar before becoming provost in 1993, the chief academic official on the Stanford campus. As an academic she began her early involvement in Washington policymaking as a Council on Foreign Relations international fellow, working with the director of the Joint Chiefs of Staff. During the first Bush administration Dr. Rice worked as director and then senior director of Soviet and East European affairs in the NSC, reporting to NSC Adviser Brent Scowcroft.

General Scowcroft, a pragmatic realist, promoted Rice's public service career, involving her in reviewing the memoir he and President George H.W. Bush wrote about the administration's foreign policy, *A World Transformed*. The senior Bush invited Condoleezza Rice to Kennebunkport in August 1998, when George W. Bush also planned to visit. One observer noted how George W. and Condoleezza "bonded at Kennebunkport," particularly through a shared love of sports and exercise.[8] Shortly afterward Bush selected Rice as his campaign's chief foreign policy adviser.

Vice President Cheney, at the beginning of the administration, attempted a power play to further enhance his role in foreign and defense policy-making. He had already created a "mini-NSC staff" in the vice president's office, twice the size of Gore's staff, hiring experienced, conservative national security experts.[9] Cheney sought to chair the principals committee, traditionally chaired by the president's NSC adviser, which would have downgraded Rice's prestige and authority. However, Rice convinced President Bush to deny the request and she continued to chair the principals meetings—although Cheney broke precedent by attending all the principals meetings.

When President George W. Bush appointed Donald Rumsfeld secretary of defense, it became his second tour of duty at the Pentagon after having also served President Ford in that post. Rumsfeld won election to Congress in 1962, served four terms in the House, and then accepted positions in the Nixon administration, including ambassador to the North Atlantic Treaty Organization. When Vice President Gerald Ford became president after Nixon's resignation, he named Rumsfeld his White House chief of staff. In 1975 President Ford appointed him secretary of defense.

After leaving government in 1976, Rumsfeld served as chief executive officer, president, and then chairman of G.D. Searle & Co., a worldwide pharmaceutical company and later as chief operating officer (CEO) of General Instrument Corporation. The elder Bush knew Rumsfeld had sidelined him from consideration for Ford's open vice presidency in 1975 by pushing his appointment as director of the CIA. During the confirmation process Bush had to disclaim any interest in the vice presidential position. As secretary of defense, Rumsfeld also criticized the CIA during Bush's tenure as Director of Central Intelligence (DCI) for underestimating the level of Soviet spending. In addition, Rumsfeld had campaigned from late 1985 to 1987 for the presidency, considering Vice President Bush a weak GOP candidate. Because of the senior Bush's bitter memories of Rumsfeld's actions, the Reagan and Bush White House years proved cool toward any hope Rumsfeld entertained about returning to public service.

Rumsfeld chaired a 1998 bipartisan U.S. Missile Threat Commission. The unanimous Commission report concluded that U.S. intelligence had underestimated the ballistic missile threat from North Korea, Iraq, and Iran.[10] Many of the Vulcan national security advisers also participated on a more secret Bush campaign group, chaired by Rumsfeld, focused on one policy—missile defense.[11] In 2000 Rumsfeld headed the U.S. Commission to Assess National Security Space Management and Organization, which also helped to restore his defense policy credentials and visibility in Washington circles. Rumsfeld had mentored and assisted Cheney in his career rise through White House and Pentagon posts, so the vice president reciprocated by promoting Rumsfeld for the Department of Defense (DoD) post. The appointment brought Rumsfeld out of the cold and back into familiar government territory.

But internal Bush administration rivalries and Republican Party factional divisions greatly contributed to Rumsfeld's Pentagon appointment. Initially Rumsfeld was considered for the position of director of the CIA, but the senior Bush urged that the current DCI, George Tenet, be kept in that position to avoid politicizing the post. When George H.W. Bush had served as DCI, newly elected President Carter had turned down his request to continue heading the CIA.

George W. heeded his father's counsel and Tenet retained the DCI leadership position on intelligence matters.

Although General Powell's prestige helped Bush win the election, Vice President Cheney and neoconservatives doubted the general's commitment to the administration's expansive foreign policy goals. Defense Secretary Cheney had rebuked General Powell during the 1991 Gulf War when Powell, as chairman of the Joint Chiefs of Staff, argued against war with Iraq, recommending that President Bush apply economic sanctions and enforce containment before resorting to military force. Cheney bluntly pointed out to Powell that war with Iraq was a political, not a military decision.[12]

Neoconservatives never forgave Powell for not urging Bush to continue the troop march to Baghdad to topple Saddam Hussein after the defeat of Iraq's military forces in Kuwait. The criticism ignored the administration's concern that the international coalition would implode if U.S. troops went beyond the UN resolution mandate, civil disorder might ensue in Iraq, and American forces might become a detested foreign occupier.[13] Neoconservatives such as Wolfowitz remained angry that Bush ended the ground war before destroying Saddam Hussein's Republican Guard divisions and tanks.[14] Bob Woodward's book, *The Commanders*, portrayed Powell as a reluctant warrior during the Gulf War deliberations, leaning toward caution in the employment of U.S. forces after a full NSC debate on policy options.[15] The new administration's hawks thus viewed Powell as a moderate, not a reliable champion of their grandiose plans to assertively project American military power around the world.

When President Bush announced General Powell's appointment as secretary of state on December 16, 2000, Powell's remarks to reporters' questions only accentuated those apprehensions, as well as raised worries about Powell's meddling with Defense Department plans.[16] Powell appeared to overshadow Bush with his commanding presence, wide knowledge of foreign affairs, and eloquence—not a comforting feeling for the new president.

Cheney and other conservatives began to promote Rumsfeld, a former Pentagon chief and ferocious bureaucratic infighter, to head the Pentagon post as a counterbalance to Powell's influence within the administration. This appointment also enhanced Cheney's White House power, since disputes between State and Defense would be pushed to the White House for resolution, where the experienced vice president held extraordinary influence, more than any prior vice president. NSC adviser Rice lacked the *gravitas* or experience to personally resolve disputes between the two bureaucratic lions—Colin Powell and Donald Rumsfeld.

The next battle over appointing new members to the Bush administration's foreign policy team occurred over the number two positions in Powell's State Department and Rumsfeld's Pentagon. As a newly commissioned Annapolis graduate, Richard Armitage had served three Navy combat tours in Vietnam, becoming fluent in Vietnamese. Armitage worked with South Vietnam's river navy, advised Vietnamese ambush teams, and served as a U.S. intelligence operative, including "black ops." In 1975 he resigned from the Navy to work in the U.S. defense attaché's office in Saigon, where he played a vital diplomatic and operational role in evacuating Vietnamese naval vessels and about 20,000 Vietnamese to the Philippines.[17] Armitage then became a Pentagon troubleshooter in Tehran, working with the Iranian Navy and special operations units in relation to U.S. arms sales.

In 1981 Armitage became deputy assistant secretary of defense for East Asia and Pacific affairs in the Reagan administration. Two years later he was promoted to assistant secretary of defense for international security, with primary responsibility for the Middle East and East Asia. Armitage attracted the enmity of Ross Perot, who viciously criticized him and sought to get Armitage fired. When George H.W. Bush won the presidency, Secretary of Defense Cheney asked Armitage to become secretary of the Army. Perot again attacked Armitage through Senator Jesse Helm, raising questions about whether the Senate Foreign Relations committee would confirm his nomination. When Cheney offered only tepid encouragement about his prospects of confirmation, Armitage angrily withdrew his name. Armitage then served as presidential special negotiator on U.S. bases in the Philippines, mediated water issues in the Middle East, and with the title of ambassador, directed foreign aid to the newly independent states of the former Soviet Union.

Early in the Reagan administration General Powell and combat veteran Armitage formed a close friendship, based upon their Vietnam military service, pragmatic policy-making approach, and nonelitist backgrounds. This friendship persisted even as their career paths diverged. This close relationship later doomed Armitage's hope to become George W. Bush's deputy secretary of defense, since Rumsfeld did not trust Armitage because of the strong tie to Powell. In spite of his background in Pentagon affairs, Armitage became Powell's undersecretary of state.

Dr. Paul Wolfowitz served as dean of the School of Advanced International Studies at Johns Hopkins University during the Clinton administration, when tapped to cochair Bush's Vulcans foreign policy advisory group. During the Nixon administration Wolfowitz had joined the Committee to Maintain a Prudent Defense Policy to develop papers and speeches in support of an antiballistic missile system on behalf of Democratic hawk Senator Henry (Scoop) Jackson. In 1972 Wolfowitz worked in the U.S. Arms Control and Disarmament Agency, where he took part in then-DCI George H.W. Bush's Team B challenge of détente era intelligence assessments of Soviet intentions, which issued dire worst-case scenarios of Soviet global aspirations.

Wolfowitz, under President Carter, became deputy assistant secretary for regional programs in the Pentagon. During this time Wolfowitz began to focus on the Middle East military threat Saddam Hussein posed to America's need for secure Persian Gulf energy resources. When Reagan came into office, Wolfowitz became the director of policy planning in the State Department, where he brought with him Lewis (Scooter) Libby, one of his students at Yale. He soon clashed with Reagan's initial secretary of state, General Al Haig, by questioning détente assumptions on the strategic need to maintain China's support vis-à-vis the Soviet Union. General Haig, rumored as ready to fire Wolfowitz for his views, was forced to resign in a dispute with the Reagan White House *troika* of top advisers. Wolfowitz then received a promotion to assistant secretary of state for East Asia and the Pacific.

Wolfowitz soon formed a working relationship with Richard Armitage, then deputy assistant secretary of defense. Secretary of State George Schultz played the lead role in finally convincing President Reagan to withdraw support for Philippine dictator Ferdinand Marcos and support democratically elected Corazon Aquino.

Analyzing the Philippine crisis in 1985, Wolfowitz wrote: "The best antidote to communism is democracy."[18] He would later adopt the same policy prescription of promoting democracy in the Middle East to create a more stable and friendly region. Wolfowitz next served three years as ambassador to the Republic of Indonesia, during the dictatorship of General Mohamed Suharto.

When George H.W. Bush entered the White House, Wolfowitz took the post of undersecretary of defense for policy under Defense Secretary Cheney. Wolfowitz grew embittered when President Bush failed to remove Saddam Hussein from power and refused to aid the uprising of Kurds and Shiites against the Iraqi dictator. As cochair of the Vulcans, Dr. Wolfowitz hoped to become undersecretary of state in the administration of George W. Bush, but his neoconservative views placed him at odds with Secretary of State Powell. Instead, he became undersecretary of defense to Secretary of Defense Rumsfeld.

Powell and Armitage shared, from their Vietnam War experience, a very cautious approach to the application of U.S. military power abroad. Powell had served as military aide to Secretary of Defense Casper Weinberger when he announced the so-called Weinberger Doctrine, calling for clear goals, support from Congress and the American people, and the application of overwhelming force to achieve military objectives.[19] Powell warmly embraced Weinberger's guidelines for the deployment of America's military forces. When serving as chairman of the Joint Chiefs of Staff, Powell added the requirement of a clear exit strategy. General Powell declared in his autobiography: "War should be the politics of last resort."[20]

The two battle-tested veterans also disdained civilian leaders who enthusiastically called for war, but had avoided military service in Vietnam. War critics often labeled such bellicose individuals as "chicken hawks." The fact that Dick Cheney, who received five deferments during his college studies, aggressively led the Pentagon into war irritated Powell.[21] Indeed, besides Powell and Armitage, only Rumsfeld had served in the regular military (Navy pilot after the Korean War). The hawkish neoconservative Wolfowitz also avoided wearing a uniform during the Vietnam era through college deferments. Powell later condemned the injustice and "antidemocratic disgrace" of America's dependence on poor, less educated, and less privileged soldiers in the Vietnam War. "I am angry that so many of the sons of the powerful and well-placed and so many professional athletes…managed to wrangle slots in Reserve and National Guard units."[22]

That criticism clearly applied to George W. Bush's privileged admission into the Texas Air National Guard's "Champaign Unit," along with the sons of two Texas senators and Dallas Cowboys professional football players. After Bush stated he supported the Vietnam War, Tim Russett asked him in a February 2004 interview: "But you didn't volunteer or enlist to go (to Vietnam)." President Bush replied: "No, I didn't; you're right. I served—I flew fighters and enjoyed it, and provided a service to our country."[23]

Other members of the Vulcan advisory group also gained positions in George W. Bush's administration. Their new responsibilities were as follows: Stephen Hadley, Rice's deputy national security adviser; Robert Zoellick, U.S. trade representative in the State Department; Robert Blackwill, ambassador to India; Dov Zakheim, undersecretary of defense (comptroller); and Richard Perle, chairman of the Defense Policy Board, an advisory post that did not require Senate confirmation—which would require an examination of his financial dealings.[24]

Strategic Ambiguity or Confusion?

George H.W. Bush had been chief of the U.S. Liaison Office to the Peoples Republic of China (PRC) before the formal reestablishment of diplomatic relations in 1979. He also enjoyed personal ties with Chinese officials that began when he served as ambassador to the United Nations and later as head of the CIA. President George Bush thought he knew China and its leaders quite well. Indeed, Bush fondly recalled when he visited China on behalf of Reagan that China's leader Deng Xiaoping called Bush "an old friend of China."[25] The senior President Bush envisioned a new "engagement" policy with China, moving beyond viewing China as a counterbalance to the Soviet Union, as viewed by President Nixon and Henry Kissinger, to a major trading partner and ally in maintaining stability in Asia.

When the Tiananmen Square student demonstrations broke out in May 1989, on the eve of a visit by Soviet President Mikhail Gorbachev, Bush watched events escalate in a manner that threatened to undermine his plans for "any influence or leverage to work for restraint and cooperation, let alone for human rights and democracy."[26] When Peoples Liberation Army troops crushed the Tiananmen Square protestors on June 3, President Bush criticized the assault but secretly sent Scowcroft and Deputy Secretary of State Lawrence Eagleburger as personal envoys to reassure the Chinese leadership of the administration's desire for improved relations. The first Bush administration continued to respond to the business community's drive to establish better investment and trade opportunities with the huge nation of China, despite the regime's brutal suppression of the Tiananmen Square pro-democracy demonstrations and continued human rights violations.

Bill Clinton campaigned against the elder Bush's policy toward China in 1992, attacking the administration's failure to utilize economic pressure to promote human rights and democracy in China. But after his inauguration President Clinton softened the tone of his rhetoric toward China, recognizing the growing importance of trade with China to boost American exports, expand investment, and (hopefully) create more jobs at home. On June 25, 1998, President Clinton arrived in China for a nine-day visit, the first by an American president since the 1989 Tiananmen Square student protests. President Bush had visited China in February 1989 prior to the violence. Defending the trip, Secretary of State Madeleine Albright declared on CNN's "Late Edition" program: "Engagement does not mean endorsement."[27]

In July 1998 the House approved Clinton's request to again grant China what had been labeled "most-favored-nation" trade status during the Cold War. Republicans had inserted an amendment in the 1998 Internal Revenue Service (IRS) restructuring bill to rename the provision "normal trade relations."[28] The growing $49.7 trade deficit with China raised concerns in both parties, but pressures from the U.S. Chamber of Commerce and National Association of Manufacturers contributed to the administration victory with GOP support. President Clinton stressed: "Our engagement with China serves American interests."[29]

The most difficult point in Sino-American relations occurred on May 8, 1999, when NATO planes mistakenly bombed the Chinese Embassy in Belgrade during the Kosovo air war. Virulent anti-American protests occurred throughout China. Nevertheless, President Clinton continued to call his policy toward China a "strategic partnership." At the end of his administration, Clinton told *New York Times* reporters that in an increasingly interdependent world, the United States had no "levers of pressure" to push China toward openness and freedom other than the ones his administration adopted. President Clinton asserted: "I don't think freedom is inevitable, or the triumph of democracy is inevitable."[30] However, Clinton felt America's example and the "strength of our engagement" increased the likelihood of progress toward democracy in China.

President George W. Bush entered office critical of his predecessor's policy toward the Peoples Republic of China—just as Clinton had hit the senior Bush's engagement policy. Bush viewed China not as a friend or "strategic ally," but as a dangerous competitor with a communist regime, a growing military capability, and a small strategic missile capability (18 to 20) that could reach the shores of America. However, Bush hedged his rhetoric on trade with China, not wishing to alienate the business community; in 2000 trade with China had reached an estimated $115 billion.[31] Bush couched his advocacy of free trade with China in moral terms, arguing that the creation of an entrepreneurial class in China over time would encourage the "habits of liberty" that lead to democracy.[32] Dr. Condoleezza Rice had argued in a *Foreign Affairs* article that "trade in general can open up the Chinese economy and, ultimately, its politics too."[33]

A series of surveys on U.S. relations with China seemed to reveal conflicting public views. In January 2000 a Gallup poll found 51 percent of respondents felt increased trade with China would "mostly help" the U.S. economy, while 38 percent felt it would mostly hurt.[34] But a January 2000 Hart Research survey revealed that 61 percent of Americans thought China had "unfair trade policies that make it difficult for American companies to sell products (there)." And three Pew surveys discovered between June 1999 and May 2001 that 47 percent of Americans disagreed with the statement that "trade between China and Western nations will lead to China becoming more democratic."

But before the new administration could launch its China policy, the collision of a U.S. Navy EP-3E Aries II surveillance plane and a Chinese F-8 jet fighter plane threw bilateral relations into a crisis. The Chinese pilot, aggressively harassing the intruding American spy plane, collided and fell into the sea. The U.S. pilot managed to make an emergency landing on the Chinese high-security island of Hainan, where Chinese authorities placed the 24-person crew in custody. American officials could not immediately reach top Chinese officials. On April 4 China's President Jian Zemin reiterated an early demand: "The U.S. side should apologize to the Chinese people."[35]

The new Bush administration, after its campaign bravado, felt it must maintain a tough stance, refusing to apologize to the Chinese as a diplomatic sign of weakness. In an April 3 Rose Garden statement, President Bush called the emergency landing on Chinese soil an "unusual situation," declaring firmly that it was time for the Chinese government to release the crew and the plane. For days afterward the president maintained a low profile to allow diplomacy to work out an acceptable solution, without admitting U.S. culpability through a formal apology.

Secretary Powell brought an end to the conflict by labeling the dispute a "tragic accident," avoiding the use of the word "apology." Instead, Powell stated: "We regret the Chinese plane did not get safe and we regret the loss of the life of that Chinese pilot."[36] Congressional GOP hard-liners and conservative commentators called for sanctions against China, such as opposing its bid to host the

2008 Olympics, reducing U.S. trade, and obstructing its admission into the World Trade Organization.

But the "regret" terminology did not work. So President Bush then agreed to the diplomatic use of "very sorry" to end the crisis with China. Ambassador Joseph Prueher delivered on April 11 a letter to China's Minister of Foreign Affairs that reiterated President Bush and Secretary Powell's expressions of sincere regret. Then the ambassador pronounced the U.S. was "very sorry" about the loss of the Chinese pilot Wang Wei and "very sorry" about entering Chinese airspace and landing without Chinese clearance.[37]

President Bush announced the agreement to release the American crew on April 11. President Bush recognized the error of his initial tough statement, acknowledged a military confrontation would be disastrous on such an issue, and flexibly moved to resolve the conflict through diplomacy.[38] The spy place crisis represented a public victory for Secretary of State Powell, who advocated a diplomatic solution over the objections of the administration's hawks.

That evening NSC Adviser Rice appeared on ABC's "Nightline" to assure critics that "under no circumstances were broader issues placed on the table or somehow bartered away with the Chinese."[39] Later the Chinese refused to allow the EP-3 plane to fly off the island. The U.S. government disassembled the spy plane, placed it in crates and returned the parts to the United States. Neoconservatives like Robert Kagan and William Kristol charged Bush's lack of action on China's treatment of the spy plane incident represented a "profound national humiliation" and "appeasement."[40]

President Bush tried to mollify Republican hard-liners by announcing on April 23 Taiwan could purchase four Kidd-class destroyers, eight diesel submarines, twelve Orion aircraft and minesweeping helicopters.[41] However, his plan would "defer" the sale of destroyers with the Aegis high-tech radar systems and Patriot PAC-3 antimissile batteries to Taiwan, weapons the Chinese deemed as serious threats to their security. Nevertheless, China issued a formal diplomatic protest on the sale as interference in China's internal affairs, representing an escalation of tensions with Taiwan. American conservatives remained upset that Taiwan would not receive the high-tech Aegis equipped destroyers.

Tensions with the PRC flared up again after President Bush responded on April 24 to a question by ABC's Charles Gibson on whether the U.S. had an obligation to defend Taiwan if attacked by China. Bush replied: "Yes, we do, and the Chinese understand that. Yes, I would." When asked whether that meant with America's full military force, the president bellicosely answered: "Whatever it took to help Taiwan defend itself."[42] With that statement the inexperienced president entered a foreign policy briar patch. President Bush's remark launched a firestorm of criticism, since it violated the two-and-a-half-decades-old U.S. policy of "strategic ambiguity" on whether the United States would go to war over Taiwan. Administrative spokesman quickly went into damage control to reassure China and America's allies that the statement did not signal a switch in existing policy.

However, the controversial remark echoed the views of administration neoconservatives, who in 1999 signed an open letter calling for the end of the "strategic ambiguity" defense policy. During the Reagan administration, Bush's Undersecretary of Defense Wolfowitz had argued that U.S. policy-makers overestimated the strategic value of China in safeguarding America's national interests in Asia.[43] The dispute reached ludicrous levels when Wolfowitz issued a May 1 Defense Department statement declaring thus: "U.S. troops shall not wear berets made in China...or with Chinese content," recalling previously distributed berets.[44] An upset White House forced Secretary Rumsfeld to quickly nullify the Pentagon policy, which Rice deemed a "mistake."

Through several other gestures—like a White House meeting with the Dalai Lama and allowing Taiwan's president to stopover in New York—the administration symbolically underscored differences with China over religious freedom, human rights, and Taiwan. But the Bush administration did not oppose China's bids to host the 2008 Olympics or join the World Trade Organization.

Most significantly, both President Bush and Secretary Powell dropped references to China as a "strategic competitor." As Secretary Powell stated on a trip to visit China, Chinese leaders had "every incentive" to maintain good relations since 40 percent of China's exports went to the United States.[45] Essentially, President Bush came to embrace his father's policy of engagement, also followed by President Clinton, by pragmatically recognizing China's importance as a major trading partner of the United States.

Missile Defense, Not Terrorism

As a presidential candidate George W. Bush called for "tough realism" in America's dealings with China and Russia, built upon a restructured, strong, and modern U.S. military. During his 1999 interview with William Safire, George W. vowed to aggressively build an American missile defense system—the "Star Wars" goal of President Reagan's Strategic Defense Initiative. Bush promised to negotiate with the Russians a revision of the 1972 Anti-ABM Treaty, but "then move forward with abrogation (of the treaty)."[46]

Governor George W. Bush rolled out his defense policy in a carefully orchestrated speech at The Citadel military college on September 23, 1999. The Bush team heavily promoted the governor's first major defense policy address, emphasizing that Bush's policy proposals were "prepared in consultation with at least eight foreign policy and military advisers."[47] The Citadel address warned of the dangers posed by the spread of missile technology and weapons of mass destruction. He noted that the post–Cold War era of American preeminence also represented "an era of car bombers and plutonium merchants and cyber terrorists and drug cartels and unbalanced dictators"—but Bush omitted the threat of terrorism.[48]

Governor Bush declared in a Reagan Library speech in November 1999, "The Empire has passed, but evil remains," evoking President Reagan's depiction of the former Soviet Union as an Evil Empire.[49] As a post–Cold War "clear-eyed realist," he criticized the Clinton administration's shifting foreign policy as moving from "crisis to crisis like a cork in a current." Governor Bush warned about the danger of "rogue regimes" and the threat of Russian nuclear weapon proliferation.

Surrounded by former GOP foreign and defense stalwarts in May 2000, Governor Bush blasted the Clinton-Gore administration for remaining "locked in a Cold War mentality" not attuned to the twenty-first century's new dangers.[50] But the threats Bush highlighted to justify the construction of a missile defense system to protect all 50 states focused on rogue nations or accidental launchings.

His realist campaign advisors emphasized dangers emanating from traditional nation-states, not amorphous international terrorist groups such as al Qaeda.

President Bill Clinton had announced on September 1, 2000, his decision to defer moving forward on deploying a national missile defense system "until we have absolute confidence that the system will work," essentially leaving the decision to his successor.[51] He pointed out that though the technology was promising, "the system as a whole is not yet proven," with only 3 of 19 intercept tests conducted at that time. He emphasized that a national missile defense could not substitute for diplomacy or deterrence, but might provide additional security against terrorists who could possibly seize control of nuclear weapons of a disintegrating or rogue state.

When Defense Secretary Rumsfeld met with European defense ministers shortly after Bush's inauguration, he reiterated: "The United States intends to develop and deploy a missile system." But, Rumsfeld insisted: "We will consult" with America's European friends and allies.[52] Secretary of State Powell also explained that "as we take their views into account, we are moving from a position of principle. We believe that theater missile defense and national missile defense is in our interest."[53] At a news conference, President Bush said: "I've assured our allies that we will consult with them. But we're moving forward to develop systems that reflect the threats of today."[54]

The Russian government countered the U.S. drive to abandon the 1972 ABM Treaty between the USSR and the United States by attempting to divide America's 19 NATO allies through a proposed mobile antimissile system alternative to shoot down missiles launched from any rogue state. NATO Secretary General Lord Robertson, meeting with President Vladimir Putin in Moscow, acknowledged that the Russian proposal offered a different plan "to deal with the same kind of perceived threat" from Iran, Iraq, and North Korea.[55] Such a mobile antimissile system, the Russian Defense Minister Igor Sergeyev argued, would be cheap and nonstrategic, thus not violating the 1972 ABM treaty.

President Bush chose the National Defense University for his May 1 speech about a U.S. missile defense system. He argued that in the post–Cold War world, deterrence should be based on more than nuclear retaliation. Bush called for a new framework that combined a national missile system with cuts in nuclear weapons: "My goal is to move quickly to reduce nuclear forces."[56] The president insisted he would hold "real consultations." President Bush portrayed the call for a new offensive and defensive missile framework with Russia as embodying vision, new thinking, and bold leadership, attempting to evoke the image of President Ronald Reagan.

White House spokesman Ari Fleischer defended the administration's plan to scuttle the 1972 ABM Treat in terms of leadership, arguing that President Bush "believes that if the United States leads and that we consult wisely, our allies and friends will find good reason to follow and to join with us."[57] However, at a May meeting of NATO foreign ministers, Secretary Powell could not obtain European support for urgent measures to deal with the "common threat" of ballistic missiles being developed in North Korea, Iraq, and Iran.[58]

During his June 2000 trip to Europe, President Bush tried to link his missile defense proposal with "being forward-thinking about fighting terrorism."[59] Since the Cold War ended, Bush called for a conclusion to "the Cold War mentality." On the eve of meeting with European Union (EU) leaders, President Bush promised thus: "I realize it's going to require a lot of consulting, but I'm willing to listen." However, at home respected former Senator Sam Nunn wrote in a *Washington Post* op-ed commentary: "The likeliest nuclear attack against the United States would come not from a missile launched by a rogue state but from a warhead in the belly of a ship or the back of a truck delivered by a group with no return address."[60] Nunn argued America would be more secure if it concentrated on reducing or safeguarding the former Soviet Union's large nuclear weapons inventory.

In the NATO summit meeting, 13 of the 19 European leaders appeared cool to Bush's missile defense plans.[61] French President Jacque Chirac stated in the closed meeting: "We need to preserve these strategic balances, of which the ABM Treaty is a pillar." German Chancellor Gerhard Schroeder also expressed reservations. Nevertheless, U.S. officials observed that Hungary, Italy, Poland, and Spain supported Bush's plan, while England was quietly supportive.

President George W. Bush and Russian President Vladimir Putin met in Slovenia on June 16, 2001. Putin affirmed the Russian position that "the 1972 ABM Treat is the cornerstone of the modern architecture of international security."[62] Putin praised Bush as a man who had studied history, and said he looked forward to a "pragmatic relationship" with the United States. President Bush described Putin in glowing terms: "He's an honest, straightforward man who loves his country. He loves his family. We share a lot of values."

At one point Bush gushed: "I looked the man in the eye....I was able to get a sense of his soul." After only a one-hour-and-forty-minutes dialogue, George W. Bush had peered positively into the eyes and soul of the former communist KGB agent and expressed trust in the man. In Condoleezza Rice's *Foreign Affairs* article, published after the 2000 election, she had criticized "the Clinton administration's embrace of (Boris) Yeltsin and those who were thought to be reformers has failed."[63] Responding to a question after the meeting as to whether Bush had also personalized U.S. diplomacy with Russia by his instant faith in Putin, Rice backtracked. She argued that having a good, warm relationship with the leader of Russia was important for U.S. interests. President Bush, with his known proclivity to give out nicknames, began referring to Putin as "Pootie-Poot."[64]

On July 22, the last day of the Group of Eight summit of industrial nations, Presidents Bush and Putin agreed to negotiations for a post–Cold War disarmament framework that linked large cuts in nuclear offensive missiles by both states, while permitting the United States to build a missile defense system. The joint statement focused upon "the interrelated subjects of offensive and defensive systems."[65] At that time the United States had about 7,300 strategic nuclear missiles and the Russians about 6,100.

President Putin had grimly warned of an arms race over the defense shield proposal a month earlier, threatening to add less-costly multiple warheads to Russian missiles if the United States went ahead with the antimissile shield. President Bush asserted the agreement with Putin: "I thought he was very forward-leaning, as they say in diplomatic nuanced circles."[66] During his second European trip in two months, Bush declared in a way some might consider arrogant: "I know what I believe...and *I believe what I believe is right*" (author's emphasis).[67]

Rejecting Clinton's Diplomacy

The effort of Secretary of State Powell to give his own imprimatur to the administration's diplomatic relations almost immediately encountered fierce opposition from the Pentagon neoconservatives as well as the White House top staff, who sought to highlight the president's central role in foreign policy-making. The conflicting early declarations on U.S. relations with communist North Korea, a so-called rogue nation with the capacity to develop nuclear weapons, manifested this internal struggle. At times the Bush administration's foreign policies appeared to reflect a knee-jerk rejection of whatever diplomatic steps President Clinton had followed prior to 2001.[68]

On March 7, 2001, the Republic of Korea's President Kim Dae-jung met with President Bush in the White House. In 2000 the South Korean president won the Nobel Peace Prize for the promotion of democracy in Asia and his "Sunshine Policy" to achieve reconciliation with North Korea. In 1998 President Kim had traveled to Pyongyang for a historic summit meeting with Chairman Kim Jong Il where initial steps were taken to reduce Korean peninsula tensions. President Kim, a Christian and longtime proponent of democracy, had spent five years in prison, faced death five times, and lived many years under house arrest or exile for his political beliefs. In his Nobel Lecture, President Kim declared: "A national economy lacking a democratic foundation is a castle built on sand."[69]

In 1994 the Clinton administration had signed the Agreed Framework with North Korea, supported by President Kim, to end an 18-month crisis after the Democratic People's Republic of Korea (DPRK) threatened to withdraw from the Nuclear Nonproliferation Treaty to develop nuclear weapons. The communist rulers of the DPRK faced serious economic problems with some Clinton advisers thinking North Korea would collapse before all elements of the Framework would be implemented.[70] The pact embodied a memorandum of understanding, not requiring Senate approval.

When the Republican Party captured control of Congress after the 1994 election, some GOP hard-liners called the Agreed Framework "appeasement." Congress reluctantly provided funding from 1996, but often not enough, adding to tensions with the DPRK regime. When North Korea test-fired a Taepo Dong-1 missile over northern Japan on August 31, 1998, the threatening action further delayed construction of the light-water reactors, already behind schedule.[71] North Korea admitted it had exported missiles to ratchet up pressure on the United States. The communist leaders called upon the United States to lift its economic embargo and compensate the DPRK for losses if it stopped selling missiles to other states.

At a State Department press conference on March 6, the day before Presidents Bush and Kim met, Powell declared, "We do plan to engage with North Korea to pick up where President Clinton and his administration left off."[72] But several hours before the president's meeting with South Korea's President Kim, Bush conferred with Vice President Cheney, NSC adviser Rice, Chief of Staff Andrew Card, and Communications Director Karen Hughes. President Bush wanted to send a loud signal to Powell and outside observers that Bush was totally in charge of his foreign policy.[73]

At a press conference with President Kim, President Bush stated: "I do have some skepticism about the leader of North Korea."[74] While Bush said Kim's

"Sunshine Policy" would contribute to peace, he expressed doubt "whether or not we can verify an agreement in a country that doesn't enjoy the freedoms that our two countries understand," hitting at the lack of "transparency" in North Korea. Speaking to the press pool immediately afterward, a subdued Powell publicly ate his words: "There was some suggestion that imminent negotiations are about to begin—that is not the case."[75] Secretary Powell's humiliating reversal was posted on the official White House web site as a warning to other cabinet officials. A senior unnamed administration official told a reporter that the United States would not walk away from the 1994 Agreed Framework, but would see whether they could "restructure it."[76]

A Unilateralist Course?

In the *Foreign Affairs* article written by Dr. Condoleezza Rice before President Bush's inauguration, she attacked the Clinton administration's rush to embrace "multilateral solutions" that led to signed agreements not reflecting America's national interests.[77] She chided Bush's predecessor for such "largely symbolic" pacts and the pursuit of "illusory 'norms' of international behavior." Rice particularly criticized the Kyoto Protocol on global warning, as Governor Bush did throughout the 2000 campaign.

However, the question of global warming, including how to deal with growing greenhouse gas omissions, became a major domestic and international issue during President Clinton's administration. On July 25, 1997, the U.S. Senate passed the Byrd-Hagel Resolution by an extraordinary 95–0 vote. The resolution rejected international limits on greenhouse gas emissions unless developing countries (like China and India) were included as well.[78] The resolution stated the United States should not sign any protocol resulting from the 1992 UN Framework Convention on Climatic Change, citing concerns that such global action would seriously harm the U.S. economy. The elder President Bush had signed the 1992 Convention, but it had included only voluntary measures to curb global warming.

The Kyoto Protocol was signed in December 1997, with countries having different emission targets. For example, the United States would reduce carbon-based emissions by 7 percent. Vice President Al Gore signed the Kyoto Protocol on behalf of the Clinton administration on November 12, 1998. However, the overwhelming opposition in the Senate convinced President Clinton not to submit it for ratification.

During the close 2000 presidential campaign, Governor George W. Bush in a September 29 Michigan speech pledged to advance cleaner air by requiring "all power plants to meet clear air standards to reduce emissions of sulfur dioxide, nitrogen oxide, mercury and carbon dioxide within a reasonable period of time."[79] After the election, Bush's new Environment Protection Agency Administrator Christine Todd Whitman told a meeting of the Group of Eight environmental ministers in Italy that Bush planned to set "mandatory reduction targets" for carbon dioxide.[80]

Nevertheless, on March 13, 2001, several weeks after Whitman's reassurance to the ministers, President Bush wrote a letter to four senators declaring: "I do not believe...that the government should impose on power plants mandatory emissions reductions for carbon dioxide."[81] Bush's policy reversal emphasized that coal generated half of America's energy supply and such a restriction would raise prices and harm consumers. Furthermore, the Bush administration formally withdrew the United States from the Kyoto Protocol.

On June 12 President Bush undertook a five-day trip to Europe, which included a NATO meeting in Brussels and an EU summit in Sweden with 15 European leaders. At a press conference in Spain on the eve of the meetings, Bush reiterated his opposition to the Kyoto Protocol. He labeled the Protocol goals unrealistic and unscientific, criticized the exclusion of developing countries, and opposed its adverse affects upon the U.S. economy.[82] Bush would argue the same points at the meeting with the European nations—in vain. The chair of the EU, Swedish Prime Minister Goran Persson, afterward declared: "The European Union will stick to the Kyoto Protocol and go for a ratification process. The U.S. has chosen another policy."[83]

In a subsequent interview with Peggy Noonan, President Bush bragged about how he sat at a dinner with the 15 EU heads of state and rejected their views, telling them, "It's right for America." He then smugly asserted: "I think Ronald Reagan would have been proud of how I conducted myself."[84] One should remember that his father, George H.W. Bush, proudly labeled himself the "environmental president."

At a July world conference on climatic change in Bonn, Germany, 178 nations supported changes in the 1997 draft Kyoto Protocol that included negotiated concessions for Japan. Olivier Deleuze, the chief EU negotiator, said: "I prefer an imperfect agreement that is living to a perfect agreement that doesn't exist."[85] Secretary of State Powell later told foreign leaders that the administration would offer its counterproposal for the October conference in Morocco, but NSC Adviser Rice quickly refuted him, stating the administration had no plans to meet that deadline.[86]

At the Group of Eight Genoa summit meeting in July, President Bush asked the leaders to wait before moving ahead on the Kyoto Protocol until he presented an alternative plan. However, he gave no indication when it would be prepared. Bush failed to have the final G-8 communiqué omit the differences over the Kyoto Protocol.

President Bush also tried to convince European leaders that the United States should be allowed to withdraw its forces from the Balkans, leaving the peacekeeping duties to NATO. In this case the Europeans made their case and Bush agreed to continue American troop participation in peacemaking operations in Bosnia and Kosovo. He told American troops in Kosovo that the United States and Europe "came in together, and we will leave together."[87] In this instance, he maintained the collaborative peacemaking mission of the Clinton administration with NATO nations, aimed at controlling the bloody ethnic conflicts in the former Yugoslavia.

In an attempt to refute the unilateralist charge, Bush administration officials pointed out that President Clinton also opposed the 1997 international ban on land mines as undermining U.S. defense plans (e.g., in South Korea) and the 1998 creation of the International Criminal Court as an infringement on American sovereignty. The Bush administration refused to resubmit the Comprehensive Text Ban Treaty to the Senate after its 1999 defeat (51 to 48) during Clinton's administration.

The administration also stood apart during debates over other international accords. U.S. officials deemed the Biological Weapons Protocol as containing problems "that we believe make it not able to achieve its current objective."[88] The U.S. opposition to provisions in the Small-Arms Control Pact that restricted civilian gun ownership and weapons sales to rebels led a UN conference to adopt watered-down language in July 2001. John Bolton, Bush's undersecretary of state for arms control and international security affairs, argued at the conference of over 140 nations that the proposal infringed on American citizens' right to keep and bear arms and prevented liberation forces from toppling illegitimate rulers.[89] Camilo Reyes of Colombia, president of the UN conference, expressed "disappointment" over how one state (United States) could block the original language to restrict weapons sales to non-state groups. However, the Bush administration received an embarrassing setback when the United States lost its seat on the UN Human Rights Commission on May 3, 2001, a commission Eleanor Roosevelt helped create in 1947.

Richard Haass, the State Department's director of policy planning, described the Bush approach as "a la carte multilateralism."[90] Condoleezza Rice defended Bush's policies as true internationalism, arguing "you will not find a more internationalist administration than this administration."[91] During a trip to Vietnam, Secretary Powell also parried critics: "I think over time people will see that we are not unilateralist, that we are deeply engaged."[92] Nevertheless, the Bush administration's rhetoric and apparent disdain of international agreements that failed to meet all their stipulations, like the Kyoto Protocol, drew angry attacks on the administration for its unilateral approach to international affairs. President Bush's drive to end the 1972 ABM Treaty with Russia particularly worried other nations—including both friends and foes.

The Bush administration's refusal to assume a lead role in achieving a Middle East peace settlement policy also generated considerable criticism at home and abroad. President Bush had criticized the personal diplomacy of President Clinton in his intense efforts to broker a peace treaty between Israel and the Palestinians. However, at Secretary Powell's January 17 Senate confirmation hearing he praised Clinton's tireless efforts to resolve the conflict, asserting that President Bush also sought to keep the peace process moving forward. However, others in the White House felt Clinton had devoted too much personal time to the thorny problem. But as violence mounted between Israelis and Palestinians in March, President Bush called for "reciprocal and parallel steps by both sides" to reduce the escalation of violence.[93] But instead of taking a broker role in peace negotiations—like Clinton—Bush declared that "this country cannot impose a timetable, nor settlement on the parties if they're unwilling to accept it."

But the ongoing Middle East violence and pressure from allies compelled President Bush in early June to send CIA Director George Tenet to the region to help restore peace, a role he played during the Clinton administration. Secretary of State Powell traveled to the Middle East for the second time in late June, largely at the behest of friendly Arab governments who felt the United States was not doing enough to end the violence. In July four EU countries (Britain, France, Germany, and Italy) proposed that the EU send observers from outside the region as a buffer force between the Israelis and Palestinians, a plan Israeli Prime Minister Ariel Sharon opposed. Later a frustrated senior Bush official said: "We've thrown Tenet at it; we've thrown Powell at it; we're not going to throw anyone else at it [Israeli-Palestinian peace settlement]."[94]

In summary, President George W. Bush sought to overcome his lack of knowledge and inexperience in foreign affairs by surrounding himself with competent advisers from prior Republican administrations. The State Department, Pentagon, and White House appointments helped to allay doubts. However, policy differences and tensions among the advisers strained the loyalty of his national security team. In particular, Secretary Powell's foreign policy role was sharply curbed when he pushed for diplomatic initiatives, such as the ones on North Korea or the Middle East, which would have implied White House acceptance of President Clinton's foreign policies.

Bush's campaign bravado toward China as a "strategic competitor" wilted as he confronted the reality of China's economic relations with the United States, leading to an engagement policy similar to that of his father and Clinton. President Bush reneged on his promise to cut carbon dioxide emissions, withdrew from the Kyoto Protocol, and stubbornly refused to seek a compromise on global warming. This intransigent policy stance angered European allies, contributing heavily to their depiction of the administration as unilateralist. However, President Bush's resistance to playing a key role in the difficult Middle East peace process only facilitated the escalating violence, encouraged greater European diplomatic efforts in the region, and provoked anger among America's Arab friends, particularly Saudi Arabia.

Bush followed through on his pledge to develop a new missile defense system, but his doggedness worried America's allies about the fallout from the abandonment of the 1972 ABM Treaty with Russia. His personal relationship with Russian President Putin—after a quick peek into Putin's soul—appeared to reflect the same style of personal diplomacy that Clinton followed vis-à-vis the prior Russian leader Yeltsen, which Bush had criticized during the election.

President Bush's smug comment about how President Reagan would have been proud of how he rejected European arguments over the Kyoto Protocol, offered insight on how George W. Bush intended to model himself after Ronald Reagan—a conservative GOP hero—in word and deed. After eight months in office, the Bush national security team had learned from its mistakes, but the future course of Bush's foreign policy would be forever changed by the events of September 11.

Chapter Six

Ignored Warnings: A Call to Destiny

Our responsibility to history is already clear:
To answer these attacks and rid the world of evil.

President George W. Bush's September 11, 2001, trip to Florida was planned as a "soft" visit, without a major speech, to meet with GOP supporters and stage a photo opportunity to support literacy at a Sarasota elementary school.[1] The visit would also underscore President George W. Bush's broader education agenda embodied in the "Leave No Child Behind Act," then weaving its way through Congress.

Bush's advance team and Secret Service detail had carefully planned the motorcade's route to the Emma E. Booker Elementary School. They had maintained security over the school since September 6; choreographed a presidential meeting with 150 selected parents, students, and teachers 2 days prior; and designed childlike decorations for the wall behind the chair where the president would sit. The students anxiously awaited President Bush's visit to the second-grade classroom of teacher Kay Daniels.

At 9:01 a.m. aide Karl Rove informed President Bush before he entered the classroom that a plane (perhaps a small twin-engine aircraft) had hit the North Tower of the World Trade Center in New York City.[2] Bush later recalled telling his Chief of Staff Andrew Card, "This is pilot error.... The guy must have had a heart attack," before being whisked into the Sarasota classroom.[3] Moments later Bush sat with a copy of *My Pet Goat* on his lap as he listened to and praised the 18 second graders reading the book out loud. At 9:07 a.m. Card whispered into the president's ear: "A second plane hit the second tower. America is under attack." Bush remained seated but his face became "visibly tense and serious" as the children read another six or seven minutes. Bush afterward commented to the class: "Really good readers! Whoo! This must be sixth-graders."[4]

When he left the classroom, Bush conferred with his aides in Florida and Washington before facing the TV cameras at 9:30 a.m. The "shaken" president voiced the same tough words his father employed after Iraq invaded Kuwait in 1990, "Terrorism against our nation *will not stand*" (author's emphasis).[5] Fearful of a terrorist attack on the White House, Air Force One flew to Barksdale Air Force Base in Shreveport, Louisiana.

At 12:36 p.m. President Bush spoke with the press again. The president declared: "Freedom itself was attacked this morning by faceless cowards."[6] Bush spoke haltingly as he read the speech notes, gaining strength as he delivered the final sentences. "The resolve of our great nation is being tested. But make no mistake: We will show the world that *we will pass this test*" (author's emphasis). Many observers viewed the president's response to the brutal terrorist assaults on the United States as not only a test of the country—but also of George W. Bush.

A Zigzag Return

The shocking events of September 11 escalated as terrorists plunged another airliner (American Airlines Flight 77) into the Pentagon at 9:45 a.m., while Secretary of Defense Donald Rumsfeld received the daily intelligence briefing in his office. He rushed to help evacuate the casualties. At 10:10 a.m. United Airlines Flight 93 crashed in a Pennsylvania field after the hostages courageously rushed the cabin to prevent the airliner from becoming a weapon against fellow citizens. People across the globe intensely watched their television sets as brave firemen and rescue workers entered the blazing World Trade Center towers, then viewed in horror as the two towers collapsed, killing about 3,000 people.

Vice President Dick Cheney heard the news about the first attack while going over a speech draft in his West Wing office. He, like others, reacted only when the second plane crashed into the World Trade Center, then recognizing the two planes as part of a terrorist attack on America. Cheney convened a meeting in the vice presidential office with National Security Adviser Condoleezza Rice and two of his top staff members. Secret Service agents quickly ordered the evacuation of the White House, fearing an attack by another hijacked airliner. The agents literally lifted and carried the vice president to the underground Presidential Emergency Operations Center in the East Wing. From that secure bunker Cheney phoned Bush and strongly urged him, "Delay your return. We don't know what's going on here, but it looks like…we've been targeted."[7]

President George W. Bush's return to the nation's capitol was further delayed when White House officials claimed a threatening phone call had warned, "Air Force One is next," allegedly using the procedural code word "Angel." Weeks later the White House admitted they could not identify any telephoned threat against Air Force One.[8]

Cheney and the Secret Service discouraged President Bush from flying directly to Washington. The Pentagon informed Andy Card that the Air Force could not provide a protecting fighter escort for another 40 to 90 minutes. Card suggested to the president: "Let's let the dust settle," before returning to Washington.[9]

After Air Force One left Louisiana at 1:37 p.m., the president flew to Offutt Air Force Base near Omaha, Nebraska. President Bush held a National Security Council (NSC) teleconference to discuss the crisis and pending security decisions, utilizing the base's sophisticated and secure communication center. The president finally returned to Washington, arriving at the White House at 7 p.m., 10 hours after he first heard about the terrorist attacks on the World Trade Center.

Five days after the 9/11 horror Vice President Cheney described his White House actions during the terrorist attacks to NBC's Tim Russert, emphasizing that the need to preserve the presidency led him to recommend that President Bush delay his return to Washington. "We don't know what's happening. We know Washington's under attack. We don't know by who, we don't know how many additional planes are coming."[10] Cheney also revealed that the Secret Service "even talked to me to try to get me to evacuate a couple of times, but I didn't want to leave the node that we'd established there, in terms of having all of this capability tied together by communications where we could, in fact, make decisions and act."

In retrospect, Cheney emerged as much more of a brave, strong, and "take charge" leader than George W. Bush on the first day of the war on terror. White House aides afterward raised Bush's leadership profile while undoubtedly encouraging Cheney to abandon the limelight for a "secure, undisclosed location."[11] Some critics unfavorably compared President Bush's initial actions with the impressive leadership of New York Mayor Rudy Giuliani at Ground Zero on the day of the attacks.

Taking Charge

Bob Woodward's book, *Bush at War*, appeared to validate a positive image of President George W. Bush as a decision-maker with his response to the 9/11 attacks, exemplifying Graham Allison's rational actor model.[12] President Bush met regularly with his war cabinet to assess threats, identify opportunities, define goals, weigh the costs and benefits of policy alternatives, and decide what actions his administration should take against al Qaeda.

Richard Clarke, chair of the administration's Counterterrorism Security Group, speculated early that the 9/11 horror manifested the characteristics of an al Qaeda operation, recalling the terrorist organization's "1998 simultaneous attacks on the American embassies in Kenya and Tanzania."[13] Central Intelligence Agency (CIA) Director George Tenet, after his agency identified known al Qaeda operatives on the passenger lists of several hijacked 9/11 planes, advised President Bush during the video-conference NSC meeting from Offutt Air Force Base that al Qaeda committed the terrorist acts.[14]

In the president's initial statement to the nation from Sarasota, Florida, after learning of the World Trade Center attack, Bush pledged "a full-scale investigation to hunt down and to find those folks who committed this act."[15] Critics later blasted Bush's temperate use of "folks" and implied classification of the bloody 9/11 terrorist strikes as merely a law enforcement problem. From Barksdale AFB the president toughened his rhetoric: "The United States will hunt down and punish those responsible for these cowardly acts."[16]

When the president returned to Washington, his chief speechwriter Michael Gerson provided him a speech draft that asserted, "this is war."[17] But Bush told his longtime aide Karen Hughes, serving as counselor to the president, that he wanted to reassure the nation in his evening address, not frighten people even more.[18] In his 8:30 p.m. address from the White House President Bush declared: "I've directed the full resources of our intelligence and law enforcement communities to find those responsible and to bring them to justice."[19]

However, a *Washington Post*/ABC News Poll conducted after Bush's evening address to the nation found 94 percent of the 608 respondents supported military action against the perpetuators of the attacks, with over 80 percent favoring military strikes even if they resulted in war.[20] In addition, 84 percent of the respondents backed military action against any countries that had aided or harbored the terrorists. The CNN/*USA Today* Poll found 86 percent of respondents considered the terrorist attacks an act of war.[21] The poll numbers seemed to fortify Bush's rhetoric toward Osama bin Laden and the al Qaeda terrorists. The next morning President Bush declared: "The deliberate and deadly attacks which were carried out yesterday against our country were more than acts of terror. They were acts of war."[22]

The news media compared the 9/11 attacks to the Japanese attack on Pearl Harbor that galvanized the United States into war with Japan. But al Qaeda was not a nation-state; it was a terrorist organization. Nineteen Islamic zealots, armed with inexpensive box cutters, had succeeded in killing about 3,000 American citizens. During the prior eight months Rice and other realist members of the war cabinet had focused most of their attention on threats emanating from traditional nation-states, the Bush administration's rationale for the development of a national missile defense system. The slow policy-making process within the Bush administration, lacking a sense of urgency about the threat of terrorism, delayed the formulation of a comprehensive policy to deal with al Qaeda. Clarke and Tenet pressed for immediate action against Osama bin Laden but Bush did not approve any strategic plan.

As Graham Allison observed, the Bush administration thus lacked a comprehensive assessment of the threat terrorism represented to the United States and had failed to craft a "coherent strategy for combating mega-terrorism."[23] As a result, the administration scrambled and galloped off "in all directions" to plan for an unexpected war. In stark contrast, Allison noted that al Qaeda had planned and trained for almost a decade to launch the devastating 9/11 attacks with a "level of imagination, sophistication and audacity" not anticipated by America's leaders.

Michael Scheuer, the head of the CIA's Osama bin Laden unit from 1996 to 1999, later faulted President Bush and his war cabinet for never fully understanding the danger that Osama bin Laden represented for the United States. Scheuer argued that "the threat Osama bin Laden poses lies in the coherence and consistency of his ideas, their precise articulation, and the acts of war he takes to implement them."[24] The CIA analyst rejected President Bush's declaration that Osama bin Laden hated America for who we are. United States policies and actions—not American values—provoked the hatred and radicalization of the Muslim public.

Scheuer also criticized the Bush administration for describing al Qaeda as simply a terrorist group, rather than recognizing that bin Laden's goals represented an Islamic insurgency in the Middle East.[25] He noted after reading *Bush at War* that the president and his war cabinet devoted little or no discussion to "the influence of Islam on the motivation, ideology, war aims, or strategy of bin Laden and the Taliban."[26] In a *New York Times* interview, Scheuer said the Bush team did not respect the threat of al Qaeda because they saw it as only a terrorist organization they could defeat by arresting or killing its operatives.[27]

Jeffrey Record, a professor at the Strategic Studies Institute of the Army War College, argued in a monograph that the administration's early broad formulation of the scope of the Global War on Terror (GWOT) was unbounded by its varied and expansive goals as voiced by President Bush. "(M)ost of the GWOT's declared objectives...are unrealistic and condemn the United States to a hopeless quest for absolute security."[28] The breadth and complexity of the administration's GWOT goals rendered them "politically, fiscally, and militarily unsustainable." He warned that "rogue states and terrorist organizations are fundamentally different in *character* and *vulnerability* to U.S. military power." Record, like Scheuer, also cautioned that al Qaeda was not a single terrorist organization, but a "global insurgency" that threatened many of America's friends in the region.[29]

Despite the lack of clarity about the strategic threat al Qaeda represented, Bush's war council members quickly reached a consensus to respond to the 9/11 attacks with swift and forceful military action against al Qaeda's bases in Afghanistan. The United States needed to mount a major U.S. military offensive in Afghanistan to deter other terrorist organizations, warn America's enemies, and reassure U.S. allies that the United States was not weak, vulnerable, and unable to strike back at foes. President Bush threatened on the evening of September 11: "We will make no distinction between the terrorists who committed these acts and those who harbor them." Those words later became the Bush Doctrine, proclaimed by the president without prior consultation with Vice President Cheney, Secretary of State Powell, or Secretary of Defense Rumsfeld.[30]

President Bush's discussions with his national security team identified a number of opportunities in the wake of the 9/11 attacks to advance U.S. interests. For example, a strong military offensive against al Qaeda would send a clear message to Syria, Iraq, and Iran—rogue regimes often supporting terrorist groups—that such behavior could lead to a military response from the United States, the world's only superpower.[31] In addition, the anger of the American people over the deadly attacks generated the public support necessary to destroy Osama bin Laden and al Qaeda through military actions in Afghanistan deemed unacceptable prior to 9/11.

The muscular application of American military power against al Qaeda would clearly give President Bush the chance to distinguish his policies from the more restrained use of force by his predecessor President Bill Clinton with his missile response to al Qaeda's 1998 terrorist attacks. The NSC discussions with President Bush also highlighted the opportunity to forge a "coalition of coalitions" to counter al Qaeda terrorist cells located already in about 60 countries, with both friendly and unfriendly regimes, as identified by the CIA.[32] And from the beginning, Rumsfeld and Deputy Secretary of Defense Paul Wolfowitz attempted to exploit the 9/11 attacks as an opportunity to invade Iraq.

The war cabinet sessions with President Bush proceeded to explore a range of policy options. One possible approach entailed pursuing Osama bin Laden through law enforcement methods to bring him to trial and imprisonment. On the other end of the policy choice spectrum loomed the deployment of 55,000 American troops to Afghanistan to destroy bin Laden and his terrorist organization on the ground, aided by U.S. airpower. The Bush administration also examined diplomatic options, such as demanding the Taliban to turn over bin Laden and his al Qaeda terrorists to the United States or face the consequences embodied in the Bush Doctrine. After reading a State Department draft of the ultimatum, President Bush decided that it "would carry more weight if it came directly from the president and it would produce a headline."[33]

However, the CIA doubted that the threat would sever the close relationship between Osama bin Laden and the Taliban's Supreme Leader Mullah Mohammed Omar, linked through their shared resistance to the Soviets in the 1980s, bin Laden's substantial financial support of the Taliban regime, and in return the Taliban's protection of al Qaeda's mountain sanctuaries. Indeed, the

Northern Alliance leader General Ahmed Shah Massoud, a longtime opponent of the Taliban, warned CIA agent Gary Berntsen that the relationship between the Taliban and Osama bin Laden and his al Qaeda organization was symbiotic, with each side receiving benefits. Massoud stated categorically: "They would both have to be destroyed together."[34]

But Osama bin Laden acted first, assassinating General Massoud, the former *mujahadin* military strategist and inspirational Afghan guerrilla leader, during a staged television interview. Two *jihadist* "journalists" exploded a bomb installed within a video camera on September 9, 2001. The killing of the charismatic guerrilla leader Massoud on the eve of the 9/11 attacks underscored that bin Laden had shrewdly calculated America might retaliate by employing the Northern Alliance to attack his Afghanistan stronghold and Taliban hosts.

When the Bush team examined military options, the only immediate response available was to launch Tomahawk cruise missiles against bin Laden's terrorist camps. But the president opposed sending "a million dollar missile to destroy a five dollar tent."[35] Furthermore, such an American military strike without "boots on the ground" would appear to merely emulate Clinton's alleged "weak" 1998 response to al Qaeda's attacks on two U.S. embassies in Africa.

In contrast, President Bush insisted that his initial military strikes should dramatically demonstrate a new, more aggressive, and robust American military riposte to terrorism. But to the dismay of the forward-leaning secretary of defense, the Pentagon possessed no off-the-shelf plan to deploy conventional ground troops to Afghanistan, forcing Rumsfeld to admit there was very little the military could effectively accomplish for up to 60 days.[36] The CENTCOM commander, General Tommy Franks, candidly acknowledged in his memoir: "There simply had been no stomach in Washington for sustained face-to-face combat in this remote, primitive, landlocked country halfway around the world."[37]

CIA Director Tenet brought his colorful Counter Terrorism Center (CTC) director Cofer Black to the White House on September 13. At that war cabinet meeting Black outlined an innovative CIA strategy to promptly send covert teams into Afghanistan to work with Northern Alliance warlords to attack the Taliban and al Qaeda forces with the help of U.S. airpower. President Clinton had authorized the CIA to reestablish its intelligence collection operations in 1999 to obtain new human intelligence (HUMINT) to facilitate the capture of Osama bin Laden. "From February 1999 to March 2001, the CIA sequentially deployed five teams into the Panjshir Valley of Afghanistan to rebuild an intelligence liaison relationship with the Northern Alliance."[38]

The CIA's proposal in the wake of the 9/11 national tragedy called for the insertion of additional CIA teams, bribing local warlords with substantial cash payouts and coordination with Special Forces teams to laser-direct U.S. smart bombs against the Taliban forces. Tenet admitted it would not be a "bloodless" operation. Black warned President Bush that bin Laden would not surrender, but the plan could destroy him and the deadly al Qaeda cadres. Black's enthusiasm and graphic portrayal of the operation from a seasoned CIA field operative won Bush's enthusiastic support. On September 17 Bush signed a finding drafted by Tenet that authorized the mission.[39] The president, anxious for a prompt response to the al Qaeda attacks, eagerly embraced the CIA's plan since it promised immediate action to destroy Osama bin Laden.

The president and his national security team also discussed the option of creating a broad coalition for the war in Afghanistan, since many nations had promptly offered to help the United States after the horrific 9/11 assault on the World Trade Center. Cheney and Rumsfeld expressed concern that maintaining a coalition might tie America's hands, but Secretary of State Powell suggested that coalition members could assume different roles within the coalition against terrorism.[40] President Bush stunned Secretary of State Powell during an NSC meeting by stating that America would pursue its goal in Afghanistan even if the United States lost all its allies. "That's okay with me. We are America."[41] Later, as criticism grew about the delayed military response to the attacks, Bush prodded the Pentagon for action because "I wanted to make sure that our coalition knew we were tough."[42] Overall, more than 80 countries offered to help the United States in its Afghanistan war, but only the British Special Air Service (SAS) commandos participated in the first wave of air strikes.[43]

Opportunity Costs

Even though CIA teams were on the ground working with Northern Alliance warlords, America's bombing campaign against al Qaeda and Taliban fixed targets did not commence until October 7. Many of the problems the Pentagon planners confronted related to logistical and diplomatic issues, such as bases for Search and Rescue units, staging rights, over-flight permission, and the support of neighboring Pakistan. But the delayed air attacks, without a major ground force operation, created "opportunity costs" for the Bush administration's chosen policy in the early weeks after the 9/11 attacks.

The Pentagon's lack of a contingency military plan involving ground forces in Afghanistan postponed a forceful response to al Qaeda's 9/11 attacks. When U.S. bombing finally began on October 7, the "window for savagery" had closed, according to the CIA's Osama bin Laden expert Michael Scheuer.[44] A quick, intensive, crippling attack on bin Laden's Afghanistan bases might have decapitated al Qaeda. Instead, Scheuer felt the "inexcusable delay afforded al Qaeda and Taliban leaders an unexpected lull to further disperse personnel, military stores and funds."[45]

Richard Clarke, Bush's White House counterterrorism coordinator, also criticized the administration's Afghanistan military effort as "slow and small."[46] Clarke felt that after 9/11 the United States should have immediately fought a "rapid, no-holds-barred operation that one might have expected."[47] Instead, the Bush administration treated the Afghanistan war as regime change, rather than seeking and destroying the terrorist sanctuaries. Indeed, General Tommy Franks' strategic plan called for only a small "footprint" of about 10,000 American ground troops in Afghanistan. The Central Command (CENTCOM) commander told Secretary Rumsfeld: "We don't want to repeat the Soviet's mistakes."[48]

Another cost of the selected policy option, the heavy reliance upon the Northern Alliance forces, centered on the questionable reliability of the warlords and whether they would honor their commitments, purchased with American dollars. One U.S. Central Command general described the National Alliance as "more of a shotgun-wedding than an alliance."[49] The first CIA Jawbreaker team leader Gary Schoen acknowledged: "Money is the lubricant that makes things happen in Afghanistan."[50] Before leaving for Afghanistan, Schoen picked up at the CIA's Counter Terrorism Center three cardboard boxes containing $3 million in used 100 dollar bills.

CIA agent Gary Berntsen recognized that the Northern Alliance forces "were no angels," with the Afghanistan warlords' well-known involvement in drug smuggling (opium) and past human rights violations.[51] From a CIA field operative's perspective, even more disconcerting was the reality that "Afghan warlords had a habit of selling out to one side or the other."[52] Nevertheless, Berntsen paid one Taliban commander a half million dollars to defect from the Taliban with his 750 soldiers—after killing the 20 Arabs bin Laden had stationed with his men to ensure his loyalty. Bernsten's Counter Terrorism Center (CTC) boss "Hank" advised him: "Continue purchasing surrenders when and where it makes sense."[53]

General Mohammed Fahim Khan, who took command of the Northern Alliance forces after the assassination of Massoud, violated the agreement he concluded with General Franks to not occupy Kabul. A personal meeting between the Afghan warlord and the American general arrived at that understanding, supposedly confirmed with a negotiated payment of $5 million for Northern Alliance military cooperation.[54] Washington feared a bloodbath if the warlords recaptured the Afghan capitol, preferring that UN multinational forces occupy Kabul. Nevertheless, on November 14 Northern Alliance troops entered Kabul, although General Khan assured Berntsen there would be no reprisal killings.

The ultimate danger of relying upon the Northern Alliance warlords centered on who would receive their loyalties when a new central government replaced the Taliban regime. However, President Bush did not raise that critical question until October 4: "Who will run the country?"[55] In other words, what would happen after U.S forces achieved the short-term goal of toppling the Taliban regime and destroying al Qaeda's sanctuary?

This vital question may have raised an embarrassing discussion of how the senior Bush administration abandoned Afghanistan after the 1989 withdrawal of Soviet armed forces. The superpowers continued to aid their proxies in the Afghan power struggle for several years. Washington's Cold War mentality meant that "Afghanistan's strategic importance to the US was not considered on its own merits, but rather how it could be best exploited as a platform to 'stick it to the Soviets.'"[56] The desire to beat the Soviets silenced the few policy-makers worried about the long-term risk of arming extremely conservative Islamic *mujahideen* guerilla groups. In late 1991 the Soviets and United States agreed to end arms support to the factions by January 1, 1992. The end of the Cold War competition over Afghanistan created a political vacuum that allowed the Taliban to seize Kabul in 1996 after a bloody civil war among the warlords. By 1998 the Taliban controlled the majority of Afghanistan's territory.

By October 4, 2001, the administration had altered Afghanistan's internal power balance through the CIA's financial deals with Northern Alliance commanders, sweetened with the promise that U.S. airpower would devastate the more numerous Taliban troops. The CIA estimated it spent $70 million in cash payments to win the loyalty and military support of the Northern Alliance leaders and Pashtun chiefs.[57]

Although the Pashtun leader Hamid Karzai courageously proved himself during the war against the Taliban, Scheuer predicted that one day the warlords would turn against the American-backed President Karzai to benefit their self-interests. Scheuer pessimistically concluded that the "nascent Afghan democracy is a self-made illusion on life-support" that ignored the realities of Afghanistan's tribal, ethnic, and religious differences.[58]

Retired Army Colonel Hy Rothstein, a Pentagon expert on unconventional warfare, questioned the Bush administration's decision to rely so heavily on a U.S. bombing campaign. Rothstein, who served over 20 years in the Army's Special Forces, traveled to Afghanistan to interview battle-tested military officers and enlisted men for a 2002 Department of Defense analysis on the planning and execution of the war in Afghanistan. In the classified report, Rothstein criticized the administration's emphasis on bombing and conventional warfare after the Taliban and al Qaeda forces retreated into the countryside in December 2001. At that point the conflict had turned into unconventional warfare, manifested by small cell operations, nightly rocket attacks, and laying mines before the guerrillas disappeared at dawn. Rothstein concluded: "What was needed after December 2001 was a greater emphasis on U.S. special operations troops, supported by light infantry, conducting counterinsurgency operations."[59]

British military officers assigned to CENTCOM had attempted to convince General Franks to stop the intense bombing campaign in Afghanistan and establish a large firebase to take the fight to the Taliban on the ground.[60] In October the United States had requested the immediate deployment of a regiment of Britain's Special Air Service (SAS) commandoes to Afghanistan.

Rothstein emphasized that a heavier reliance on the use of Special Forces, with their training emphasizing winning the hearts and minds of the population, would have advanced U.S. interests more than the intensive bombings that contributed to over 1,000 civilian casualties in the early months of the war. He also faulted the administration for ignoring the possibility of creating divisions within the Taliban through a political-military effort directed by Special Forces on the ground. Instead, Rothstein concluded that the U.S. campaign in Afghanistan created a power vacuum that gave "warlordism, banditry and opium production a new lease on life." Indeed, a November 2006 report by the UN Office of Drugs and Crime and the World Bank reported a 59 percent increase in opium production in Afghanistan. The report concluded that Afghanistan provided over 90 percent of the world's opium supply.[61]

On December 18, 2002, Secretary Rumsfeld optimistically told CNN's Larry King: "They have elected a government through the Loya Jirga process. The Taliban are gone. The Al Qaeda are gone."[62] The advantage of hindsight allows one to appreciate Scheuer's prophetic rebuttal to Rumsfeld's premature declaration of victory: "America's Afghan war is still in its infancy."[63]

A Flawed Process

Perhaps the most critical finding employing Graham Allison's Government Organization Model lens involved the painfully slow NSC process in formulating the Bush administration's policy toward the growing terrorist threat of al

Qaeda prior to the 9/11 attacks. President Clinton's NSC Adviser Sandy Berger had warned his successor Condoleezza Rice that she "would be spending more time on terrorist and al Qaida than any other issue."[64] CIA Director Tenet and White House counterterrorism chief Clarke pushed for a tough policy toward bin Laden from the beginning of the Bush administration. But Bush's NSC Advisor Condoleezza Rice established a NSC process that required the deputies' committee to first review Clarke's proposals to deal with the al Qaeda terrorist threat, which then went to the principals' committee, and finally to the president.

Clarke briefed Vice President Cheney, Secretary of State Powell, and Rice on the threat of terrorism early in the administration, but he did not get permission from Rice to brief President Bush on terrorism until September 11.[65] Even Tenet's CIA warning in summer 2001 about "hair raising" intelligence reports on looming al Qaeda terrorist attacks failed to accelerate the Bush administration's national security policy process on how to handle al Qaeda and the mounting threat of a terrorist attack.[66]

Secretary of State Colin Powell explained that the new administration had other compelling issues on its agenda: collapsed Middle East policy, unraveling sanctions against Iraq, relations with Russia, and the U.S. spy plane collision with a Chinese fighter in April.[67] Civilian officials in the Pentagon focused on restructuring the American military and ending the 1972 ABM Treaty's restrictions on a national missile defense system. Pursuing those agenda goals took most of the time of the Bush national security team. Nevertheless, one 9/11 Commission member pointed out that the principals met 33 times in 7 months without 1 meeting dedicated solely to terrorism, even though threats dramatically escalated in the summer of 2001.

Perhaps, as Clinton's NSC Adviser Sandy Berger suggested in his testimony to the 9/11 Commission, the relative modest cost of terrorism before the September 11 attacks contributed to the low priority accorded to a policy aimed at non-state terrorist groups. Despite the growing violence al Qaeda mounted against U.S. targets, such as the bombings of the American embassies in Kenya and Tanzania and the *U.S.S. Cole* in 2000, fewer than 50 Americans had died in the attacks.[68] Berger observed that in the 1980s almost 500 Americans were killed in overseas terrorist attacks, "yet counterterrorism was not a priority of our government."[69] Clarke testified that the low number of American deaths prior to 9/11 made it more difficult to convince officials of the potential catastrophic damage al Qaeda could inflict upon the United States. Berger sagely observed, "History is written through a rearview mirror, but it unfolds through a foggy windshield."[70]

NSC Adviser Condoleezza Rice testified that President Bush wanted a new, comprehensive strategy rather than responding tit-for-tat to attacks. Bush told Rice he was "tired of swatting flies."[71] But the *9/11 Commission Report* found more than 40 intelligence articles in Bush's President's Daily Briefs (PDB) from January 20 to September 10, 2001, related to bin Laden.[72] By July 2001, CIA Director Tenet told the commission, "the system was blinking red."[73]

The CIA proposed arming the National Alliance at the NSC's deputies' committee meeting in April 2001.[74] At the July meeting the deputies' committee recommended a comprehensive plan to deal with al Qaeda. The NSC principals' committee did not approve a "strategic" policy toward al Qaeda until September 4, which included a recommendation giving the CIA $125–$200 million a year for arming the Alliance.[75] The draft National Security Presidential Directive (NSPD) rested on President Bush's desk awaiting his approval at the moment the hijacked airliners crashed into the World Trade Center and Pentagon.

Dr. Rice defended the administration's NSC policy process in the *Washington Post*: "Our plan called for military options to attack Al Qaida and Taliban leadership, ground forces and other targets, taking the fight to the enemy."[76] But Deputy Secretary of State Richard Armitage, testifying on behalf of Rice, acknowledged in the 9/11 hearings that the more aggressive tactics were added after the horror of 9/11. For example, counterterrorism coordinator Clarke tried to insert the objective to "eliminate" al Qaeda into the draft NSPD, but the deputies' committee reduced the goal to "significantly erode."[77] Clarke bitterly recalled that only after the 9/11 terrorist attacks "we were able to go back to my language of eliminate, rather than significantly erode."

A major controversy erupted over whether the administration had ignored a Presidential Daily Brief (PDB) prepared by the CIA on August 6, 2001, ominously titled "Bin Ladin Determined to Strike US," which remained classified until Rice's testimony before the 9/11 Commission. Rice described the August 6 PDB as a response to questions asked by President Bush. But Commissioner Richard Ben-Veniste pointed out that the commission had received a written CIA document showing that the August 6 PDB "was initiated by individuals within the CIA and not as a direct request from the national security advisor."[78]

Sensing a political landmine, Dr. Rice downplayed the August 6, 2001, PDB as only "a historic memo," an "analytic piece" without evidence of specific threats to the U.S. homeland, such as terrorist suicide attacks using hijacked American airliners. Rice asserted that the administration's policy, not yet approved by the president, placed al Qaeda in a stronger regional context. However, an "all-out invasion of Afghanistan," she admitted, "was not recommended" before the 9/11 terrorist attacks.

The application of Allison's Government Organization Model also revealed how the Department of Defense played a secondary role in the Afghanistan response to the al Qaeda attacks because of the Pentagon's aversion to developing a contingency plan for a major ground offensive against al Qaeda's Afghanistan stronghold. President Bush, impatient for a more immediate, visible, and muscular policy against bin Laden, quickly adopted the CIA's novel plan for toppling the Taliban through CIA field teams working with National Alliance warlords, while Special Forces directed U.S. airpower at Taliban forces. Bush rejected Rumsfeld's efforts to scale back the CIA plan on September 17: "I want the CIA to be first on the ground."[79]

Quite clearly, the unsuccessful Soviet experience in fighting the Afghan *mujahidine* from 1979 to 1989 greatly influenced Pentagon planners. The Soviet Union had introduced 620,000 troops into Afghanistan without defeating the *mujahidine*. During the 10-year struggle 15,000 Soviet troops were killed and 55,000 wounded.[80] General Franks, CENTCOM commander, concluded that the "implicit lesson of Afghanistan's recent history was not to put large numbers of American troops on the ground to accomplish the mission—unless absolutely necessary."[81]

But during the 9/11 Commission hearings, top officials from both the Clinton and Bush administrations emphasized that the American public, Congress, or U.S. allies would not have supported a policy to invade Afghanistan with ground forces prior to the World Trade Center and Pentagon attacks. Clinton's advisor Berger declared: "I do not believe before September 11th that the American people or the international community would have supported an invasion and occupation of Afghanistan." Clinton's secretary of defense, former Republican Senator William Cohen, described the prevailing "Wag the Dog" cynicism in the House of Representatives. Cohen felt Congress would have "overwhelmingly rejected" any substantial American military invasion of Afghanistan before 9/11.

Secretary of Defense Donald Rumsfeld emphasized he knew of no actionable intelligence after President Bush's January 20 inauguration that "would have allowed the U.S. to capture or kill bin Laden."[82] Rumsfeld asserted that if President Bush had appeared before Congress and the world calling for an invasion of Afghanistan to overthrow the Taliban and destroy al Qaeda before 9/11, not many countries would have joined the U.S. coalition. Secretary of State Powell also stressed that without the support of the surrounding countries, an invasion of Afghanistan during the first seven months of the Bush administration lacked "a sufficient cause and justification" to take such military action.

Some other factors preventing the Department of Defense from playing an early role on the ground in Afghanistan included diplomatic obstacles, such as "overshoot rights" to launch Tomahawk attacks across Pakistan's territory, and the Pentagon's standard operating procedures.[83] General Henry Shelton, chairman of the Joint Chiefs of Staff, warned the president that air combat operations could not begin until Combat Search and Rescue helicopter teams were in place. This "bedrock doctrine" recognized that captured American airmen behind enemy lines could become potential hostages with a serious negative political impact.[84] Indeed, Rice feared that if al Qaeda captured a downed pilot as a hostage it would give bin Laden considerable leverage.[85] The administration required permission to use bases in Pakistan, Uzbekistan, and Tajikistan to stage Combat Search and Rescue activities to bring out downed aircraft crews.

Although the CIA had covert teams on the ground since 1999 to reestablish intelligence contacts with Northern Alliance commanders, Secretary Rumsfeld impatiently waited for Special Forces teams to be inserted into Afghanistan. In fact, the "Ten Days from Hell," as General Franks described the delays caused by logistics, weather, and equipment problems, only ended on October 19 when a Special Forces A-Team joined National Alliance forces commanded by General Abdul Rashid Dostrum in northern Afghanistan.[86] On each of those 10 days Rumsfeld questioned the CENTCOM commander when the Special Forces would enter Afghanistan. Although the coalition had been bombing Taliban targets for over a week, Rumsfeld wanted to report to President Bush "tangible achievements—something beyond the airdrops of humanitarian daily rations," namely Special Forces boots on the ground.[87] As a clear sign of the bureaucratic rivalry Graham Allison's Governmental Politics Model highlighted, Rumsfeld bluntly told his top generals: "Every CIA success is a DoD failure."[88]

From an organizational point of view, the Bush administration's plan to attack Afghanistan and its al Qaeda bases broke new ground by requiring unprecedented close coordination between the CIA and Pentagon. General Richard Myers, who became chair of the Joint Chiefs on October 1, 2001, admitted to President Bush: "We're not really experienced at it." However, the CIA and Special Forces had worked together in Bosnia on capturing war criminals.[89]

When CIA agent Berntsen received his briefing before leaving to lead the Jawbreaker team in Afghanistan, his CTC boss Hank emphasized that on this mission he must share everything with the military, including sources. Hank stressed that Berntsen should provide General Franks whatever he requested "and then inform me. We have to be married to CENTCOM."[90]

However, Schoen later recalled the difficulty in getting a Special Operations officer to accompany the CIA's Jawbreaker team into Afghanistan, as spelled out in the presidential finding, An unresolved debate raged within the Pentagon over what the mission of Special Operations should be in Afghanistan. Schoen noted: "The bottom line was that no SpecOps personnel would accompany JAWBREAKER into Afghanistan. The official reason given was that without SAR [Search and Rescue] capability, the mission was considered 'too dangerous' for U.S. military personnel."[91] Nevertheless, the CIA team courageously took a helicopter into Afghanistan. Feeling pressure from President Bush to move ahead, the CIA's seventh-floor managers were no longer "risk-averse."

Personality and Politics

Graham Allison's Governmental Politics lens provides different insights into the president's decision to topple Afghanistan's Taliban regime and destroy al Qaeda's sanctuary. President Bush shared Rumsfeld's impatience over the Pentagon's delayed response to his marching orders. Rice warned the president that his time expectations for military action in Afghanistan and the military's timetable to begin attacks were not in sync. Bush exclaimed: "That's unacceptable."[92] Bush later told Woodward: "I'm ready to go..... Sometimes that's the way I am—fiery. On the other hand [Rice's] job is to bear the brunt of some of the fire...to take the edge off a bit."[93] The president admitted: "I was growing a little impatient. I can be an impatient person." Rice called Rumsfeld to have him provide the president with a realistic timetable the following day.

Gary Schoen had to leave Washington two days before they had planned, on September 19 rather than September 21, to head CIA's Jawbreaker team in Afghanistan. President Bush had pressured CIA Director Tenet for an earlier departure date.[94] Bush once exclaimed in his frontier style: "We're steady, clear-eyed and patient, but pretty soon we'll have to *start displaying scalps*" (author's emphasis).[95]

President George W. Bush, possibly trying to recover from his less than stellar performance on September 11, sought to improve his image as a hands-on leader. Bush rejected Vice President Cheney's offer to chair the war cabinet meetings.[96] Cheney had framed the suggestion as developing options to streamline the president's decision-making process. One could argue that President John F. Kennedy utilized his brother, Attorney General Robert Kennedy, in the same manner by having him chair the ExComm meetings during the October 1962 Cuban Missile Crisis.

But President Bush had already denied Cheney's power-seeking effort to chair the principals' committee. Nevertheless, even though NSC adviser Rice chaired the principals' committee, Cheney became the first vice president to regularly attend its meetings. After the 9/11 attacks, President Bush recognized that he needed to be viewed at home and abroad as clearly in charge of crafting America's response to the al Qaeda terrorists. Europeans only knew him as the "toxic Texan," Bush complained, because of his opposition to the Kyoto Protocol.[97]

Bush insisted that his war cabinet provide him with action and solutions. He demanded 100 percent commitment to the plan the NSC team adopted. The president explained to Woodward that he felt his job entailed providing the calcium in the backbone of the team, demonstrating steadfast pursuit of the outlined policy goals without looking backward with regrets. "If I weaken, the whole team weakens.... If my confidence level in our ability declines, it will send ripples throughout the whole organization."[98]

Despite President Bush's earlier speeches criticizing President Johnson for micromanaging the Vietnam War, at times Bush had to be checked from involving himself too much in the details of the Afghanistan mission. Chief of Staff Andy Card warned Bush he was becoming too interested in tactics. "Don't be a general, be a president."[99] Rice once reminded Bush that he was the coach not the quarterback of the team.[100]

The president knew he had to rely on his principals' expertise, which surpassed his own foreign policy knowledge and experience at that point in his first term. However, Bush demonstrated a keen interest in an area where he felt uniquely qualified: handling the public relations aspect of the war. President Bush established a daily meeting with Karen Hughes to shape his message on the imminent war. He explained that the administration was fighting a two-front war—Afghanistan and at home. Bush placed Hughes in charge of communicating the administration's goals and actions in the war effort, asserting that the Vietnam War was not effectively explained to the American people.[101] He directed the Pentagon to work with Hughes on the "themes" in the announcement of military action.[102]

Bush insisted upon personally announcing from the Rose Garden his Executive Order directing the Treasury Department to freeze terrorist assets, describing the action as "a major thrust of our war on terrorism [begun] with the stroke of a pen."[103] President Bush also suggested a humanitarian food drop in north and south Afghanistan, coordinated with the military. Bush later explained in an interview, "I was sensitive to this [accusation] that this was a religious war, and that somehow the United States would be the conqueror. And I wanted us to be viewed as the liberator."[104] After public criticism of the administration's delayed military response, Bush told the NSC principals on October 3: "We're losing the public relations war."[105] He then proposed a humanitarian donors' conference prior to the Muslim holiday of Ramadan.

When Donald Rumsfeld took charge of the Department of Defense in 2001 for the second time in his career, he demanded complete control over the Pentagon, leading to numerous clashes with the uniformed service chiefs. Rumsfeld at one point suggested that General Shelton should give his military advice to the president through him. Shelton refused, pointing out that the law made him, as chairman of the Joint Chiefs of Staff, the "principle military adviser" to the president.[106] One senior general tactfully noted: "He's [Rumsfeld] got a weakness in wanting to have his hands around everything." Thus, when President Bush asked General Franks his opinion during a NSC meeting, the CENTCOM commander deferentially replied: "Sir, I think exactly what my secretary thinks, what he's ever thought, what he will ever think, or whatever he thought he might think."[107]

Despite President Bush's approval of the plan for close coordination among the CIA teams, Special Forces, and attacking U.S. aircraft, Secretary Rumsfeld maneuvered to have the Defense Department placed clearly in charge of the Afghanistan operation. Rumsfeld expressed his unease about the "blurring of operational lines between CIA and Defense."[108] In a secret meeting in the White House living quarters, General Franks briefed President Bush on his Afghanistan war plans. Secretary Rumsfeld addressed the issue of the fuzzy lines of authority; he recommended the president grant "operational control of the CIA...to the Department of Defense."[109] General Franks later acknowledged that CENTCOM had received full operational control over CIA activities in the war theater, including the use of Predator drones armed with Hellfire missiles.[110]

In conclusion, President George W. Bush's decision-making in the days following the disastrous 9/11 terrorist attacks generally manifested the desirable features described in Graham Allison's Rational Actor Model. After all, Bush had been taught in Harvard's prestigious MBA program, which through its case studies emphasized the importance of an executive's rational, value-maximizing decisions.

Nevertheless, President Bush voiced overly expansive goals for his war on terror that created problems in crafting workable strategies. Carefully developed goals would have led to "bounded" strategies to attain the administration's objectives. Although Bush's hot rhetoric, in the emotional wake of the World Trade Center's collapse, called for an ambitious campaign to eliminate all terrorism from the world, eradicate evil, and destroy the evil ones, his more pragmatic advisers recognized that such goals were too broad and unrealistic.

Another problem emerged from the Bush administration's understandable concentration on retaliation to destroy bin Laden, al Qaeda, and its Taliban hosts—but without a full examination of what type of Afghanistan government would replace the Islamist regime. The Bush administration chose to back the India-educated Hamid Karzai, a Pashtun leader who spoke fluent English and enjoyed support in the West, to become the new president of Afghanistan. But the limited forces the United States sent to Afghanistan—because President Bush disdained nation-building and anticipated a war with Iraq—meant that President Karzai became essentially the "mayor of Kabul."[111] The powerful but corrupt tribal warlords continued to dominate their respective regions throughout Afghanistan. Secretary Rumsfeld's upbeat December 2002 declaration that both the Taliban and Al Qaeda "are gone" reflected his desire to avoid nation-building with additional U.S. forces, rather than the political and military reality on the ground in Afghanistan.

Some terrorism experts argued that the Bush NSC team never fully recognized that al Qaeda represented an Islamic insurgency in the Middle East, a much more profound threat to America's interests in the strategic region. Since President Bush lacked knowledge and background in foreign affairs, making him dependent upon their expertise, his advisers' myopia served the president poorly.

Behind the scenes President Bush demonstrated considerable impatience, prodding his war cabinet to act faster. His emphasis on teamwork led to a demand for consensus and a total commitment to the adopted war plan, creating the danger of *groupthink*, when alternative views become silenced.[112] And Bush learned, through planning his response to the al Qaeda attacks, that early contingency planning expedited the execution of policy, particularly to mobilize America's powerful military machine. That lesson contributed to Bush's long media campaign and drawn-out Pentagon planning for the 2003 invasion of Iraq.

Chapter Seven

New Kind of War: Breaking the Rules

This will be a different kind of conflict against a different kind of enemy.

President Bush recognized after the 9/11 terrorist attacks the importance of forceful military action against al Qaeda in Afghanistan, both from a political standpoint and as a powerful message to America's foes and friends. Bush told the American people that the conflict would be without battlefields or beachheads, involving a series of actions against terrorist organizations and their supporters. He predicted: "This will be a different kind of conflict against a different kind of enemy."[1] President Bush acknowledged later that the war on terrorism "has a multiple of fronts."[2]

On the domestic front, President Bush signed into law on October 26, 2001, the USA Patriot Act, crafted to assist domestic law enforcement agencies "to identify, to dismantle, to disrupt, and to punish terrorists before they strike."[3] The House and Senate approved the 342-page law with little debate in the face of Attorney General John Ashcroft's pressure for immediate action, FBI warnings of a possible second terrorist attack, and a deadly anthrax mailing to Senator Tom Daschle's office.[4]

The bill bypassed the usual House and Senate committee process "in favor of high-level, closed-door, executive-legislative negotiations."[5] Although the House Judiciary Committee had unanimously approved a bipartisan bill, the full House voted on a different version (with the same bill number) secretly agreed to by Speaker Dennis Hastert and the White House without the full Judiciary Committee's knowledge.[6] The Bush administration negotiated with the Senate Judiciary Committee leaders on the upper chamber's version, not allowing the full committee to examine the bill before the Senate floor vote.

Early in the congressional deliberations, Senate Judiciary Committee Chairman Patrick Leahy warned that "if the Constitution is shredded, the terrorists win." Nevertheless, in the wake of 9/11 the Justice Department obtained through the Patriot Act many of the strong law enforcement tools Congress had rejected in prior years, thwarted through the strong opposition of congressional civil rights and privacy advocates in both parties.[7] The Patriot Act expanded law enforcement's power to spy on possible terrorist with "roving wiretaps," conduct black-bag "sneak-and-peek" searches without notifying the suspect, monitor Internet traffic, strengthen money-laundering laws, and criminalized knowingly harboring a terrorist.

Attorney General Ashcroft declared at a 2002 judicial conference: "The mission of the Department of Justice has been transformed from a focus on prosecution of illegal acts to a focus on the prevention of terrorist acts."[8] He blasted opponents of the administration's antiterrorism policies, charging that such criticisms only "aid terrorists" and "erode our unity."[9]

President Bush secretly approved a number of controversial policies—not passed by Congress—that reflected his willingness to embrace extreme actions on both the foreign and domestic fronts of his war on terrorism. These aggressive policies relied upon an expansive "unitary" concept of the president's commander-in-chief powers as the nation's Executive. The tough policies also reflected Bush's perception of the conflict with Islamic *jihad* extremists as a moral struggle against the menacing forces of evil.

The "Quaint" Geneva Conventions

President Bush's call for a new type of warfare against al Qaeda terrorists opened the door to a number of radical policy changes. In particular, Bush abandoned the restrictions in the 1949 Geneva Conventions on the Treatment of Prisoners of War ratified by the U.S. Senate. Six days after the horrific 9/11 attacks, President George W. Bush signed a secret finding giving the CIA broad authority for antiterrorist activities, including permission to kill, capture, and detain members of al Qaeda anywhere in the world. The September 17 finding triggered the CIA's proposed "Worldwide Attack Matrix," aimed at terrorist networks in 80 countries.[10]

The original order focused on the capture and interrogation of about two dozen al Qaeda leaders "believed to be directly responsible for the Sept. 11 attacks, or who posed an imminent threat, or had knowledge of the larger al Qaeda network."[11] The CIA applied to these "high-value detainees (HVDs)" the "most aggressive interrogation techniques" to uncover intelligence to prevent an imminent follow-up attack, according to CIA Director George Tenet.[12] But as intelligence leads grew, the CIA began apprehending individuals with weaker links to terrorism and less useful intelligence.

In November 2001 CIA Director Tenet told the Agency's general counsel: "We need guidance from Justice and the White House on what we're allowed to do."[13] Where would detainees be held for interrogation and what standards should guide the interrogators? Within the CIA, some cautioned about the need for a standard of evidence before resorting to "expedient action," while others argued torture was justified if a terrorist had intelligence that could save many lives.

Vice President Dick Cheney supported the latter viewpoint. "If there's a one percent chance that Pakistani scientists are helping al Qaeda build or develop a nuclear weapon we have to treat it as a certainty in terms of our response."[14] Essentially, Cheney's "One Percent Doctrine" dramatically lowered the threshold for the employment of "expedient action." As a result, solid analysis became secondary to the imperative of a quick response to potential threats to U.S. interests.[15]

The Justice Department responded to the CIA's request for guidance in late fall 2001 with a narrow interpretation of the restrictions on torture in the Third Geneva Convention, giving the CIA the green light to employ sleep deprivation, use of phobias, and "stress factors" in the interrogation of al Qaeda suspects. According to a former administration official, the only limits concerned "causing severe physical or mental pain."[16]

The legal underpinning of the Bush administration's rejection of the 1949 Third Geneva Convention on the Treatment of Prisoners of War and the 1997 War Crimes Act's constraints (which incorporated provisions of the treaties into U.S. law) appeared in the January 9, 2002, memorandum of John Yoo, deputy assistant attorney general, and Special Counsel Robert J. Delanhunty. Addressed to the Defense Department's General Counsel William Haynes, the memorandum concluded that international treaties did not protect al Qaeda members as non-state actors or the Taliban militia, since Afghanistan was a failed state and the Taliban forces had become functionally indistinguishable from al Qaeda's members. Yoo and Delanhunty further contended:

> The President...has the constitutional authority as Commander in Chief to interpret and apply the customary or common laws of war in such a way that they would extend to the conduct of members of both al Qaeda and the Taliban, and also to the conduct of the U.S. Armed Forces towards members of those groups taken prisoner in Afghanistan.[17]

On January 18, 2002, President Bush followed the advice of the Justice Department and White House Counsel Albert Gonzales by determining that the 1949 Geneva Convention on prisoners of war did not apply to al Qaeda or the Taliban. However, Secretary of State Colin Powell requested the president to reconsider his decision.

Gonzales sent a January 25, 2002, memorandum to President Bush endorsing Yoo's Department of Justice legal opinion that the Third Geneva Convention did not apply to the conflict with al Qaeda. Gonzales asserted that the "new kind of war" after 9/11 required an innovative paradigm that "renders obsolete Geneva's strict limitations on questioning of enemy prisoners and renders *quaint*" some of its provisions for the treatment of captured enemies (author's emphasis).[18]

The White House attorney emphasized that the war against terrorism placed a premium on quickly obtaining information from terrorist prisoners to avoid further atrocities against American civilians. Gonzales underscored the need for flexibility, since "it is difficult to predict the needs and circumstance that could arise in the course of the war on terrorism." President Bush's counsel stated that the United States would continue to treat detainees humanely, but only "to the extent appropriate and consistent with military necessity"—leaving a significant "military necessity" loophole for the use of extreme interrogation methods to obtain actionable intelligence to save American lives.

Secretary of State Powell outlined the pros and cons of the options available to President Bush. He warned that for the administration to assert the inapplicability of the Geneva Convention to the Afghanistan conflict would "reverse over a century of U.S. Policy" designed to protect American troops under the international laws of war, create an international reaction to U.S. foreign policy, and undermine support from critical allies.[19] Powell argued in favor of applying the Geneva Convention to the Afghanistan conflict, recommending that the president should then assert that the al Qaeda and the Taliban do not enjoy POW status under the treaty. However, the retired four-star general emphasized: "Treat all detainees consistent with the principles of the GPW."

Attorney General John Ashcroft addressed the issue on February 1, 2002. Ashcroft, citing the Supreme Court case of *Clark v. Allen*, declared that if the president judged Afghanistan represented a failed state, the Taliban would not be legally entitled to protection under the Geneva Convention on Prisoners of War. That stance would provide the United States with "the highest level of legal certainty available under American law."[20] Ashcroft warned that the alternative legal opinion that the Geneva Convention applied to the Afghanistan conflict but would not protect unlawful Taliban combatants (Powell's position), "could well expose our personnel to a greater risk of being treated improperly in the event of detention by a foreign power."

The State Department's legal adviser sent a February 2 memorandum to Gonzales challenging his legal brief on the Geneva Conventions. William H. Taft IV warned that not applying the Geneva Conventions to the Afghanistan conflict would overturn 50 years of "unvaried practice" when sending U.S. troops into conflict.[21] He cautioned that American soldiers might be deprived of the protection of the Geneva Convention if they were captured.

Taft also included an attachment summarizing the positions of lawyers from the Departments of Justice, State, White House Counsel, and Office of the Vice President that highlighted the differences within the administration over the applicability of the Geneva Convention on Prisoners of War. The outline showed that lawyers from Justice, Defense, White House, and the Vice President's office concurred that the conflict with al Qaeda was not covered by the Geneva treaty. Lawyers from the Joint Chiefs of Staff and the State Department emphasized the need to treat all detainees as the Conventions specified and emphasized all other countries should treat American troops "consistent with the convention."

On February 7, 2002, President Bush signed a memorandum calling for U.S. armed forces to treat detainees humanely "to the extent appropriate and consistent with military necessity."[22] Bush asserted that the war on terrorism ushered in a new paradigm against "groups with broad, international reach [that] commit horrific acts against innocent civilians," which required a fresh approach to the law of war. He stated the Geneva Convention did not apply to the conflict in Afghanistan, determining that the Taliban and al Qaeda prisoners were unlawful combatants not qualified for prisoner-of-war status. Thus, President Bush overrode the voices emanating from the State Department and Joint Chiefs advocating caution on violating the Geneva Convention's ban on the treatment of prisoners of war.

Walk on the Dark Side

Rendition, the process of turning over suspects to a foreign government outside of the formal extradition process, began during the Reagan administration in 1986. President Bill Clinton also authorized renditions in the mid-1990s to transfer drug lords and terrorists to other countries or the United States for military or criminal trials.[23] Michael Scheuer, the chief of the CIA's Bin Laden Unit, designed the Clinton administration's rendition program. In an interview Scheuer outlined the requirements of Clinton's rendition program: an "outstanding legal process" against the suspect, usually for terrorist offenses; a CIA dossier on the person based on intelligence; a country willing to help apprehend the suspect on its territory; and "somewhere to take him after he was arrested."[24] But Scheuer emphasized that the pre-9/11 goal of the Clinton administration's rendition operations was not to gather intelligence. "Success…was to get someone, who was a danger to us or our allies, 'off the street' and, when we got him, to grab whatever documents he had with him."

The Council of Europe's critical report on the Bush administration's rendition program by Swiss senator Dick Marty acknowledged thus: "The act of rendition may not *per se* constitute a breach of international human rights law."[25] The report noted that the U.S. Supreme Court had upheld other renditions or abductions to bring a man to trial under the concept of "rendition to justice," which some legal experts support if the judicial process respects human rights. For example, in 1995 the FBI resorted to "irregular rendition" to arrest Ramzi Yousef in Pakistan to stand trial for his key role in the 1993 World Trade Center bombing plot.[26] Condoleezza Rice defended the Bush administration after revelations of its rendition activities in Europe, pointing to the 1994 French rendition of Carlos the Jackal from Sudan.[27] However, a French court tried, sentenced, and imprisoned the terrorist Carlos for his terrorist acts—rather then sending him to a third country for harsh interrogation.

Scheuer recalled that in 1995 the CIA established its rendition program with Egypt, although the State Department knew the *Mukhabarat* (secret police) employed brutal interrogation techniques. He acknowledged the law required "assurances" that suspects would not be tortured, but Scheuer was "not sure" the documents offering assurances were signed.[28] Scheuer, tasked by the CIA with finding the terrorist leader Osama bin Laden, frankly admitted to an interviewer: "I check my moral qualms at the door."[29] Another CIA agent involved in the rendition of terrorist suspects described the formal assurances from other countries as "a farce."[30]

In 2000 CIA Director George Tenet claimed that "renditions have shattered terrorist cells and networks, thwarted terrorist plans, and in some cases even prevented attacks from occurring."[31] Tenet later disclosed that the CIA had ordered 70 renditions prior to the 9/11 terrorist attacks, under Clinton's Presidential Decision Directive 39 and PDD 62 as part of *The Plan*.[32] But about four years later Tenet ruefully admitted at a 9/11 Commission hearing: "Disruptions, renditions and sensitive collection activities no doubt saved lives.…However, we never penetrated the 9/11 plot overseas."[33]

Congress expressed its concern about certain forms of rendition in the Foreign Affairs Reform and Restructuring Act of 1998. The law declared: "It shall be the policy of the United States not to expel, extradite, or otherwise effect the involuntary return of any person to a country in which there are substantial grounds for believing the person would be *in danger of being subjected to torture*, regardless of whether the person is physically present in the United States" (author's emphasis).[34] In the 109th Congress opponents of rendition introduced several bills against outsourcing torture and rendition to Syria and other countries that practiced torture.[35]

After the horrifying events of 9/11, the Bush administration sought actionable intelligence through "extraordinary rendition" to countries that practiced torture in order to swiftly obtain information about any future attacks. President Bush signed a secret finding on September 17, 2001, authorizing the CIA "to kill, capture and detain members of al Qaeda anywhere in the world."[36] Vice President

Cheney hinted at the policy change in a "Meet the Press" interview five days after the attacks: "*We also have to work…the dark side*, if you will…It is a mean, nasty, dangerous dirty business out there, and we have to operate in that arena" (author's emphasis).[37]

President Bush's September 17 finding authorized renditions, lethal measures, disinformation, and cyber attacks by the CIA.[38] Scott Horton estimated 150 people had been rendered since 9/11 in a report on rendition he prepared for the New York City Bar Association. Suspects were captured and sent to Egypt, Syria, Saudi Arabia, Jordan, and Pakistan—all countries the State Department listed for routinely applying torture in their prisons.[39]

The CIA established a Rendition Group comprising CIA case officers, paramilitaries, analysts, and psychologists to identify key terrorists, plan their capture, and render the suspects to another country for interrogation. The Rendition Group standardized the procedures: "Dressed head to toe in black, including masks, they blindfold and cut the clothes off their new captives, then administer an enema and sleeping drugs. They outfit detainees in a diaper and jumpsuit for what can be a day-long trip."[40]

In April 2005 a reporter asked President Bush how he could justify the rendition of suspects to a third country for interrogation. Bush called the question "a hypothetical," stating the United States sends people to countries where they say they will not torture people. Nevertheless, the president defended the detention of dangerous suspects: "We—we still at war."[41] However, the following month a spokesperson for Amnesty International described U.S. human rights violations as "atrocious" and portrayed the Guantanamo detention facility as "the gulag of our times."[42]

Because of the waves of negative publicity around the world over the CIA's extreme interrogation measures and risk of lawsuits, the CIA suspended such activities until the president issued new rules for the CIA. The U.S. Army revised its field manual in September 2006 to ban interrogation techniques, such as waterboarding, as "cruel, inhumane and degrading treatment" forbidden by Common Article 3 of the Geneva Accords. General John F. Kimmons, Army deputy chief of staff for intelligence, declared that "no good intelligence is going to come from abusive practices. I think history tells us that. I think the empirical evidence of the last five years, hard years, tells us that."[43]

Nevertheless, in an October 2006 radio interview Vice President Cheney agreed with a conservative host that a "dunk in water" was a no-brainer, igniting protests from human rights advocates.[44] Cheney overlooked the fact that the United States declared waterboarding a war crime in 1947, convicting a Japanese officer of employing the coercive technique against an American in World War II. In addition, the Army court-martialed American soldiers for waterboarding captives during the Vietnam War.[45]

President Bush issued an executive order on July 20, 2007, outlining new interrogation guidelines for the CIA—but classified the detailed list of approved interrogation techniques. The new rules prohibit "acts of violence serious enough to be considered comparable to murder, torture, mutilation and cruel and inhuman treatment."[46] The guidelines also ban "willful and outrageous acts of personal abuse done for the purpose of humiliating or degrading the individual" beyond the bounds of decency. However, as Jane Mayer observed, "Bush's order pointedly did not disavow the use of 'enhanced interrogation techniques' that would likely be found illegal if used by officials inside the United States."[47]

In the future the CIA director must personally approve all "enhanced interrogation" procedures. CIA chief Michael Hayden stated: "There will be no lone wolves, interrogations will always be conducted by a team, and anybody on the team can knock it off at any time."[48] Nevertheless, a former CIA official expressed grave concern over the lasting psychic damage to the American interrogators themselves, even when operating as a team. He observed: "When you cross over that line of darkness, it's hard to come back. You lose your soul."[49]

Hidden from View

The international spotlight focused on another tactic of the Bush administration's war on terror in late 2005: CIA secret prisons in third countries. According to Dana Priest, who broke the explosive story, the CIA had established "black site" prisons shortly after 9/11 in eight countries, including Thailand, Afghanistan, and "several democracies in Eastern Europe."[50] Those countries were later revealed as Poland and Romania, although their leaders denied the allegations.[51] The top-secret CIA prisons were known to only a handful of American officials. James Risen explained that the CIA sought secret locations to have complete control over the interrogations and debriefings, free from the prying eyes of the international media, human rights groups, and "most important, far from the jurisdiction of the American legal system."[52]

A first tier of secret prisons held about thirty high-value terrorist suspects, financed and managed by the CIA itself. However, the CIA closed the Thailand prison in 2003 after disclosures in the press; the special prison (Camp X-Ray) at Guantanamo shut down in 2004. A second tier of prisons housed 70 detainees assessed to hold a lower terrorist intelligence value. The host country ran the black sites in Egypt, Jordan, Morocco, and Afghanistan, but they received funding and often directions from the CIA. Only the House and Senate Intelligence Committee chairmen and vice chairmen received general briefings about the program. A senior intelligence official admitted that before 9/11 the idea of detaining and interrogating people was never discussed. "It was against the culture and they believed information was best gleaned by other means."[53]

The disclosure of secret CIA prisons in Eastern Europe and the collaboration of European Union (EU) governments with the CIA's rendition program sparked anger throughout Europe. An April 24, 2006, report of the European Parliament found that "30 to 50 people have been rendered by the CIA in Europe."[54] In February 2007 the European Parliament approved the controversial report on CIA activities in Europe by a 382–256 vote, with 74 abstentions.[55]

The Parliamentary Assembly of the Council of Europe passed on April 26, 2005, a resolution that charged "the United States has engaged in the unlawful practice of secret detention," urging the United States to respect the principles of the rule of law and human rights.[56] The EU investigation also found that the CIA conducted over 1,000 clandestine flights in Europe, with some planes transporting suspects to secret prisons for torture.[57] Allegedly, the EU secretly approved letting the United States land at European airports to transfer "criminal/ inadmissible aliens" at a January 22, 2003, meeting in Athens, Greece.[58]

Marty's Council of Europe report described the CIA's rendition program as a "global 'spider's web.'" Secret prisons throughout the world held terrorist suspects who became trapped in a spider's web, never facing the justice system to determine their guilt or innocence.[59] The report examined in detail 10 cases of rendition involving 17 individual detainees.[60]

Stephen Grey, a reporter for the London *Sunday Times*, began analyzing flight logs to track the movement of CIA planes and their prisoners. After a Swedish TV station published details of the CIA's kidnapping of several alleged terrorists in Sweden, obtaining the U.S. registration number of a CIA Gulfstream jet, Grey began a series of collaborations that involved the Swedish TV journalists, *New York Times* and *Washington Post* reporters. He matched more than 15 different flight logs to the accounts of rendition by prisoners.[61] In *Ghost Plane*, Grey concluded that the CIA operated a fleet of 26 planes. The CIA fleet appeared reminiscent of the Agency's use of Air America during the Vietnam War.

CIA officials underscored to Grey that all the renditions and techniques of interrogation received the approval of CIA headquarters—and the White House. NSC Adviser Condoleezza Rice and Attorney General John Ashcroft signed off on specific operations. "Our backs were relentlessly covered," one former CIA official assured him.[62]

On September 6, 2006, President George W. Bush announced from the White House that 14 high-value detainees would be transferred from secret CIA overseas prisons to Guantanamo Bay, Cuba, for prosecution through U.S. military tribunals. Bush explained: "Captured terrorists have unique knowledge about how terrorist networks operate. They have knowledge of where their operatives are deployed, and knowledge about what plots are underway."[63] For the first time Bush acknowledged the existence of the CIA's "black site" prisons:

> In addition to the terrorists held at Guantanamo, a small number of suspected terrorist leaders and operatives captured during the war have been held and questioned outside the United States, in a separate program operated by the Central Intelligence Agency. This group includes individuals believed to be the key architects of the September the 11th attacks, and attacks on the USS Cole, an operative involved in the bombings of our embassies in Kenya and Tanzania, and individuals involved in other attacks that have taken the lives of innocent civilians across the world.[64]

Just hours before the president's speech, the U.S. Army released its new rules for the treatment of prisoners that banned "degrading, humiliating" treatment on detainees, including "water-boarding."[65] However, the new rules on interrogation did not apply to CIA activities.

Despite the president's acknowledgment of the CIA rendition program and secret prisons, the issue would not go away, straining U.S. diplomatic relations with its allies. Daniel Coats, U.S. ambassador to Germany, informed the German interior minister that the CIA had wrongfully imprisoned one of its citizens, Khaled al-Masri, releasing him after five months of interrogation in Afghanistan as an "erroneous rendition."[66] In January 2007 German prosecutors issued arrest warrants for 13 CIA operatives suspected of kidnapping al-Masri from the Balkans in 2004, flying him to Afghanistan for torture and then, discovering he was the wrong suspect, dumping him on a hillside in Albania.[67]

Italian prosecutors sought the indictment of 25 CIA operatives and a U.S. Air Force colonel, along with Italy's former intelligence head, for the 2003 kidnapping of militant Egyptian cleric Abu Omar from the streets of Milan.[68] Admiral Gianfranco Battelli, former head of Italy's military intelligence agency, testified in a deposition on how the CIA station chief in Rome approached him a few days after the September 11, 2001, attack. The CIA official requested assistance in kidnapping terrorist suspects and flying them to other countries for interrogation. General Gustavo Pignero, another top Italian intelligence officer, recalled: "It was clear that this was an aggressive search project (for ten dangerous terrorist suspects in Europe), that their (CIA) willingness to employ illicit means was clear."[69]

After a long governmental investigation, Canadian Prime Minister Stephen Harper formally apologized to Canadian citizen Maher Azar—and agreed to give him $9 million in compensation—after the CIA seized him from a New York airport and rendered him to Syria, where Azar was tortured.[70] The compensation sought to end Azar's legal action blaming Canadian intelligence agencies for participation in the abduction. The head of the Royal Canadian Mounted Police resigned over the issue.

The CIA operations led to the seizure of at least 10 European citizens or legal immigrants, with 4 renditions occurring in Sweden, Macedonia, and Italy, with the assistance of European intelligence agencies in 5 cases. By 2006 a dozen countries had initiated legislative inquiries into the involvement of their spy agencies in the CIA's rendition program. John B. Bellinger III, the State Department's legal adviser, acknowledged that the European outcry over the rendition operations have "undermined cooperation and intelligence activities," while heightening suspicion and anti-Americanism in Europe.[71]

Big Brother is Listening

On December 16, 2005, the *New York Times* revealed that the Bush administration had been spying on "hundreds, perhaps thousands, of people inside the United States without warrants over the past three years" to uncover links to al Qaeda terrorists.[72] The monitoring by the National Security Agency (NSA) of phone calls and e-mail messages occurred without the approval of the special court Congress created in the 1978 Foreign Intelligence Surveillance Act (FISA) to approve warrants for such domestic spying. At any time up to 500 Americans might be spied upon by NSA, which by statute normally limited its message intercepts to overseas threats. The *New York Times* delayed publication of the story for a year, after administration officials argued its release would alert possible terrorists of the communication monitoring.

After the disclosure of the program, President George W. Bush admitted he had authorized the NSA to intercept communications to Americans from overseas suspected terrorists "to detect and prevent" another terrorist attack on the United States.[73] Bush stated he had reauthorized this "vital tool" against terrorism over

30 times since the 9/11 attacks, with congressional leaders briefed on the activities more than a dozen times. The president claimed his authority derived from the Joint Authorization for Use of Military Force (AUMF) passed immediately after the 9/11 attacks as well as his constitutional commander-in-chief powers.

Attorney General Alberto Gonzales and General Michael Hayden, the former head of NSA, held a press briefing to describe the legal basis of the warrantless surveillance program. Gonzales asserted the AUMF resolution established statutory authority "to engage in this kind of signals intelligence."[74] He argued that in the 2004 *Hamdi* case the Supreme Court's majority opinion, written by Justice Sandra Day O'Connor, found that even though detention was not mentioned in the AUMF resolution, detention of combatants was fundamental to conducting war, and hence legal although not specifically authorized. Gonzales maintained: "For the same reason, we believe signals intelligence is even more a fundamental incident of war," and thus authorized by Congress.

However, Gonzales ignored the core of the *Hamdi* decision that rejected the administration's claim that Hamdi, an American "enemy combatant," could not invoke his constitutional right to due process. Justice O'Connor wrote: "We have long since made clear that *a state of war is not a blank check for the President* when it comes to the rights of the Nation's citizens" (author's emphasis).[75]

General Hayden argued that while the Foreign Intelligence Surveillance Act (FISA) has been helpful, "it doesn't provide the speed and the agility" required for coping with the new threat of terrorism.[76] He maintained that the administration needed a more "aggressive" program devised to detect, deter, and demolish planned attacks. Hayden contended: "FISA involves marshaling arguments; FISA involves looping paperwork around," a process too slow to deal with immediate threats. When a reporter asked why the administration did not seek new authorization to avoid those delays, Gonzales replied that certain members of Congress advised "that was not something we could likely get, certainly not without jeopardizing the existence of the program."

On February 6, 2006, Attorney General Gonzales testified before the U.S. Senate Judiciary Committee on the domestic spying program, which he had earlier dubbed as NSA's "terrorist surveillance program."[77] The attorney general justified the surveillance by emphasizing that "this new kind of war" required taking all possible steps to detect and prevent any enemy plots. He described the domestic monitoring as "an early warning system designed for the 21st century," with the speed, agility, and secrecy necessary to fight the war with terrorists. In a later written response to a senator's question, the attorney general acknowledged that President Bush authorized the NSA surveillance program in October 2001—before his October 26 signing of the Patriot Act—but declined to give the exact date.[78]

In a town hall meeting in Cleveland, President Bush recalled how the idea of NSA surveillance of overseas calls to American citizens arose. In speaking to a number of frontline officials shortly after September 11, Bush asked: "[I]s there anything more we could be doing, given the current laws?"[79] NSA chief Hayden proposed a "hot pursuit" tactic of monitoring calls from suspected terrorists overseas to persons inside the United States to facilitate a quicker response to such threats. Hayden told the president that the FISA restrictions were slow, cumbersome, and designed for another era. Bush said he asked government attorneys about whether such a program would be legal, and they later concluded he could authorize such surveillance.

However, the plan to go ahead with domestic surveillance on U.S. citizens met major objections from NSA attorneys, who were worried about repeating the scandal of the 1970s when NSA garnered criticism for its domestic spying—resulting in passage of the 1978 FISA law. Two senior intelligence officials later revealed that a major internal struggle resulted, pitting NSA lawyers against Vice President Cheney and his counsel David Addington, both staunch advocates of the president's unlimited wartime powers as commander-in-chief. Cheney and Addington believed warrantless surveillance "could be done and should be done," relentlessly pushing the NSA lawyers to approve the plan and ignore the FISA statute.[80] Hayden succeeded in persuading the NSA attorneys to accept the proposal, but with the condition that one side of the phone call or e-mail must involve suspected terrorists in another country.

The White House decision-making, as in the approval of other extraordinary measures adopted for the "new kind of war," omitted key players. For example, Cheney and Addington excluded the Pentagon lawyer Richard Shiffrin, assigned responsibility to supervise the NSA lawyers, from the discussions. Shiffrin doubted that the NSA attorneys had sufficient expertise to challenge the contentions of Cheney and Addington about the president's constitutional war powers.

Vice President Cheney, NSA Director Hayden, and CIA Director Tenet met the Republican chairs and ranking Democratic members on the Senate and House Intelligence Committees in the vice president's office to brief them on the surveillance program on October 25, 2001, shortly after President Bush signed the new directive.[81] The White House later emphasized that Cheney announced the administration's decision—not asking for congressional permission. However, the leaders of the Intelligence Committees found themselves bound by secrecy and barred from discussing the program with staff or House and Senate colleagues. Thus, the administration strangled any effective congressional oversight—while proclaiming later that these secret, "gagged" briefings constituted congressional review.

Cheney vigorously defended the NSA surveillance program. In an address to the conservative Heritage Foundation, Cheney declared that if the wiretapping had been in place before 9/11, the Bush administration may have been able to thwart the September 11 terrorist attacks.[82] Speaking to the Conservative Political Action Conference on February 11, the vice president suggested the Republican Party should wield the surveillance program as a 2006 midterm election issue against the Democrats. In the spring Cheney told Navy midshipmen that members of Congress from both parties had received over a dozen briefings on the Terrorist Surveillance Program. "The reason I know this is that I'm the one who presided over most of those briefings."[83]

Members of Congress and civil rights advocates attacked the Bush administration for bypassing the FISA Court, established by Congress to secretly approve surveillance over American citizens on national security matters. The Congressional Research Service (CRS) drafted a legal brief analyzing President Bush's professed authority to conduct warrantless surveillance. The CRS attorneys observed that FISA contained three provisions for foreign intelligence surveillance without a court order: first, upon certification by the attorney general; second, emergency authorization of electronic surveillance for up to 72 hours while seeking approval from a FISA court judge; and lastly, electronic surveillance without a court order for 15 days following a declaration of war by Congress.[84]

The CRS brief concluded that FISA's statutory language and legislative history "reflect the Congress's stated intention to circumscribe any claim of inherent presidential authority to conduct electronic surveillance...to collect foreign intelligence information."[85] Furthermore, the FISA provision permitting surveillance for 15 days after a declaration of war demonstrated that Congress "seems clearly to have contemplated that FISA would continue to operate during war."[86] The CRS lawyers noted that the legal cases the Department of Justices cited to support the concept of the president's inherent power to order surveillance occurred *before* FISA was enacted.

Critics argued that the secret FISA court generally granted the government's requests for foreign intelligence wiretaps, rejecting only 5 of 18,748 requests since 1978.[87] Under the president's program, "only the presiding judge of the secret court was allowed to hear cases in which warrantless surveillance may have played a role."[88] During the first four years of warrantless surveillance, just the two federal judges who presided sequentially over the FISA Court knew about the program.

Both of the FISA Court judges raised questions about the constitutionality of the new NSA surveillance program. When U.S. District Judge Colleen Kollar-Kotelly became the presiding FISA court judge in May 2002, her complaint that warrantless surveillance might be providing information later presented to the FISA Court led to changes in the program. Henceforth, a high-ranking official had to certify—under threat of perjury—that "information presented to the FISA court was totally independent of any information gleaned in warrantless surveillance," to avoid tainting the FISA Court's proceedings.

On August 17, 2006, Detroit U.S. District Judge Anna Diggs Taylor ruled that the five-year-old Terrorist Surveillance Program was unconstitutional, violating the First and Fourth Amendments, the separation of powers doctrine, and the 1978 FISA statute. Judge Taylor wrote in her 43-page opinion: "It was never the intent of the Framers to give the President such unfettered control, particularly where his actions blatantly disregard the parameters clearly enumerated in the Bill of Rights."[89] Taylor emphasized: "There are no hereditary Kings in America and no powers not created by the Constitution. So all 'inherent powers' must derive from that Constitution."[90] Vice President Cheney labeled Judge Taylor's decision "an indefensible act of judicial overreaching" that tied the hands of the president in the conduct of the war on terror.[91]

In 2007 a major fight within the administration came to light revealing serious divisions among Bush officials over the legality of the NSA domestic surveillance program. Justice Department officials had refused to reauthorize new features of the NSA domestic surveillance program, which they considered illegal, igniting the administration's internal conflict.

A dramatic showdown occurred on March 10, 2004, at the hospital where Attorney General John Ashcroft lay in intensive care recovering from gallstone surgery. Alerted by Ashcroft's wife, Deputy Attorney General James Comey raced to the hospital to prevent then-White House Counsel Gonzales and Bush's Chief of Staff Andy Card from pressuring the ailing Ashcroft to override his staff and reauthorize the program. Ashcroft rallied enough to assert his support of the

Justice Department's position. Comey testified: "I was angry...I thought I just witnessed an effort to take advantage of a very sick man, who did not have the powers of the attorney because they had been transferred to me."

Shortly thereafter, Comey, FBI Director Robert Mueller and Ashcroft's Chief of Staff David Ayres prepared to resign from the Justice Department in a mass protest, but Attorney General Ashcroft sent word to wait until he recuperated sufficiently to tender his resignation with them. On March 12 Card invited acting-Attorney General Comey to the White House, but Comey insisted Solicitor General Ted Olson attend the meeting as a witness. After the White House discussion, Comey met privately with President Bush in the president's study for a "full exchange" on the issue. President Bush soon authorized the changes insisted upon by the Justice Department officials to ensure the legality of the NSA surveillance program.

The White House could ill-afford the publicity of President George W. Bush's top Justice and FBI officials collectively resigning to protest a controversial, possibly illegal NSA domestic spying program. The media would immediately compare the resignations to President Nixon's "Saturday Night Massacre" on October 20, 1973, when Attorney General Elliot Richardson and Deputy Attorney General William Ruckelshaus resigned rather than fire independent special prosecutor Archibald Cox during the Watergate scandal.

Creating a New Paradigm

President George W. Bush's decisions to essentially ignore the Third Geneva Convention, to permit the extreme rendition of terrorist suspects, to maintain CIA "black site" prisons, and to authorize NSA to conduct domestic surveillance in waging the war on terror represented significant steps in the administration's campaign against al Qaeda and Osama bin Laden. Through the lens of Allison's Rational Actor Model it becomes clear that the perceived threat of a follow-up attack on American soil by al Qaeda operatives armed with a weapon of mass destruction propelled these actions.

Vice President Cheney's One Percent Doctrine aimed at preventing terrorists from acquiring a nuclear capability, but the anthrax attacks on Washington offices raised fears of biological weapons. Cheney, overseeing intelligence and WMD matters for the administration, stressed: "It's important we have a sense of urgency." The Federal Bureau of Investigation (FBI), trained to obtain admissible evidence for criminal prosecutions, succumbed to the CIA's demand for extreme interrogation procedures to obtain immediate results. However, FBI agents had concluded that a persuasive approach that developed a relationship with a prisoner yielded more useful intelligence.[92] A FBI official explained: "We don't believe in coercion..... Our goal is to get information and we try to gain the prisoners' trust."[93] But the impatient White House backed CIA efforts to quickly obtain the elusive actionable intelligence.

Nevertheless, a March 9, 2007, report by the Justice Department's Inspector General Glenn A. Fine, found that the FBI also employed shortcuts over three years, disregarding privacy safeguards when using national security letters to obtain telephone records, e-mail addresses, employment records, and the credit history of Americans deemed relevant to terrorism investigations.[94] The Patriot Act stipulated that national security letters were not subject to judicial review or public disclosure. But the investigation found the FBI substantially underreported the number of national security letters their agents employed, often issuing false claims or inaccurately asserting a subpoena had been requested. Both Attorney General Gonzales and FBI Director Robert Mueller apologized to Congress for the misuse of the exigent circumstance letters.

The debate within the administration provided President Bush with policy alternatives, with Secretary Powell and the State Department's legal adviser suggesting a course of action toward al Qaeda and Taliban detainees less likely to provoke international criticism of the United States for abandoning the Geneva Convention. The president made a value-maximizing decision in an effort to collect critical intelligence that might better safeguard American citizens in the short term. Bush shunted aside warnings of the long-term consequences of weakening the ban on torture in the Geneva Convention, extreme renditions, and secret overseas prisons that subsequently provoked international protests after revelations of prisoner abuse at Iraq's Abu Ghraib prison. The decisions also reinforced the world community's hostile view of the Bush administration's unilateralist approach to international affairs, undermining future diplomatic and military support.

President Bush's hot rhetoric toward the "evil ones" symbolized his call for a dramatic new tack in the war on terror, contributing to the radical changes in U.S. policy. The shifts also reflected Bush's propensity to accept risk in confronting this new type of enemy, allowing the president to follow his gut instincts through these uncharted waters. Vice President Cheney's advocacy of the "One Percent Doctrine" and a New Paradigm of an unfettered commander-in-chief provided fertile soil for such controversial policies in advancing the war on terror.

Bush liked to personalize matters. For example, he designed for himself a chart with pictures of the top al Qaeda leaders which he could mark out with an "X" when killed or captured. CIA analysts found President Bush preferred making broad, complex matters personal, connecting them "to his gut, his instinct, for swift decisions."[95] Bush's decision style, favoring bold actions, undermined the impact of legal arguments that stressed the damaging long-term effect of such policies on the safety of American troops, weakening of disciplined procedures for interrogation, and diplomatic "high ground" advantage of adhering to international norms. However, as the CIA's counterterrorist director Cofer Black testified at a 2002 joint hearing of the House and Senate Intelligence Committees: "After 9/11 the gloves came off."[96]

Allison's Government Organization Model lens revealed strong differences within the Pentagon over the Geneva Convention's restrictions on the treatment of prisoners of war. Secretary Rumsfeld, critical of the CIA's failure to produce actionable intelligence, dramatically increased the role of Special Forces in gathering intelligence on terrorist networks. In early 2002 President Bush authorized the Defense Department to create a top-secret special-access program (SAP) of Special Forces teams to snatch high-value al Qaeda operatives throughout the world for intense interrogation or assassination. According to a former intelligence official, the rules were: "Grab whom you must. Do what you want."[97] The clandestine program reflected "forward-leaning" Rumsfeld's ongoing campaign to prod senior uniformed officers to accept more risks. The defense secretary scorned the international outcry over the U.S. rejection of the Geneva Convention's guidelines for the treatment of al Qaeda and Taliban prisoners, calling the protests only "isolated pockets of international hyperventilation."[98]

Deputy Assistant Attorney General Yoo assured White House Counsel Gonzales on August 1, 2002, that the methods used to interrogate al Qaeda prisoners would not violate the 1984 Torture Convention. He opined that persons undertaking such actions could not be prosecuted under the International Criminal Court, "although it would be impossible to control the actions of a rogue prosecutor or judge."[99]

The White House queried the Justice Department over the standards constituting torture under the 1984 Torture Convention. Assistant Attorney General Jay Bybee replied that interrogations outside of the United States must be of an extreme nature to fall under the Convention's definition of torture. Bybee declared: "Physical pain amounting to torture must be equivalent in intensity to the pain accompanying serious physical injury, such as organ failure, impairment of bodily function, or even death."[100] Purely mental pain had to create "significant psychological harm of significant duration," lasting months or years.

Bybee also proffered a broad, unrestricted interpretation of the president's commander-in-chief power, especially during a war resulting from a direct attack upon America. Since information gleaned from interrogations might prevent future enemy attacks, any legal effort "that interferes with the President's direction of such core war matters as the detention and interrogation of enemy combatants thus would be unconstitutional."[101]

Secretary of Defense Rumsfeld approved on December 2, 2002, a list of "counter-resistance techniques" for the Army's Joint Task Force 170 interrogators to overcome the defiance of al Qaeda and Taliban detainees at Guantanamo Bay.[102] The guidelines permitted hooding of prisoners, exploitation of phobias (fear of dogs), and deprivation of light and auditory stimuli, all coercive techniques forbidden in the Army Field Manual. However, the new DoD rules required special permission for Category III techniques for high-value "exceptionally resistant" prisoners: threats implying imminent death or great pain for him and/or his family; exposure to cold weather or water; and the controversial employment of "wet towel and dripping water to induce the misperception of suffocation (water-boarding)."

Two weeks before the United States invaded Iraq, Secretary Rumsfeld released a memorandum soon dubbed the "Torture Memo." The Justice Department legal brief, written for the Defense Department, rejected the notion that Congress could limit the employment of interrogation techniques by the president in his role as commander-in-chief. "Congress may no more regulate the President's ability to detain and interrogate enemy combatants than it may regulate his ability to direct troop movements on the battlefield."[103]

The Torture Memo argued the relevance of the "necessity defense" when confronting the evil of terrorism. The memo restated the administration's legal stance that none of the provisions of the Third Geneva Convention applied to al Qaeda and Taliban detainees. The Department of Justice's guidelines concluded: "Customary international law cannot bind the Executive Branch under the Constitution, because it is not a federal law." Furthermore, the Torture Statute did not apply to the conduct of U.S. personnel at Guantanamo.

Considerable dissent arose within the Pentagon, especially by the Judge Advocate General (JAG) attorneys in each of the services, over the new, aggressive torture standards that abandoned traditional Geneva Convention restrictions. A memo by Alberto J. Mora, general counsel for the Navy, chronicled a three-year effort to halt what he characterized as an illegal policy of cruel torture for terrorist suspects. Mora argued that circumventing the Geneva Convention represented "an implicit invitation to abuse."[104] He warned such actions were unlawful, dangerous, and erroneous in their legal reasoning, which could one day subject U.S. military personnel to subsequent criminal prosecution.

Nevertheless, the top Pentagon officials ignored Mora's warnings, aided by the machinations of the Vice President's Counsel David Addington. Even though the vice president held no statutory role in the military chain of command, Addington's tenacity, knowledge of national security legal issues, and strong backing from Cheney meant he "played a central part in virtually all of the Administration's legal strategies, including interrogation and detainee policies."[105]

Top Pentagon officials approved a secret detention policy without the knowledge of Mora and the other military legal advisers. This policy granted "legal indemnity to engage in cruel interrogations, and, when the Commander-in-Chief deemed it necessary, in torture."[106] These same extreme interrogation techniques, employed by General Geoffrey Miller at Guantanamo, later were applied in Iraq. Sent to Baghdad to review interrogation procedures, Miller recommended that U.S. military commanders put military intelligence in charge of the Abu Ghraib prison to elicit more actionable intelligence on the growing Iraqi insurgency. The subsequent Taguba Report on prisoner abuse at Abu Ghraib noted that General Miller suggested that "detention operations must act as an enabler for interrogation."[107]

Graham Allison's Governmental Politics lens pointed out how the administration's "action channel" in developing the policy for the harsh interrogation of al Qaeda and Taliban detainees excluded JAG lawyers from the military services, the Department of State, and other key officials. The Governmental Politics Model underscored the pivotal role of Vice President Cheney and his counsel David Addington in overriding the constraints in the Third Geneva Convention and U.S. laws. Admiral Stansfield Turner, President Jimmy Carter's CIA director, caustically called Cheney the "vice president for torture."[108]

The Navy's Chief Counsel Mora noted that State Department lawyers, familiar with the laws of war, treaties, and Nuremburg trials, were left out of the deliberations on this sensitive and controversial issue. "The State Department wasn't just on the back of the bus—it was left off the bus."

Retired Army Colonel Larry Wilkerson, Secretary of State Powell's chief of staff during Bush's first term, later asserted: "There's no question in my mind where the philosophical guidance and the flexibility in order to do so (torture detainees) originated—in the vice president of the United States' office."[109] Wilkerson believed that Cheney provided political cover for Secretary Rumsfeld to have the freedom of action to utilize cruel torture techniques in the interrogations of detainees.

After leaving the State Department, Wilkerson charged that a cabal controlled U.S. foreign policy: "What I saw was a cabal between the vice president of the United States, Richard Cheney, and the secretary of defense, Donald Rumsfeld."[110] Wilkerson faulted President Bush for allowing the Cheney-Rumsfeld cabal to take charge, because Bush was "not versed in international relations and not too much interested."

New Yorker reporter Jane Mayer traced the close collaboration of Cheney and Addington, Cheney's counsel in the Office of the Vice President and then chief of staff, in promoting a New Paradigm or unitary executive theory, a debatable constitutional interpretation that stressed "the idea that congressional checks on the president's power are limited."[111] The two men worked together since the 1980s and shared a common view, in the aftermath of the Watergate scandal, that Congress had usurped or undermined the president's constitutional power as commander-in-chief. The shock of the 9/11 terrorist attacks accorded Cheney and Addington the opportunity to implement this concept when crafting the administration's aggressive policies on torture, surveillance, and military tribunals.

Mayer concluded that since none of the top national security team members held law degrees—Bush, Cheney, Powell, Rumsfeld, or Rice—Addington's expertise in national security law stampeded the administration into embracing the New Paradigm following the al Qaeda terrorist attacks. Although Gonzales had served Bush during his governorship, the White House Counsel's lack of knowledge on national security issues permitted Addington to dominate White House deliberations on the relevance of the Geneva Convention, according to a former high-ranking administration lawyer.[112] The Bush administration's memos dealing with torture, often drafted in secret, sidestepped the "customary interagency debate and vetting procedures." Addington purposely excluded key officials and their legal advisers in the formulation of these new polices. An administration lawyer felt that the January 2002 legal memo dismissing the Geneva Conventions as quaint and obsolete in the war on terror, although signed by Gonzales, reflected the efforts of Addington to give the president "maximum flexibility."

President Bush signed the executive order creating military commissions (November 13, 2001) to try al Qaeda and Taliban detainees without consulting Secretary of State Powell; NSC adviser Rice; the top lawyer at the CIA; Michael Chertoff, the head of the Justice Department's criminal division; John Bellinger II, the NSC legal adviser and deputy White House Counsel; or any of the chief JAG lawyers in the military.[113] Rear Admiral Donald Guter, the Navy's top JAG officer until June 2002, emphasized that he and other JAG experts on the laws of war "were marginalized."

Graham Allison's decision-making analytical approach emphasized that the personalities of key actors represented the "hard core" of the Governmental Politics Model. Certainly Vice President Cheney (aided by his counsel David Addington) played a crucial role in the Bush administration's adoption of the aggressive "new kind of war" tactics discussed in this chapter. During a trip from Pakistan to Oman in December 2005, Cheney acknowledged to reporters on Air Force Two: "I believe in a strong, robust executive authority, and I think that the world we live in demands it."[114] The vice president stated that although he respected Congress, "I do believe that especially in the day and age we live in, the nature of the threats we face, the president of the United States needs to have his constitutional powers unimpaired, if you will, in terms of the conduct of national security policy." Cheney argued that Watergate and the Vietnam War in the 1970s served "to erode the authority I think the president needs to be effective, especially in the national security area."

Jack Goldsmith, who headed the Office of Legal Counsel in the Justice Department, challenged the legality of the so-called torture memos and tried to convince the White House to get congressional authority for NSA domestic surveillance. He concluded, after a series of court decisions undercutting the Bush administration's claim of unfettered presidential authority, thus: "The central irony is that people whose explicit goal was to expand presidential power have diminished it."

President Bush never signed any authorization concerning interrogation tactics, nor was he officially briefed on interrogation methods, according to the CIA's Office of Inspector General.[115] CIA Director Tenet gave his briefings on interrogations to Vice President Cheney, NSC Adviser Rice, Attorney General Ashcroft, and White House Counsel Gonzales. The CIA also defined interrogation tactics as encompassed under their normal "intelligence collection" duties, not as covert action that required a presidential finding.[116] These procedures provided the president with "deniability" on this controversial issue. Thus, when the Abu Ghraib prisoner abuse scandal became public in June 2004, Bush could declare: "We do not condone torture. I have never ordered torture. I will never order torture."[117]

Chapter Eight

March to War: Vision or Vengeance?

In my judgment you don't contain Saddam Hussein.
You don't hope that therapy will somehow change his evil mind.

The September 11, 2001, al Qaeda terrorist attacks upon America resulted in President George W. Bush dramatically altering the course of his administration's foreign policy from the traditional approach of Republican realists, like his father. The first step in President Bush's proclaimed war on terror, an innovative Central Intelligence Agency (CIA) and a U.S. military assault on Osama bin Laden and his Taliban hosts in Afghanistan, won broad support in the United States and abroad. Angry public calls for retaliation and the immediate offers of military assistance from America's North Atlantic Treaty Organization (NATO) allies and friends made uncertain only the timing of the initial strikes upon Afghanistan.

The second step in the global war on terrorism proved far more controversial: a preemptive invasion of Iraq to end the threat posed by Saddam Hussein's alleged weapons of mass destruction (WMD) and links to al Qaeda terrorists. No longer would U.S. foreign policy focus on the limited realist goal of the containment of Saddam Hussein. The Bush administration would pursue an aggressive foreign policy aimed at achieving "regime change" in Baghdad.

The administration's concentration upon removing Saddam Hussein from power reflected a perception that the 9/11 attacks provided an opportunity for President Bush to advance his mission against the worldwide threat of terrorism, pursue the muscular agenda of neoconservatives within the Bush administration, and respond to the president's deep hatred of Saddam Hussein for his 1993 attempt to assassinate Bush's revered father.[1] However, often bitter and conflicting memories of the aftermath of the senior President Bush's "victory" over Saddam Hussein in the 1991 Gulf War also colored the post-9/11 debate on Iraq.

Victory or Unfinished Business?

The 1991 Gulf War, launched by President George H.W. Bush in response to Iraq's brutal aggression against Kuwait on August 2, 1990, represented the high point in the senior Bush's White House years; Bush's job approval rating skyrocketed to 89 percent. President Bush won accolades from all quarters for his diplomatic orchestration of the UN Security Council and congressional resolutions supporting military action to end Iraq's occupation of Kuwait.

The Iraqi dictator threatened President Bush that if U.S. troops engaged Iraq's war-hardened armed forces, America would experience the "mother of all battles." Despite Saddam Hussein's bravado, Bush crafted a broad international coalition which, combined with the Pentagon's creative air and ground strategy, defeated Iraqi tanks and armed forces after only 100 hours of combat. American airpower battered Iraq's defense of dug-in tanks, Iraqi soldiers surrendered *en masse* to swiftly advancing coalition troops, and thousands of Iraqi soldiers retreated in disarray after sustaining major casualties.

The successful 32-nation international coalition included armed forces from neighboring Middle East states: Saudi Arabia (118,000), Egypt (40,000), United Arab Emirates (40,000), Syria (17,000), and Oman (25,000). Great Britain provided 43,000 and France 18,000 troops, in addition to their naval and air support. The United States deployed 540,000 troops and suffered 148 casualties.[2] In addition, allied governments paid almost 80 percent of the estimated $82 billion cost of the war, with Saudi Arabia contributing $29 billion, Kuwait $22 billion, and Japan $13 billion.

The senior President Bush's studious effort to avoid politicizing the Gulf War issue in the 1990 mid-year election also resulted in solid bipartisan backing to drive Saddam Hussein's military from Kuwait after the conflict began. Thus, President George H.W. Bush's impressive 1991 Gulf War victory could have served as a guide for his son's military and diplomatic campaign against Saddam Hussein's armed forces 12 years later. Indeed, Marine General Anthony Zinni, the former chief of the Middle East Command, maintained that the senior President Bush's model for post–Cold War foreign intervention, with its "remarkable coalition" and international framework, should have been embraced by the second Bush administration in dealing with Saddam Hussein.[3]

The elder President Bush skillfully developed bipartisan and public support, despite the initial skepticism of Democrats. When Iraq occupied Kuwait in August 1990, a Gallup poll found that over two-thirds (68 percent) of respondents opposed immediate "direct U.S. military intervention in Kuwait."[4] This aversion to war in Kuwait contributed to the elder President Bush's rhetorical efforts to demonize Saddam Hussein to generate public support for the Gulf War. He labeled the Iraqi dictator as a man of evil, "Hitler revisited," and a despot whose actions were worse than Hitler's.[5] Then, when polls still showed only one in four Americans favored war in Kuwait, Bush sought counsel from his advisers. Pollster Bob Teeter counseled the president that he had employed too many themes.

Subsequent polls found public backing for the war rose when the administration framed the war's objective as preventing the dictator Saddam Hussein from acquiring nuclear weapons.[6] President George H.W. Bush declared in a November 20, 1990, address that "every day that passes brings Saddam Hussein one step closer to realizing his goal of a nuclear weapon arsenal." The younger President Bush adopted the same rhetorical tactic to boost public support for the second war with Iraq. The swift 1991 coalition victory over Saddam Hussein's forces, with minimal American losses, brought about a dramatic reversal in the polls, with 78 percent of respondents approving the Bush administration's decision to "go to war with Iraq in order to drive the Iraqis out of Kuwait."[7]

However, after the February 28, 1991, cease-fire with Iraq, a growing number of critics began to attack the Bush administration for its failure to march to Baghdad, capture Saddam Hussein, and prosecute the cruel Iraqi dictator for his war crimes. Nevertheless, President Bush and his realist National Security Adviser, retired General Brent Scowcroft, repeatedly defended the decision. In *A World Transformed* they emphasized that the American-led coalition had achieved the limited UN Security Council mandate of expelling Iraqi forces from Kuwait. Crossing into Iraq to capture Saddam Hussein would have fractured the coalition, increased American casualties, and compelled the United States to occupy a hostile country.[8] The former president opposed the idea of "mission creep."[9] Scowcroft emphasized in a 2002 TV interview: "The objective in the Gulf War was not to take out Saddam. It was to liberate Kuwait."[10] The younger Bush acknowledged to Rice during the 2000 campaign that his father "did the right thing at the time," considering the limited UN mandate.[11]

The senior President Bush later admitted that after the defeat of the Iraqi armed forces in Kuwait, "we thought Saddam Hussein would leave power," overthrown by the Iraqi military. He explained that the "miscalculation" grew from an underestimation of Hussein's brutality toward his own people in suppressing a Shiite and Kurd uprising in the wake of his defeat in Kuwait.[12] Ironically, the elder Bush's secretary of defense at the time, Dick Cheney, also defended the administration's decision not to attack Baghdad. Cheney declared the United States should not act as "an imperialist power, willy-nilly moving into capitals in that part of the world, taking down governments."[13]

The Neoconservatives' Moment

Despite the impressive Desert Storm battlefield victory, an April 1991 Gallup Poll found that a strong majority (57 percent) of Americans felt the cease-fire in the Gulf War had been ordered too soon.[14] In mid-August 1992, on the eve of the presidential election, almost two-thirds (65 percent) of respondents supported U.S. forces resuming military action against Iraq to force Hussein from power.[15]

Criticism of the first Bush administration's failure to topple Saddam Hussein's regime, particularly after the Iraqi dictator brutally crushed the uprisings of Shiite Muslims in southern Iraq and Kurds in the north, fueled a growing rift within the Republican Party between traditional realists and neoconservatives. In a PBS interview Richard Perle, former assistant secretary of defense in the Reagan administration, acknowledged that he was "uncomfortable" with the Iraqi regime even during the eight years of Reagan-Bush *realpolitik* collaboration with Saddam Hussein aimed at preventing Iranian troops from defeating Iraq. "(T)he right course immediately after the end of that war would have been to say to Saddam, now we've had enough of you, and we're not gonna to tolerate it."[16] Tenet later recounted how Perle, the day after the 9/11 attacks, startled the CIA chief by telling him: "Iraq has to pay a price for what happened yesterday. They bear responsibility."[17] Tenet was focused on al Qaeda as the culprit.

Paul Wolfowitz, who worked under then-Defense Secretary Cheney in the senior Bush's Pentagon during the Gulf War, became the leading neoconservative advocating war with Iraq. However, Wolfowitz confessed that he did not support marching into Iraq to capture Saddam Hussein at the end of Operation Desert Storm: "I don't think we needed to go to Baghdad."[18] He shared President Bush's surprise "that Saddam managed to survive a defeat of that magnitude." Indeed, no senior member of President George H.W. Bush's foreign policy team favored going to Baghdad.[19]

However, Wolfowitz blasted the first Bush administration for permitting Saddam Hussein to fly helicopter gunships against the revolts of the Iraqi Shiites and Kurds. Wolfowitz increasingly voiced dismay at President Bush's failure to backup his idealistic rhetoric of February 15, 1991—inviting Iraqis to "take matters into their own hands, to force Saddam Hussein the dictator to step aside"—with forceful American military steps to protect the insurgents.[20] But Wolfowitz admitted in 1994 that a full-scale occupation of Iraq would have been very difficult: "Even if easy initially, it is unclear how or when it would have ended."[21]

The memories of Saddam Hussein's brutal suppression of the 1991 revolt, combined with worries about Iraq's weapons of mass destruction, provoked Wolfowitz to declare in 1997: "It was a grave mistake not to provide such support when Iraqis rose up against Saddam in 1991."[22] Wolfowitz rejected the containment strategy embraced by the senior Bush and the Clinton administration, arguing the overall U.S. strategy should seek "the liberation of Iraq from his tyranny."

In a 1994 assessment of Clinton's first year in office, Wolfowitz faulted the Democratic president for doing "virtually nothing to call Iraq to account for its renewed claims on Kuwait, its border incursions, its oppression of Shia in the south, or its war crimes in Kuwait."[23] He later mocked President Clinton's retaliation against Saddam Hussein for the Iraqi regime's April 1993 attempted assassination of former President Bush during a visit to Kuwait. Wolfowitz labeled the night strike on the Iraqi intelligence headquarters with Tomahawk missiles as only a "pinprick use of force."[24]

In a 1999 letter in *Foreign Affairs*, Wolfowitz and former Democratic Congressman Steven Solarz argued that the "United States should be prepared to commit ground forces to protect a sanctuary in southern Iraq where the opposition could safely mobilize."[25] Saddam Hussein had conceded substantial control over northern Iraq to the Kurds with "very modest American efforts," thus they contended a U.S. protected sanctuary in the south would yield even more territory to anti-Hussein Iraqis. Nevertheless, Wolfowitz and Solarz expressed the caveat that "a much more direct commitment of U.S. force" might be required as the resistance spread.

Wolfowitz strongly backed the exile Iraqi National Congress (INC) president, Ahmed Chalabi. In 1998 Chalabi told a Senate hearing: "Give the Iraqi National Congress a base protected from Saddam's tanks, give us the temporary support we need to feed and house and care for the liberated population, and we will give you a free Iraq, an Iraq free of weapons of mass destruction."[26] General Zinni derisively dismissed this strategy as the "Bay of Goats" plan, destined to fail like the CIA-orchestrated Bay of Pigs invasion of Castro's Cuba in 1961.[27]

The outline of the neoconservatives' post–Cold War national security strategy, following the Persian Gulf defeat of Saddam Hussein's forces, first emerged in a 46-page draft of the 1992 Defense Planning Guidance, when Dick Cheney headed the Pentagon. Neoconservative Wolfowitz, assisted by Lewis "Scooter" Libby, supervised a draft of the Defense Planning Guidance, which someone leaked to the press. The document bluntly declared: "Our first objective is to prevent the re-emergence of a new rival."[28]

The Planning Guidance added: "If necessary, the United States must be prepared to take unilateral action," perhaps bolstered by *ad hoc* coalitions. There was no mention of collective action through the United Nations. The post–Cold War plan ignited a firestorm of protests, forcing the senior Bush administration to issue a watered-down version of the draft Defense Guidance. Nevertheless, the core ideas reemerged in George W. Bush's September 17, 2002, *National Security Strategy*, following the 9/11 attacks.

Two other neoconservatives, William Kristol (often labeled the "godfather" of neoconservatism) and Robert Kagan, called for the establishment of an American "benevolent global hegemony."[29] They argued that a neoReagan policy of military supremacy and moral confidence after the Cold War represented "the only reliable defense against a breakdown of peace and international order." The authors asserted that a natural harmony existed between America's moral goals and fundamental national interests, attacking the prudence of traditional conservatives for backing a deterrence policy that manifested "cowardice and dishonor." Kristol, who had served as Vice President Dan Quayle's chief of staff, bellicosely told a reporter in 2000: "What's the point of being the greatest, most powerful nation in the world and not having an imperial role?"[30]

One year after the neoconservatives founded the Project for the New American Century (PNAC), they sent an open letter on January 26, 1998, to President Clinton urging that he adopt a strategy aimed at "the removal of Saddam Hussein's regime from power."[31] They rejected the policy of containing Iraq, declaring America "can no longer depend on our partners in the Gulf War coalition to continue to uphold the sanctions." The letter stressed that only the removal of Saddam Hussein from Baghdad would eliminate the threat posed by the Iraqi dictator's desire to acquire weapons of mass destruction. Of the 18 individuals signing the letter, 10 received positions in the administration of George W. Bush.

In 1998 the Republican-controlled Congress passed the Iraq Liberation Act. The House overwhelmingly approved the legislation (360 to 38) on October 15, followed two days later by unanimous Senate passage. President Clinton signed the measure into law on October 31. The 1998 Iraq Liberation Act declared that U.S. policy should support efforts "to remove the regime headed by Saddam Hussein from power in Iraq and to promote the emergence of a democratic government to replace it." Significantly, the measure did not authorize the employment of U.S. military forces. Instead, it provided financial assistance for Iraqi democratic opposition groups and funding for radio and television broadcasts into Iraq.

When Saddam Hussein kicked out UN weapons inspectors in 1998, President Clinton launched Operation Desert Fox. In the three-day attack on Iraq, 600 bombs and 415 cruise missiles fell on 97 suspected Iraqi weapons of mass destruction production or storage sites.[32] Indeed, then-CENTCOM Commander General Zinni concluded that the raids almost toppled the Hussein regime.

In *America Unbound*, Ivo Daalder and James Lindsay labeled Wolfowitz and Perle, with their neoconservative views, as "democratic imperialists." They advocated remaking the world in America's image, calling for the toppling of tyrants to create more democratic governments. However, Daalder and Lindsay underscored that initially a majority of Bush's security advisers were not democratic imperialists, especially Cheney and Rice. "They were instead assertive nationalists deeply skeptical of nation-building, especially when it involved the U.S. military."[33]

The 9/11 attacks permitted the neoconservatives to "hijack" the Bush administration's foreign policy, according to Stefan Halper and Jonathan Clarke.[34] After the horror of the al Qaeda terrorist attacks on America, "the neo-conservatives were ready with a detailed, plausible blueprint for the nation's response."[35] The authors identified 3 key themes developed during the 30-year evolution of the neoconservative movement: a religious belief in mankind's choices between good and evil, the will to exercise armed force to determine the relations among nation-states, and a focus on the Middle East and global Islam as pivotal to America's national interests.[36]

The neoconservatives' emphasis on America's moral right to pursue its interests through military means—as the world's only superpower—produced the preemption doctrine. The Bush administration's 2002 *National Security Strategy* baldly declared: "To forestall or prevent such hostile acts by our adversaries, the United States will, if necessary, act preemptively."

"The Iraq War started as a war of ideas," George Packer stated in *The Assassins' Gate*, forever linked to the advocacy of neoconservatives.[37] The rhetoric and policies of the Reagan administration became central to the neoconservatives in formulating their democratic idealism, resting upon the belief in the transformative power of American values throughout the world. Neoconservative Robert Kagan told Packer that the 9/11 attacks converted the neoconservatives' carefully nurtured ideas into the Bush administration's policies. "September 11 is the turning point. Not anything else. This is not what Bush was on September 10."[38] Kristol concurred with Kagan's assessment: "I think you could make the case that on Sept. 10, 2001, it's not clear that George W. Bush was, in any fundamental way, going in our direction in foreign policy."[39]

In 2002 neoconservative William Kristol testified before the Senate Foreign Relations Committee as chairman of the Project for the New American Century. Kristol responded, when asked about the second step in the war on terrorism: "The short answer is that Iraq is next."[40] He asserted that the Bush Doctrine should recast the Middle East from a breeding ground of terror into a region based on embracing the principles of liberal democracy—fostered through American military power. Kristol optimistically predicted that America and its allies "will be welcomed in Baghdad as liberators." He also claimed that the reconstruction of Iraq would be less difficult than rebuilding Afghanistan into a viable state.

The neoconservatives' agenda, with its dire warnings and rosy scenarios, thus morphed into the post 9/11 foreign policy of the Bush administration. President George W. Bush brashly adopted the neoconservatives' radical, muscular foreign policy stance, rejecting the prudent realist approach favored by his father and other traditional Republicans.

Next Step in War on Terror

When President George W. Bush entered the White House, Saddam Hussein and his Baathist party still held dictatorial control over Iraq, despite President Clinton's missile attacks in 1998 and repeated American and British air strikes in Iraq's "no-fly zones." International criticism was building over the adverse impact of UN sanctions upon the Iraqi people, while smugglers obtained lucrative Iraqi oil deals outside of the Oil-for-Food program of the United Nations. In February 2001, over six months *before* the terrifying September 11 terrorist attacks, a Gallup poll found that 85 percent of Americans expressed unfavorable views of Iraq, with Iraq rated below Iran and Libya on a list of 26 countries.[41] At his Senate confirmation hearing, Secretary of State Colin Powell told the Senate committee that

Iraq was "a failed state with a failed leader," pledging that the new administration would reenergize the UN sanctions against Saddam Hussein's regime.[42]

Treasury Secretary Paul O'Neill served as one of the principals on the National Security Council. At the Bush administration's first NSC meeting on January 30, 2001, Condoleezza Rice brought up the agenda topic: "How Iraq is destabilizing the region." A surprised Secretary O'Neill observed after the NSC meeting adjourned: "Ten days in, and it was about Iraq."[43] The treasury secretary noted that the NSC discussions focused on *how* to weaken or end Hussein's regime—not why Saddam, why now, and why was it central to U.S. interests.

The day after the 9/11 terrorist attacks on American soil, the NSC met on the afternoon of September 12 to formulate a policy response. Secretary of Defense Rumsfeld proposed attacking Iraq, not just al Qaeda. Secretary Powell responded, "The American people want us to do something about al Qaeda"—and al Qaeda maintained its base in Afghanistan.[44]

Indeed, a *TIME*/CNN poll on September 13, 2001, found 92 percent agreement that Osama bin Laden played a pivotal role in the horrific acts of terrorism.[45] But the survey also revealed that 78 percent of interviewed Americans (34 percent "very likely" and 44 percent "somewhat" responses) felt it was likely that Saddam Hussein was "personally involved in Tuesday's terrorist attacks." A September 21–22 Gallup poll reported that over two-thirds (68 percent) of respondents favored removing Saddam Hussein from power in Iraq.[46] When the Taliban government in Afghanistan crumbled in mid-December, a *Washington Post*-ABC News poll revealed that 61 percent of the respondents believed Saddam Hussein had to be removed from power for the war on terror to be a success.[47]

Richard Clarke, who served as counterterrorism chief to Presidents Bill Clinton and George W. Bush, chaired the Bush administration's immediate responses to the 9/11 attacks. Clarke was stunned on September 12 when he walked into a NSC meeting where, instead of dealing with al Qaeda, the discussion focused on Iraq. "Then I realized with almost a sharp physical pain that Rumsfeld and Wolfowitz were going to try to take advantage of this national tragedy to promote their agenda."[48] Rumsfeld argued: "There aren't any good targets in Afghanistan, and there are lots of good targets in Iraq." Clarke angrily responded that there were lots of targets everywhere, "but Iraq had nothing to do with it (9/11 attacks)."[49]

Even more disconcerting for Clarke, President Bush on September 12 pulled him into a room near the Situation Room and asked Clarke: "See if Saddam did this. See if he's linked in any way." The startled counterterrorism expert replied: "But, Mr. President, al Qaeda did this."[50] President Bush reiterated his order to look into Iraq's involvement and Clarke subsequently reviewed the intelligence concerning Saddam Hussein's possible involvement in the 9/11 terrorist attacks.

After Clarke reexamined the data, he consulted with CIA and FBI experts and they all signed off on a report to the president indicating there was no evidence linking the Iraq dictator to 9/11. Clarke later noted: "It got bounced and sent back saying, 'Wrong answer,'"[51] Rice's NSC deputy, neoconservative Steve Hadley, told CBS reporter Leslie Stahl that Clarke was wrong in his account of that brief meeting with President Bush. However, Stahl replied to Hadley, "We have two sources who tell us independently of Dick Clarke that there was this encounter. One of them was an actual witness."[52]

During a September 13 Pentagon briefing, Deputy Secretary of Defense Wolfowitz assumed the forward-leaning style favored by his boss, Don Rumsfeld. Wolfowitz brazenly declared that the war on terror would focus on "ending states who sponsor terrorism," a goal not approved by the president.[53] At the Saturday September 15 Camp David war cabinet meeting with the president, Wolfowitz argued that although Afghanistan could bog down U.S. troops in the mountains, Iraq represented a brittle, harsh regime that would easily fall to American forces. Wolfowitz estimated there was a 10–50 percent chance that Saddam Hussein was involved in the September 11 terrorist attacks.[54] Secretary Powell cautioned that America had many allies for a strike at Afghanistan, "but they will go away if you hit Iraq."[55]

One of the major impediments to ordering an immediate attack on Iraq, as Powell pointed out, was the Pentagon's lack of a military plan to achieve that goal. President Bush later told Woodward that he thought if the administration tried to attack both Afghanistan and Iraq, "the lack of focus would have been a huge risk."[56] Chief of Staff Andy Card informed the national security team the president wanted no more debate about Iraq. However, according to a senior administration official, a September 17 top-secret document, besides outlining a plan for the Afghanistan campaign, directed the Pentagon to begin planning a military option for the invasion of Iraq.[57] Vice President Cheney joined Powell, Tenet, and Card in opposing simultaneously military action against Afghanistan and Iraq during the early Camp David war cabinet meetings.

In an interview with Woodward, President George W. Bush expressed his aversion to following his father's foreign policy approach. Recognizing that Cheney, Powell, and Wolfowitz had served the elder Bush during the Gulf War, the president declared: "(W)e weren't going to let their previous experiences in this theater dictate a rational course for the new war."[58] Subsequent events suggest the president did not want to be tied to his father's model of waging war with Saddam Hussein—either in crafting a coalition for a looming conflict, winning the backing of the United Nations, or pursuing the limited objective of destroying Iraq's weapons of mass destruction—that stopped short of regime change.

On September 19 and 20 the Pentagon's Defense Policy Board, chaired by neoconservative Richard Perle, emphasized the importance of dealing with Iraq after ending the war with al Qaeda and the Taliban in Afghanistan. Both Secretary Rumsfeld and his deputy Wolfowitz attended the sessions. Former House Speaker Newt Gingrich, a neoconservative member of the board, stated: "If we don't use this as the moment to replace Saddam after we replace the Taliban, we are setting the stage for disaster."[59] Shortly afterward the Pentagon authorized former CIA Director James Woolsey, a neoconservative member of the board, to fly to London on a government plane to find evidence linking Saddam Hussein to the September 11 attacks. Meanwhile, President Bush assured Americans that his administration remained focused on Afghanistan "right now," but described the Iraqi leader as "an evil man" that the administration would carefully watch.[60]

Words of War

After the fall of the Taliban's Kandahar stronghold on December 7, with al Qaeda and Taliban forces fleeing into the mountains, the internal debate within the Bush administration once again turned toward Iraq. The silhouette of Bush's expansive war on terror appeared in the president's 2002 State of the Union Address when he targeted Iraq as a member of a dangerous "axis of evil," which also included Iran and North Korea.[61] The speech essentially kicked off the Bush administration's political offensive for the planned war with Iraq.

The 2002 State of the Union speech featured many of the key arguments and rhetorical techniques President George W. Bush would employ during the next 14 months to build public and congressional support for an Iraq war. The oratorical framework of Bush's case for war generally included the following elements: arousing the fears created by the horrific 9/11 terrorist attacks, warning about the growing danger of Islamic terrorism, highlighting Saddam Hussein's cruelty and aggression against neighboring states, emphasizing Iraq's relentless drive to acquire weapons of mass destruction, and finally implying linkage between the 9/11 attacks and the Iraqi dictator through alleged pre-9/11 contacts with al Qaeda members. On the eve of the U.S. invasion of Iraq in March 2003, 51 percent of Americans believed Saddam Hussein was involved in the 9/11 attacks.[62]

The president sent Vice President Cheney to the Middle East in March 2002 to obtain Arab support for military action against Iraq, depicting the 12-country trip as manifesting his diplomatic approach of consulting with allies and friends. Cheney declared during the journey: "The United States will not permit the forces of terror to gain the tools of genocide."[63]

However, the Bush administration's regime change approach to Iraq failed to gain the backing of Arab leaders. Shortly after Cheney's visit, the Arab League approved the Beirut Declaration that rejected "the threat of an aggression on some Arab countries, particularly Iraq."[64] Undaunted, President Bush asserted during an April visit of British Prime Minister Tony Blair to his Crawford, Texas, ranch that "the policy of my government is the removal of Saddam Hussein," with all options on the table.[65] Bush conceded, however, that the term "regime change sounds a lot more civil."

President Bush unveiled his acceptance of the neoconservative idea of preemptive attacks during his June 1, 2002, commencement address at West Point. He told cadets that the Cold War doctrines of containment and deterrence applied in some cases, but the nation required a new strategy to meet the threat of terrorism. Bush avowed: "Containment is not possible when unbalanced dictators with weapons of mass destruction can deliver those weapons or missiles or secretly provide them to terrorist allies."[66] The president declared that the United States could not base the war on terrorism on a defensive strategy; America must "disrupt his (the enemy's) plans, and *confront the worst threats before they emerge*" (author's emphasis).

During the early debate on war with Iraq, Bush rejected the charge that his administration simply postured on the issue. "We don't take a bunch of polls and focus groups to tell us what...we ought to do in the world," a slap at the Clinton administration.[67] However, in July 2002 the Bush administration formed the White House Iraq Group (WHIG) to create a Madison Avenue style media strategy to market a preemptive war with Iraq. Members of the WHIG group included Condoleezza Rice, Stephen Hadley, Scooter Libby, Dan Bartlett, Karen Hughes, Michael Gerson, Karl Rove, and White House's legislative lobbyist Nick Calio.[68]

The coordinator of the media campaign, Chief of Staff Card, told a reporter: "From a marketing point of view...you don't introduce new products in August."[69] The administration kicked off its campaign to sell war with Iraq on September 11, 2002, with President Bush delivering a national address from Ellis Island, framed by the illuminated Statue of Liberty behind the president.

The Bush administration's rush to war worried many traditional Republican realists. General Brent Scowcroft, the elder Bush's national security adviser, cautioned that although the United States military could "take him (Saddam Hussein) out," the task would not be a cakewalk. He warned that an Iraq invasion to achieve regime change would lead to a Middle East explosion, turning the region into a caldron.[70] The *Wall Street Journal* published Scowcroft's August 15 Op-Ed commentary, which also warned that an attack on Iraq would "seriously jeopardize, if not destroy, the global counterterrorism campaign we have undertaken."[71]

James Baker, the senior Bush's secretary of state, wrote a *New York Times* commentary warning that an Iraq war could harm other Americans interests, including relations with allies and Arab friends, as well as endanger the nation's top priority—the war on terror.[72] Baker urged President Bush to reject the counsel of his advisers who urged that the United States should "go it alone" or with only a few allies.

Vice President Cheney launched a counterattack upon critics of the administration's dogged advance to war. Cheney also sought to undermine Secretary Powell's growing collaboration with Prime Minister Tony Blair in urging President Bush to obtain UN Security Council approval for war with Iraq and renewed UN inspections for weapons of mass destruction. In an August 26 address to the Veterans of Foreign Wars (VFW) the vice president unequivocally declared, *"we now know"* that Saddam Hussein resumed his efforts to acquire nuclear weapons (author's emphasis).[73] Tenet later noted that the CIA had not cleared Cheney's VFW speech, which went beyond the intelligence community's facts.[74]

Cheney also scorned the call for renewed UN inspections in Iraq to search for weapons of mass destruction. The vice president charged that prior to 1998 "the inspectors missed a great deal," asserting that sending UN inspectors back to Iraq would create the false comfort that Saddam Hussein was again "back in his box." In a September 9 "Meet the Press" interview, Cheney admitted he could not "make a specific allegation that Iraq was somehow responsible for 9/11....I can't say that."[75] Nevertheless, the vice president mentioned that U.S. intelligence reports after September 11 disclosed "a number of contacts over the years," hinting at an unproven link between Saddam Hussein and the 9/11 attacks.

Observers began to remark upon Vice President Cheney's power within the administration as the "fulcrum of Bush's foreign policy."[76] Cheney had assembled a staff of 14 hard-line foreign policy specialists in the vice president's office to rival the NSC staff. He maneuvered to have his neoconservative Chief of Staff Scooter Libby appointed as assistant to the president so Libby could participate in NSC discussions. In 2002, 17 foreign presidents or prime ministers scheduled visits with Cheney in recognition of the vice president's influence in the Bush White House. Treasury Secretary O'Neill, who had worked with Cheney in the Nixon administration, portrayed Cheney as a puppeteer in how he manipulated policy, "all done with strings and suggestions. In the end, there are no fingerprints. No accountability."[77]

The Bush national security team, in a rare moment of agreement between Cheney and Powell, decided to have President Bush speak to the United Nations to insist that the Security Council enforce the 16 post–Gulf War resolutions imposed on Saddam Hussein to disarm, throwing the responsibility for eliminating Iraq's WMD back upon the UN Security Council.[78] On September 12, 2002, President George W. Bush addressed the UN General Assembly to present America's case against Saddam Hussein's violations of Iraq's UN obligations in the manner of a prosecutor. Bush stirred emotions through graphic depictions of Hussein's cruelty: "Wives are tortured in front of their husbands, children in the presence of their parents."[79] President Bush mentioned Hussein's attempt to assassinate "a former American President"—his father.

Bush issued a qualified warning about a nuclear-armed Saddam Hussein: "*Should* Iraq acquire fissile material, it would be able to build a nuclear weapon within a year" (author's emphasis). President Bush reminded the UN delegates that Saddam Hussein had pursued weapons of mass murder even while inspectors were inside Iraq's borders. Bush starkly concluded: "Saddam Hussein's regime is a grave and gathering danger." However, to the relief of the delegates who feared an imminent American preemptive attack on Iraq, Bush pledged to "work with the U.N. Security Council for the necessary resolutions." Neoconservatives high in the administration had attempted to delete the sentence calling for a UN resolution from the draft speech. Nevertheless, President Bush left the threat of unilateral U.S. military action on the table.

On August 11 the UN Security Council approved Resolution 1441 holding Iraq in "material breach" of its obligations under prior resolutions, granted Saddam Hussein a "final opportunity to comply" with the disarmament resolutions, and warned of serious consequences for noncompliance.[80] In an effort to thwart the U.S. drive to war, Saddam Hussein notified UN Secretary General Kofi Annan in late September that Iraq would allow UN weapons inspectors to return "without conditions." Pressure from Arab states trying to avert a war contributed to Hussein's concession, which only angered Bush administration officials who insisted upon unfettered access for UN weapons inspectors.[81]

The reluctance of congressional Democrats to accept the administration's draft of a new Homeland Security bill, because of weak worker protection provisions, enabled President Bush to initiate a preelection partisan assault questioning the patriotism of his opponents. Bush charged that the Democratic-controlled Senate was "more interested in special interests in Washington and not interested in the security of the American people."[82] The harsh attack reflected Bush political adviser Karl Rove's comments to the Republican National Committee in January 2002 that the administration would brandish the terrorism issue to win seats in the November election.[83] The Republican National Committee e-mailed a fund-raising letter to 2 million contributors on September 25 with a provocative headline that blared: "Democratic Senators Put Special Interests over Security," quoting the president's incendiary September 23 comment.[84]

The next step in the determined movement toward war involved the strategy of winning support from Congress for preemptive military action against the threat of Iraq's WMD, thereby gaining leverage over the UN Security Council to push a resolution authorizing the employment of force.[85] When a Gallup poll showed only a bare majority (53 percent) favored the invasion of Iraq with U.S. ground forces to remove Saddam Hussein from power, the Bush team hastily arranged for the president to deliver an October 7 speech in Cincinnati that ratcheted up the political pressure on Congress to approve the resolution authorizing war with Iraq. Responding to the insistence of the Bush administration, Congress had scheduled the votes on the resolution before the November mid-term election.

In the Cincinnati speech Bush evoked painful memories of the September 11 horror, when "America felt its vulnerability."[86] President Bush suggested a link between Saddam Hussein and al Qaeda by arguing that they shared a common enemy—the United States. The president alleged that Iraq and al Qaeda maintained "high-level contacts" over a decade, with Iraq training al Qaeda members in bomb-making and poisons, while providing medical treatment to a senior al Qaeda leader. Bush employed a worst-case scenario to direly warn that an Iraqi alliance with terrorists "*could* allow the Iraqi regime to attack America without leaving any fingerprints" (author's emphasis).

The president used what Secretary Rumsfeld called the potent nuclear "energizer" argument to stir fears of a nuclear-armed Saddam Hussein, but this time without any qualification.[87] "The evidence indicates that Iraq *is reconstituting its nuclear weapons program*" (author's emphasis). Bush described a frightening scenario that *if* Iraq obtained a small amount of highly enriched uranium, it could have a nuclear weapon in less than a year. Bush asked Congress to authorize American military force to enforce UN Security Council resolutions, while assuaging public fears by stating that the passage of the resolution "does not mean that military action is imminent or unavoidable."

President Bush's October 7, 2002, Cincinnati speech actually led to a five-point drop in his overall job ratings, which rebounded to 67 percent in the October 21–22 Gallup poll. Support for sending U.S. ground troops to remove Saddam Hussein from power rose by three points to 56 percent favoring such military action, but dipped in the following poll. But most significantly, the combination of President Bush's overall popularity in the mid-sixties percentile and his aggressive promotion of the Joint Resolution to Authorize Use of Force against Iraq—with the backdrop of an election the following month—led the House to approve the measure 296 to 133 and the Senate to pass it by a 77 to 23 vote on October 11, 2002.[88] During the House debate, Speaker Dennis Hastert posed the rhetorical question: "Is there a direct connection between Iraq and al Qaeda? The president thinks so."[89]

Democratic leaders decided to avoid a fight with the popular president on the war question, saving their campaign ammunition for a clash with the administration on the troubled domestic economic front. Among the 50 incumbents assessed by *Congressional Quarterly* to face competitive House races, only 10 voted against the Iraq war resolution.[90] And in 18 competitive Senate races, just 1 candidate cast a vote against the resolution. Congressional acquiescence to President Bush on the authorization for force against Iraq validated the conclusion of Paul Brace and Barbara Hinkley: "Congress...can be expected to follow the polls—to be, on average, more timid when opposing a popular president and more courageous against an unpopular one."[91]

The battlefield shifted to the United Nations as the Bush administration and the British government sought Security Council approval for military action to eliminate Iraq's alleged WMD. A stalemate developed until the United States agreed to drop its insistence that a UN resolution contain an automatic trigger for military action.[92] On the campaign stump, Bush bashed the United Nations by calling for it to become "more than just a debating society," derisively comparing it to the failed League of Nations.[93] Bush ominously warned: "If the U.N. can't make its mind up, if Saddam Hussein won't disarm, we will lead a coalition to disarm him."

However, Secretary Powell's statements increasingly downplayed regime change and emphasized the goal of removing Iraq's weapons of mass destruction capability. On ABC's "This Week," Powell declared: "Either Iraq cooperates, and we get this disarmament done through peaceful means; or they do not cooperate, and we will use other means to get the job done."[94] But neoconservative John Bolton, undersecretary of state for arms control and international security, voiced a hard-line message underscoring the continuing tug-of-war within the administration: "There will be no stability in the region until he's gone."

President Bush's vigorous campaign in the last five days of the 2002 campaign reversed the usual off-year loss of congressional seats for the president's party, retaining a Republican majority in the House and recapturing control of the Senate. But despite the success of Bush's hot rhetoric on the campaign trail, the administration failed to achieve its goals in the Security Council. On January 9, 2003, UN weapons inspector Hans Blix told reporters before meeting with the Security Council, "We haven't found any smoking guns."[95] Ari Fleischer, Bush's press spokesman, shot back: "We know for a fact that there are weapons there."

Wolfowitz and Rice pounded the war drums with fearsome rhetoric. Wolfowitz told the Council of Foreign Relations: "Iraq's weapons of mass terror and the terror networks to which the Iraqi regime are linked are not two separate themes—not two separate threats. They are part of the same threat."[96] NSC adviser Rice wrote a *New York Times* Op-Ed titled: "Why We Know Iraq Is Lying." Rice described Iraq's weapons disclosure to the United Nations as "a 12,200-page lie," reflecting a material breach of UN Security Council Resolution 1441.[97]

But reports from UN weapons inspections undercut the administration's push for another resolution authorizing war. Director General Dr. Mohamed ElBaradei of the International Atomic Energy Agency (IAEA) reported in late January: "We have to date found no evidence that Iraq has revived its nuclear program."[98] The European Parliament adopted a resolution that declared that breaches of UN resolutions by Iraq "do not justify military action," although Great Britain and seven other E.U. members backed a war with Iraq.[99] Because of the vocal opposition of France and Germany to an Iraq war, Secretary Rumsfeld disdainfully labeled these NATO allies as "old Europe."[100] But huge protest rallies in London, Paris, Rome, and Barcelona on February 15 revealed the deep European opposition to a preemptive war with Iraq.

In his 2003 State of the Union Address, President Bush maintained the drumbeat for war with Iraq, warning that Saddam Hussein aided and protected terrorists, including members of al Qaeda. Bush's speechwriters cleverly stirred up the painful memories of the 9/11 attacks and implied links to Iraq: "*Imagine* those 19 hijackers with other weapons and other plans—this time armed by Saddam Hussein. It would take one vial, one canister, one crate slipped into this country to bring a day of horror like none we have ever known" (author's emphasis).[101] Several days later President Bush ridiculed the concept of containment: "You don't contain Saddam Hussein. You don't hope that therapy will somehow change his evil mind."[102]

Bush announced that his popular Secretary of State Colin Powell would document before the UN Security Council on February 5, 2003, America's evidence of Iraq's deadly weapons of mass destruction. On the eve of the secretary's Security Council presentation, a phenomenal 86 percent of respondents in a CNN/ *USA Today*/ Gallup Poll expressed a favorable opinion of Secretary Colin Powell. The president used Powell's credibility to sell the case for war. Indeed, a Gallup poll found that 63 percent of Americans chose Powell over Bush (24 percent) as the leader they trusted the most in making decisions about U.S.-Iraq policy.[103] Vice

President Cheney, who scoffed at his own low ratings, told Powell: "You can afford to lose some poll points."[104]

After Powell's February 5 presentation to the UN Security Council supporting the administration's charges against Iran, 61 percent of respondents felt he clearly made the case for the use of force, a seven-point increase from a February 1 poll.[105] Bush's State of the Union address, bolstered by Powell's UN speech, had succeeded in building public confidence that the administration had clearly explained why the United States might use military force to remove Saddam Hussein from power. The ever-loyal soldier Colin Powell expended some of his impressive political capital to sell the war to the American people, based on what he then believed was sound intelligence data. Indeed, Secretary Powell insisted that CIA Director Tenet sit directly behind him during the UN speech.

On February 23 President George W. Bush's rhetoric pivoted in a new direction, altering his core message from Saddam Hussein's weapons of mass destruction and terrorism to endorse the goal of promoting democracy in Iraq and throughout the Middle East.[106] The call for democracy in Bush's American Enterprise Institute (AEI) speech attempted to counter rising European protests against a preemptive war with Iraq, mollify Arab criticism by supporting the resolution of the Israeli-Palestinian conflict, and broaden Bush's appeal to more Americans by casting the war's goal in terms of fostering democratic governments. However, on February 15, 2003, an estimated 100 million people in 600 European cities protested the imminent war with Iraq.[107]

Decision-Making in the Shadows

President George W. Bush's decision to launch a preemptive war with Iraq seems to violate many of the core tenets of Graham Allison's Rational Actor Model. In particular, the Bush administration inflated the immediate threat of Saddam Hussein's regime, restricted the consideration of policy goals to only regime change (rejecting containment), and concentrated on the policy of a preemptive military invasion of Iraq.

When President Bush decided to go to war in Iraq remains shrouded in mystery, since Bush isolated many key advisors from that pivotal decision, particularly Secretary of State Colin Powell and CIA Director George Tenet. Indeed, the paper trail and the administration's internal politics suggest that the only officials privy to Bush's critical decision were Vice President Cheney, NSC Advisor Condoleezza Rice, Chief of Staff Andy Card, and Defense Secretary Don Rumsfeld, the man charged with implementing the war order. Tenet recalled no "serious debate about the imminence of the Iraqi threat" or a cost/benefit analysis of the policy alternatives containment versus regime change in Baghdad.[108] Once the president made that decision, *groupthink* shunted aside warnings, contrary data, and less optimistic assumptions that disputed the president's preferred policy.

In late spring 2002 President Bush probably made his critical decision to go to war with Iraq without informing many key administration national security officials. Richard Haas, director of policy planning at the State Department, visited NSC Adviser Rice in the White House to give reasons to avoid a war with Iraq. Rice stopped him: "Save your breath.... The President has already made up his mind."[109] An astonished Haas recalled: "A decision was not made—a decision happened, and you can't say when or how." The final process had excluded Secretary of State Colin Powell, who often found himself frozen out of White House decision-making in the administration's "icebox."[110]

The next month British officials concluded that President Bush had decided to go to war with Iraq, as documented in the Downing Street Memorandum published in Britain's *The Sunday Times* in 2005. The July 23, 2002, memorandum included Sir Richard Dearlove's (Head of British Intelligence MI6) report to Prime Minister Blair of his recent visit with Bush administration intelligence and NSC officials. The memorandum summarized Sir Dearlove's conclusions:

> Military action was now seen as inevitable. Bush wanted to remove Saddam, through military action, justified by the conjunction of terrorism and WMD. *But the intelligence and facts were being fixed around the policy* (author's emphasis). The NSC had no patience with the UN route, and no enthusiasm for publishing material on the Iraqi regime's record. There was little discussion in Washington of the aftermath of military action.[111]

According to Tenet, Dearlove believed "the crowd around the vice president was playing fast and loose with the evidence."[112] Of course, publicly President Bush maintained the stance that no decision had been made on the question of whether the United States would preemptively invade Iraq. Furthermore, authorization had not been sought from either Congress or the UN Security Council. Bush spokespersons later claimed that the president's decision to launch Operation Iraqi Freedom occurred after Secretary of State Powell documented the administration's charges against the Iraqi regime before the Security Council on February 5, 2003.

But another British memorandum later surfaced describing a January 31, 2003, Oval Office meeting between President Bush and Prime Minister Blair. David Manning, then serving as foreign policy adviser to Blair, authored a five-page memo that recalled: "Our diplomatic strategy had to be arranged around the military planning." President Bush indicated that the military campaign would commence on March 10.[113] The two leaders agreed to seek a second UN resolution authorizing war with Iraq. But Bush declared that if the diplomatic initiative failed, "military action would follow anyway." When Prime Minister Blair asked about postwar planning, Condoleezza Rice assured him a great deal of work had been done. President Bush confidently predicted that internecine warfare between religious and ethnic groups was "unlikely."

George W. Bush set the course to topple Saddam Hussein commencing with his first NSC meeting, 10 days after the 2001 inauguration. The horrific 9/11 terrorist attacks contributed to President Bush's tendency to increasingly make high-risk decisions, partially based upon the administration's initial military success in Afghanistan, Bush's astronomical job approval ratings, and an aggressive neoconservative agenda that meshed with Bush's Righteous Hawk persona. In addition, the post-9/11 political environment afforded President Bush with an opportunity to avenge Saddam Hussein's attempted assassination of his father. The successful removal of the dictator from power would also manifest a foreign policy achievement surpassing the senior President Bush's victory in the 1991 Gulf War.

The administration deliberately ignored the victorious model pursued by the senior President Bush in the 1991 Gulf War. Indeed, George W. Bush's advisors seemed to purposely choose a different strategy and tactics. For example, the senior President Bush delayed the war authorization vote in Congress until after the 1990 midterm election to avoid politicizing such an important issue. As a result, the senior President Bush enjoyed tremendous support for the 1991 war from both Republicans (94 percent) and Democrats (81 percent).[114]

However, President George W. Bush, encouraged by Cheney and Rove, forced a congressional vote on the Iraq War authorization resolution before the 2002 midterm election to compel Democrats to back the war and win firm Republican control over Congress. A Bush aide later admitted: "The election was the anvil and the president was the hammer. That was when we had the most leverage."[115] While the senior Bush received overwhelming Democratic backing in the 1991 Gulf War because of his bipartisan approach, George W. Bush's administration confronted growing distrust, bitterness, and opposition from Democrats over the Iraq War. Although 93 percent of Republicans backed George W. Bush's 2003 war with Iraq, only 50 percent of Democrats supported the conflict, a huge 43-point partisan gap.[116]

President George H.W. Bush, a former UN ambassador, respected the international body and lobbied his former diplomatic colleagues for a supporting Security Council resolution. He called in favors from both the Russians and the Chinese to win the Security Council authorization to use "all necessary means" to drive Saddam Hussein's forces out of Kuwait.[117] As a result of the United Nation's legitimization of the war against Hussein's brutal act of aggression, the elder Bush found American armed forces fighting in tandem with thousands of troops from neighboring Arab countries as well as French and British soldiers. Furthermore, Saudi Arabia, Kuwait, and Japan paid the bulk of the Desert Storm costs, thus avoiding placing a larger national debt on the American taxpayer.

In contrast, George W. Bush adopted the thinking of the neoconservatives, demonstrating disdain toward the United Nations, disrespect toward many of America's historic allies, and derision toward diplomacy in general. As a superpower, the neoconservatives arrogantly proclaimed that the United States could and should impose its agenda upon the world. However, the political, economic, and human costs of such a go-it-alone foreign policy soon became evident.

The ideological beliefs underlying the neoconservatives' foreign policy stance provided President Bush with a strategic vision that matched his moral outrage at the forces of evil operating in the Middle East. The neoconservative prism differentiated Bush's audacious approach to world affairs from too-cautious realists—like his father. George W. Bush considered his proclaimed doctrine of preemption a bold, forward-leaning stance. However, "prudent" realists disparaged Bush's policy change as provocative, precedent-setting, and dangerous.

While both Democratic and Republican realists called for keeping Saddam Hussein "in his box" through sanctions and airpower, Bush chose the more belligerent course of a preemptive war to bring about regime change in Iraq. President George W. Bush's February 2003 AEI speech highlighted his vision of a peaceful, democratic Middle East, created through the establishment of a democratic Iraq. However, traditional realists felt that the more limited goal of a stable region, even if dominated by nondemocratic governments, better safeguarded America's vital national interests in the Middle East.

Chapter Nine

Bush's War: Break It...and It's Yours

Facing clear evidence of peril, we cannot wait for the final proof—
the smoking gun—that could come in the form of a mushroom cloud.

The Bush administration's call for a preemptive war against Iraq—replete with frightening warnings about Iraq's weapons of mass destruction, Saddam Hussein's links to al Qaeda and hints of the Iraqi dictator's role in the 9/11 attacks on America—created a powerful juggernaut toward a "war of choice" with Iraq.[1] Despite President George W. Bush's October 7, 2002, assurance that approval of the congressional resolution authorizing war "does not mean that military action is imminent or unavoidable," military plans for an invasion to topple Saddam Hussein gained deadly traction.[2]

However, the U.S. Central Command's (CENTCOM) military planning to invade Iraq confronted repeated "iterations" to downsize the requisite troop levels through persistent pressure from Defense Secretary Donald Rumsfeld with his "snowflake" memos.[3] Secretary Rumsfeld micromanaged the formation of the Bush administration's new preemption strategy against Iraq, predicated upon rosy scenarios and optimistic assumptions. The Pentagon's civilian leadership repeatedly shoved aside war plans calling for more robust troop levels, "worst case" contingency plans, and caveats about possible post-conflict dangers generated by other departments and outside experts.

The neoconservatives' upbeat projections for both the Iraqi battlefield and postwar security smothered the U.S. military's traditional planning procedures. In addition, Secretary Rumsfeld's quest to achieve a "21st century transformation" of the Department of Defense (DoD)—creating a leaner and more flexible military force—imposed further restrictions upon the CENTCOM strategic planners. The reduced size of America's invasion ground force also generated difficulties for the Coalition Provisional Authority (CPA) after U.S. troops imposed "regime change" in Iraq.

Shock, Awe, and Chaos

Graham Allison's Government Organization Model, which focuses upon a bureaucracy's standard operating procedures, revealed how Secretary of Defense Donald Rumsfeld's controlling administrative style disrupted the Pentagon's normal war planning process. Rumsfeld framed the strategic objectives, insisted upon rosy assumptions, and prevented General Tommy Franks from independently developing an invasion plan. A senior Pentagon planner on the Joint Staff revealed that Secretary Rumsfeld on six occasions insisted upon a reduced number of troops when presented with operational plans for the Iraq War.[4] Secretary of the Army Tom White acknowledged: "Rumsfeld just ground Franks down."[5]

An important decision in the war on terror occurred in December 2002 when President George W. Bush approved the launching of the war on Iraq with the "Running Start" strategy advanced by General Franks and Defense Secretary Rumsfeld, featuring pared-down troop levels for the offensive. Under pressure from Rumsfeld, the CENTCOM planners consciously crafted a strategy that would repudiate the 1991 model of Operation Desert Storm. The successful Desert Storm strategy applied the so-called Powell Doctrine which stipulated that the United States should field an overwhelming number of ground forces. Contrasting his 2003 war plan to the Desert Storm model, CENTCOM commander Franks bragged: "We would go into Iraq fast and hard, not slow and heavy."[6]

President Bush and Secretary Rumsfeld wanted the second step in the war on terror—toppling Saddam Hussein—to manifest the administration's new approach to warfare, founded upon America's technological advantages of "smart" weaponry and lean, highly mobile armed forces. Rumsfeld perceived the 9/11 terrorist attacks as "a transformational event" that required an updated defense strategy after the end of the Cold War.[7]

A successful request through the Freedom of Information Act provided the National Security Archive with the CENTCOM PowerPoint slides used in 2002 briefings for President Bush and his national security team on the assumptions and troop requirements for the code-named POLO STEP plan to invade Iraq. Thomas Blanton, executive director of the Archive concluded: "First, they [CENTCOM planners] *assumed* that a provision government would be in place by 'D-Day,' then that the Iraqis would stay their garrisons and be reliable partners, and finally that the post-hostilities phase would be a matter of mere 'months.' All of these [assumptions] were delusions."[8] Furthermore, the PowerPoint presentation (Tab K, Slide 10) estimated that the postwar Phase IV would last a maximum of 45 months, leaving only 5,000 U.S. troops in Iraq by December 2006.

President Bush and his Pentagon chief vociferously opposed nation-building, particularly as conducted by President Bill Clinton in Somalia, Haiti, Bosnia, and Kosovo. In the second 2000 presidential debate, then-Governor Bush declared: "I don't think our troops ought to be used for what's called nation-building. I think our troops ought to be used to fight and win war."[9] Defense Secretary Rumsfeld, in a *Washington Post* Op-Ed commentary published after the fall of Saddam Hussein, categorically stated: "We are not in Iraq to engage in nation-building— our mission is to help Iraqis so that they can build their own nation."[10]

Defense Secretary Rumsfeld wrestled with unenthusiastic top military officers to impose his "transformation" vision on the Pentagon. The secretary anticipated that a victory in Iraq, won with high-tech weaponry and a lean invasion force, would forever silence the Army generals who advocated higher troop levels. At a September 10, 2001, Pentagon town hall meeting, Secretary Rumsfeld described an adversary that represented a significant threat to U.S. national security. To a shocked audience, Rumsfeld declared: "The adversary's closer to home. It's the Pentagon bureaucracy."[11]

Studies conducted by the U.S. Central Command, CIA, National Security Council (NSC), RAND Corporation think tank, and Council on Foreign Relations recognized the immediate postwar imperative of overpowering ground forces to maintain order, prevent an insurgency, and provide a stable transition to an Iraqi interim government. These analyses calculated troop recommendations based upon U.S. peacekeeping experiences in other postwar settings, such as in Bosnia and Kosovo.

The Bush administration inherited the Central Command's OPLAN 1003–98, an Iraq war contingency plan calling for up to 500,000 troops, which Franks scornfully dubbed "Desert Storm II."[12] When Major General Greg Newbold, chief operations deputy of the Joint Chiefs of Staff, briefed Secretary Rumsfeld on OPLAN 1003–98 in December 2001, Rumsfeld stunned General Newbold by stating that only 125,000 troops would be required—perhaps even less.[13] A frustrated Joint Chiefs planner subsequently observed: "He thought he knew better. ...He was the decision-maker at every turn."[14]

General Anthony Zinni, who served as the U.S. CENTCOM commander from 1997 to 2000, had recognized after the extensive 1998 Desert Fox bombings on Iraq's WMD facilities the fragility of Saddam Hussein's regime. The general felt the United States and Britain had successfully contained the Iraqi dictator. Zinni observed that Saddam Hussein's military had shrunk by half since the 1991 Gulf War, with obsolete equipment, poorly trained soldiers, high absenteeism, and low morale further weakening the Iraqi army. General Zinni concluded: "We didn't see the Iraqis as a formidable force. *We saw them as a decaying force*" (author's emphasis).[15]

General Zinni ordered a 1999 Desert Crossing exercise to explore the requirements for postwar reconstruction in Iraq. The exercise recommended 400,000 armed forces to invade and stabilize Iraq. General Zinni explained: "We knew the initial problem would be security."[16] The "After Action Report" of Desert Crossing anticipated many of the problems that regime change in Iraq would precipitate: the dangers of fragmentation along religious and/or ethnic lines, Iraq's neighbors taking advantage of the chaos, and rival internal forces creating domestic and regional problems.[17] When Joint Chiefs of Staff officers mentioned Desert Crossing's findings, the Bush administration's civilian Pentagon leaders dismissed the study because "its assumptions are too pessimistic."[18]

Marine Major Jeff Kojac, an officer on the staff of the NSC, prepared a briefing addressing the required level of U.S. forces in postwar Iraq.[19] Kojac pointed out that if the Bush administration's postwar Iraq planning focused on the number of peacekeepers utilized in Kosovo, the United States would need 480,000 troops. His examination of the Bosnia peacekeeping operation suggested that the United States should deploy 364,000 troops to Iraq. Major Kojac underscored that three-quarters of Iraq's population lived in urban areas, which closely reflected the population distribution in Kosovo and Bosnia, rather than Afghanistan. Nevertheless, the NSC principals ignored his provocative findings.

Former diplomat James Dobbins had served as President Bush's first envoy to Afghanistan, playing a pivotal role in the formation of the new Karzai government. His RAND Corporation study concluded that there should be 20 occupying troops for every 1,000 people in the country occupied, recommending 526,000 coalition troops for postwar Iraq duty.[20] Dobbins presciently warned: "Only when the number of stabilization troops has been low in comparison to the population have U.S. forces suffered or inflicted significant casualties."[21]

The Council on Foreign Relations and the James A. Baker III Institute for Public Policy published recommendations in early 2003 for America's post-conflict policy in Iraq. The former ambassadors who wrote the report opened with a stark warning, "The United States may lose the peace, even if it wins the war."[22] The report opposed the creation of a post-conflict government dominated by Iraqi exile leaders who "would lack internal legitimacy."[23] The authors emphasized that the Iraqi army "remains one of the country's more respected institutions" and could play a key reconstruction role after purging its top leaders.[24]

An important question arises from Allison's Rational Actor Model. How could President Bush and his national security team discard the warnings and dismiss the advice of experienced realists from inside and outside of the administration? The disgraceful treatment of General Erik Shinseki, Secretary of the Army Tom White, and White House economic adviser Lawrence B. Lindsey revealed the tactics the administration hawks employed to repress the doubts and flow of facts upward that differed from the administration's sanguine projections.

At a February 2003 hearing of the Senate Armed Services committee, General Eric K. Shinseki, the Army chief of staff, candidly answered a question from Democratic Senator Carl Levin about how many troops would be needed for the looming war with Iraq. General Shinseki, who formerly commanded the North Atlantic Treaty Organization (NATO) peacekeeping operation in Kosovo, stated: "I would say what's been mobilized to this point—something on the order of several hundred thousand soldiers—are probably, you know, a figure that would be required."[25] The general explained that Iraq was a country with "the kinds of ethnic tensions that could lead to other problems," thereby requiring more U.S. troops to maintain order.[26]

Several days later Deputy Secretary of Defense Paul D. Wolfowitz blasted General Shinseki's troop estimate, calling it "wildly off the mark." Secretary Rumsfeld also dismissed Shinseki's assessment that the war would take more than 100,000 troops as "far off the mark." Rumsfeld announced General Shinseki's replacement over a year and a half before his scheduled retirement, humiliating and effectively making the Army chief of staff a lame duck.

Retired General Tom White, the civilian secretary of the Army, also clashed with Rumsfeld over his plans to reduce the size of the Army. Secretary White loyally defended General Shinseki for honestly presenting his professional military judgment in response to a senator's direct question. Two weeks after the fall of the Baghdad regime, Rumsfeld fired Army Secretary White.[27] Rumsfeld sought to eliminate or intimidate into silence any Pentagon opponents of the proposed invasion of Iraq with limited ground troops or critics of his "transformation" vision of a leaner twenty-first-century Army.

And when White House economic adviser Lawrence B. Lindsey told a *Wall Street Journal* reporter that the cost of a war with Iraq could rise as high as $200 billion, the Bush administration fired him several months later. Lindsey's estimate contradicted the Pentagon's optimistic low-ball estimate of a $40 billion Iraq war.[28] Mitchell E. Daniels Jr., director of the Office of Management and Budget (OMB), was a more supportive team player. He estimated the cost of the Iraq war at $50–$60 billion, more in line with the Pentagon's cost projection.[29]

The estimated cost of the Iraq war on the fourth anniversary of the invasion was estimated at $532 billion by fall 2008.[30]

President George W. Bush announced the kick-off of Operation Iraqi Freedom on the evening of March 19, 2003. The start of the war, several days earlier than planned, began with "decapitation" air and missile strikes on a Baghdad location where the CIA reported a meeting of Saddam Hussein and his sons Uday and Qusay with top Iraqi advisers. The military leaders directed precision missile and bomber strikes on Iraqi Republican Guard and Army units as well as command-and-control targets.

In the 1991 Gulf War American "smart" missiles and bombs comprised only 10 percent of the weaponry. However, in the 2003 war against Iraq 70 percent of the air strikes comprised high-tech "smart munitions."[31] General Franks, in his first military briefing from the Central Command headquarters in Qatar, described the just-launched campaign against Iraq as "characterized by shock, by surprise, by flexibility, by the employment of precise munitions on a scale never before seen."[32]

The initial number of pinpoint air strikes suggested to some observers that Rumsfeld had adopted a 1996 National Defense University study advocating the employment of a "shock and awe" strategy to win wars quickly. The strategy emphasized the goal of destroying or confounding the enemy's will to resist through technological superiority, so an adversary "will have no alternative except to accept our strategic aims and military objectives."[33]

The Kuwait-based ground invasion of Iraq commenced with a combined American and British assault force of 145,000 troops, with additional units arriving daily.[34] U.S. Army soldiers and Marines rapidly advanced toward Baghdad, while British forces approached Basra in southern Iraq, the two cities Franks viewed as Iraq's "centers of gravity."[35] The Phase III ground combat stage of the Central Command's war plan lasted 21 days. British military writer John Keegan lauded Operation Iraqi Freedom: "(T)he Americans had achieved a pace of advance unprecedented in history."[36] The coalition sustained low casualties (122 Americans and 33 British) and almost no equipment losses.

Worldwide television broadcasts on April 9 featured the moment when Iraqi citizens in central Baghdad toppled a 40-foot statue of Saddam Hussein—with the help of U.S. Marines. The dramatic event symbolized the fall of the Iraqi dictator's regime. Widespread looting in Baghdad followed this incident, with 17 of 27 Iraqi ministries sacked by crowds.

The "off-ramping" of the First Calvary Division reinforcements after toppling the Hussein regime meant the Pentagon found itself without sufficient ground forces in Baghdad to prevent the looting of Iraqi government facilities, secure the stocks of weaponry stashed by the Hussein regime (that soon fueled the insurgency), or guard Iraq's borders from the entry of Islamic *jihadists* from other Arab states.[37]

Secretary Rumsfeld dismissed the importance of the looting: "Stuff happens."[38] However, the Pentagon had assigned American troops to prevent the looting of the Iraqi Ministry of Oil, an obvious signal to many observers around the world as to the "real" goal behind the invasion of Iraq. A 2004 Pew poll found majorities in the Muslim countries of Jordan (71 percent), Morocco (63 percent), Turkey (64 percent), and Pakistan (54 percent) felt America's war on terror sought to control Mideast Oil.[39] But German (60 percent), French (58 percent), and Russian (51 percent) respondents also viewed U.S. foreign policy goals as focused upon Mideast oil.

Viceroy in Combat Boots

Graham Allison's Governmental Politics lens offers further insights into why President Bush assigned Rumsfeld and the Department of Defense the lead role in the occupation of Iraq, normally the responsibility of the State Department. Rumsfeld and Douglas Feith, Undersecretary of defense for policy, had disparaged the State Department for allegedly mismanaging postwar Afghanistan by sharing responsibilities with other departments and allies, without one department clearly in charge.[40]

The NSC drafted and President Bush signed on January 20 National Security Directive 24 (NSD-24) to establish the Office of Reconstruction and Humanitarian Assistance (ORHA) in the Defense Department.[41] Neither Secretary Powell nor his deputy Richard Armitage objected to Pentagon control over post-conflict Iraq. Powell had warned President Bush in August 2002 that if the U.S. invaded Iraq: "You will own all their [25 million Iraqis] hopes, aspirations and problems. You'll own it all."[42] Powell and Armitage called this the Pottery Barn rule: You break it, you own it.

Dov Zakheim, one of President Bush's Vulcan advisers in the 2000 campaign, observed the interdepartmental conflict from his Pentagon post as Comptroller. Zakheim flatly stated: "State and Defense were at war—don't let anyone tell you different."[43] The split began at the top over policy issues, evoking "knee-jerk venom" in both departments that trickled down to the working level.

The Department of State had initiated "The Future of Iraq Project" in October 2001, almost one and a half years before the invasion of Iraq. Over 200 Iraqi exiles and Mideast experts focused on involving professional Iraqi exiles in practical planning for the situation after regime change in Iraq. The State-led planning omitted any Iraqi exile politicians on the assumption that "most Iraqi professionals are not involved in Iraqi opposition politics."[44] This approach also reflected the negative opinion of Ahmed Chalabi held by the State Department and CIA. Congress approved $5 million for the Future of Iraq Project in May 2002.

The Army's Strategic Studies Institute's January 2003 report underscored the significant postwar challenges the United States would face after toppling Saddam Hussein's regime: a strong tradition of instability and violence; tension among Iraq's religious, ethnic, and tribal communities; inexperience with national power sharing, and a scary scenario of growing terrorist attacks upon the occupying coalition forces.[45] The SSI analysis suggested that during the Phase IV post-hostilities stage, "U.S. should recognize that the [Iraq] military is a national institution and one of the few forces for unity within the country."

In January 2003 the CIA's analysts prepared an analysis on postwar Iraq, cautioning that the goal of turning Iraq into a liberal democracy would entail a "long, difficult and probably turbulent challenge."[46] The report worried about possible religious and ethnic conflicts unless the United States stationed enough forces in Iraq to suppress any outbreak of violence. The Bush administration's response was as follows: "You guys just don't see the possibilities. You're too negative."[47]

Secretary of Defense Rumsfeld selected retired Army Lieutenant General Jay M. Garner to head the postwar operation under NSD-24 in early January 2003—only two months before the Iraq invasion began. While commanding Operation Safe Comfort after the 1991 Gulf War, Garner had protected the Kurds from Saddam Hussein's forces. Secretary Powell sent to the Pentagon the 13-volume Future of Iraq report for General Garner's consideration, accompanied by the names of about seventy-five State Department Arab experts. General Garner acknowledged that the Future of Iraq report "wasn't well received" within the Pentagon or the NSC.[48]

Rumsfeld quickly vetoed the State Department's Thomas Warrick, the director of the Future of Iraq project, from holding any position with OHRA, despite the request of General Garner and the angry response of Secretary Powell. General Garner later discovered that the order to exclude Warrick originated from "a higher authority"—Vice President Dick Cheney.[49] Rumsfeld also scrubbed the names of other experienced State Department Arab experts from General Garner's Iraq reconstruction team.

When briefing President Bush the second week of March, just before the Iraq War, General Garner told the president that "we were going to use most of the Iraqi army for reconstruction, we were going to hire them and make them…reconstruction battalions." President Bush voiced no objections to the post-conflict plan. Even though the statue of Saddam Hussein fell on April 9, CENTCOM's security concerns about conditions in Baghdad kept Garner and his team stuck in Kuwait until April 19.

General Garner had anticipated and prepared for a worst-case scenario: a humanitarian crisis sparked by fleeing Iraqi refugees, treatment of Saddam Hussein's victims from a chemical attack; torched oil fields; blown dams, and the outbreak of an epidemic. However, the swiftness of the coalition offensive helped prevent those calamitous events—combined with the Iraqi dictator's belief that he would survive the war with the United States and might face an internal revolt.[50] When Garner and 19 members of his team arrived in Baghdad, 17 of 23 ministries were unusable to locate governmental services in the reconstruction phase because of the looting, destruction, and burning of official buildings.

The day General Garner landed in Baghdad, Secretary Rumsfeld phoned him and said: "Jay, the president's appointed Jerry Bremer to come over and be the special envoy as part of the plan."[51] In a BBC interview the following year, General Garner claimed that the Bush administration ousted him from the OHRA post because of his support for free elections and opposition to a CPA imposed program of privatization.[52]

Ambassador Bremer had served 23 years as a career diplomat, but he specialized in counterterrorism. Bremer had little knowledge of Middle East affairs and did not speak Arabic. Some labeled Paul Bremer as America's "viceroy." On May 9 President Bush appointed Bremer his presidential envoy to Iraq, "with full authority over all U.S. government personnel, activities and funds there."[53] Bremer typically wore a coat and tie, despite the heat and dust, along with distinctive combat-style boots given to him by his son.

During his tenure as the CPA administrator, Bremer made three controversial decisions that gravely impacted upon the situation in post-conflict

Iraq—andthegrowing—butunacknowledgedinsurgency.Thefirstdecisionimposed de-Baathification on March 16, 2003. Bremer explained that before leaving for Iraq, Undersecretary of Defense Feith showed him a draft of the de-Baathification order aimed at Saddam's key supporters, mostly Sunnis who held most government positions. Bremer assured his concerned CPA aides: "The White House, DOD, and State all signed off on this."[54]

But many senior CPA staff, working with former-Baathist bureaucrats to reestablish Iraq's essential public services, strongly objected. One warned: "We can't run our ministries now."[55] The CIA's Baghdad chief vainly cautioned Bremer about a backlash from the de-Baathification order: "By nightfall, you'll have driven 30,000 to 50,000 Baathists underground. And in six months, you'll really regret this."[56]

CENTCOM commander General Abizaid later told a Senate committee that the de-Baathification order "was too severe."[57] British Prime Minister Tony Blair subsequently acknowledged: "I think that probably in retrospect—though at the time it was very difficult to argue this—could have done the de-Baathification in a more differentiated way than we did."[58] In April 2004, before leaving Iraq, even Ambassador Bremer admitted: "The de-Baathification policy was and is sound. . . . But it has been poorly implemented," blaming Chalabi for the zealous application of de-Baathification for personal political gain.[59]

Bremer made a second mistake a week later by announcing CPA Order No. 2, which disbanded the Iraqi military, intelligence service, Republican Guards, and police forces. General Garner, in a February 19, 2003, briefing for NSC adviser Rice, had warned against any immediate demobilization of the Iraqi army that would place 300,000–400,000 unemployed, trained military men on the streets.[60]

The demobilization of the Iraqi army also directly contravened Doug Feith's March 7, 2003, presentation to President Bush on the Pentagon's postwar plan to convert three to five Iraqi army divisions as a "national reconstruction force," incorporating the suggestions of CENTCOM planners and General Garner.[61] President Bush had approved Feith's March 2003 proposal, but he never countermanded Bremer's order.

State Department officials affirmed that neither Secretary Powell nor NSC Adviser Rice received advance notification of Bremer's fateful decision to dissolve the Iraqi army.[62] Furthermore, even though the CPA order directly affected Pentagon plans for reconstruction and redeployment, Bremer failed to consult with the Joint Chiefs.[63] General Zinni later recalled that CENTCOM always assumed that the Iraqi army could serve as a "ready-made force to pick up some of the security requirements"—after the selective purge of the top Baathist officers and retraining.[64]

Generals Abizaid, Franks, and David McKiernan, the top three U.S. commanders in the region, viewed a functioning Iraqi army as a key component for postwar reconstruction, security, and exit strategy. After the dissolution of the Iraqi army, an American Special-Forces officer in Baghdad said: "I had my guys coming up to me and saying, 'Does Bremer realize that there are four hundred thousand of these guys out there and they all have guns?'"[65]

The third error committed by CPA administrator Bremer involved the decision to delay the formation of a provisional government led by Iraqis, a goal General

Garner had promoted. Presidential envoy Zalmay Khalilzad had even told Iraqi exile leaders that a transitional government would be established by mid-May 2003. Bremer told the exile leaders on May 16: "I want to reemphasize that the path to representative government will be incremental."[66] He noted the group included no Arab Sunni, no Turkmen, no Christians, and no women.

Bremer established a broader, more representative Governing Council, but only to serve in an advisory capacity to himself, as CPA administrator. This led Ahmed Chalabi to return to Washington to lobby for a "sovereignty now" campaign targeted for April 2003, apparently backed by Wolfowitz, Feith, and John Hannah in Vice President Cheney's office. Rumsfeld called to urge Bremer to grant sovereignty sooner, which Bremer interpreted as the "creeping air of desperation about the troop rotation."[67] Bremer ridiculed the Iraqi advisory Governing Council members: "Those people couldn't organize a parade, let alone run a country."[68]

Dissatisfaction with the handling of the turbulent situation in Iraq led President Bush to transfer authority for reconstruction from Secretary of Defense Rumsfeld to NSC Adviser Condoleezza Rice, who he placed in charge of a new Iraq Stabilization Group. An upset Secretary Rumsfeld admitted he was not involved in the decision: "You don't understand English? I was not there for the backgrounding."[69]

Bremer scheduled the transfer of sovereignty to Prime Minister Ayad Allawi and a 16-member Governing Council for June 30, 2004. Rice called Bremer to arrange a secret transfer several days earlier to thwart insurgent attacks. The transfer of sovereignty occurred on June 28, with Bremer immediately leaving Baghdad. He used subterfuge to confuse insurgent plotters, faking his departure in a C-130 and then dashing to a Chinook helicopter.[70] Bremer's unceremonious exit from Iraq illustrated the dangerous environment in Iraq after 14 months of the U.S. occupation.

A Bloody Cakewalk

The Bush administration's momentous failure to immediately recognize and take military action to suppress the growing postwar Sunni insurgency represented another mistake during the occupation of Iraq, not originating with Ambassador Bremer. The administration's unwillingness to acknowledge the insurgency early—and send more troops to crush the insurrection in its most vulnerable stage—stemmed partly from the rosy pictures administration officials painted for Congress and the American people of troops hailed as liberators. The administration's prewar hype thus restricted Bush officials from acknowledging the extent of their misstatements, misjudgments, and mistakes.

In a prewar *Washington Post* commentary, neoconservative Kenneth Edelman, a member of the Pentagon's Defense Policy Board under Rumsfeld, predicted: "I believe demolishing Hussein's military power and *liberating Iraq would be a cakewalk*" (author's emphasis).[71] Vice President Dick Cheney, in a televised interview three days before the invasion, confidently stated that "my belief is we will, in fact, be *greeted as liberators*" (author's emphasis).[72]

President Bush triumphantly declared on May 1 aboard the aircraft carrier *USS Abraham Lincoln*: "Major combat operations in Iraq have ended."[73] A large

"Mission Accomplished" banner hung behind him. But burgeoning insurgent attacks and accidents killed 54 American troops between May 1 and June 18. Nevertheless, Defense Secretary Rumsfeld scornfully depicted the Iraqi resistance as only "pockets of dead-enders."[74] Rumsfeld portrayed the violence as the "untidy" aftermath of regime change.[75] Undersecretary of Defense Wolfowitz also downplayed the threat from insurgents in congressional testimony, describing them as the "last remnants of a dying cause."

Defense Secretary Rumsfeld refused to recognize the swelling potency of the Sunni insurgency: "I don't use the phrase 'guerrilla war'... because there isn't one."[76] But General John Abizaid, in his first Pentagon press conference after assuming the CENTCOM command in July 2003, candidly described the situation in Iraq as "a classical guerrilla-type campaign against us." Although the insurgency represented a low-intensity conflict, Abizaid flatly stated, "It's war, however you describe it."[77]

Ambassador Bremer later admitted: "We really didn't see the insurgency coming."[78] Bremer wrote in his memoir that he repeatedly tried "to reach the president's ear" to stress the need for more U.S. troops to stabilize postwar Iraq.[79] Bremer called Rice to reinforce his warning that "the Coalition's got about *half* the number of soldiers we need here and we run a real risk of having this thing go south on us."

President Bush brashly told reporters in July 2003: "There are some who feel...that the conditions are such that they can attack us there. My answer is, *bring them on*" (author's emphasis).[80] The statement reflected the president's *macho* Bombastic Bushkin persona, which sparked criticism that his bellicose words only encouraged more attacks upon American troops.

In October 2003 a new National Intelligence Estimate (NIE) found that the insurgency had gained support from local conditions and grievances, such as the presence of occupying U.S. troops—rather than foreign terrorists. The analysts also pointed to signs of an "incipient civil war." Significantly, the CIA and intelligence community's assessment of the increasing violence in Iraq was requested by the U.S. Central Command—not the White House.[81] Robert Hutchings, chairman of the National Intelligence Council from 2003 to 2005, remembered the cool reception the 2003 NIE estimate received in the White House and Pentagon. "Frankly, senior officials simply weren't ready to pay attention to analysis that didn't conform to their own optimistic scenarios."[82]

As late as May 2005, Vice President Cheney declared: "I think they're *in the last throes*, if you will, of the insurgency" (author's emphasis).[83] However, with the insurgency augmented by growing sectarian violence, Cheney admitted a year later: "I don't think anybody anticipated the level of violence we've encountered."[84]

But the vice president's statement blatantly ignored the many reports warning about postwar violence, drawn from Iraq's history and the bitter sectarian splits among Iraqis. Cheney's uncritical acceptance of the neoconservative vision of a "cakewalk" victory followed by a warm welcome by the Iraqi people—advanced by Ahmed Chalabi to encourage an American invasion to topple Saddam Hussein—contributed to the self-delusion in the White House.

Former Secretary of State Colin Powell disclosed in an April 2006 London television interview: "I made the case to General Franks and Secretary Rumsfeld *before the president* that I was not sure we had enough troops.... A judgment was made by those responsible that the troop strength was adequate" (author's emphasis).[85] Powell wryly noted: "They were anticipating a different kind of immediate aftermath of the fall of Baghdad; it turned out to be not exactly as they had anticipated."

A Futile Search

Graham Allison's Government Organization lens provides an excellent tool to evaluate why the Central Intelligence Agency (CIA) presented such an inflated assessment of Saddam Hussein's inventory of weapons of mass destruction. The agency's top Middle East analyst described the normal intelligence process: "The intelligence community collects information, evaluates its credibility, and combines it with other information to help make sense of situations abroad that could affect U.S. interests."[86]

The CIA's organizational culture stressed the need to separate the collection and analysis of raw intelligence from the political process of policy-making. The strong presumption of Iraq possessing an expanding WMD arsenal tainted the process and its conclusions. When UN arms inspectors were forced out of Iraq in 1998, the CIA had no human assets inside Iraq monitoring Saddam Hussein's WMD program. Nevertheless, CIA Director George Tenet confidently told President Bush prior to the war that proving Iraq possessed a WMD arsenal would be a "slam dunk," a comment he later labeled the "two dumbest words I ever said."[87]

Deputy Secretary of Defense Wolfowitz explained after the toppling of Saddam Hussein's regime why the Bush administration selected Iraq's WMD program as the key rationale for the war: "We settled on the one issue that everyone could agree on which was weapons of mass destruction as the core reason."[88] Major bureaucratic disagreements over the extent of Iraq's support for terrorism weakened that argument for war. The third rationale for war, Iraq's criminal treatment of the Iraqi people, Wolfowitz felt was "not a reason to put American kids' lives at risk, certainly not on the scale we did it."

Taking advantage of Colin Powell's popularity at home and respect abroad, President Bush asked his secretary of state to present America's case against Saddam Hussein's dangerous WMD program to the UN Security Council. Secretary Powell's February 5, 2003, presentation included satellite photos, taped communication intercepts, human intelligence, and findings from foreign intelligence services to dramatically highlight the threat of Saddam Hussein's WMD arsenal.

Powell disclosed that eye witness accounts described "biological weapons factories on wheels and on rails" that could produce anthrax and botulinum toxin.[89] The secretary displayed satellite photos allegedly revealing how Iraq hid its illicit chemical weapons production within dual-use civilian factories. Furthermore, Powell warned that Iraq had developed small unmanned aerial vehicles (UAVs) that could deliver biological agents and chemical weapons to its neighbors, or if transported, even against the United States.[90]

Secretary of State Powell charged that Saddam Hussein never abandoned his nuclear weapons ambition. He pointed to Iraq's "repeated covert attempts to acquire high-specification aluminum tubes from 11 different countries," showing pictures of aluminum tubes the CIA had seized en route to Iraq. Powell emphasized that most U.S. experts concluded that the tubes would serve as centrifuge rotors to enrich uranium. Secretary Powell concluded: "Leaving Saddam Hussein in possession of weapons of mass destruction for a few more months or years is not an option, not in a post-September 11th world."

However, Secretary Powell's UN Security Council presentation excluded any mention of Iraq's alleged attempt to obtain yellowcake uranium from Niger. Eight days earlier President Bush had declared in his 2003 State of the Union Address: "The British government has learned that Saddam Hussein recently sought significant quantities of uranium from Africa."[91] Those 16 words sparked a major controversy, which compelled the White House to recant the assertion, CIA Direct Tenet to issue a public apology, and NSC Deputy Director Stephen Hadley to admit his error of including the statement in the president's annual address. The CIA had warned Hadley before Bush's October 7 speech in Cincinnati that they had grave reservations about the documents, later deemed as forgeries.

In January 2003 the director general of the International Atomic Energy Agency (IAEA), Dr. Mohamed Elbaradei, reported to the UN Security Council as follows: "We have to date found no evidence that Iraq has revived its nuclear weapons program since its elimination of the program in 1990s."[92] ElBaradei gave an updated report to the UN Security Council about two weeks before the United States invaded Iraq, presenting his agency's assessment that the "documents, which form the basis for reports of recent uranium transactions between Iraq and Niger are, in fact, not authentic."[93] The IAEA and a team of international centrifuge experts also found that the high-strength aluminum tubes were intended for rocket production, not uranium enrichment.

The Bush administration dispatched its highest-ranking hawk, Vice President Dick Cheney, to discredit the IAEA. Cheney stated on March 16: "We believe he [Hussein] has, in fact, reconstituted nuclear weapons. I think Mr. ElBaradei frankly is wrong."[94] After the war Cheney admitted to Tim Russert: "I did misspeak.... We never had any evidence that he had acquired a nuclear weapon."[95]

Secretary of State Powell's speech to the UN Security Council embraced many of the findings in the intelligence community's October 2002 National Intelligence Estimate (NIE). A senior intelligence official revealed that the White House had avoided requesting a NIE because Bush's advisers knew "there were disagreements over details in almost every aspect of the administration's case against Iraq."[96] The White House admitted that President Bush never read the 2002 NIE.[97]

The October 2002 NIE, with an unclassified version released later that month, buttressed the Bush administration's contention that Saddam Hussein's WMD program represented a growing threat to the United States and its friends. However, caveats and disagreements from various intelligence participants, particularly by the State Department and Energy Department, were not easily found, often appearing as footnotes. Among the NIE document's key judgments appeared the incendiary statement that Iraq was reconstituting its nuclear weapons program, and if it obtained weapons grade uranium from abroad, "it could make a nuclear weapon within several months to a year."[98]

The NIE analysis declared Iraq's attempts to obtain high-strength aluminum tubes manifested Saddam Hussein's goal of building a centrifuge uranium enrichment program. However, the State Department's Bureau of Intelligence and Research (INR) offered an alternative view that the tubes were intended for Iraq's conventional artillery rockets. Iraq's clandestine purchase of high-strength aluminum tubes, combined with Iraq's alleged efforts to obtain yellowcake uranium in Africa, became a pivotal argument supporting the Bush administration's emotional contention that Saddam Hussein sought to build a nuclear arsenal.

The White House Iraq Group's (WHIG) strategy to market the war with Iraq began on September 8, 2002, with speeches warning about the aluminum tubes and frightening "mushroom cloud" imagery, later evoked in speeches by NSC Adviser Rice and then President Bush.[99]

However, the Energy Department's nuclear centrifuge experts at the Oak Ridge National Laboratory and Livermore National Laboratory flatly rejected the CIA's conclusion. In 2001 Houston G. Wood III, acknowledged as among the most eminent living experts on centrifuge physics, concluded that the aluminum tubes were "too heavy, three times too thick and certain to leak" if Iraq utilized them as centrifuges to enrich uranium.[100] Other analysts pointed out that the specialized aluminum tubes matched the dimensions and alloy used in the Italian-made Medusa 81 rocket, which Iraq had copied.[101]

After the collapse of the Hussein regime, CIA Director Tenet named David Kay, a former UN weapons inspector, to head the CIA's 1,400 person Iraq Survey Group (ISG) in its search for Iraq's alleged weapons of mass destruction. When Kay later delivered his interim report to a closed session with the House and Senate intelligence committees, he informed them that the ISG had found no chemical or biological weapon stockpiles in Iraq. Furthermore, Iraq's nuclear program existed in only "the very most rudimentary" state, less advanced than the programs of Libya or Iran.[102] Dr. Kay subsequently told the Senate Armed Services Committee: "It turns out we were all wrong."[103]

Kay believed the intelligence failure arose because the CIA lacked its own spies on the ground in Iraq, spoiled by the high-quality intelligence obtained from UN arms inspectors inside Iraq. This forced the agency after 1998, when Saddam Hussein kicked out the UN monitors, to become too dependent upon "spy satellites, intercepted communications and intelligence developed by foreign spies and by defectors and exiles."[104] Kay underscored the certainty within the CIA about the existence of a growing Iraqi WMD program and stockpiles of unconventional weapons—decision-making characteristics found in *groupthink*. "Alarm bells should have gone off when everyone believes the same thing....No one stood up and said, 'Let's examine the footings for these conclusions.'"

Charles A. Duelfer, who replaced Kay, issued a three-volume report to Congress in October 2004. The ISG director concluded that in 1996 the Iraqi government had destroyed the last factory capable of producing militarily significant quantities of chemical or biological weapons.[105] When America and its allies invaded Iraq, Saddam Hussein's regime did not possess large stockpiles of deadly WMDs, nor was it attempting to produce them. Furthermore, Duelfer stated it would have taken Iraq years to develop a nuclear weapon.

Duefler also debunked a May 2003 CIA assessment that several trailers found in Iraq after the war proved that Iraq planned to produce biological agents for weapons. The ISG chief concluded that the mobile labs were designed to produce hydrogen for weather balloons used in artillery practice, contrary to the sole eye-witness report of an Iraqi exile in Germany code-named Curveball.

The Blame Game

CIA Director Tenet loyally defended the CIA's role in the WMD intelligence flap in a February 2004 speech at Georgetown University. He argued his "provisional bottom line" was that Saddam did not have a nuclear weapon although he wanted one, "but we may have overestimated the progress Saddam was making."[106] Tenet acknowledged "discrepancies" in the claims of a key human source (Curveball) on the existence of Iraqi mobile biological weapons labs, but his "bottom line" suggested that Iraq intended to develop biological weapons.

More pointedly, Tenet emphasized the intelligence community never portrayed Iraq as an imminent threat to the United States. Left unstated but central to the rush to war was President Bush's UN declaration that Saddam Hussein's regime represented "a grave and gathering danger."[107] Tenet announced his resignation as DCI on June 3, 2004.

On July 7, 2004, the Senate Select Committee on Intelligence issued a scath-ing report on the intelligence community's inaccurate assessment of Iraq's WMD program. The investigators found the major judgments in the October 2002 NIE—Iraq was reconstituting its nuclear program, possessed biological and chemical weapons, and was developing an unmanned aerial vehicle for biological agents—"either overstated, or were not supported by, the underlying intelligence reporting."[108] The committee blamed the intelligence community for professional lapses in its "analytic trade craft."

The Senate report directly faulted *groupthink* for the intelligence community's exaggerated findings and general acceptance of the worst-case scenario that Iraq possessed an active and expanding WMD program. "This 'group think' dynamic led Intelligence Community analysts, collectors and managers to both interpret ambiguous evidence as conclusively indicative of a WMD program as well as ignore or minimize evidence that Iraq did not have active and expanding weapons of mass destruction programs."

In March 2005 the commission appointed by President Bush prior to the 2004 presidential election, headed by Judge Laurence Silberman and former Senator Charles Robb, issued its finding on U.S. intelligence capabilities and failures. The presidential commission found the intelligence community's prewar Iraq assess-ments "riddled with errors."[109] The 2002 NIE findings on Iraq's nuclear arms program, biological and chemical weapons, and unmanned aerial vehicles all reached wrong conclusions. The commission criticized the CIA's tardiness in not authenticating the "transparently forged documents purporting to show that Iraq had attempted to procure uranium form Niger."[110]

The presidential commission report identified as the central flaw in the 2002 NIE analysis the stress on supporting dire assumptions about Iraq's WMD with uncritical acceptance of nearly worthless or misleading information, while "they explained away or simply disregarded evidence that pointed in the other direction."[111] The presidential commission tactfully concluded: "Intelligence analysts worked in an environment that did not encourage skepticism about the conventional wisdom." However, instead of labeling the flawed process *group-think*, the commission described the focus on existing assumptions as "tunnel vision."[112]

Paul Pillar, the CIA's top Middle East analyst, criticized the "upside-down relationship between intelligence and policy" on Iraq during the Bush administration. Pillar charged that the administration "used intelligence not to inform decision-making, but to justify a decision already made."[113] He maintained that the Bush national security team "cherry-picked" intelligence data to win public backing for war with Iraq. Although the Silberman-Robb commission found no evidence of administration pressure, Pillar argued that intelligence analysts "felt a strong wind consistently blowing in one direction."

Graham Allison's Governmental Politics Model provided further key insights into the intelligence failure. Vice President Cheney visited the CIA's headquarters eight times to press for information backing the administration's conclusions.[114] Cheney's Chief of Staff Scooter Libby also kept asking questions about existing data, seeking supporting intelligence to bolster the White House's prevailing assumptions.

Over nine months in 2003 Scooter Libby sent requests to the CIA "that generated between three hundred and five hundred documents."[115] Tenet pointed out that Wolfowitz and Libby "were relentless in asking us to check, recheck, and recheck."[116] These unique visits by a vice president pursuing intelligence leads, submitting analysts to "withering interrogation," and repeated demands to recheck data generated the "strong wind" blowing toward making a case for war.

Richard Kerr, a retired analyst who served twice as the CIA's deputy director for intelligence, led an internal investigation (still classified) of the CIA's analysis of Iraq's WMD program and the October 2002 NIE. Kerr found: "We may have relied too heavily on our prior knowledge and were not as careful as we should [have been]."[117] Kerr indicated that the basis for the yellowcake uranium portion of the NIE reflected extremely meager and very thin data. He particularly faulted the agency for not handling Curveball's information on Iraq's mobile biological lab more skeptically, particularly since he was the only source for the intelligence. Furthermore, no CIA agent ever interviewed Curveball to vet the information and veracity of the single source, who some labeled a fabricator.

Presidential scholar James Pfiffner examined the issue of whether President Bush misled the United States into a war with Iraq, particularly through allegations of a link between Saddam Hussein and al Qaeda's 9/11 attack on America. In his October 7 Cincinnati address, Bush stated, "We know Iraq and al Qaeda had high-level contacts over a year."[118] In late 2001 Vice President Cheney said an alleged meeting between al Qaeda plotter Mohamed Atta and an Iraqi agent in Prague was "pretty well confirmed." Defense Secretary Rumsfeld declared that the evidence of a tie between Saddam Hussein and al Qaeda appeared "bulletproof."

However, after the war President Bush acknowledged: "No, we've had no evidence that Saddam Hussein was involved with September the 11th."[119] Pfiffner observed: "We can conclude that his [President Bush] statements were misleading and deceptive, though not outright lies."[120]

The Governmental Politics lens also highlights how the neoconservatives ratcheted up pressure on CIA analysts when Defense Secretary Rumsfeld created the Office of Special Plans (OSP), to select raw data supporting the purported ties between Saddam Hussein and al Qaeda as well as Iraq's WMD program. A Pentagon adviser acknowledged: "The goal of Special Plans [was]...to put the data under the microscope to reveal what the intelligence community can't see."[121] Undersecretary of Defense for Policy Douglas Feith directed the secretive Office of Special Plans.

The Pentagon's civilian leaders thus bypassed their own intelligence experts. The former chief of Middle East intelligence of the Defense Intelligence Agency (DIA) bitterly noted: "The Pentagon [civilian leadership] has banded together to dominate the government's foreign policy....They're running [INC head Ahmed] Chalabi. The D.I.A. has been intimidated and beaten to a pulp."[122]

After the fall of Saddam Hussein and the failure to find WMDs in Iraq based on information provided to Feith and Cheney by the INC, its head Ahmed Chalabi proudly declared: "We are heroes in error."[123] The Iraqi refugees' agenda had succeeded—at the expense of the lives of U.S. soldiers, taxpayers' dollars, and America's reputation in the Middle East.

Most significantly, the OSP's selectively chosen data bypassed the normal give-and-take evaluation by the full intelligence community. Instead, Special Plans "stovepiped" the unvetted information to the Office of the Vice President. The unchecked information provided by Chalabi's Iraqi National Congress also reached top Bush administration officials, bolstered by a long-standing bond among Chalabi, Wolfowitz, and Libby.[124] The Special Plans findings were then used by the war supporters to demand that the CIA follow up the OSD's new intelligence leads.[125] The neoconservatives, backed by Rumsfeld and Cheney, thus succeeded in marginalizing the CIA.

In February 2007 the Pentagon's inspector general released a report that concluded that the Office of Undersecretary of Defense for Policy did not provide "the most accurate analysis of intelligence" to senior decision-makers.[126] The report described the disseminated "alternative intelligence assessments" of Doug Feith's office as "inconsistent with the consensus of the Intelligence Community." The DoD inspector general's report asserted that Undersecretary of Defense Feith's 2002 briefing to the White House "undercuts the Intelligence Community" and drew conclusions not fully backed by the available intelligence.

The Director of Central Intelligence (DCI), as the head of the intelligence community at that time, prepared summaries of intelligence findings in the President's Daily Brief (PDB), which circulated to other top national security officials. As a result of the failure to warn about the 9/11 terrorist attacks and inaccurate assessments of Iraq's WMDs, the 2004 Intelligence Reform and Terrorism Prevention Act transferred this overall intelligence authority from the CIA director, with the influential access to the president, to a new Director of National Intelligence (DNI). The CIA no longer stands first among equals in the intelligence community. The politicization of the CIA's intelligence on Iraq thus undermined the central role the CIA played since its creation in 1947 in the collection of intelligence and analysis of international threats to America's interests.

In summary, Graham Allison's Rational Actor Model emphasizes the importance of examining all possible policy alternatives and carefully evaluating the costs and benefits of each option. However, President Bush and his national security team rejected any policy recommendations that diverged from their focus on toppling Saddam Hussein with a minimum number of U.S. troops. Anxious to launch the historic second step in the war on terror, President Bush flatly rejected the advice of realists that containment had effectively diminished the threat of Iraq through no-fly zones, the UN oil embargo, and the inability of Saddam Hussein to rebuild his shattered military after the 1991 Gulf War.

The policy myopia over adequate forces for post-hostilities security in Iraq also suggested that Deputy Defense Secretary Wolfowitz and Rumsfeld, backed by Vice President Cheney, assumed they could arrange for a quick handover of power in Baghdad to the INC's Ahmed Chalabi, thereby facilitating a quick exit of U.S. troops. CIA Director Tenet viewed the Office of the Vice President (OVP) and Pentagon moves as "thinly veiled efforts to put Chalabi in charge of post-invasion Iraq."[127] In early April 2003, the Pentagon flew Chalabi and 570 of his untrained INC supporters to southern Iraq without the advance knowledge of the State Department and the strong misgivings of the CIA.[128] Wolfowitz countermanded a CENTCOM order refusing to transport Chalabi and his men to Iraq.[129]

CPA Administrator Bremer's orders for total de-Baathification and disbanding of the Iraqi army only fueled the rage in the Sunni towns and villages, providing trained military men and youth with jobs in the insurgency. However, Ahmed Chalabi and his neoconservative supporters in the Pentagon and OVP believed that weakening the Baathists and the Army as a national institution would facilitate Chalabi's rise to power over Iraq. NSC members expected the order would specify that Iraqi military members below the rank of lieutenant colonel could apply for reinstatement, but Bremer's pronouncement did not mention that provision.[130]

During his July 2007 confirmation hearings to become chairman of the Joint Chiefs of Staff, Admiral Michael Mullen listed seven administration mistakes, including an assessment that the disbanding of the entire Iraqi Army undermined security, reconstruction, and provided a "recruiting pool" for extremist groups.[131] He also faulted the de-Baathification process as more divisive than helpful.

Graham Allison's Governmental Politics lens revealed how the so-called cabal between Rumsfeld and Cheney reduced Secretary of State Colin Powell's influence in White House deliberations, while NSC Adviser Condoleezza Rice never weighed-in to balance the policy debate with the inexperienced president. Rumsfeld often would not even answer Rice's calls, arrogantly ignoring many NSC decisions.[132] The Pentagon Office of Special Plans "stovepiped" upward the most threatening, unchecked intelligence data to the White House without review by the intelligence community. Special Plans thus undermined the pivotal role of the CIA in the established intelligence assessment process.

Allison's Government Organization model disclosed how the Bush administration promoted the case for an immediate preemptive war with Iraq by politicizing the CIA, ignoring intelligence challenging its most compelling arguments for war, and cherry-picking the most threatening raw data. As official investigations subsequently discovered, *groupthink* developed within the CIA that discouraged any questioning of the underlying assumption that Iraq posed an immediate threat to the United States.

As a result of the administration's wielding of frightening, inaccurate, and hyped intelligence, President Bush created a "credibility gap" between himself and the American people after the Iraq Survey Group's postwar investigation discovered no weapons of mass destruction. A February 2007 *Washington Post*-ABC

News Poll found 63 percent of respondents stated they cannot trust the Bush administration to report potential threats from other countries honestly and accurately.[133] This unfortunate state of affairs resulted from what arms expert Greg Thielmann aptly called "faith-based intelligence"—only accepting data that backed the Bush administration's march to war with Iraq.[134]

Part III

Pursuing a Vision

Chapter Ten

Axis of Evil: An Inverted Threat Matrix

States like these, and their terrorist allies, constitute an axis of evil, arming to threaten the peace of the world.

President George W. Bush's 2002 State of the Union Address greatly expanded the war on terror from a focus on al Qaeda and its Afghan Taliban hosts to three rogue states seeking dangerous weapons of mass destruction: Iraq, Iran, and North Korea. Bush labeled these countries "an axis of evil" that threatened world peace: "By seeking weapons of mass destruction, these regimes pose a grave and growing danger. They could provide these arms to terrorists, giving them the means to match their hatred. They could attack our allies or attempt to blackmail the United States."[1]

President Bush had already ordered the Pentagon to secretly plan a preemptive invasion of Iraq, his major objective, so including Iran and North Korea in the malevolent bloc of nations camouflaged the administration's immediate target for regime change. Indeed, since Iraq and Iran had fought a bloody eight-year war and North Korea maintained an isolated posture in Asia, a common tie appeared nebulous to most informed observers.

Bush speechwriter David Frum had initially crafted the metaphor "axis of hatred," but Bush's chief speechwriter Michael Gerson changed it to "axis of evil" for the more "theological language" Bush favored in his good versus evil war against terrorism.[2] Frum proudly observed that President Bush soon embraced "axis of evil" as his personal epithet, defiantly repeating it despite international criticism of the phrase. Bush later explained: "It just kind of resonates."[3] President Bush also believed the phrase manifested the same tough tone as President Ronald Reagan's depiction of the Soviet Union as the "Evil Empire."

Although the expression "axis of evil" symbolized the new thrust of Bush's post-9/11 foreign policy, critics such as Harvard's Graham Allison called the clever rhetoric "harmful both conceptually and operationally." The rhetorical use of "axis" suggested an alignment that did not exist and operationally the harsh depiction provoked adverse reactions in Iran, North Korea, and throughout the world.[4]

Furthermore, the Bush administration's concentration upon Iraq inverted the threat matrix employed by the intelligence community to prioritize national security dangers. The Bush national security team's virtual obsession with Iraq ignored the reality that Iran and North Korea had surged ahead in the pursuit of weapons of mass destruction, while Iraq remained militarily crippled after the 1991 Persian Gulf War and the subsequent UN oil embargo.

Friends to Bitter Foes

The United States and Iran experienced a roller-coaster ride in their diplomatic relations after World War II, featuring highs of friendly dealings followed by lows of hostility.[5] The 1953 CIA-backed coup that toppled the democratically elected government of Prime Minister Mohammad Mossadeqh symbolized to Iranians America's meddling in their domestic affairs. The 1951 nationalization of the Anglo-Iranian Oil Company, even though Mossadeqh offered compensation, triggered the events leading to the ouster of Prime Minister Mossadeqh, resulting in Mohammad Reza Shah Pahlavi assuming autocratic powers. The subsequent close American relations with the increasingly repressive shah ensured a dominant role for the United States in safeguarding Iran's security against Cold War threats, building the Iranian military into a formidable regional power, and cementing commercial relations with the oil-rich Persian Gulf nation.

The second dramatic event undermining America's relations with Iran occurred after the 1979 Islamic Revolution forced the shah to flee Iran. Student radicals seized and held 52 American embassy hostages for 444 days, as televised images of the blindfolded American hostages—surrounded by demonstrators chanting "Death to America"—became seared into the memories of Americans. Anger toward Iran steadily intensified, driven by the daily reports on the humiliating Iran hostage crisis and the Carter administration's inability to free the U.S. diplomats and Marine guards at the embassy.

President Jimmy Carter had emphasized human rights as the cornerstone of his foreign policy. However, he ignored the abuses under the shah and his SAVAK (secret police), acknowledging the vital strategic importance of the U.S. alliance with the shah. President Carter memorably declared in a 1977 New Years Eve toast to the shah: "Iran, under the great leadership of the Shah, is an island of stability in one of the more troubled areas of the world."[6]

The Carter administration broke diplomatic relations with revolutionary Iran, froze an estimated $14 billion in Iranian assets, and approved a failed hostage rescue. Nevertheless, Ayatollah Ruhollah Khomeini refused to release the hostages until January 20, 1981—after the inauguration of President Ronald Reagan, who narrowly defeated Carter in the 1980 election, aided by the Iranian hostage issue.

The Iraqi dictator Saddam Hussein launched a September 22, 1980, preemptive attack on Iran, attempting to take advantage of the revolutionary turmoil within the Islamic Republic and the collapse of Iranian military collaboration with the United States. Even though Iraq was the aggressor state, the UN Security Council and other nations refused to assist Iran until Ayatollah Khomeini released the American hostages. The war with Iraq increased pressures on the Islamic regime to free the hostages, win international backing against the aggressor Iraq, and recover Iran's seized assets in the United States in order to purchase more arms.

President Reagan, concerned about the danger of the Iranian Islamic Republic spreading its Shiite revolutionary influence throughout the oil-rich region, reversed America's hostile relations with the Iraqi dictator as a sponsor of terrorism, ordering covert support of Saddam Hussein's regime during the bloody war with Iran. However, the Iran-Contra Affair revealed the Reagan administration sold missiles to Iran (using Israel as an intermediary), despite President Reagan's strong admonitions against dealing with terrorist states such as Iran. The scandal marred President Reagan's second term.

During his first term President Bill Clinton followed a policy of "dual containment" toward both Iran and Iraq. Anthony Lake, Clinton's assistant for national security affairs, listed Iran with Cuba, North Korea, Iraq, and Libya as an aggressive, outlaw "backlash" state seeking to develop weapons of mass destruction.[7] The Clinton administration sought a favorable regional balance of power in the post–Cold War era without depending on either Iraq or Iran. His national security team viewed Iran as a lesser threat than Iraq because its WMD program appeared at an earlier stage of development. Lake favored dialogue with the Iranian Islamic regime and positive inducements such as trade and aid to change Iran's unacceptable support of terrorism, quest for weapons of mass destruction, and opposition to the Israeli-Palestine peace process.

After Republicans won control of Congress in the 1994 elections, Clinton faced GOP efforts to ratchet up pressures on Iran and Libya. President Clinton issued two Executive Orders in spring 1995 that banned U.S. investment in Iran's energy sector and forbade U.S. trade and investment in that nation.[8] In 1996 he signed the Iran and Libya Sanctions Act (ILSA) that mandated U.S. sanctions against any foreign firm investing over $40 million in a year in either state. However, ILSA's secondary sanctions against countries investing in the Iranian oil and gas industry generated "universal, immediate and unequivocally hostile" international attacks, with the European Union (EU) filing a formal protest.[9]

The May 1997 landslide election victory of the reformist President Mohammad Khatami, with his call for a "dialogue among civilizations," encouraged the Clinton administration to initiate steps for renewed engagement with the Islamic Republic of Iran. President Khatami called for a crack in the "bulky wall of mistrust between us and the U.S. Administration."[10]

Clinton's Secretary of State Madeleine Albright responded to Iranian President Khatami's call for a new dialogue in June 1998: "As the wall of mistrust comes down, we can develop with the Islamic republic, when it is ready, a road map leading to normal relations."[11] She applauded Khatami's rejection of terrorism and Iran's record of opposition to Afghanistan's export of drugs. Secretary Albright acknowledged in March 2000 America's role in "orchestrating the overthrow of Iran's popular Prime Minister, Mohammed Massadegh," recognizing Iranian resentment of this U.S. intervention in their internal affairs.[12] She further conceded America's "regrettably short-sighted" support of Saddam Hussein during the Iran-Iraq war. However, Albright did not apologize: "Neither Iran, nor we, can forget the past. It has scarred us both."

Even though President Khatami faced increasing Iranian conservative opposition to his reform agenda and called for improved diplomatic relations with the United States, the Clinton administration indicated an interest in restoring ties. In September 2000 Secretary Albright rushed back to New York to sit in the front row during the Iranian president's address to UNESCO. The next day President Khatami arrived at the United Nations six hours earlier than scheduled to listen to President Clinton's speech to the General Assembly; Clinton remained in the hall to hear Khatami's address.[13] In addition, for the first time since the 1979 embassy takeover, on September 15, 2000, Secretary Albright and Iran's Foreign Minister Kamal Kharrazi sat together at a UN six-nation meeting on Afghanistan and its Taliban rulers. Iran almost went to war with Afghanistan in 1998 after the Taliban regime killed 10 Iranian diplomats and a journalist.[14]

Rejecting Engagement

The Bush administration often appeared to automatically disparage and derail the foreign policies initiated by President Clinton. President George W. Bush's relations with Iran manifested this tendency. In Condoleezza Rice's 2000 *Foreign Affairs* article outlining the foreign policy a Bush administration would follow, she blasted Iran's attempts to destabilize Saudi Arabia, support terrorism against America, develop sensitive military technologies, and threaten Israel.[15] Rice questioned how much authority Iran's moderate President Khatami really exercised in the Islamic Republic. But in June 2001 President Khatami won reelection with over 20 million votes, despite the vigorous opposition of Iranian conservatives.

On June 22, 2001, Bush's Attorney General John Ashcroft announced the federal indictments of 13 Saudis and a Lebanese man for the 1996 tanker truck bombing of the Khobar barracks in Saudi Arabia that killed 19 U.S. servicemen. At a joint press conference with FBI Director Louis Freeh, Ashcroft charged that the "Iranian government inspired, supported and supervised members of Saudi Hezbollah."[16]

The 2001 debate over renewal of the Iran-Libya Sanctions Act found the Bush administration advocating only a two-year extension, but Congress passed a five-year extension of the ILSA sanctions, again angering the Iranian government. However, a 2006 report to Congress found that between 1999 and 2004 foreign firms invested $11.5 billion in Iran's energy sector, despite the ILSA sanctions. Over $7 billion in foreign investment in Iran occurred after President Bush took office.[17] The fear of international retaliation and objections by key U.S. allies resulted in the United States not sanctioning any foreign firms under the ILSA law through 2006.

Initially some Iranians felt the new Bush administration, with the oil industry backgrounds of Bush and Cheney, would seek to restore American private investment in Iran's lucrative oil sector. Indeed, while serving as the chief executive officer (CEO) of Halliburton in 1996, Dick Cheney declared: "We seem to be sanction-happy as a government.... The problem is the good Lord didn't see fit to always put oil and gas resources where there are democratic governments."[18] Halliburton opened a Tehran office in 2000 using a subsidiary incorporated in the Cayman Islands and based in the United Arab Emirates that generated $30–$40 million a year in profits. In January 2005 it won a contract to drill for oil in a large Iranian gas field called Pars.[19] However, when Cheney became vice president, he became a key hard-line opponent of diplomatic steps to improve relations with Iran.

The Bush administration opened "secret, back-channel talks in Geneva" with Iran on Afghanistan and the Taliban.[20] The Iranian government had long opposed Saudi Arabia's efforts to export the radical Wahabi view of Islam to Afghanistan—that viewed Shiites as infidels—and the Pakistan intelligence agency, Inter-Services Intelligence (ISI), for backing of Taliban forces. Iran was the Northern Alliance's major supporter in its struggle against the Taliban. When war loomed in 1998, Ayatollah Hashemi Rafsanjani counseled against a military conflict: "Afghanistan is like a swamp; anyone can fall into it, but a few can get out of it safely and undamaged."[21]

After the horrific 9/11 terrorist attacks, the Iranian people emotionally took to the streets to show sympathy with Americans. Iranians stood at a soccer game for a moment of silence remembering the victims of the 9/11 attacks.[22] President Khatami not only condemned the 9/11 attacks, he labeled them anti-Islamic and barbaric. Soon Iranian advisers in Afghanistan operated close to American CIA and military personnel in the Northern Alliance-controlled areas. Iran also announced it would assist downed American pilots on Iranian soil and allowed the United States to transport food and humanitarian goods to Afghanistan through Iran's territory.

Iranian diplomats played a key role in the December 2001 Bonn Conference to establish a new Afghanistan government headed by Hamid Karzai. James Dobbins, President Bush's special envoy to Afghanistan, publicly acknowledged Iran's role as very helpful at the Bonn Conference, obtaining support for the Karzai regime from a recalcitrant Northern Alliance representative.[23] At the January 2002 Tokyo donors' conference, Iran pledged $500 million in aid for reconstruction in Afghanistan, a greater amount than other neighboring states. In March Iran offered to quarter, clothe, and train as many as 20,000 new Afghan army soldiers. Milani concluded that Iran's "overall Afghan policy has contributed more to moderation and stability than to extremism and instability."[24]

Despite the shared goals of the United States and Iran in dealing with Afghanistan—plus Iran's help in creating the Karzai government—the Bush administration restricted its diplomatic dialogue with Iran for the next year to "infrequent, low-level and inconclusive exchanges."[25] In early January 2002 Israel boarded a Palestinian Authority-owned freighter, the *Karine A*, carrying 50 tons of weapons with Iranian markings. Although the Palestinian captain of the *Karine A* did not directly implicate Iran, he described a tie to the Lebanese Hezbollah terrorist group that Iran backed. The seizure of the weapons shipment halted the budding relationship between the United States and Iran.[26] One Bush administration official later stated that despite Iran's cooperation on Afghanistan, the Iranian arms shipment to Palestine "was a sign to the president that the Iranians weren't serious."[27]

President Bush's "axis of evil" address slammed the door on *rapprochement* with Iran. The supreme leader, Ayatollah Ali Khamenei, warned Iranians to prepare to repel a U.S. military attack: "The arrogant enemy also must know that Iran is neither Afghanistan nor Iraq."[28] CIA Director George Tenet interpreted Iran's contradictory behavior as reflecting "a deep-seeded suspicion among Tehran's clerics that the United States is committed to encircling and overthrowing them." Indeed, neoconservatives Richard Perle and David Frum asserted that Iran's mullahs represented a threat that would not end by simply bombing their nuclear facilities: "The regime must go."[29]

In the National Intelligence Council's January 2003 pre-Iraq war assessment of the "Regional Consequences of Regime Change in Iraq," the analysts cautioned that a quick victory over Iraq "would increase the fears of Syria and Iran that they would become targets of future US military operations."[30] The Intelligence Community assessment warned: "The degree to which Iran would pursue policies that either support or undermine US goals in Iraq would depend on how Tehran viewed specific threats to its interests and the potential US reaction."

As a result of the positive cooperation between the United States and Iran on the issue of Afghanistan, several dinner meetings were held in the United States involving former U.S. ambassadors, the Iranian ambassador to the United Nations, and the head of the American Iranian Council. At one dinner, Iran's Foreign Minister Kamal Kharrazi responded to a question: "Yes, we are ready to normalize relations."[31] In May 2003 Iran faxed the secret Iranian proposal for improved relations—approved by the supreme leader Ayataolla Khamenei, President Khatami, and Foreign Minister Kharrazi—to the U.S. State Department, and sent it through an intermediary to the White House, to settle outstanding issues.[32]

New York Times reporter Nicholas Kristof posted the Iranian proposed "Grand Bargain" document on his blog. The Swiss ambassador to Iran, who represented U.S. interests in Tehran, also conveyed the text of an Iranian proposal to Washington with a cover letter that paraphrased key points, which the Bush administration rejected. Kristof's "final clean version as transmitted" identified Iran's diplomatic objectives: the United States removing the Islamic republic from its "axis of evil" and terrorism lists, ending economic sanctions on Iran, granting full access to peaceful nuclear technology, and disarming anti-Iranian terrorists (MKO) in Iraq. In return, Iran agreed to discuss "full transparency" to reassure the United States that it did not seek or possess WMD, pledged decisive action against al Qaeda terrorists on Iranian territory, and promised support for the stabilization of Iraq. Iran would also agree to end its aid to Hamas, transform Hezbollah into a Lebanon political organization, and endorse the Saudi two-state solution to the Israeli-Palestinian conflict.

Flynt Leverett, a former CIA analyst who served as senior director for Middle East policy on President Bush's National Security Council until 2003, underscored the divisions within the Bush administration that contributed to a "fundamental strategic deficit" on how to deal with Iran.[33] The lack of coherence in U.S. policy toward Iran, according to Leverett, resulted from the conflicting approaches of Secretary of State Rice, who viewed negotiations as a tactic to manage the Iranian nuclear issue; Vice President Cheney, who "strongly opposed" any grand bargain, calling for a "more coercive approach" to Iran; and Defense and Treasury Department officials, who focused upon economic, financial, and nonmilitary sanctions to pressure Iran.

Leverett thought President Bush concentrated on keeping all his key foreign policy advisors "on board" in backing his Iran policy, while he tried to keep his options open. The inclusion of Iran in the "axis of evil" reflected Bush's "own deep-seated reluctance to go down a road that would require him ultimately to extend some sort of security guarantee toward Iran, thereby legitimating a political order he considers fundamentally illegitimate."[34]

In July 2002 the respected Ayatollah Jalaleddin Taheri blasted Ayatollah Khomeini's conservative successors for "crookedness, negligence, weakness.... Genghis-like behavior."[35] Taheri's charges reinvigorated the reform movement as students began to demonstrate for reforms. President Bush attempted to bolster Iran's resurgent reformers through a July 12 statement that criticized the "unelected people who are the real rulers of Iran."[36] Iran's conservative leaders portrayed Bush's words as America once again meddling in their domestic affairs and launched retaliatory attacks that torpedoed the reform movement's growing protests. Ansari felt Bush's "clumsy intervention" revealed the administration's "woeful ignorance" of the internal dynamics of Iranian politics.[37] President Bush expressed no regret for his incendiary remarks, declaring: "My job isn't to nuance.... My job is to say what I think. I think *moral clarity* is important" (author's emphasis).[38] The statement reflected Bush's Righteous Hawk persona.

The National Council of Resistance of Iran revealed on August 14, 2002, what U.S. Intelligence had not discovered: Iran had developed a top-secret uranium enrichment facility in Natanz and a heavy water production facility in Arak.[39] The Bush administration charged that the construction indicated Iran's intent to develop nuclear weapons, which violated the Non-Proliferation Treaty Iran had signed. The administration sought to move the issue from the International Atomic Energy Agency (IAEA) to the UN Security Council for punitive action. Director General Mohammed ElBaradei and some of his IAEA inspectors began a series of trips to examine suspected Iranian nuclear construction sites. The Iranian regime argued that the United States acted hypocritically, since it had supported Iran's nuclear development under the shah, approving a $15 billion agreement to construct eight nuclear plants in 1975.

The Iranian and American governments sparred diplomatically over Iran's efforts to advance its nuclear program, which Iran claimed focused on the production of peaceful nuclear energy. France, Germany, and Britain, the so-called EU-3, engaged Iran on the nuclear issue, hoping to eventually include the United States in the talks. The United States played the bad cop, insisting upon tough UN language in resolutions. The EU-3 nations assumed the good-cop role, gaining the support of Russia and China by diluting the conditions Bush demanded.

The presidential election of Mahmoud Ahmadinejad, the former mayor of Tehran, in June 2005 further aggravated relations with Washington. Ahmadinejad staunchly defended Iran's right to pursue nuclear conversion, even in an address before the United Nations. His harsh rhetoric, calling for Israel to be "wiped of the map" and depicting the Holocaust as a "myth," intensified American antagonism toward the Iranian regime. President Ahmadinejad proudly disclosed in June 2006: "I'm announcing officially that Iran has now joined the countries that have nuclear technology," but only for the purpose of peace, he hastily added.[40] Facing stronger sanctions in the United Nations, an Iranian spokesman cautioned that the United States could cause harm and pain to Iran: "But the United States is also susceptible to harm and pain."[41]

The American public appeared to back the tough talk of the Bush administration against Iran, still reflecting the negative feelings generated by the 1979 hostage crisis. A February 2006 Gallup Poll found 86 percent of Americans expressed an unfavorable view of Iran. Iran had risen to the status of America's greatest enemy in the minds of almost one-third of the respondents, replacing North Korea and Iraq.[42] However, a *New York Times*/CBS News Poll in March 2007 found that 65 percent of respondents felt Iran could be contained with diplomacy.[43]

The Bush administration's 2006 "National Security Strategy" starkly declared: "*We may face no greater challenge from a single country than from Iran*" (author's emphasis).[44] In addition to the threat Iran's nuclear development program represented to U.S. interests, the document charged that the Iranian regime also sponsored terrorism, threatened Israel, opposed Middle East peace, and disrupted democracy in Iraq.

John Negroponte, director of national intelligence, told a congressional hearing that Iran possessed "the largest inventory of ballistic missiles in the Middle East."[45] Negroponte portrayed the Tehran regime as "more confident and assertive" due to rising oil prices, bolstering its conventional military strength "to threaten to disrupt the operations and reinforcement of U.S. forces based in the region." However, the intelligence chief doubted Iran had a nuclear weapon or produced or acquired the necessary fissile material.

John Rood, assistant secretary of state of international security and nonproliferation told Congress on May 3, 2007, that Iran could acquire a long-range missile capable of attacking Europe and the United states in less than eight years. Iran might develop such a missile on its own or "Iran could procure a completed system from North Korea as it has done in the past."[46]

Nevertheless, stories proliferated about Bush administration plans to launch a military attack on Iran's suspected nuclear installations before leaving office. Cheney told an American Israel Public Affairs Committee (AIPAC) audience: "We will not allow Iran to have a nuclear weapon."[47] Seymour Hersh identified Vice President Cheney and his neoconservative staffer David Wurmser as staunch proponents of military action. A Pentagon consultant told Hersh: "More and more people see the weakening of Iran as the only way to save Iraq."[48] Some viewed air strikes on Iran as an explicit warning to the mullahs against continuing Iran's quest for nuclear weapons. Others, such as Cheney and Wurmser, felt "there can be no settlement of the Iraq war without regime change in Iran."[49]

The belief that bombing Iran would lead the Iranian people to rise up and topple the Islamic regime—a belief held by neoconservatives and some in the White House—"is a fool's errand," according to Bush's former Deputy Secretary of State, Richard Armitage.[50] Nevertheless, Cheney direly warned on January 2007 of the need to prevent "a nuclear-armed Iran, astride the world's supply of oil, able to adversely impact the global economy, prepared to use terrorist organizations, and/or their nuclear weapons to threaten their neighbors and others around the world."[51] A retired intelligence official told Hersh of a special Joint Chiefs of Staff planning group assigned the task of picking bombing targets in Iraq to strike within 24 hours of the president's command.[52]

The question of whether the United States possesses adequate intelligence on the exact location of all the nuclear program's facilities poses a critical challenge to such a military operation. Furthermore, underground tunnels made it doubtful whether all the major nuclear facilities could be destroyed, particularly without tactical nuclear warheads.[53] Critics stressed that an attack on Iran would rally the Iranian people behind the hard-line clerics, provoke Iran into working with Shiite militias to increase American casualties in Iraq and Afghanistan, encourage Hezbollah to attack American interests, and boost anti-American sentiment in the Middle East.

Iran's supreme leader, Ayatollah Ali Khamenei, threatened that if the United States attacked the Islamic republic, "Iran.will retaliate by damaging U.S. interests worldwide twice as much as the U.S. may inflict on Iran."[54] The senior commander of Iran's Revolutionary Guards ominously threatened that "the first place we target will be Israel."[55] A government spokesman forewarned that Iran could also cut oil production to drive up the world price for a barrel of oil, creating serious economic repercussions in the industrialized nations.

The British opposed military action against Iran. Foreign Secretary Jack Straw explained, "Because it's an infinitely worse option and there's no justification for it."[56] President Bush sought to quell the rumors of a pending U.S. military strike on Iran as "wild speculation."[57] In congressional testimony in February 2007, Secretary of Defense Robert Gates asserted, "We are not planning for a war with Iran."[58]

In May 2006 President Ahmadinejad sent an 18-page letter to President Bush that included religious references, criticism of the U.S. invasion of Iraq, and objections to the abuse of detainees. The letter represented the first top-level government-to-government communication since the 1979 hostage crisis. Many observers felt it presented President Bush an opening to resume a dialogue with Iran on pressing issues. But President Bush, still opposed to direct bilateral negotiations with Iran, dismissed the letter. On his May 2007 trip to the Middle East, Vice President Cheney, aboard a U.S. aircraft carrier in the Persian Gulf, bluntly warned Iran: "With two carrier strike groups in the Gulf, we're sending clear messages to friends and adversaries. We'll keep the sea lanes open."[59] During the vice president's trip, Egyptian President Hosni Mubarak and Jordan's King Abdullah II warned Cheney against a U.S. military attack on Iran.

Despite the call for tougher sanctions on Iran, President Bush opened the door a crack to diplomatic contacts with the Islamic regime, approving Secretary of State Rice's proposal for direct talks between American and Iranian officials in Baghdad on improving Iraqi security. On May 28, 2007, U.S. Ambassador to Iraq Ryan Crocker held a four-hour meeting with the Iranian ambassador in Prime Minister al-Maliki's office in Baghdad's fortified Green Zone. The change to permit bilateral talks reflected the impact of the firing of Defense Secretary Donald Rumsfeld, a key ally of Vice President Cheney, a hard-line opponent of diplomatic contact with Iran and North Korea that would "reward bad behavior."[60]

The diplomatic breakthrough appeared to indicate that President Bush was inching toward the bipartisan recommendations of the December 2006 Iraq Study Group (ISG). The ISG report recommended a "New Diplomatic Offensive" involving Iraq's regional neighbors, including Iran and Syria.[61] The report's Recommendation 9 underscored that the United States and Iran had cooperated in Afghanistan, suggesting the United States adopt a diplomatic incentive emphasizing political and economic reforms, rather than regime change, "as Iran now perceives it."[62]

Commentary published an inflammatory article in June 2007 titled, "The Case for Bombing Iran." Norman Podhoretz, a neoconservative advocate of the war in Iraq, compared Iran's President Ahmadinejad to Adolph Hitler: "Like Hitler, he is a revolutionary whose objective is to overturn the going international system and to replace it in the fullness of time with a new order dominated by Iran and ruled by the religio-political culture of Islamofascism."[63] Pohhoretz pleaded for President Bush to bomb Iran before leaving office to ensure "the survival of Israel, a country to which George W. Bush has been friendlier than any other President before him," and to avert a Middle East arms race.

The issue of Cheney's opposition to a diplomatic tack toward Iran broke out in June 2007, when remarks by his hawkish National Security Assistant David Wormser appeared on The Washington Note blog, suggesting a military approach over so-called failed diplomatic efforts to check Iran. Then IAEA director ElBaradei, the recipient of the 2005 Nobel Peace Prize for trying to slow the Bush administration's rush to war over Iraq's WMD, warned of "new crazies who say, 'Let's go and bomb Iran.'"[64] Secretary Rice felt compelled to affirm: "The president of the United States has made it clear that we are on a course that is a diplomatic course.... That policy is supported by all of the members of the cabinet, and by the vice president of the United States."[65]

A Diplomatic Agreement

When creating a threat matrix among the "axis of evil" states, North Korea clearly represented the greatest danger to U.S. interests with over 50 years of a hostile relationship marked with war, an extremely explosive Demilitarized Zone with almost 37,000 U.S. troops in "harm's way," and North Korea's advanced ballistic missile and nuclear program. At the time President Bush took office, the communist Democratic People's Republic of Korea (DPRK, also called North Korea) fielded an army of over 1 million soldiers—the fifth largest in the world—with over 800 ballistic missiles targeting the Republic of Korea (ROK, also called South Korea) and Japan.[66] North Korea's 12,000-plus artillery weapons, located within range of the Demilitarized Zone and the South Korean capital of Seoul, greatly imperiled forward-stationed U.S. and South Korean forces and "threatens all of Seoul with devastating attacks" in the event of war.[67]

General Gary Luck, the former commander of U.S. forces in Korea, estimated another Korean war could result in 1 million casualties—52,000 of them Americans.[68] During a May 1994 crisis with the DPRK over the removal of nuclear fuel rods, a Joint Chiefs contingency plan estimated a war with North Korea would require the deployment of "roughly half of all U.S. combat forces" to Korea.[69]

Created in 1948 after World War II, the DPRK's founding ruler Kim Il-Sung became a personal favorite of Joseph Stalin. When the DPRK invaded South Korea in June 1950 to reunite the two Koreas, President Harry Truman ordered General Douglas MacArthur to repel the invasion, obtained UN Security Council authorization to drive back the aggressor and subsequently approved—after Gen. MacArthur's bold amphibious landing at Inchon split the DPRK army—crossing the 38th parallel into North Korean territory. However, as American-led UN multinational forces approached the Yalu River, Chinese troops entered the war, prolonging the conflict.

The Korean War, which cost 36,574 American lives, ended with the July 27, 1953, armistice obtained under newly elected President Dwight Eisenhower.[70] North Korea remained an isolated totalitarian communist state after the collapse of the Soviet Union, a major source of its support. In the late 1980s the United States placed North Korea on the list of states that sponsor terrorism.

The United States kept approximately 680 nuclear weapons in South Korea during the 1970s, declining to about 150 by 1981.[71] The DPRK signed the International Nuclear Non-Proliferation Treaty in 1985 but refused to allow inspections of its nuclear capabilities as long as the United States maintained nuclear weapons in South Korea. On September 27, 1991, President George H.W. Bush dramatically declared that America would "eliminate its entire worldwide inventory of ground-launched short-range, that is, theater nuclear weapons."[72] The elder President Bush's 1991 policy change removed approximately 100 American tactical nuclear weapons from South Korea, putting pressure on North Korea to then allow weapons inspections. On January 31, 1991, the two Korean governments signed the Joint Declaration on the Denuclearization of the Korean Peninsula.

In January 1994 CIA Director James Woolsey told the Senate Select Committee on Intelligence that North Korea's military buildup constituted one of his major concerns. The CIA estimated the DPRK had built one or two nuclear weapons, produced weapons-grade plutonium, and exported missiles with a range of 625 miles or more. General James Clapper, head of the Defense Intelligence Agency, described North Korea as one of the intelligence community's biggest challenges because of "mysteries—things that are not predictable, not even knowable."[73]

North Korea announced in spring 1994 the removal of fuel rods from its Yongbyon nuclear reactor that could be processed into plutonium. The DPRK action sparked a crisis that led President Bill Clinton to threaten UN sanctions and order Stealth bombers and other military forces into South Korea to deter a North Korean preemptive attack on the ROK.[74] President Clinton received a military briefing on the possibility of a war with North Korea that projected "staggering losses for both sides."[75]

Clinton approved former President Jimmy Carter's unofficial trip to the North Korean capitol of Pyongyang to meet with President Kim Il Sung, who had invited Carter to assist in defusing the conflict. The North Korean leader expressed to Carter his willingness to freeze the DPRK's nuclear program at Yongbyon, permit IAEA inspectors to check the site, and initiate direct talks with South Korea.[76]

The Clinton administration followed up Carter's trip, engaging in talks with DPRK officials in Geneva, resulting in an August 12, 1994, preliminary understanding that outlined what would become the Agreed Framework.[77] Even after the death of the DPRK's founding president Kim Il Sung, with Kim Jong Il succeeding his father, negotiations continued.[78] In October 1994 the Agreed Framework was signed.

Clinton called the 1994 Agreed Framework a "good deal for the United States," which unfolded in three stages.[79] The first stage entailed North Korea not refueling its Yongbyon reactor and stopping construction on two larger reactors. The removed 8,000 fuel rods, if enriched, could have generated enough plutonium for five bombs.[80] In return, the United States and its allies would begin construction of a light-water reactor for energy—largely financed ($4 billion) by South Korea and Japan. A light-water reactor produces reactor-grade plutonium, not weapon-grade plutonium, as generated by the Yongbyon reactor.[81]

The American government also promised to send at least 50,000 metric tons of heavy fuel oil annually to provide the DPRK with energy until the reactors came on line. In the second phase North Korea would allow IAEA inspectors to monitor the waste sites and the DPRK would begin sending their fuel rods to a third country. The final phase involved the dismantling of the DPRK's nuclear reactors and the United States completing the construction of the second light-water reactor. The detailed, synchronized steps for each side reflected an acknowledgment that the 1994 Agreed Framework was based upon a "foundation of mutual distrust."[82]

In the mid-1990s North Korea suffered a famine that, combined with its inefficient agricultural system, killed an estimated one to two million people. The United States sent $615 million in food assistance to the DPRK through the UN World Food Program between 1996 and 2002.[83] America provided about $400 billion for heavy fuel oil shipments after the 1995 freeze of North Korea's reactors and construction of a light-water reactor.[84] Although the Clinton administration claimed its food assistance was humanitarian aid, the administration used food aid to leverage greater North Korean cooperation and participation in multilateral security talks.[85]

Despite the hopes for improved relations and peace on the Korean Peninsula, another crisis arose in late August 1998 when North Korea fired a three-stage Taepo Dong-I ballistic missile that flew over Japan. CIA Director George Tenet told Congress in February 1999 that with improvements the Taepo Dong-I could deliver small payloads to parts of Alaska and Hawaii. He cautioned that Pyongyang's Taepo Dong-2, when provided with a third-stage, could deliver larger warheads to the United States, although not with great accuracy. Tenet also warned that North Korea's internal situation "has become more volatile and unpredictable."[86]

President Clinton named former Secretary of Defense Dr. William Perry to head an interagency review of U.S. policy toward North Korea in November 1998. The following May, as part of his policy analysis, Perry visited Pyongyang as Clinton's envoy for talks that proved "constructive and entirely without polemics."[87] Perry's October 1999 unclassified report called for a "two-path strategy" toward dealing with North Korea. One track called for comprehensive, integrated, and synchronized "step-by-step" reciprocal diplomacy toward the DPRK, offering normalization of diplomatic relations and the end of most sanctions—conditioned upon North Korea abandoning its programs to build long-range missiles and nuclear weapons. If North Korea refused, the other path involved reinforcing America's military deterrent against the DPRK.

At his 1998 inauguration, South Korea's President Kim Dae-jung announced his "sunshine policy" calling for improved relations with North Korea through cooperation, reconciliation, and eventual peaceful reunification. In a June 2000 summit, Kim Dae-jung and Kim Jong Il met in Pyongyang, signing an agreement for reuniting families and other exchanges. Perry's visit to Pyongyang and the joint summit resulted in the October 2000 visit of the first high-level North Korean official to Washington, Vice Marshal Jo Myong Rok. Two weeks after Roc's visit, Secretary of State Madeline Albright traveled to North Korea to pave the way for an anticipated summit between President Clinton and Chairman Kim Jong Il. However, because of intense Middle East peace negotiations and the legal battle after the close 2000 election, President Clinton could not visit North Korea in December.

A Visceral Enemy

When President Bush entered the Oval Office in January 2001, the 1994 Agreed Framework was still in place and high-level bilateral diplomacy had developed between the two long-term foes. Cha and Kang maintained that if Clinton had not succeeded in freezing North Korea's Yongbyon reactor for nine years, "North Korea would today [2003] have enough plutonium for at least 30 nuclear weapons rather than one or two bombs' worth."[88] However, many of the new Bush administration officials opposed "rewarding" North Korea's bad behavior with economic assistance and light-water nuclear reactors, advocating a tough "strangulation strategy" toward the DPRK to remove the communist regime.

On the eve of South Korean President Kim Dae-jung's initial meeting with President Bush, Secretary of State Colin Powell told reporters: "We do plan to engage with North Korea *to pick up where President Clinton and his administration left off....* Some promising elements were left on the table" (author's emphasis).[89] However, after meeting with the South Korean president, George W. Bush stated: "I do have some skepticism about the leader of North Korea."[90] Bush emphasized that because of the nature of the DPRK and its leader, in any agreement "we must be able to verify that it is more peaceful." Secretary Powell swallowed his words from the prior day: "If there was some suggestion that imminent negotiations are about to begin—that is not the case."[91] Powell, trumped by White House hardliners, wryly admitted later: "I got a little too far forward on my skis."[92]

President Bush harshly highlighted the DPRK in his 2002 State of the Union address as part of the "axis of evil." Bush declared: "North Korea is a regime arming with missiles and weapons of mass destruction, while starving its citizens."[93]

George W. Bush's feelings toward the North Korean dictator manifested an extreme personal antipathy. According to *Newsweek*, in a 2002 closed meeting with Republican senators Bush mocked the diminutive (5 foot 3 inches) Kim as a "pygmy," who behaved like "a spoiled child at a dinner table."[94] The president later told Woodward: "I loathe Kim Jong Il...I've got a visceral reaction to this guy, because he is starving his people." Bush added, "'Yes, it appalls me'....'It is visceral. Maybe it's my religion...but I feel passionate about this.'"[95] In January 2003 President Bush publicly stated: "Kim Jong-Il is somebody who starves his people."[96]

During an October 2002 visit to the North Korean capital, James Kelly, assistant secretary of state for East Asian and Pacific Affairs—the highest-level Bush administration official to travel to North Korea—was told by the DPRK's Deputy Foreign Minister Kang Sok Joo that North Korea possessed a nuclear program.[97] The North Korean officials also "nullified" the 1994 Agreed Framework.

Despite this real threat to U.S. interests and American forces stationed in South Korea, the normally bellicose White House issued a muted response, reflecting a realistic assessment of the costs of war with North Korea. When asked by a reporter why the United States should worry more about Saddam Hussein, who had no nuclear weapons, rather than the unstable Kim Jong Il, who possessed nuclear weapons, President Bush evasively replied, "It's important to remember that Saddam Hussein was close to having a nuclear weapon."[98] The president added that an attack by Saddam Hussein or a surrogate "would cripple our economy." Bush continued to prudently describe the North Korean crisis as a diplomatic issue, rather than a military threat.

The Bush administration's concentration on the preemptive invasion of Iraq in March 2003 missed an opportunity to increase international pressure on the North Korean regime. In late December 2002 North Korea ordered IAEA inspectors—monitoring the DPRK's nuclear facilities and fuel rods—to quickly leave the country. On January 10, 2003, North Korea announced its withdrawal from the Nuclear Non-Proliferation Treaty (NPT), effective January 11, even though the treaty required 90 days notice. Nevertheless, President Bush made no effort to impose economic sanctions on the DPRK through the UN Security Council or push China and Russia to order sanctions on North Korea.

In July 2003 John Bolton, the neoconservative undersecretary of state for arms control and international security, delivered an address that described life in North Korea as a "hellish nightmare" and attacked the "failed policies of Kim Jong Il."[99] The DPRK regime bitterly replied to Bolton's personal remarks about their leader. When Secretary of State Powell proposed a 2004 agreement in Beijing to establish steps to resolve the stalemate over North Korea's nuclear weapons, the proposal lacked the tough language demanded by neoconservative administration officials. Vice President Cheney bypassed the State Department to convince President Bush to kill the proposal, which Bush ordered.[100]

The head of the Defense Intelligence Agency, Vice Admiral Lowell Jacoby, told Congress in 2005 that the intelligence community believed North Korea had harvested enough plutonium from the Yongbyon reactor's fuel rods to produce nine nuclear weapons.[101]

But despite the Bush administration's general disdain for diplomacy, preferring to act unilaterally with a few allies, President Bush persistently pursued the difficult path of multilateral talks with North Korea that included South Korea, Japan, China, and Russia. He explained in 2006 that "the best way to solve the problem diplomatically is for all of us to be working in concert and to send one message." The normally impatient president admitted, however, "diplomacy takes a while."[102] Bush hoped that China, North Korea's longtime military ally, would play a pivotal role in resolving the nuclear and missile dispute. Beijing supplied the North Koreans with about 90 percent of its energy supplies and 38 percent of imports.[103] China also feared that famine or political instability in the DPRK could produce a flood of North Korean refugees flowing into China.

The North Koreans test-fired seven missiles on July 4, 2006. Indeed, it often appeared that North Korea's diplomatic strategy aimed at capturing the attention of the Bush administration through provocative actions to divert Washington's focus from Iraq or Iran. The Pyongyang regime sought direct bilateral talks with the United States, normalized relations, and possible economic assistance. Despite the potential consequences of the missile launchings, President Bush stated he would not "get caught in the trap of sitting alone with South Korea at the table."[104]

Conservative Nicholas Eberstadt later wrote in the *Wall Street Journal* that North Korea had achieved more "strategic successes" under President Bush than President Clinton.[105] Neoconservative William Kristol went so far as to label Bush's foreign policy as "Clintonian," the ultimate Republican insult. One Bush official later acknowledged: "The decisions we made then narrowed our options now."

But President Bush's prudent diplomacy and toned-down rhetoric toward the North Korean regime of Kim Jong Il reflected the reservations of the American people toward another military conflict with North Korea. Almost half of polled Americans in July 2006 considered North Korea as an enemy, with another one-third depicting the regime as unfriendly. However, almost three-fourths of the respondents favored the United States exerting diplomatic pressures and imposing economic sanctions.[106] Only 9 percent of the interviewed Americans supported air or missile strikes on North Korea.

The North Korean government announced on March 9, 2006, its first underground nuclear test, an event the Bush administration could not spin, downplay, or finesse. President Bush's strategy of relying upon six-party diplomacy had failed to prevent the DPRK from reaching this plateau—entry into the exclusive global club of nuclear-armed states. The administration's strategy had assumed China could prevent such a technological breakthrough, recognizing a North Korean nuclear test might provoke a threatened Japan and South Korea to develop nuclear arsenals. China called the test a "flagrant and brazen" violation of international opinion and firmly opposed North Korea's conduct.[107]

President Bush immediately announced the United States "condemns this provocative act," criticizing North Korea's shipment of missile technology to Iran and Syria.[108] The week before Bush's envoy Christopher Hill stated the United States "could not live" with a nuclear North Korea, which echoed a 2003 bellicose statement by President Bush pledging to not "tolerate" a nuclear-armed Pyongyang.[109] However, Secretary of State Rice quickly assured the DPRK that the United States embraced no plan to invade or attack North Korea.[110]

The UN Security Council unanimously voted on October 14 to impose tough sanctions on North Korea because of its nuclear test. However, to avoid a veto by either China or Russia, the resolution excluded the threat of military force.[111] A highly debated clause in the resolution authorized the inspection of cargo to and from North Korea to locate illegal weapons. However, the Chinese UN ambassador flatly stated shortly afterward that China would not participate in the inspection regime that could result in a confrontation. In 2005 the trade between North Korea and China totaled $1.7 billion, reflecting a major loophole in the inspection regime.

In the wake of the 2006 congressional elections, which resulted in Democrats gaining control of both the House and Senate, President Bush approved a quiet bilateral diplomatic approach toward North Korea recommended by Secretary Rice. In January 2007 North Korea's Vice Foreign Minister Kim Kye-gwan and Assistant Secretary of State Christopher Hill held three days of meetings in Berlin. President Bush gave Secretary of State Rice and her envoy Hill considerable leeway in negotiating a new agreement with the DPRK. Hill and Victor Cha, NSC director for Asian Affairs, approved the agreement in Beijing during a February meeting of the six parties.

The agreement specified that in the 60-day initial phase, the DPRK would close its Yongbyon nuclear facility, allow IAEA inspectors to verify its actions, and provide a list of all its nuclear programs and plutonium extracted from used fuel rods.[112] In return, bilateral talks with the United States would move toward restoring normal diplomatic relations, remove North Korea from the list of state sponsors of terrorism, and begin emergency shipments of 50,000 tons of heavy fuel oil to the DPRK within 60 days. As a means of reassuring each party, the phased steps would be implemented under the "principle of 'action for action.'"

Attempting to distinguish the Bush administration's agreement with North Korea from Clinton's 1994 Agreed Framework, Hill emphasized that "as opposed to previous deals with North Korea, this is not a bilateral U.S.-North Korean deal. This is a multilateral deal."[113] The Bush envoy also emphasized that China worked very hard and closely with the U.S. envoys to obtain the agreement.

The Bush administration's shift from a refusal to engage in bilateral talks and stringent conditions for any agreement angered neoconservative John Bolton, who just stepped down as the American ambassador to the United Nations. "This is a very bad deal," Bolton stated.[114] Deputy National Security Advisor Elliot Abrams sent e-mails to other administration officials protesting the removal of North Korea from the list of state sponsors of terrorism before its nuclear program was completely ended. A *Wall Street Journal* editorial labeled the administration's agreement as "faith-based nonproliferation."[115] And the neoconservative *National Review* blasted the agreement with Kim Jong Il as "a promise from a liar."[116]

Despite the opposition of neoconservatives, the diplomatic agreement launched the process of denuclearization with North Korea. On June 21 the U.S. chief negotiator Christopher Hill made a surprise trip to Pyongyang, the first high-ranking American official to visit Pyongyang in almost five years. The dispute over frozen North Korean funds in a Macao bank was resolved when about $23 million was wired to Russia's central bank and transferred to a Russian bank where North Korea had an account.

The Pyongyang government closed down its Yongbyon nuclear reactor when a South Korean tanker delivered its first shipment of heavy fuel oil as part of the February agreement of 50,000 tons of fuel oil. Mohamed ElBaradei, head of the UN IAEA, announced in mid-July: "Our inspectors are there. They verified the shutting down of the reactor yesterday."[117]

Democratic critics charged that the Bush administration could have obtained the agreement with North Korea years earlier if it demonstrated diplomatic flexibility. Instead, the Bush-DPRK agreement came after the accumulation of 50 kilos of plutonium (Hill's appraisal), development of about 10 nuclear weapons, long-range missile firings, and a nuclear test. Many observers argued that President Bush should demonstrate similar adaptability by permitting direct negotiations with Iran.

A Revised Approach

President George W. Bush's formulation of an "axis of evil" appears at first glance to upend Graham Allison's Rational Actor model. Instead of a focus on the two states representing the greatest military danger to American interests—North Korea and Iran, with their advanced weaponry capabilities—the Bush administration concentrated on Saddam Hussein from its first days in office, despite Iraq's weakened military and staggering economy.

In a September 14, 2002, meeting in the White House Situation Room, Bob Walpole, the national intelligence officer for strategic programs, argued that Iraq's WMD arsenal should not be used to justify war. He pointed out that North Korea was ahead of Iraq in every category of WMD. Other CIA analysts emphasized that Iran's support for international terrorism was greater than Iraq's. Nevertheless, the Pentagon's Doug Feith dismissed these fact-based objections as "persnickety."[118]

Robin Cook, Britain's former foreign minister, noted: "The truth is that the U.S. chose to attack Iraq not because it posed a threat but because the U.S. knew Iraq was weak and expected its military to collapse."[119] In the July 2002 Downing

Street memorandum, written after talks in Washington, British Foreign Minister Jack Straw saw the case for war as thin because "Saddam was not threatening his neighbors and his W.M.D. capability was less than that of Libya, North Korea or Iran."[120]

President Bush's personal views may have clouded his calculations, restricting diplomatic options. Indeed, the coined phrase "axis of evil" appealed to Bush's good-versus-evil fundamentalist view of the world. In confronting evil, compromise was unforgivable in his black-and-white worldview. When George W. Bush disdainfully called Kim Jong Il a "pygmy," his words echoed the Bombastic Bushkin persona's tendency to employ sarcasm to belittle people.

When the president admitted to Woodard he loathed the DPRK ruler for starving the North Korean people, Bush manifested his Righteous Hawk persona, attributing his visceral feelings toward Kim Jong Il to his born-again Christian religious beliefs. In either case, such deeply held views contributed to Bush's embrace of a hard-line approach to North Korea and early abandonment of Clinton's 1994 Agreed Framework. Of course, the Bush administration sought to avoid following any policy course charted by the "weak" Clinton administration.

Rational decision-making assumes a full review of all information and an unemotional assessment of threats, alternatives, and risks. Despite the Bush administration's tough rhetoric toward North Korea and its leader, U.S. policies and actions under Bush reflected a pragmatic acknowledgment of the heavy human and economic costs of a war with North Korea. To break out of the stalemated situation with the DPRK, as the Pyongyang regime kept escalating its provocations to seize the president's attention, Bush agreed to explore bilateral negotiations. The context of that decision demonstrated an awareness of the Democrats' control of both chambers of Congress, the explosion of the civil war in Iraq, and dimming prospects for diplomatic successes in the final two years of the Bush administration.

Allison's Government Politics Model points to how the change of key actors in the Bush administration provided an opportunity to pursue diplomatic solutions to problems long opposed by neoconservatives. In particular, Secretary of State Condoleezza Rice maintained close personal relations and the confidence of President Bush that Colin Powell never enjoyed. Her advocacy of greater diplomatic flexibility eventually won Bush's approval. Defense Secretary Rumsfeld, fired after the 2006 election, could no longer ally with Vice President Cheney to sustain hard-line policies. His successor, the more pragmatic Secretary Robert Gates, concentrated on the Iraq war. The departure of John Bolton and Paul Wolfowitz also muted two strong voices within the administration's neoconservative camp.

Another key change in the internal deliberations was the elimination of the "layers of interagency discussion" that thwarted previous debate over North Korea policy.[121] Bush set the broad parameters for the bilateral discussions with the DPRK and Rice delegated discretion within those boundaries to Assistant Secretary Hill. NSC Adviser Hadley went over the draft agreement in detail with President Bush. Cheney had lost his influential chief of staff, Scooter Libby, in the investigation of the White House leak of CIA agent Valarie Plame's name. A federal judge found Libby guilty of lying to a grand jury. Cheney pessimistically said about the agreement with North Korea: "We go into this deal with our eyes open."[122]

In dealing with the Islamic Republic of Iran, the other major "axis of evil" state, the Bush administration initially embraced an intransigent neoconservative policy opposed to direct negotiations with Tehran. However, in the wake of the 9/11 attacks, the Iranians backed the U.S. attack upon al Qaeda and its Taliban hosts, supported the Northern Alliance, and provided vital assistance to install President Hamid Karzai over the Afghanistan government. Nevertheless, President Bush declined the historic opportunity in early 2003 to pursue negotiations, which would have addressed the major policy concerns of the administration. Although President Bush appeared not to hold visceral feelings toward Iran's mullahs, his attitude toward the regime stemmed from his fear of giving legitimacy to the revolutionary Islamic rulers, with their hostility toward Israel.

But once again the unwillingness to initiate bilateral negotiations failed to halt Tehran's drive toward nuclear power. Furthermore, America's embroilment in Iraq provided new challenges, particularly the alleged Iranian collaboration with Shiite militias and supplying Iraqi extremists with powerful new "shaped" improvised explosive devices. Rumors of impending attacks of Iran's nuclear facilities generated counterthreats from the Iranians, consolidating public support for the clerical hard-liners in Tehran.

Using the Rational Actor lens, President Bush appeared to exercise constraint based upon a cost-benefit calculation of Iran's mountainous terrain, conventional missile capability, the likelihood of retaliatory terrorist attacks on U.S. forces in Iraq and Afghanistan, and possible Iranian actions to drive up the price of oil. Although the most ardent neoconservatives advocated regime change, President Bush recognized the difficulty and high costs of such a venture—particularly with Pentagon manpower already stretched thin by the Iraq war.

The Governmental Politics Model again revealed how the decline of Vice President Cheney's influence, as neoconservatives left the administration, allowed Secretary of State Rice to quietly promote diplomatic contacts through her close personal friendship with President Bush. The May 2007 talks between American and Iranian diplomats over the security situation in Iraq revealed Bush's new flexibility, similar to the administration's more conciliatory approach toward North Korea.

President Bush appeared to abandon his stubborn refusal to negotiate in a *de facto* acknowledgment that more pragmatic policies might avert dangerous military confrontations over nuclear programs. The neoconservatives' emphasis on unilateral actions, insistence on stiff preconditions for talks, and downplaying of the value of diplomacy had produced the quagmire in Iraq and escalating danger of confrontations with Iran and North Korea. Bush thus backed into the realists' approach to diplomacy, a pragmatic course he belittled in the heady days after 9/11.

Chapter Eleven

Ending Tyranny: Bush's Democracy Agenda

*So it is the policy of the United States to seek and support the growth of
democratic movements and institutions...
with the ultimate goal of ending tyranny in our world.*

In his February 26, 2003, address to the American Enterprise Institute (AEI)—less
than a month before the Iraq War began—President Bush claimed a free Iraq
would provide a "dramatic and inspiring example of freedom for other nations
in the region," thus setting the stage to move forward on the "road map to
peace" between Israel and the Palestinians.[1] Critics viewed President Bush's shift
from the rhetoric of fear—with its focus on Saddam Hussein's weapons of mass
destruction—to the rhetoric of freedom as a calculated effort to boost public support for his march toward war with Iraq. But after the "coalition of the willing"
toppled the Hussein regime, President Bush's vision of a democratic Middle East
developed into a "forward strategy of freedom."[2]

On the twentieth anniversary of the National Endowment for Peace—
established in 1983 by President Ronald Reagan—President Bush blasted realists
(like his father) for only pursuing stability in the vital region without pressing for
democratic reforms. He charged that cynical approach had only produced "stag-
nation, resentment, and violence ready for export."

Thus, when President George W. Bush highlighted in his Second Inaugural
Address the goal of "ending tyranny in our world," the 2005 declaration only formalized a belief Bush regularly voiced after the 9/11 terrorist attacks on America.[3]
The expansive goal manifested President Bush's fundamentalist religious view of
a violent world where good constantly battled evil. Bush avowed that in history,
only the force of human freedom could defeat hatred, resentments, tyrants, and
terrorists. Lauding President Bush's idealist vision, Secretary of State Condoleezza
Rice, a self-described realist, later gushed about Bush's idealism: *"We have a
President who doesn't just see the world as it is, but the world as it can be"*
(author's emphasis).[4]

The administration's democracy agenda also allowed George W. Bush to present himself to Republicans as the standard bearer of Reagan's legacy of fostering democracy throughout the world. However, a democratic Iraq—the pivotal
Middle East domino in President Bush's vision for the region—remained wobbly,
despite increased military deployments, expenditure of billions of taxpayer dollars,
and pressures on Iraq's elected rulers.

Controlled Path to Democracy

On the same day President Bush delivered his AEI address on democracy, the State Department's Bureau of Intelligence and Research issued an analysis titled: "Iraq, the Middle East and Change: No Dominoes."[5] The report concluded that liberal democracy would be difficult to achieve in Iraq and the region, warning that electoral democracy "could well be subject to exploitation by anti-American elements." The author, then-Deputy Director Wayne White, warned that even a successful effort in Iraq "would not only fail to trigger a tsunami of democracy in the region, but potentially could endanger longstanding U.S. allies in the Middle East."[6]

Nevertheless, after the fall of Saddam Hussein's government Pentagon neoconservatives and Vice President Cheney's office hoped to quickly turn over power to the Iraqi National Congress' leader Ahmed Chalabi. The CIA favored the exile leader Ayad Allawi, who headed the Iraqi National Accord party, while some in the State Department leaned toward Iraqi exile Adnan Pachachi, a secular nationalist.[7] Larry Diamond, serving as a senior advisor on governance to the Coalition Provisional Authority (CPA), faulted President Bush for not picking one of the postwar plans before the dictator's regime fell, thereby creating even greater uncertainty on how to proceed in the chaotic environment after hostilities.

Disagreement arose early in the occupation over the best path to create a democratic Iraq, whether through tight control by Washington and the CPA or by promptly allowing Iraqis to select their leaders. Ambassador Paul Bremer, who favored a highly controlled process, clashed with Iraq's preeminent Shiite leader, Ayatollah Ali Sistani, who called for an early extension of voting rights to Iraqis—since Shiites comprised 60 percent of the population. The core problem, according to Diamond, was the Bush administration's "obsession with control" throughout the U.S. occupation.[8]

After a three-month delay, Ambassador Bremer named an Iraqi Governing Council (GC) comprising handpicked Iraqis, which overrepresented controversial Iraqi exiles and assigned them highly visible roles. However, the CPA never delegated to the Governing Council any real authority, since Bremer considered the Governing Council as solely an advisory body. Ahmed Chalabi would later complain: "It was a puppet show! The worst of all worlds.... We were blamed for everything the Americans did, but we couldn't change any of it."[9]

In June 2003 the United Nations established a mission in Baghdad under Sergio Vieira de Mello. De Mello quickly recognized the need for greater substantive Iraqi participation in the interim government. But the horrific terrorist bombing of the UN headquarters on August 19, 2003, which killed de Mello and over 12 other UN staffers, resulted in the United Nations withdrawing its personnel from Iraq.

Bremer's original seven-step path to return sovereignty to the Iraqi people envisioned a lengthy political process.[10] But as the insurgency grew more violent, Washington demanded a faster route to restore Iraq's sovereignty. Ayatollah Sistani issued a June 2003 *fatwa* (religious decree) stating that popularly elected Iraqis must draft the new Iraqi constitution, blindsiding the Bush administration. Afterward the new UN envoy, Lakhdar Brahimi, met with Sistani and persuaded him to accept a compromise that scrapped Bremer's complicated caucus method of selecting an interim government to write the constitution.

President Bush's vision of a democratic Iraq received a major boost on January 30, 2005, when over 8.5 million Iraqis courageously went to the polls—a 58 percent turnout. Many Iraqis proudly held up a finger colored with purple ink to signify they had voted. Not unexpectedly, the Shiites' United Iraqi Alliance won 130 seats in the 275-person Transitional National Assembly, Kurds 70 seats, and interim Prime Minister Ayad Allawi, a secular Shiite, 40 seats. Most Sunnis failed to vote because of a Sunni boycott of the election.

Behind the scenes the Bush administration considered covert action during the January 2005 election to reduce the influence of the religious Shiite coalition—with its ties to Iran. The CIA estimated Iranian covert funding to a coalition of Shiite parties at $11 million a week for media and political operations.[11] Diamond had sent a memo to Bremer cautioning that Iran was funneling resources to the Supreme Council for the Islamic Revolution in Iraq Party (SCIRI), Islamic Dawa Party (Dawa), and other Shiite groups that would provide them with an electoral advantage. He wanted the CPA to provide financing to all political parties to level the playing field, not just help Allawi. "We had to be fair and transparent in everything we did, if we were really interested in promoting democracy," Diamond argued.[12]

Deputy Secretary of State Richard Armitage recalled that President Bush said several times: "We will not put our thumb on the scale." Nevertheless, a highly classified presidential "finding" in fall 2004 directed the CIA to provide approximately $20 million and support to selected Iraqi moderate candidates. But one week after President Bush signed the finding, the authority was canceled due to the objections of NSC Adviser Rice and Minority Leader Nancy Pelosi, a member of the House Intelligence Committee, to manipulating the Iraqi election while touting democracy.

Allawi recalled to a reporter August 28, 2007: "The initial attitude of the U.S. was to support moderate forces, financially and in the media. . . . This was brought to a halt, under the pretext that the U.S. does not want to interfere."[13] The situation thus involved the idealism of promoting democracy against the practical advantage Iran-supported candidates would enjoy without U.S. covert financial assistance to balance Iran's manipulation of the January 2005 election.

The next hurdle facing President Bush's vision of a democratic Iraq occurred on October 15, 2005, when a referendum was held on the draft constitution. The Iraqi election commission reported that 63 percent of registered voters turned out to cast ballots on the ratification of the new Iraqi constitution. Most of the increased turnout came from Sunni voters, who had boycotted the January election but went to the polls in October to vote against the proposed constitution. To defeat the draft constitution, two-thirds of voters in three provinces had to vote against it. A hefty 79 percent of all Iraq voters approved the constitution, with Shiite and Kurdish provinces voting overwhelmingly to ratify it. However, the three Sunni provinces voted against the constitution—but only two of the Sunni-dominated provinces opposed it with a two-thirds majority vote. The Iraqi people narrowly adopted the new constitution, but Sunni opposition foretold of future battles over its provisions.[14]

The final step in the structured democratic course occurred on December 15, 2005, when Iraqis voted for a permanent 275-seat Council of Representatives to form a parliamentary government under the new constitution, with 25 percent of the seats reserved for female candidates.[15] The United Iraqi Alliance of Shiites won 48 percent of the popular vote and 128 seats, surprising many observers who assumed they would receive a clear majority. The Kurdistan Alliance won 53 seats and the Sunni Iraqi Accordance Front took 44 seats, with another Sunni party winning 11 seats. The party of Shiite cleric Moqtada al-Sadr, whose Mahdi Army militia launched two rebellions against U.S. troops in 2004, won 32 seats, placing him in a kingmaker position among the competing Shiite factions. The former Prime Minister and secular Shiite Ayad Allawi, favored by Washington and the CIA, won only 25 seats. The postelection jockeying among the parties delayed the selection of the new prime minister, Nouri al-Maliki, a top official in the Shiite Dawa Party, until April 22, 2006.

Ahmed Chalabi, the favorite of the Pentagon neoconservatives and the Office of the Vice President, found his Iraqi National Congress party failing to win a single seat in the Iraqi National Assembly, garnering only 0.5 percent of the cast votes.[16] The ambitious Chalabi had withdrawn from the Shiite alliance when they refused to guarantee him the top job of prime minister. Chalabi's campaign posters brazenly proclaimed: "We Liberated Iraq."[17] Later Chalabi bitterly blamed the Pentagon's neoconservative civilian leaders for his failure to gain power after the fall of Saddam Hussein: "They chickened out. *The Pentagon guys chickened out*" (author's emphasis).[18]

Even though President Bush established a good personal rapport with Prime Minister al-Maliki, the sectarian divisions prevented the new Iraqi government from moving ahead on key reforms sought by the Bush administration. In August 2006 General John Abizaid, CENTCOM commander, told the Senate Armed Services Committee that if the sectarian violence was not stopped, "it is possible that Iraq could move toward civil war."[19]

The specter of a looming civil war would not disappear. Central Command's intelligence directorate presented an assessment in an October 18, 2006, briefing with a slide showing Iraq sliding toward chaos, driven by the "expanding activity of the militias."[20] A CENTCOM officer stated that since the February 2006 bombing of the sacred Shiite gold-domed al-Askari Mosque in Samara, "it has been closer to the chaos side than the peace side."

On November 7 America's voters went to the polls and delivered what President Bush candidly called a "thumping" to Republican candidates, switching control of Congress to the Democrats.[21] Recognizing that the Iraq War cost his party dearly, President Bush announced the replacement of Secretary of Defense Donald Rumsfeld with Robert Gates, a former CIA chief in his father's administration. The ever-loyal Bush had ignored the "generals' revolt" in the spring, when six retired generals called for Rumsfeld's dismissal, but he heard and heeded the voters' ballot message in November.

But news from Iraq only worsened. Defense Intelligence Agency (DIA) Director Michael Maples told Congress in mid-November: "Sectarian violence, a weak central government, problems in basic services, and high unemployment are causing more Iraqis to turn to sectarian groups, militias, and insurgents for basic needs, imperiling Iraqi unity."[22]

On October 30, NSC Advisor Stephen Hadley met privately with Prime Minister al-Maliki in Baghdad to push for reconciliation reforms and Iraqi action to curb sectarian violence. The following month the White House leaked Hadley's secret, five-page memorandum expressing doubts on whether Maliki had the will or ability to control sectarian violence. Hadley rhetorically asked in the memo: "Do we and Prime Minister Maliki share the same vision for Iraq? If so, is he able to curb those who seek Shia hegemony or the reassertion of Sunni power?"[23] Republican Senator John Warner, then-chair of the Armed Services Committee, after returning from a trip to Iraq critically observed: "The situation is simply drifting sidewise."[24]

On December 6 President Bush formally received the report and recommendations of the bipartisan Iraq Study Group (ISG). The president stated that his administration would take the report seriously and "we'll act on it in a timely fashion."[25] Bush then ignored the recommendations. The Iraq Study Group Report opened with a stark, pessimistic evaluation: "The situation in Iraq is grave and deteriorating."[26] The ISG called for the phased withdrawal of U.S. combat troops over the following 15 months.

On January 10, 2007, President Bush announced his new "surge" strategy in Iraq, rejecting the Iraq Study Group's call for an immediate phased withdrawal of American combat forces. Instead, Bush announced an increased deployment or surge of U.S. forces, eventually reaching 30,000 troops, to provide greater security in Iraq, primarily in Baghdad. However, the president warned Prime Minister al-Maliki: "America's commitment is not open-ended."[27]

This decision represents what political psychologist Renshon called Bush's psychological pattern of "right back at you."[28] It reflected Bush's strong convictions about the Iraq war as well as defiance of his realist critics. Bush challenged Congress to fight him on his proposed surge strategy, looking forward to the fight since he held the hole card of a presidential veto. Bush's decision flatly rejected the advice of his father's pragmatic advisers, such as cochair James Baker, who suggested the "prudent" course laid out in the ISG recommendations, including an emphasis on regional diplomacy that included Syria and Iran. Once again, Bush rebelled against those who lacked faith in his judgment.

A *Washington Post*-ABC News poll after the president's speech found 61 percent of the respondents opposed the force increase, with 52 percent "strongly" against the U.S. force escalation. Only 36 percent of those interviewed supported sending additional troops to Iraq.[29] Clearly, President Bush's defiant rejection of calls for phased withdrawal also ignored public skepticism about his strategy for the controversial war.

Bush called for benchmarks to measure the Iraqi government's compliance with reforms to improve the security and political situation—but provided no penalties. American drafted mandates proved quite unpopular in "sovereign" Iraq. Prime Minister al-Maliki declared: "I affirm that this government represents the will of the people, and no one has the right to impose a timetable on it."[30]

The Democrat-controlled Congress failed in its first attempt to impose a timetable for the withdrawal of U.S. forces from Iraq through a war-funding measure. The House of Representatives approved a $124 billion war-spending bill with benchmarks by a close 218 to 212 vote. The bill required troop withdrawals to start by March 2008, setting a timetable for the withdrawal of all combat troops by August 31, 2008. The Senate approved its war-spending bill on April 26, including a binding troop withdrawal timetable. President Bush vetoed the bill on May 1, 2007, arguing: "It makes no sense to tell the enemy when you plan to start withdrawing."[31] However, the *New York Times/* CBS News Poll found that 63 percent of respondents agreed that the United States should set a timetable for withdrawal of troops by 2008.[32]

On May 24 Congress sent Bush a $120 billion war-funding bill without the troop withdrawal deadlines, but it included 18 benchmarks to measure the progress of the Iraq government on vital reforms. President Bush signed the bill into law. On July 12, 2007, President Bush presented an interim report to Congress that evaluated Iraqi progress on 8 of the 18 benchmarks as "satisfactory," but "unsatisfactory" or mixed results on the remaining 10 guideposts.[33]

A democratically elected Iraqi legislature thus stymied the political objectives of President Bush in that fractured nation as it lurched toward either civil war or a *de facto* division into three autonomous states.[34] In 2006 Senator Joseph Biden and Leslie Gelb had proposed partitioning Iraq into three largely autonomous regions with a central government, using war-torn Bosnia as a model.[35] A Pentagon commissioned war-game exercise concluded that if U.S. combat forces withdrew in the near future from Iraq, "Iraq would effectively become three separate nations."[36] A large plurality (48 percent) of the American public told *Newsweek* pollsters in July 2007 that they would favor breaking Iraq into Sunni, Shiite, and Kurdish states.[37] As the war dragged on, with the sectarian conflicts growing bloodier, many Americans viewed the partition of Iraq as a reasonable solution to end the violence and instability.

Israel in His Heart

Richard Haass, former State Department director of policy planning in George W. Bush's administration until 2003, maintained that George W. Bush's 2003 invasion of Iraq produced the end of U.S. primacy in the Middle East. He observed: "It is one of history's ironies that the first war in Iraq, a war of necessity, marked the beginning of the American era in the Middle East and the second Iraq war, a war of choice, has precipitated its end."[38] Haass pointed to the growing regional influence of Iran, mushrooming appeal of radical Islam, and rising anti-American sentiment. Indeed, the findings of the June 2007 Pew Global Attitudes poll underscored that anti-Americanism was "abysmal in most Muslim countries in the Middle East and Asia."[39]

President George H.W. Bush, in the victorious wake of the Gulf War, had convened the three-day Madrid Conference on October 30, 1991, jointly sponsored with the Soviet Union, to work for a Middle East peace. The conference represented the first time that Israel directly negotiated with Syria, Lebanon, and Jordan—and indirectly with the Palestinians. The elder Bush's diplomacy led to the 1994 Israel-Jordan peace treaty, the second treaty Israel signed with an Arab neighbor. The Madrid Conference also generated the secret 1993 Oslo negotiations between Israel and the Palestinians.

President Bill Clinton hosted the formal signing ceremony of the Oslo Accords on September 13, 1993. At this historic occasion, Palestinian Liberation Organization (PLO) Chairman Yasser Arafat and Israeli Prime Minister Yitzhak Rabin cautiously shook hands—two longtime enemies. The Oslo Accords outlined general principles for a five-year interim period of Palestinian self-rule, with negotiations commencing in the third year to formulate an agreement for "permanent status."

Clinton convened Israeli-Palestinian negotiations, which resulted in the signing of the October 23, 1998, Wye River Memorandum by Chairman Arafat and Israel's new Prime Minister Benjamin Netanyahu. President Clinton addressed the Palestinian Legislative Council (PLC) in Gaza, after witnessing the PLC vote in December 1998 to reject conflict with Israel and revoke the article in the Palestinian Charter calling for the destruction of Israel.[40]

The Democratic president began another round of negotiations between Israel's new Prime Minister Ehud Barak and PLO Chairman Arafat in his last year in office at the Camp David presidential retreat over the contentious issues of the right of return for Palestinian refugees and the status of Jerusalem. According to the United Nations, the 1948 and 1967 wars made four million Palestinians homeless refugees who, if they returned to Israel, would outnumber Jewish citizens.[41] But despite President Clinton's last-minute efforts in December, Arafat rejected any trade-offs without the right of Palestinian refugees to return to Israel, even though they could be settled elsewhere with compensation.[42] But despite President Clinton's vigorous, personal diplomacy to achieve a peace agreement between Israel and the Palestinians, his efforts failed.

George W. Bush approached the Middle East from a much different perspective than either his realist father or Democrat Bill Clinton. Ten days after his 2001 inauguration, President Bush told members of his National Security Council: "We're going to correct the imbalances of the previous administration on the Mideast conflict. *We're going to tilt it back toward Israel*" (author's emphasis).[43] According to Treasury Secretary Paul O'Neill, Bush then observed: "Clinton overreached, and it all fell apart....If the two sides don't want peace, there's no way we can force them." Bush startled Secretary Powell by proposing a U.S. hands-off policy, rather than the nation's traditional "honest broker" role to stop violent outbreaks. Bush told the NSC principals: "Sometimes a show of strength by one side can really clarify things."[44]

George W. Bush's tilt toward Israel reflected both a reaction to Clinton's inability to reach a settlement through personal diplomacy and Bush's fundamentalist biblical view of God's covenant with Israel as the stage before the prophesied "second coming" of Jesus Christ. Bush had forged earlier a personal tie with former Israeli General Ariel Sharon. In 1998 Texas Governor Bush met then-Foreign Minister Sharon during a trip to Israel with three other Republican governors. Sharon served as guide during a helicopter tour over Israel and Palestine territory, impressing Bush with Israel's vulnerability to its hostile neighbors.

Matthew Brooks, a prominent Jewish Republican who accompanied Bush in 1998, recalled: "He brought Israel back home with him in his heart."[45] Brooks observed eight years later, as executive director of the Republican Jewish Coalition: "He is not only the most pro-Israel president, he's redefined what it means to be pro-Israel."

Jewish leaders had worried that President George W. Bush might follow his father's middle-of-the road course—not always siding with Israel. They remember when violent demonstrations occurred on the Temple Mount in Jerusalem in October 1990 and Israeli troops fired into a crowd killing 21 Palestinians. The first Bush administration joined the British in condemning Israel for using excessive force in a UN resolution. Bush and Scowcroft recalled: "With the introduction of the US-supported resolution, our relations with Israel hit a new low."[46] In 1992 the elder Bush's administration also threatened to withhold U.S. loan guarantees from Israel unless the government halted the construction of new Jewish settlements in the occupied West Bank.[47]

A provocative visit by Ariel Sharon, the Likud opposition leader, to East Jerusalem's Temple Mount—also the site of Islam's Al-Aqsa Mosque—sparked in September 2000 the second *intifada* (uprising) of Palestinians against Israeli occupation. The four-year *intifada* resulted in over 1,000 Israeli and more than 3,000 Palestinian deaths. Ariel Sharon, Bush's 1998 guide, won election to become Israel's prime minister only weeks after George W. Bush's January 2001 presidential inauguration.

At a White House news conference in March 2001, President Bush stated that the United States "cannot impose a timetable, nor settlement on the parties if they're unwilling to accept it."[48] The president sent CIA Director George Tenet to the Middle East to negotiate a cease-fire and Secretary Powell to assuage friendly Arab governments who believed the United States was not doing enough to stop the Israeli-Palestinian violence. Saudi Arabia's Crown Prince Abdullah ibn Abdulaziz emotionally told a *Financial Times* reporter: "Don't they see what is happening to Palestinian children, women and the elderly?"[49]

During a meeting with reporters at his Crawford ranch on August 24, Bush emphasized he had urged Sharon to exercise restraint, but then pointed out: "Israelis will not negotiate under terrorist threat."[50] Crown Prince Abdullah watched Bush's August 24 press conference and interpreted the president's remarks as "absolving Israel and blaming Yasser Arafat…for worsening conditions."[51] The angry Saudi leader sent a message, delivered to Rice and Powell, which a senior Saudi official summarized: "We believe there has been a strategic decision by the United States that its national interest in the Middle East is 100-percent based on Israeli Prime Minister Ariel Sharon." The bitter crown prince ominously warned: "From now on, we will protect our national interests, regardless of where America's interests lie in the region."

The Saudi ruler's threat landed like a bombshell at Bush's Crawford ranch, energizing the Bush team to calm the crown prince. Former President Bush assured the crown prince that his son's "heart was in the right place." Finally, a two-page personal letter from President George W. Bush delivered 36 hours later satisfied the Saudi crown prince. In the letter Bush wrote: "I firmly believe that the Palestinian people have a right to self-determination and to live peacefully and securely in their own state in their own homeland."[52] This was the first U.S. public support for a Palestinian state in writing.

Over the weekend of September 8 and 9, both Saudi and U.S. officials pondered the next step, including the possibility of a Bush-Arafat meeting at the United Nations. However, the September 11 terrorist attacks changed the priorities of the Bush administration and Saudi Arabia, as Saudi diplomats worked to immediately return home Saudi royals and bin Laden family members who were then visiting the United States. The Saudi diplomats also deflected American questions about why 15 Saudi Arabian *jihadists* participated in the hijacked airliner attacks.

President Bush affirmed to the UN General Assembly on November 10, 2001: "We are working toward a day when two states, Israel and Palestine, live peacefully together within secure and recognized borders as called for by the Security Council resolutions."[53] President Bush became the first U.S. president to publicly endorse a two-state solution to the conflict.

The Saudi crown prince formally presented his proposal to end the Israel-Palestine violence at an Arab summit, resulting in the 2002 Beirut Declaration calling upon Israel to withdraw from Arab territories taken in the 1967 war, adhere to UN General Assembly Resolution 194 to solve the refugee problem, and create a sovereign state of Palestine.[54] In return, the Beirut Declaration promised that Arab states would deem the Arab-Israeli conflict over, sign a peace treaty with Israel, and establish normal relations with the Jewish nation. President Bush praised Abdullah's proposal.

However, after a Hamas suicide bombing, Israeli troops moved into the West Bank, laying siege and shelling Chairman Arafat's Palestinian Authority headquarters compound in Ramallah. Prime Minister Sharon and his cabinet labeled Arafat "the enemy," declared the Israeli government's intent to "isolate" Arafat, and charged that Arafat led a "coalition of terror."[55] Secretary Powell cautioned Prime Minister Sharon: "Chairman Arafat is the leader of the Palestinian people, and his leadership is now even more central to trying to find a way out of this situation."

Secretary of State Powell issued a White House-crafted statement calling upon Palestinian Authority Chairman Arafat to act against the groups responsible for terrorist acts against Israel. According to administration sources, the hard-line statement reflected the position of Vice President Cheney and Secretary of Defense Rumsfeld, who opposed getting more deeply involved in the Middle East conflict or opposing Sharon, the conservative Likud leader.[56] Prime Minister Sharon assured the Bush administration that the Israeli Defense Forces (IDF) did not seek to capture or kill Arafat—only to isolate him.

President Bush then said: "I fully understand Israel's need to defend itself." The comment generated worldwide criticism for its apparent one-sided assessment of the conflict. Initially, the president had restricted his war on terror to terrorist groups with "global reach" who might attack the United States or targeted Americans abroad, purposely excluding organizations such as Fatah, Hamas, Hezbollah, and the Muslim Brotherhood.[57] But over time Bush came to view the terrorist strikes on America the same as Palestinian terrorist acts against Israel, forging a closer bond with Prime Minister Sharon.

President Bush soon adopted Sharon's strategy of isolating Arafat, calling for new Palestinian leadership: "I call on the Palestinian people to elect new leaders, leaders not compromised by terror."[58] The president criticized the fact that the unelected Palestinian legislature had no authority, with the Palestine Authority's power "concentrated in the hands of an unaccountable few."

Crown Prince Abdullah asked President Bush to bring immediate pressure upon Israel to end the siege of Arafat's headquarters in Ramallah and restart peace negotiations. The Saudi leader warned Bush during a visit to his Crawford ranch that U.S. policy was biased toward Israel.[59] Indeed, Prime Minister Sharon acknowledged during a 2002 visit to the Oval Office: "We never had such cooperation in everything as we have with the current administration."[60]

Bowing to American pressure, Yasser Arafat named Mahmoud Abbas the first prime minister of the Palestinian Authority in March 2003. Abbas sought to implement the American designed "road map" to peace, backed by the "Quartet" of the United States, European Union, Russia, and the United Nations.[61] But Arafat balked at granting Abbas full authority as prime minister; so after only four months in office, Abbas resigned.

In November 2004 the longtime Palestinian leader Yasser Arafat died, still isolated in his partially destroyed Ramallah compound. Palestinian voters elected Mahmoud Abbas president of the Palestinian Authority on January 9, 2005, with 62 percent of the ballots. Abbas campaigned in favor of coexistence but refused to renounce the Palestinian refugees' "right of return" or call for exclusive Palestinian sovereignty over Jerusalem's holy sites.

In order to protect Israel from Palestinian terrorists, Prime Minister Sharon ordered the 2002 construction of a security wall between Israel and Palestinians in the West Bank. Yitzhak Rabin had constructed the Israeli Gaza strip barrier in 1994. But President Bush publicly recognized during a July 2003 White House meeting with Sharon that the Israeli wall signified "an international problem."[62]

Indeed, the International Court of Justice ruled 13 to 1 on July 9, 2004, that the construction of the Israel wall in the Occupied Palestinian Territory was "contrary to international law."[63] The court felt the wall created a *fait accompli* on the ground, "tantamount to de facto annexation." On July 20, 2004, the UN General Assembly overwhelmingly adopted (150 to 6) a nonbinding resolution calling on Israel to tear down the security barrier—over the negative votes of Israel and the United States.

Prime Minister Sharon announced in December 2003 his "Disengagement Plan" for a unilateral security withdrawal from Gaza and the northern part of the West Bank.[64] The new strategy recognized that the West Bank and Gaza Strip territories no longer provided strategic depth against attacks from Arab states, who demonstrated little desire to launch a conventional attack on Israel.[65] By withdrawing Israel settlers, pulling back the dispersed IDF troops, and completing the security wall, Israel would establish a stronger defensive line against Palestinian terrorists.

President Bush later praised Sharon's disengagement plan as a "bold and courageous decision to withdraw from Gaza and the northern part of the West Bank."[66] The Israeli Knesset approved Sharon's plan by a 67 to 45 vote in October 2004, with 23 of the prime minister's fellow-Likud party members supporting the plan and 17 voting against disengagement. The Likud revolt spurred Sharon to leave the conservative party to form the Kadima Party, flanked by Likud on the right and the Labor Party on the left. In January 2005 Sharon suffered a major debilitating stroke, with power transferred to his Deputy Prime Minister Ehud Olmert. Israeli voters in March made Olmert prime minister as the head of the Kadima-led coalition. However, Ehud Olmert lacked the political clout of General Ariel Sharon—and the long, personal friendship with George W. Bush that Sharon enjoyed.

Democracy Boomerangs

The political arm of Hamas emerged in 1987 from the Muslim Brotherhood, a pan-Islamic movement originating in Egypt. The Council on Foreign Relations described

Hamas as combining "Palestinian nationalism with Islamic fundamentalism."[67] The 1988 Hamas covenant called for abolishing the state of Israel by the sword, declaring that peace among Muslims, Christians, and Jews could only be permitted "under the wing of Islam."[68] The organization's social wing operated religious, cultural, and educational institutions and charities, while the military wing of Hamas conducted suicide bombings and rocket attacks on Israel.

After the death of Arafat, Hamas engaged more heavily in the political arena, successfully running many candidates in the municipal elections in Gaza and the West Bank. Hamas campaigned vigorously in the January 2006 Palestinian Legislative Council elections. Israeli Prime Minister Sharon, during a September 2005 visit to Washington, threatened to halt the Palestinian parliamentary elections if Hamas ran candidates, but assented under pressure from President Bush. Sharon advocated blocking the participation of Hamas unless it disbanded its militia and accepted Israel's right to exist. But Secretary of State Condoleezza Rice objected: "Elections are fundamental to the continued evolution and development of the Palestinian process."[69]

The *Washington Post* reported that the Bush administration clandestinely spent $2 million to promote the Palestinian Authority and Fatah in the final weeks of the campaign.[70] But when the ballots were counted, Hamas had won a majority of 76 seats in the 132-member Palestinian parliament, with Fatah acquiring only 43 seats. Over three-fourths of the 1.3 million registered Palestinian voters turned out to vote. Palestinian voters had dramatically rebuffed—through the ballot box—President Bush's call for a reformist, secular government to negotiate peace with Israel.[71]

The Palestinian election results stunned and embarrassed the Bush administration. Secretary of State Rice admitted, "Nobody saw it coming."[72] But Bush had shunted aside Prime Minister Sharon's warnings in his visionary desire to highlight a victory of democracy over Islamic extremists. President Bush initially tried to put a positive spin on the unsettling ballot results: "You see, when you give people the vote…and if they're unhappy with the status quo, they'll let you know."[73]

Regardless of their election victory, President Bush blasted Hamas for its armed wing: "If your platform is the destruction of Israel, it means you're not a partner in peace." Rice warned: "You cannot have one foot in politics and another in terror."[74] Hamas leader Khaled Meshal later affirmed that Hamas "would not submit to pressure to recognize Israel, because the occupation is illegitimate and we will not abandon our rights."[75]

In retrospect, the Bush administration had failed to encourage Israel to take steps for improving Abbas's standing as a Palestinian leader, such as ending settlement expansion or releasing Palestinian prisoners. President Abbas had warned Sharon that a unilateral Israeli disengagement from Gaza, without a political or security agreement with the Palestinian Authority, would only strengthen Hamas in Gaza.[76] Indeed, Hamas claimed that its attacks on Israel had forced Israel to disengage from Gaza, contributing to the Hamas upset victory.

In a defensive mode, the White House revealed that President Bush had personally appealed to Abbas during an October 2005 White House meeting to disarm the Hamas militia as a condition for participation in the 2006 legislative election. An administration official revealed the Palestinian leader's honest response: "He said he wouldn't do it, because he said he couldn't do it."[77] Indeed, President Abbas admitted his apprehension that Fatah could lose control of the Palestinian parliament, several times asking for a delay in the scheduled Palestinian elections.[78]

Israel announced after the Hamas victory a freeze of about $50 million in taxes and customs it collected on behalf of the Palestinian Authority, undercutting the ability of the Palestinian administration to pay its 135,000 employees. The United States also stopped aid to the Palestinians, which in 2005 totaled $403 million.[79] However, Secretary Rice's appeals to staunch Arab allies such as Saudi Arabia and Egypt to cut economic assistance to the Palestinian Authority proved futile. The Saudis gave the Palestinian government $15 million per month.

Observers noticed that Secretary Rice had eased public pressure on the two autocratic states to institute democratic reforms, with Egypt's Mubarak government canceling local elections on the eve of Rice's visit. Rice angrily denied the charge, asserting the United States remained "strongly committed" to democracy.[80] However, in April President Hosni Mubarak extended a 25-year-old emergency law by two years. Nevertheless, the United States continued to provide Egypt with $2 billion per year as a vital strategic ally in the region.

Rising tensions and street battles between Fatah and Hamas led the Saudis to broker a power-sharing deal between the two Palestinian factions in February 2007. President Abbas asked Palestinian Prime Minister Ismail Haniyeh of Hamas to form a cabinet and divide ministerial portfolios between the parties. However, both Israel and the United States rejected the new coalition government led by Hamas, refusing to end the economic boycott of the Palestinian Authority.

Pitched battles between Fatah and Hamas in the Gaza Strip broke out in June, culminating in the defeat of Fatah forces and the supremacy of Hamas in Gaza. President Abbas, with the support of the Bush administration, dissolved the Palestinian coalition government, declared a state of emergency, and consolidated Fatah's control over the West Bank. The White House accepted the separation of Hamas-led Gaza as an opportunity to showcase President Abbas as a moderate Palestinian leader willing to negotiate with the Israeli government for peace—a West Bank-first strategy.

Attempting to bolster President Abbas in his conflict with Hamas, the United States restored aid to his embattled government and Israel returned to the Palestinian Authority about $700 million in collected tax and custom revenues. The administration also provided Abbas with $80 million in aid to strengthen his Palestinian Authority security forces. In another effort to strengthen President Abbas, Israel agreed to remove 178 Fatah militiamen from its wanted list and release 250 Palestinian prisoners.[81]

President Bush also called for a fall 2007 international peace conference to work toward creation of an independent Palestinian state. But unlike his father's 1991 Madrid Conference, Bush only invited nations that "recognize Israel's right to exist"—excluding Iran and Hamas.[82] In 2007 Secretary Rice made four trips to Israel and the Palestinian territories and engineered six meeting between Olmert and Abbas to set the stage for a possible "Israeli-Palestinian reconciliation."[83] But Thomas Friedman lampooned Secretary Rice's quick-in-and-out trips to the Middle East to negotiate a significant peace settlement as simply "drive-by-diplomacy."[84]

The Hezbollah Challenge

After its 1982 invasion of Lebanon to stop Palestinian terrorists from attacking Israeli settlements, Israeli Defense Force (IDF) soldiers remained in Lebanon to secure Israel's northern border until 2000. Hezbollah (Party of God), a Lebanese Shiite militia and political organization, was created in 1982 to drive out the Israeli forces stationed in Lebanon. When the Israeli military withdrew in 2000, Hezbollah claimed that its battles with Israeli troops and attacks on Israel forced the departure of the IDF from Lebanon's soil. Hezbollah received support from both Syria and Iran for its militant activities against Israel. According to one source, Iran annually gave Hezbollah $100 million in financial and military aid.[85] Hezbollah held 13 seats in Lebanon's 128-member parliament by 2005.

The February 14, 2005, car bomb assassination of former Prime Minister Rafiq Hariri, who had resigned from the government to protest Syrian domination of Lebanese politics, triggered massive anti-Syria demonstrations. Syria had kept about 14,000 military troops in Lebanon since 1976, when it intervened to stop a civil war. The United Nations began a high-profile investigation of Syrian involvement in the Hariri assassination.

President Bush joined the international diplomatic offensive against Syria's troop presence in Lebanon, declaring: "Syria must...end its occupation of Lebanon."[86] The Bush administration launched a three-prong strategy that stressed American condemnation of Syria's occupation of Lebanon, diplomatic coordination with European allies such as France, and mobilization of Arab regimes with influence over Iraq, particularly Saudi Arabia and Egypt.[87] Syria succumbed to international pressure and withdrew its forces in April.

In 2005 Lebanon held its first democratic election, without Syrian domination, in 29 years. The anti-Syrian Cedar Revolution coalition won 72 seats, the Hezbollah and Shiite Amal parties gained 35 seats, and the Maronite Christian Free Patriotic Movement (FPM) obtained 21 seats. On July 19 Fouad Siniora became prime minister. Siniora included in his cabinet ministers from FPM and Hezbollah to make his government representative of the nation. President Bush backed the new Siniora administration, praising it as a sign of the forward momentum of democracy in the region.

Hezbollah mounted a cross-border raid on July 12, 2006, kidnapping two Israeli soldiers and killing eight others. Sheik Hassan Nasrallah, secretary-general of Hezbollah, offered to trade the captured prisoners for three Lebanese prisoners in Israeli jails. Prime Minister Olmert's government reacted to the kidnappings with massive air attacks on Hezbollah guerrilla positions and Shiite areas in Beirut and southern Lebanon, partly to provoke Sunni and Christian anger at Hezbollah for igniting the conflict.[88] Israel's bombing strategy aimed at crippling Hezbollah's arsenal of over 12,000 rockets, killing or capturing Nasrallah, and attempting to "neutralize" Hezbollah.

The Bush administration faced a win-win situation.[89] If Israel disabled Hezbollah, listed as a terrorist organization by the State Department, Bush could claim a victory in the global war on terrorism. If Israel failed to achieve its objectives, the administration could use the Hezbollah Shiite threat to rally Arab Sunni nations against Iran, Hezbollah's major sponsor.

Once again the Bush administration's foreign policy response to a crisis differed from the preference for diplomatic solutions of President Bill Clinton. When a 1996 16-day conflict broke out after an Israeli retaliation against Hezbollah's rocket barrages, Clinton's Secretary of State Warren Christopher had engaged in shuttle-diplomacy between Israel and Syria to obtain a cease-fire agreement that lasted until the 2006 kidnapping. Instead, in this crisis, Secretary Rice opposed talks with Syria and stalled UN actions to establish a cease-fire.

The Bush administration opposed imposing a cease-fire from the beginning of the conflict to give Israel time to achieve its objectives. Secretary Rice resisted pressures to stop the fighting: "I have no interest in diplomacy for the sake of returning Lebanon and Israel to the *status quo ante.*"[90] But as the destruction in Lebanon increased, Arab and international opposition to the Israeli bombings rose. French President Jacques Chirac called the Israeli response to the kidnappings as "completely disproportionate."[91]

Secretary Rice declared that the 2006 violence represented the "birth pangs of a new Middle East"—symbolized by the freely elected Lebanese government—that extremists wanted to strangle in its crib.[92] Rice portrayed the Israeli-Hezbollah face-off as a test of President George W. Bush's transformational vision for the region: "It is time for a new Middle East."[93] Although President Bush supported Prime Minister Siniora as a democratic ally, he ignored the Lebanese leader's plea for an immediate UN-imposed cease-fire.

On August 11 the Security Council voted unanimously to end the 33-day war and deploy 15,000 UN Interim Force in Lebanon (UNIFIL) troops to southern Lebanon. Security Council Resolution 1701 included no arrangements for disarming Hezbollah. The Lebanese Army would assume security duties along the Israel-Lebanon border, reinforced by UN peacekeepers. Israel agreed to the cease-fire even though it had just sent Army troops into Lebanon to destroy Hezbollah's short-range Katyusha rockets.

Hezbollah leader Nasrallah described the outcome of the conflict with Israel as a "divine victory." However, Sheik Nasrallah later admitted that he had miscalculated the Israeli reaction to the kidnappings: "We did not think, even 1 percent, that the capture would lead to a war at this time and of this magnitude."[94] The guerrilla group's bunkers, tunnel system, communications, and discipline grimly impressed the IDF, which had lacked intelligence on Hezbollah's capabilities. Despite Israel's punishing air attacks, Hezbollah fired 3,500 rockets into Israel. Significantly, Hezbollah had punctured the IDF's "aura of invincibility."[95]

The Lebanese government reported about 1,200 citizens killed and over 4,000 wounded. The Siniora government faced the momentous postwar challenge of rebuilding destroyed homes and businesses, with the damage estimated at $7 billion. In early December 2006, Hezbollah and Amal ministers left the Siniora cabinet, after trying to obtain a greater share of governmental power. Nevertheless, Siniora emerged from the 2006 crisis as a stronger, more effective, and persuasive leader, winning accolades at home and abroad.

Israeli Prime Minister Olmert faced extensive criticism after the Hezbollah conflict for not attaining a quick, decisive victory over the guerrilla force. Israeli casualties included 119 soldiers and 41 civilians from combat and rocket attacks. An official Israeli investigation blamed IDF Chief of Staff Dan Halutz for placing too much emphasis on airpower to stop the Hezbollah rocket attacks, accused the

Olmert government of failing to develop an effective strategy, and criticized the government's war goals as "too ambitious."[96]

President Bush chose to interpret the outcome of the summer war as a victory over Hezbollah in the wider struggle "between freedom and terrorism."[97] He placed responsibility for Lebanon's destruction upon Iran and Syria, Hezbollah's state sponsors. However, the reputation of the United States suffered throughout the region from the Bush administration's unwillingness to rein in Israel's heavy bombing of civilian areas. In contrast, Hezbollah acquired respect, even in Sunni states, for standing up to Israel's military might longer than any previous Arab combatants. Some observers viewed Iran, Hezbollah's major sponsor, as the big winner in the 33-day conflict.

Clashing Goals

President Bush's idealistic call to end tyranny in the world often clashed directly with the realpolitik strategy undergirding the war against global terrorism. This clash appeared constantly in the Bush administration's dealings with General Pervez Musharraf, the president of Pakistan. President Musharraf—at both a personal danger to himself (three assassination attempts) and at the risk of provoking an Islamic popular revolt against his regime—agreed shortly after 9/11 to play a key role in supporting the U.S. war against terrorism in Afghanistan.

However, the army general had seized power from a democratically elected government in 1999 through a military coup, declared himself president in 2001, and won a mandate in a 2002 national referendum with only his name on the ballot. In 2004 the Pakistan parliament gave him a vote of confidence. Despite General Musharraf's lack of democratic credentials, the Bush administration provided Pakistan with over $10 billion between 2001 and 2007 for its help with the war on terror, despite misgivings over Musharraf's military rule.

President Musharraf visited the White House in September 2006 to explain his arrangement with the largely autonomous tribal chiefs to keep al Qaeda fighters out of Waziristan, a remote Pakistan region bordering Afghanistan. Afterward, President Bush declared: "When the President [Musharraf] *looks me in the eye* and says, the tribal deal is intended to reject the Talibanization of the people, and that there won't be a Taliban and won't be al Qaeda, I believe him" (author's emphasis).[98]

Nevertheless, despite the eyeball-to-eyeball assurance, Vice President Dick Cheney secretly traveled to Pakistan in February 2007 to inform President Musharraf that al Qaeda had rebuilt its networks and training facilities in the mountainous tribal area. Cheney also warned Musharraf that the new Democratic Congress might cut aid to Pakistan unless the army more aggressively attacked al Qaeda sanctuaries in his country.[99] A National Intelligence Estimate later concluded that al Qaeda "has protected or regenerated key elements of its Homeland attack capability" in its Pakistan safe haven, thereby restoring its ability to attack the U.S. Homeland.[100]

But President Musharraf confronted a number of domestic challenges, some stemming from his maneuvers to retain power and others from his support of the Bush administration's war on terror policies. He suspended Pakistan's Chief Justice Iftikhar Mohammed Chaudhry in March 2007, whose support of constitutional restrictions on military government posed a challenge to the general's bid for reelection. When the Supreme Court overturned the suspension, Musharraf reluctantly accepted the decision. A poll by the International Republican Institute found that 72 percent of Pakistani respondents did not support President Musharraf's suspension of the chief justice.[101]

The Pakistani president's falling poll numbers also reflected public anger over the army's July attack on the Red Mosque in the capital city of Islamabad, when over 100 people died in fighting with Islamic extremists. Then a series of July terrorist bombings rocked the capital. By July 2007 President Musharraf's job approval ratings had plummeted to 34 percent, down 20 points from his job approval rating in February.[102]

The Pakistan media reported in August that Musharraf was deliberating over a presidential proclamation of a national state of emergency, which could postpone or suspend the scheduled October 2007 elections. Opposition to the emergency decree arose throughout the country, even reverberating in Washington. The White House worried that the action could unleash an Islamic uprising in Pakistan, a nation with nuclear missiles and materials that could land in the hands of Islamic extremists if the government fell. An Islamabad newspaper later reported that Secretary Rice phoned President Musharraf to convince him an emergency decree was not necessary.[103] Shortly afterward, Musharraf declared he would not issue an emergency decree.

The Bush administration's war on terror policies also created considerable Pakistani unease about President Musharraf's partnership with the United States. A Pew Research Center poll found 59 percent of Pakistani respondents opposed the U.S. war against terrorism, over three-fourths felt America should withdraw troops from Iraq, and three-fourths favored U.S. and NATO forces leaving Afghanistan.[104] But most disturbing, the presence of U.S. troops fighting in neighboring Muslim countries influenced 72 percent of respondents to declare they were very or somewhat worried the United States might soon target Pakistan as a threat.

President Musharraf's delicate domestic situation often tempered the Bush administration's leverage on the Pakistani ruler to more vigorously attack the tribal safe havens where al Qaeda and Taliban forces were regrouping. The White House encouraged President Musharraf's negotiations with exiled opposition leader Benazir Bhutto to form a coalition government. The two met secretly in Abu Dhabi on July 27 for a face-to-face discussion of conditions for a power-sharing agreement. Subsequently America's UN Ambassador Zalmay Khalilzad met privately with Bhutto to indicate U.S. support for such a political arrangement to preserve the cooperative Musharraf regime.[105] Even though Bhutto insisted President Musharraf must resign as army chief of staff before seeking reelection, as required in Pakistan's constitution, General Musharraf told supporters on August 16 that he would run for reelection in uniform.[106]

The Pakistani Supreme Court ruled in July 2007 that former prime minister Nawaz Sharif, toppled in General Musharraf's 1999 military coup, could return from forced exile to run for president in October. However, when Sharif's plane landed in Islamabad, commandos in black uniforms surrounded his plane. An investigator offered Sharif the choice of prosecution for alleged corruption charges or exile. A government spokesman declared: "He opted to go abroad." Four hours after landing in his native land, Sharif flew to Saudi Arabia. Sharif's supporters have appealed to the Supreme Court, which will continue to stir Pakistani passions about the autocratic rule of President Musharraf.

A Defense Department official acknowledged the tension between the Bush administration's war on terror objectives and support for democratically elected leaders. America's dealings with General Musharraf manifested that tension: "He's not perfect....But we have to get away from the view that other countries need to see the world exactly as we do."[107]

In summary, President George W. Bush's transformational call for democracy throughout the Middle East encountered the obstruction of sectarian militias intent on subverting the U.S.-birthed democratic regime in Iraq, repudiation in the stunning Hamas election victory, and the undermining of a democratic Lebanese government by an ascendant Hezbollah. The military ruler of Pakistan played a pivotal strategic role in the war on terror, which the Bush administration could not overlook. The visionary idealism of President Bush thus collided with the complex realities of the region.

An assessment of President Bush's campaign to promote democracy in Iraq and Palestine applying Graham Allison's Governmental Politics lens—with its recognition of the importance of the personality of key actors—offered insights on the genesis and failure of many of the administration's policies in postwar Iraq and in the Israel-Palestine conflict. In formulating U.S. policy toward Iraq, the internal conflicts between the neoconservatives in the Vice President's Office and the Pentagon, who favored a swift turnover of power to Iraqi exile leader Ahmed Chalabi, and the State Department and CIA, who distrusted Chalabi, resulted in a disastrous occupation. The mistakes made in those early days—particularly inadequate coalition forces to guard Iraq's borders, prevent looting, deter an insurgency, and halt sectarian violence—sabotaged President Bush's idealistic vision of a model Iraqi democratic government as the key domino to advance democracy throughout the Middle East.

The obsessive controlling personality of Paul Bremer, America's "viceroy" in Iraq, matched the White House intent to direct the occupation. However, the existing public record indicates the president often found his NSC decisions ignored by Bremer and Rumsfeld—yet he issued no reprimands or countervailing orders.

The administration's prewar planning had arrogantly rejected the warnings of governmental and other experts anticipating the likelihood of postwar violence among Iraq's Sunnis, Shiites, and Kurds. The key actors in the Bush administration thus ignored the emphasis in Graham Allison's Rational Actor Model on accurate risk assessment in decision-making. The neoconservatives' rosy scenario, which dismissed pessimistic projections about postwar conditions, justified the Pentagon's decision to slash the number of troops required to topple the Iraqi dictator. That critical decision, endorsed by President Bush as commander-in-chief, proved disastrous in maintaining security in the wake of the ground victory—as quickly proven by widespread looting, the disastrous breakdown of law and order, and the rise of the insurgency.

The absence of a secure environment encouraged the major sectarian groups to unleash their militias to expand their power, rather than relying on the political process. Shiites, Sunnis, and Kurds aggressively maneuvered for advantage in the drafting of the new constitution and subsequent debate over the Bush administration's proposed reconciliation reforms. Even after President Bush approved in January 2007 a surge of almost 30,000 U.S. troops, administration prodding for passage of vital Iraqi reforms—to weaken the insurgency and reduce sectarian violence—found only minimal traction.

In addition, President Bush had pledged to spend his political capital after his 2004 reelection to establish a democratic, independent Palestinian state in his final four years in office.[108] But an analysis of the administration's decisions in the Israeli-Palestinian conflict revealed that George W. Bush's fundamentalist beliefs, empathy primarily for beleaguered Israel, and aversion to emulating Clinton's personal diplomacy combined to discourage any sustained, even-handed initiative aimed at a comprehensive peace settlement.

Cheney and Rumsfeld reinforced Bush's outlook, opposing any deeper engagement in the conflict, thereby giving conservative Prime Minister Sharon a free hand. Secretary of State Powell expressed unease about the obvious tilt toward Israel's foreign policies, but as in the formulation of Iraq policy, the Cheney-Rumsfeld axis outflanked him. The 9/11 terrorist attacks on American soil allowed Sharon to portray Israel's vulnerability to Palestinian terrorists as similar to U.S. fears of another al-Qaeda attack, trumping calls for more balanced American diplomacy toward the Israel-Palestine conflict.

The summer 2006 battle between Hezbollah and Israel also underscored the extent of Bush's one-sided support of Israel's policies, rejecting America's usual diplomatic quest for a swift end to the bloodshed. However, few administration voices cautioned Bush about the impact of Secretary Rice's diplomatic campaign to thwart a UN cease-fire before Israel achieved its battlefield objectives, despite the outpouring of anti-American protests in the region. Indeed, Hezbollah surfaced from its guerrilla tunnels a stronger force in Lebanese politics, emerging as a significant threat to the fragile democratic government of Prime Minister Siniora, who President Bush lauded as a symbol of his democracy vision for the Middle East.

President Bush's self-confidence in his determined drive for a democratic Middle East—despite the quagmire in Iraq, persistent violence in the Israeli-Palestinian situation, and resilient strength of Hezbollah—appeared founded upon his Christian fundamentalist beliefs. The president told David Brooks in a 2007 interview: "It's more of a theological perspective. I do believe there is an Almighty, and I believe a gift of that Almighty to all is freedom. And I will tell you that is a principle that no one can convince me that doesn't exist."[109] By interpreting his Middle East mission for democracy as performing God's will, George W. Bush's Righteous Hawk persona could resolutely pursue his vision despite setbacks and the realities on the ground.

However, the debacle in the January 2006 election victory of Hamas—followed by the Islamic party seizing full control over the Gaza Strip—clearly revealed the fundamental flaw in President Bush's optimistic assumption that democracy would bring into power secular, peace-loving governments attuned to American interests. President Bush declared after the Hamas election victory, "We're watching liberty begin to spread across the Middle East." Nevertheless, a mist of spent gunpowder hovered over the Middle East, making it unclear whether the Bush administration's legacy would generate more stable, democratic nations in the region.

Conclusion

Chapter Twelve

Tested by Fire: Mixed Legacy

I'm here for a reason…and that is going to be how we are going to be judged.

Test by Fire highlights George W. Bush's initial triumphs as a War President in achieving "regime change" in Afghanistan and Iraq, as well as his subsequent mistakes, disappointments, and failures in the global war on terror. The examination of George W. Bush's development into a War President revealed how his beliefs and decision-making style dramatically changed after 9/11, leading to the expansive war on terror, preemptive invasion of Iraq, and visionary goal of ending tyranny throughout the world.

President George W. Bush does not deserve to be either demonized or canonized, despite partisan portrayals. The forty-third president's legacy will not simply reflect failures nor will it manifest a clear beacon of success for future presidents to follow. In *Test by Fire* President Bush emerges as a War President with a mixed record in accomplishing his ambitious foreign policy agenda, which historians will debate for decades as more documents from this very secretive administration become declassified. Bush's three personas influenced his perception of events, impacted upon his decision-making, and made him resolute—and stubborn—in his "forward-leaning" pursuit of terrorists and visionary ideals.

President Bush essentially emulated his father's pragmatic foreign policy course—*until* the September 11 terrorist attacks. Thereafter, Bush's more aggressive foreign policies reflected a fresh assessment of international challenges through "the prism of 9/11." The nation's fear, anger, and cry for vengeance after the attacks evoked a new persona in the forty-third president—the Righteous Hawk—as Bush transcended the modest expectations of his capabilities prior to 9/11 to comfort a stricken nation and demonstrate firm leadership in responding to the horrific events. In other words, George W. Bush faced a profound *personal* "test by fire" when he turned into the War President of the United States.

President Bush embraced the neoconservatives' muscular worldview partly because he felt the context after 9/11 demanded a strong military response against the forces of evil that had attacked America. This policy shift also allowed the administration's top officials to portray President George W. Bush as reflecting President Ronald Reagan's principled, resolute, and tough approach toward international challenges. In an August 2007 poll, 65 percent of Iowa Republicans stated they wanted a 2008 Republican presidential candidate in the mold of conservative Ronald Reagan. However, 78 percent of the interviewed Iowa Republicans then stated George W. Bush did not fit that role, despite his actions over the prior six years.[1]

History will, as George W. Bush often stated, provide the final judgment on his two terms as president. However, in the shorter term we can evaluate how well the forty-third president met the test of fire in his self-proclaimed role as a War President.

Progress or Morass?

After achieving "regime change" in Iraq, President Bush encountered an insurgency, burgeoning sectarian strife, and escalating *jihadist* bombings, which compelled him to embark upon an ambitious nation-building operation unthinkable before 9/11. Soon American troops became mired in a costly campaign to quell a mushrooming civil war. The turbulence and violence hampered reconstruction plans and threatened Iraq's new but fractured democratic government, the keystone for fulfilling President Bush's vision of a democratic Middle East. The 2006 resurgence of the Taliban in Afghanistan also demanded an about-face on President Bush's early opposition to nation-building activities involving U.S. armed forces.

Likewise, the Bush administration's stress on coercive diplomacy—as the world's only superpower—lost its luster when the overextension of U.S. military forces in Iraq and Afghanistan undermined the credibility of threats calling for regime change in Syria, Iran, and North Korea. Furthermore, prudent calculations of the potential costs of military action against the "axis of evil" nations—Iran and North Korea—also reduced the efficacy of such tactics, despite the administration's often bellicose rhetoric. These factors led President Bush to abandon his opposition to direct negotiations with Iran and North Korea, resulting in progress on curbing North Korea's nuclear program. However, despite diplomatic contacts, Iran remains a problem because of its enhanced influence in the region and continued drive for a nuclear capability.

Most importantly, President George W. Bush's success as a War President will hinge upon the outcome of his wars in Afghanistan and Iraq. The resurgence of the Taliban in Afghanistan and the bloody civil strife among Iraq's sectarian militias continue to erode the legacy of President Bush as the clock runs out on his years as War President.

Afghanistan War

President George W. Bush initially succeeded in toppling Afghanistan's harsh Islamic regime and forcing al Qaeda and Taliban leaders to flee into neighboring Pakistan. But by early fall 2007 resurgent Taliban and al Qaeda forces threatened to reverse America's gains in Afghanistan, despite the introduction of NATO troops to stabilize the nation.

President Bush grandly promised a Marshall Plan to rebuild Afghanistan in April 2002 "to build an Afghanistan that is free from this evil."[2] Nevertheless, the burgeoning costs of the Iraq war compelled the Bush administration to cut assistance to Afghanistan from $4.3 billion to $3.1 billion in fiscal 2006.[3] But when the Taliban began its 2006 offensive against American and NATO troops,

U.S. aid jumped to $9 billion in 2007. Former U.S. ambassador to Afghanistan Ronald Neumann observed: "The idea that we could just hunt terrorists and we didn't have to do nation-building...that was a large mistake."[4]

This mistake resulted from President Bush's aversion to nation-building, which symbolized an aspect of President Clinton's foreign policy that Governor Bush had derided throughout the 2000 presidential campaign. Indeed, Secretary of Defense Donald Rumsfeld squelched Secretary of State Colin Powell's February 2002 proposal to establish an international peacekeeping force of Americans and Europeans to extend President Hamid Karzai's control throughout Afghanistan.[5]

In July 2006 NATO troops took over command of the fighting in Afghanistan. NATO forces totaled 34,000, including 14,000 American soldiers, with another 11,000 U.S. forces engaged in training Afghan forces and conducting counterterrorism activities.

However, some of America's 26 NATO allies insisted upon less dangerous assignments in the country, with German, Italian, and French troops deployed to the least violent areas of Afghanistan.[6] President Bush appealed to NATO political leaders to raise the number of deployed NATO troops and share the risks more equitably, but he received a cool reception in many European capitals—largely because of continuing resentment over the administration's preemptive war in Iraq.

The government of President Karzai still lacks control over most of Afghanistan's territory, divided among provincial warlords and the Taliban who both profit from opium drug trafficking. Opium production provides about one-third of Afghanistan's gross national product (GDP) and, according to the UN Office on Drugs and Crime, Afghanistan supplies 92 percent of the world's opium.[7] CIA Director Michael Hayden explained the U.S. dilemma that attacking Afghanistan's drug trade "actually feeds the instability you want to overcome," possibly pushing poor farmers into the Taliban's arms.[8]

President Bush invited President Karzai to Camp David in August 2007, an honor Bush bestowed on selected leaders to signal personal friendship and commitment. President Karzai candidly acknowledged in a CNN interview the evening before meeting President Bush: "The security situation in Afghanistan over the past two years has definitely deteriorated.... There is no doubt about that."[9] But President Karzai also challenged the Bush administration's assertion of Iranian meddling of Afghanistan, stating, "so far Iran has been a helper and a solution."

The Taliban by September 2007 had driven out government forces in about half the territory in southern Afghanistan that the United States and NATO troops had cleared the prior fall. The United Nations reported that incidents from bombings, firefights, and coercian rose 20 percent a month in 2007, while American and NATO fatalities grew by 20 percent.[10]

The jury remains out as to whether the United States and NATO can prevent the Taliban from again imposing its harsh Islamic rule over the Afghan people. Most hopeful for the Bush administration, the U.S. struggle against the Taliban and al Qaeda forces in Afghanistan retains the solid support of the American people, unlike President Bush's second war in Iraq. An August 2007 *USA Today/Gallup* Poll found a hefty 70 percent of respondents stating the United States did not make a mistake by sending military forces to Afghanistan in October 2001.[11] Furthermore, a solid majority favored sending additional troops to Afghanistan or moving troops from Iraq to Afghanistan.

But the terrorist who sparked the war on terror, al Qaeda leader Osama bin Laden, continues to avoid apprehension six years after the terrible 9/11 attacks on America, despite President Bush's bravado about placing bin Laden on an Old West "Wanted: Dead or Alive" poster—and offering a $50 million reward. On the eve of the 2007 anniversary of the 9/11 attacks, Osama bin Laden appeared in two televised videotapes to remind Americans he still posed a menace. When Afghan President Karzai spoke with CNN's Wolf Blitzer, he admitted that in the hunt for Osama bin laden, "we are where we were a few years ago," not closer or further away from capturing or killing him.[12]

Iraq War

Like the proverbial Sword of Damocles, the outcome of the Iraq war hangs ominously over the legacy of President George W. Bush. Six Iraqi cabinet members loyal to radical cleric Moqtada al-Sadra had left the government in April 2007 to protest against the failure to set a timetable for the withdrawal of U.S. troops.[13] In early August five Sunni members of Prime Minister Nouri al-Maliki's cabinet withdrew from the Shiite-dominated government. They all belonged to the Sunni Accordance Front party, which held 44 seats in the parliament.[14]

Secretary of Defense Robert Gates admitted: "We probably all underestimated the depth of the mistrust and how difficult it would be for these guys to come together on legislation."[15] In a press conference eight days later, President Bush suggested that the Iraqi leaders "need to trust each other more."[16]

But the issue of trust reflects the core of Iraq's problems generated from centuries of Sunni dominance over Shiites in the region, Saddam Hussein's brutal oppression of Iraq's Shiite majority, and a Shiite perception that the United States betrayed them after the elder President Bush called for an uprising following the 1991 Persian Gulf War. Most pre-Iraq war analyses that projected conditions the United States might confront after hostilities warned the Bush administration that these long-simmering conflicts could erupt into violence.

The Sunni insurgency initially attacked coalition forces and Shiites, provoking Shiite militias to retaliate with the ethnic cleansing of Sunni neighborhoods and death squad executions. Nevertheless, President Bush tended to attribute the violence primarily to al Qaeda in Iraq (AQI), a largely foreign-run Sunni group that employed spectacular suicide bombings to ignite a civil war in the fractured country.

President George W. Bush proclaimed in July 2007: "We are fighting bin Laden's al Qaida in Iraq; *Iraq is central to the war on terror*" (author's emphasis).[17] However, when pollsters for the *New York Times*/CBS News Poll asked respondents two months later whether the war with Iraq was part of the war on terror, 60 percent felt the Iraq war was not part of the war on terror or only a small part.[18]

Highlighting al Qaeda in Iraq's connection to Osama bin Laden's terrorist organization, President Bush portrayed the unpopular war in Iraq as closely linked to the Islamic terrorists who attacked America. Fighting terrorism aimed at avenging the 9/11 horror presented a more appealing rationale to voters than sending American soldiers to become embroiled in a bloody civil war in Iraq. A senior White House official explained the tactic: "The average person doesn't understand why the Sunnis and Shia don't like each other. They don't know where the Kurds live…And al-Qaeda is something they know. They're the enemy of the United States."[19]

Analyst Anthony Cordesman of the Center for Strategic and International Studies observed in a July 16 report, however, that al Qaeda in Iraq represents "only one part of a mix of different Sunni Islamist Extremists and more nationalist groups."[20] He estimated AQI conducted only 15 percent of the terrorist attacks, cautioning that al Qaeda in Iraq "does not dominate the Sunni insurgency."[21] Other U.S. intelligence sources assess al Qaeda in Iraq as accounting for "less than 10 percent of the approximately 1,000 incidents in a week."[22]

Making the Iraq quagmire even more complex, the bloody free-for-all among the militias also occurs *within* the same sectarian groups, as their respective leaders attempt to seize control of territory, lucrative resources, and government jobs. As the British drew down their Basra forces to 5,500 troops in preparation for turning over control of the city to the Iraqi government, three competing Shiite militias battled for dominance.

The street fights and political maneuvering involved radical cleric Moqtada al-Sadr and his Mahdi Army, the Fadhila (Islamic Virtue Party), and the largest Shiite party, the Supreme Islamic Iraqi Council (formerly the SCIRI party).[23] A report by the International Crisis Group concluded that Basra had experienced "the systematic misuse of official institutions, political assassinations, tribal vendettas, neighborhood vigilantism," as well as the rise of criminal mafias tied to the political actors.[24]

Fighting broke out in the Iraqi holy city of Karbala in late August 2007 between the Mahdi Army of Moqtada al-Sadra and the Badr Organization of the Supreme Islamic Iraqi Council. The clash occurred during the holy pilgrimage of Shiites to a sacred shrine, killing 50 people and injuring 149 in the gun battles between the rival Shiite militias.[25] Tensions between the two groups had grown after the assassination of two Supreme Islamic Iraqi Council governors two weeks prior, with the Mahdi Army considered the murderers.

The January 2007 National Intelligence Estimate, produced by the U.S. intelligence community, described three "prospective security paths" in Iraq, none very encouraging. The first scenario involved chaos leading to partition; second, the emergence of a Shia strongman; and last, an anarchic fragmentation of power.[26] The intelligence community warned that unless actions were undertaken to reverse conditions in Iraq within the next 12–18 months, "we assess that the overall security situation will continue to deteriorate."

The ongoing bloody morass compelled President Bush to reverse his position on several fronts: restoring formal diplomatic talks with the Iranian government to seek cooperation on Iraqi security issues and enlisting the United Nations to play a greater role in mediating among sectarian groups and enhancing regional security for Iraq. Since May 2007 Ambassador Ryan Crocker met twice with his Iranian counterpart, the first public contact between American and Iranian diplomats in 28 years. Ambassador Crocker pressed the administration's claim that Iranian aid to Shiite militias accounted for one-third of U.S. combat deaths in July, many from Iranian-designed roadside bombs armed with explosively formed penetrators (EFPs).

On August 10 the Security Council unanimously approved sending a UN diplomatic mission to advance Iraq's "inclusive political dialogue and national reconciliation."[27] In pushing for UN help, America's ambassador to the United Nations Zalmay Khalilzad acknowledged that the United Nations was "uniquely suited" to work out a Middle East solution to stabilize Iraq, including dealing with neighboring Syria and Iran.[28]

Nevertheless, Iraq's situation on the ground remained perilous, with a stalemated government in Baghdad lacking the will or votes to enact reconciliation measures. President Bush, the "decider," had arrived at a critical crossroad in his war in Iraq.

The Decider

When President George W. Bush ordered the "surge" of American troops in Iraq in January 2007, he told reporters: "I'm the decision maker."[29] However, Senator Arlen Specter, a senior member of his own party promptly cautioned: "I would suggest respectfully to the president that he is not the sole decider."[30] Specter emphasized: "The decider is a joint and shared responsibility" between the president and Congress.

When President George W. Bush announced his decision to deploy more U.S. troops to Iraq, he explained the surge strategy as a choice between three alternatives. First, President Bush acknowledged that continuing "what we're doing"—the stay-the-course option he urged for months—could result in "a slow failure."[31] The second alternative of withdrawing combat troops from Baghdad, the Iraq Study Group recommendation, "would be expedited failure." Therefore, he chose the third course of action: safeguarding the Iraqi government by providing greater security in Baghdad with an additional 30,000 U.S. troops. Bush concluded: "I think it's going to more likely be successful."

In making this decision President Bush downplayed the potential costs of sending U.S. soldiers and Marines to impose order on Iraq's militias engaged in a violent civil war. The president also dismissed Pentagon doubts that a "surge" could be sustained long enough to be effective, given the Pentagon's already stretched manpower resources. Furthermore, many of the troops would be scheduled for rotation home in April 2008 after serving a combat tour in Iraq already extended from 12 to 15 months.

When President Bush initially campaigned for the presidency he affirmed that he would listen keenly to his generals, criticizing President Lyndon Johnson for not letting his generals run the Vietnam War. President Bush once told lawmakers that unlike President Johnson, "I'm not going to sit around some map room micromanaging the war."[32] As the nation's War President, Bush liked to depict himself as following the recommendations of his generals regarding troop requirements. For example, in July 2006 President Bush said at a press conference that when it came to troop levels, he told the commander of the American forces in Iraq, General George Casey, "You decide, General."[33]

Dismal poll numbers reinforced the political necessity of President Bush's claim that the generals set troop levels, especially as opposition to the Iraq war rose and Bush's job approval ratings plummeted. A December 2006 Gallup Poll asked respondents how much they trusted the recommendations of various groups and individuals regarding "the right thing for the United States to do in Iraq." A significant 81 percent of the respondents indicated they had a great deal or a fair amount of trust in recommendations from the U.S. military and Defense Department, with two-thirds expressing trust in the Iraq Study Group's recommendations.[34]

But significantly, only 46 percent of respondents trusted President Bush's recommendations on Iraq. Later, in a May 2007 interview, President Bush wryly observed: "I've been here too long.... Every time I start painting a rosy picture, it gets criticized and then it doesn't make it on the news."[35] He hoped General Petraeus could reassure Americans that the surge of U.S. forces was achieving progress in Iraq.

Anticipating that the Iraq Study Group's December 2006 report would call for troop withdrawals from Iraq, President Bush began a well-publicized review of his Iraq policy to identify options and showcase his openness to advice from many quarters, rather than listening only to those within his so-called "bubble."[36] In April 2007 Bush's former White House aide Matthew Dowd, who joined the Bush team in 1999, described President Bush as having become "secluded and bubbled in," especially on the Iraq war.[37]

However, America's top generals disagreed with Bush's plan to increase U.S. troops in Iraq, preferring to downscale the mission. General John Abizaid, head of the U.S. Central Command for four years, opposed raising the number of American troops in Iraq, favoring the Iraqi military assuming the country's security burden and diplomatic steps "to internationalize the problem."[38] General Casey, the senior commander in Iraq, recommended gradually reducing U.S. combat troops from 14 to 6 combat brigades and redefining America's role as training Iraqi armed forces to handle security matters.[39] A smaller U.S. footprint, Casey argued, would make the presence of American forces appear less like an occupation.

The Joint Chiefs unanimously opposed sending a significant number of additional troops to Iraq, preferring steps to accelerate the training of the Iraqi army to provide more security, increase U.S. pressure on Iraq's sectarian factions for political reconciliation, and bolster economic reconstruction activities to create jobs.[40] The generals and chief of naval operations underscored their concern that the war in Iraq had eroded the Pentagon's ability to handle other crises around the world. Indeed, Army Chief of Staff General Peter Schoomaker testified that troop demands from the wars in Afghanistan and Iraq "will break" the active-duty Army unless the size of the Army was increased and the Army's presence in Iraq reduced.[41]

President Bush's redefined mission for the U.S. forces in Iraq won the grudging acceptance of the Joint Chiefs. But President Bush answered the generals' concerns about readiness by agreeing to enlarge the overall size of the Army and Marine Corps to fight Islamic extremists around the world in the "long war."[42] Thus, the Joint Chiefs did not emerge empty-handed in negotiating the Iraq troop level issue. Furthermore, President Bush essentially ditched his initial vision of a restructured, lean, and flexible U.S. military. The Pentagon transformation concept pushed by Secretary Rumsfeld had relied heavily on smart weaponry to offset sharply trimmed Army forces—another casualty of the war in Iraq.

If the top generals expressed opposition to the surge strategy, then *who* tilted the scale toward sending more troops to Iraq? The previous chapters have shown the bitter struggles within the Bush administration that intensified after 9/11. In particular, the hard-line influence of Defense Secretary Rumsfeld and Vice President Cheney (the so-called cabal) outflanked the more temperate proposals and caveats of Secretary of State Powell.

Vice President Dick Cheney tenaciously advanced the idea of a unitary executive to justify the radical new policies the Bush administration embraced in the battle against Islamic terrorists. For example, Congress overwhelmingly passed (90 to 9) Senator McCain's Detainee Treatment Act in 2005 by a veto-proof margin to curb the administration's extreme interrogation tactics.

But Cheney's counsel David Addington surreptitiously added a sentence to the signing statement just hours before Bush signed the bill. The late addition asserted the president would interpret the new law "in a manner consistent with the constitutional authority of the President to supervise the unitary executive branch and as Commander-in-Chief."[43] Therefore, every law containing such a signing statement becomes provisional, based upon the president's discretion. The signing statement undermined the Constitution's grant of all legislative power to Congress in Article I, thus side-stepping a veto-override fight or court review.

In essence, Vice President Cheney and his staff—through stealth, command of details, focus on pivotal issues, and marginalizing opponents—overrode all skeptics. In the view of Cheney and his hawkish supporters, Congress and the courts should not hinder the all-powerful War President through investigations, restrictive laws, and legal proceedings.[44] The venerable institutions of Congress and the Supreme Court should become simply spectators sitting on the sidelines of the war on terror.

Former Senator Bob Graham, chairman and later ranking minority member of the Intelligence Committee, confirmed that President Bush told him that Cheney "has the portfolio for intelligence activities."[45] The broad authority President Bush delegated to Vice President Cheney in the national security arena meant that the vice president could channel information supporting a war with Iraq to the president, hyping the supposed presence of weapons of mass destruction in Saddam Hussein's armory. Thus, although President Bush remained the decider, "the vice president often serves up his menu of choices."[46]

The vice president, along with the Defense Department's Office of Special Plans contrived "alternative intelligence," ultimately making the CIA complicit in promoting the preemptive war with Iraq. Under those pressures, *groupthink* resulted. The CIA ignored serious flaws in the gathering and interpreting of intelligence dealing with the alleged weapons of mass destruction, thereby fortifying the Bush administration's case for war. However, President Bush resented the criticism that *groupthink* produced the administration's decision to invade Iraq: "This group-think of 'we all sat around and decided'—there's only one person that can decide, and that's the president."[47]

During President Bush's second term, Condoleezza Rice's appointment as secretary of state, especially after the December 2006 replacement of Rumsfeld with Gates at the helm of the Pentagon, provided a more effective counterbalance to the influence of Cheney over the president's foreign policy decisions. For example, Rice won Bush's consent to initiate the bilateral negotiations with North Korea that achieved an initial breakthrough on dismantling Pyongyang's nuclear program.

Secretary Rice also sought to deflect the campaign within the administration of Vice President Cheney and neoconservatives to launch military attacks upon Iran, winning President Bush's grudging approval to begin diplomatic talks on shared Iraqi security issues. But as the administration's rhetoric heated toward Iran, the State Department pressed for President Bush to designate Iran's Revolutionary Guard Corps as a "specially designated global terrorist."[48]

Although Secretary Rice sought to thwart Vice President Cheney's strong advocacy of air attacks on Iran's nuclear sites through such a diplomatic move, it worried European and Middle East allies who feared the Revolutionary Guards' terrorist designation might trigger a war with Iran that could embroil the entire region.[49] A September 2007 *New York Times*/CBS News Poll found 59 percent of respondents felt Iran could be diplomatically contained, while only 9 percent favored military action now.[50] Many Americans clearly doubted the wisdom of the administration launching a *third war* on President Bush's watch before concluding the wars in Afghanistan and Iraq.

With the Bush administration's clock ticking down, Vice President Cheney and his allies appear determined to strike at Iran, regardless of the consequences. Cheney expressed disdain toward presidents who stick their "finger in the air and figure out which way the winds are blowing, and then try to get in front of the herd."[51] The vice president lauded President Bush as representing "leadership going forward," which ignored poll numbers. Indeed, Vice President Cheney received only an 18 percent favorable rating in a *New York Times*/CBS News Poll in March 2007, while President Bush received a 30 percent favorable rating.[52]

Vice President Cheney exerted unprecedented influence within the White House, an outgrowth of Cheney's delegated national security role, ability to control the flow of information, wide network of administration allies, and access to "every table and every meeting," according to White House Chief of Staff Joshua Bolten.[53] President Bush's lack of curiosity, combined with inattention to detail, have bolstered Cheney's opportunities to steer Bush's decision-making. Columnist David Broder, after reading the *Washington Post* series on Cheney's White House influence, concluded tellingly: "He could exercise this power only with the compliance of the president," who permitted it and enabled it.[54]

A Last Hurrah

President George W. Bush faced considerable pressure as his administration prepared a required report to Congress on Iraq's progress toward meeting 18 benchmarks to improve security and achieve political reconciliation. When President Bush announced his new surge strategy on January 10, 2007, he firmly declared: "America will hold the Iraqi government to the benchmarks it has announced."[55]

As the scheduled September 15 deadline approached, President Bush turned to his military commander and his ambassador in Iraq—General David Petraeus and Ambassador Ryan Crocker—to convince a hostile Congress and skeptical public that the surge of an additional 30,000 U.S. troops had brought greater security to Baghdad. When President Bush explained the purpose of the surge in January, he stressed that the additional American troops in Baghdad would give

Iraqi politicians "breathing space" from sectarian violence to enact legislation aimed at political reconciliation among Shiites, Sunnis, and Kurds.

But a series of reports on Iraq's security and movement toward reconciliation raised doubts about the effectiveness of the surge. The intelligence community released an unclassified National Intelligence Estimate (NIE) on August 23, the first since the announcement of the surge, offering a mixed assessment: "The level of overall violence…remains high; Iraq's sectarian groups remain unreconciled…and to date Iraqi political leaders remain unable to govern effectively."[56]

The intelligence experts concluded that the surge temporarily stopped the decline in security but underscored that the political reconciliation process stood at a "standstill." Although the NIE analysis praised the "bottom up" cooperation of Sunnis tribes in Anbar Province in fighting Al Qaeda in Iraq (AQI), the report cautioned it "has not yet translated into broad Sunni Arab support for the Iraqi government" or willingness to work with the Shiites.[57] In other words, the United States could be arming Sunnis who might later direct their fire at the Shiite-dominated government in Baghdad—a palpable fear among Shiite politicians.

The Government Accountability Office (GAO) released its required report on September 4, although an earlier draft was leaked to the press to prevent the White House and Pentagon from watering down its gloomy findings. The GAO report found "as of August 30, 2007, the Iraqi government met 3, partially met 4, and did not meet 11 of its 18 benchmarks."[58]

Comptroller General David Walker told Congress that the Iraqi "government is dysfunctional."[59] The Baghdad government had met only one of its eight legislative benchmarks, failing to enact laws on de-Baathification, oil revenue sharing, provincial elections, militia disarmament, or amnesty. The GAO analysts underscored that a boycott by 15 of 37 members of the Iraqi cabinet diminished the likelihood of the government enacting the reconciliation measures.

Only two of nine security benchmarks had been met. The GAO report noted sectarian militias still controlled or significantly influenced local security in Baghdad and other parts of Iraq. The Pentagon insisted that the GAO omit from its final report the initial draft's finding that the number of Iraqi army units capable of operating independently had fallen from 10 in March to 6 in August. Obviously, that decline raised questions about how soon the Iraqi army could take over security responsibilities without U.S. military backing.

Another independent commission report on Iraq's security forces, chaired by retired Marine General James Jones, concluded that although the Iraqi armed forces continued to improve, they would not attain the ability to operate independent of U.S. forces for the next 12–18 months.[60] The Jones commission blasted Iraq's National Police as operationally ineffective because of sectarianism. The report starkly recommended: "The National Police should be disbanded and reorganized."[61]

On the eve of the testimony of General David Petraeus and Ambassador Ryan Crocker, several national surveys revealed the challenges the two men faced to overcome public cynicism about the Iraq war. On September 9 the *Washington Post*-ABC News Poll found almost two-thirds of respondents disapproved President Bush's handling of the situation in Iraq, 62 percent felt the war in Iraq was not worth fighting, and a majority felt General Petraeus would try to make things look better than they are in Iraq.[62]

The *New York Times*/CBS News Poll, released on September 10, found 64 percent of respondents felt U.S. efforts to bring stability and order to Iraq were going somewhat or very badly.[63] But when asked who they trusted to successfully resolve the war with Iraq, over two-thirds favored military commanders. *Significantly, only 5 percent trusted the Bush administration to successfully resolve the Iraq war.* That distrust probably stemmed from the credibility gap created by how the Bush administration made its case for war with Iraq, since 60 percent of the respondents felt the administration had "intentionally misled" the public on Iraq.

The formal statement of General Petraeus in his congressional testimony opened with a disclaimer that the White House had not helped craft nor cleared his assessment of the security situation in Iraq, an attempt to dampen public doubts about his objectivity. The general gave a bottom-line assessment that the military objectives of the surge in U.S. forces were being met, with improvements in the security arena. General Petraeus highlighted the progress in Anbar Province, where Sunni tribes joined coalition and Iraqi forces in the fight against al Qaeda in Iraq.

General Petraeus announced his recommendation to reduce U.S. forces to the pre-surge level (130,000) by July 2008, with the withdrawal of a brigade combat team in mid-December 2007. He warned that a premature drawdown of the remaining troops "would likely have devastating consequences."[64] General Petraeus stressed: "The fundamental source of the conflict in Iraq is competition among ethnic and sectarian communities for power and resources."[65] The fulfillment of U.S. goals in Iraq would require a "long-term effort. There are no easy answers or quick solutions."

Ambassador Ryan Crocker, an experienced State Department Arabist, testified that "a secure, stable, democratic Iraq at peace with its neighbors is attainable."[66] Progress would not be quick or even, possibly even featuring setbacks. But Ambassador Crocker admitted to Senator Hegal: "The government, in many respects, is dysfunctional, and members of the government know it." Crocker hedged on the importance of Iraq meeting the 18 benchmarks—perhaps heralding a new Bush administration tactic to downplay the importance of unmet critical benchmarks—calling them a "potential misleading indicator."

General Petraeus and Ambassador Crocker's presentations to Congress set the stage for President Bush's prime-time television address to the nation on September 13. President Bush began his speech by referring to Iraq as an "ally of the United States," even though America has no treaty with the fractured nation it has invaded and occupied.[67] Nor was it clear the various Iraqi sectarian groups desired such an alliance.

Bush focused on General Petraeus's report as demonstrating Iraq's increased security, downplaying concerns about sectarian violence and militia control over local areas. The president acknowledged, however, that the Iraqi "government has not met its own legislative benchmarks." Bush pointed to General Jones's commission finding of the Iraqi army becoming more capable, but he ignored the prediction that it would take 12–18 months for Iraq's army to have the capability to fight without U.S. support. The president also disregarded the Jones commission's call to disband the militia-infiltrated National Police.

President Bush "accepted" the recommendation of General Petraeus to delay the withdrawal of U.S. surge forces until July 2007. Bush appealed to Congress to support the troop-level request by General Petraeus, who enjoyed more credibility and clout than Bush himself did as War President. However, Bush made no mention of the Pentagon imperative of redeploying the surge forces by April 2008, at the end of their extended 15-month tours in Iraq, which was a condition for the initial surge.

Instead of saying American forces would stand down as Iraqi army units stand up, President Bush coined a fresh marketing slogan: Return on Success. But during the September 11 Senate hearing, Republican Senator Lisa Murkowski told General Petraeus that his strategy "sounds identical to what President Bush has been saying all along that U.S. forces will draw down as the Iraqis are able to stand up." Two-thirds of respondents in the September *Washington Post/* ABC News Poll felt President Bush would stay with his Iraq policy—no matter what the Petraeus report said, a clear sign of the public's cynicism. Indeed, the testimony of General Petraeus allowed the War President to maintain his policy course.

President Bush had found a general who agreed with his Iraq strategy. The Joint Chiefs of Staff again expressed reservations about the high level of troops deployed in Iraq. U.S. Middle East commander Admiral William Fallon worried about limited forces to deal with other challenges in the Middle East, such as Afghanistan and Iran. And General George W. Casey, head of the Army, warned in an August 31 speech: "Our force is stretched and out of balance.... The tempo of our deployments are not sustainable, our equipment usage is five times the normal rate and continuously operating in harsh environments."[68]

The net result of President Bush's speech, using General Petraeus to support his strategy in Iraq, would leave 130,000 U.S. forces in Iraq until July 2008. This represents the same number of troops in Iraq as when voters repudiated Bush's "stay the course" Iraq policy in November 2006.

Furthermore, in 2008 the United States should complete the construction of a $592 million American embassy in Baghdad—21 buildings on a 104-acre complex inside the Green Zone—the largest U.S. embassy in the world. This underscored the dominant concern in 14 of 22 countries surveyed by the BBC that the United States planned to keep permanent bases in Iraq.[69]

The winner of the 2008 presidential election would thus face the challenge of withdrawing U.S. forces—and any subsequent chaos and violence—which President Bush would avoid. Democratic critics viewed Bush's maneuver as a way to shift blame for Bush's risky venture in Iraq to his successor. President Bush would also finesse the recommendations of the realist Iraq Study Group, led by his father's old friend. Therefore, George W. Bush and his neoconservative defenders could claim his administration did not "lose" the war in Iraq.

Thus, in mid-September 2007 the Democrat-controlled Congress faced a dilemma. President Bush effectively marshaled the prestige of General Petraeus to support his long-standing strategy to "win" in Iraq. On one hand, polls revealed that over 60 percent of the American people oppose the war in Iraq. Democrats confronted additional pressure from MoveOn, a well-funded liberal antiwar group, to force an immediate withdrawal from Iraq. However, many voters express caution toward a precipitous removal of U.S. forces.

On the other hand, although Democrats controlled Congress, they enjoyed only a 51 to 49 majority in the Senate, where approval of a controversial measure requires 60 votes to overcome a filibuster. Even if the Democrats forge a solid 60-vote coalition with some Republican senators to further reduce America's combat forces in Iraq, 67 votes would be required to override a veto by President Bush. Historically, Congress has overridden less than 10 percent of presidential vetoes.

Therefore, President George W. Bush stands a good chance of handing over the fractious, controversial Iraq war for his successor to resolve. The War President thus resolutely—or stubbornly—"stayed the course" in Iraq.

Assessment of the War President

President Bush told his political adviser Karl Rove after the 9/11 terrorist attacks: "I'm here for a reason." How he handled the war on terror "is going to be how we are going to be judged."[70] Taking Bush at his word, *Test by Fire* focused on how George W. Bush, a self-proclaimed War President, met the 9/11 challenge and expanded retaliation against al Qaeda into a global battle against terrorism.

War is not the only criteria for evaluating America's great presidents. Indeed, studies of presidential greatness find that a president's "performance within the context of his times" played a major role in predicting a president's rankings.[71] General George Washington's service as a military leader in the battle for America's independence earned him great esteem, but as president, Washington's major accomplishment comprised his actions to create a respected national government. President Franklin Roosevelt, also listed among great U.S. presidents, assumed the mantle of a War President after the 1941 attack on Pearl Harbor. However, historians and the public especially applaud his hopeful, innovative, and pragmatic leadership in the 1930s to pull America out of the Depression with his New Deal programs.

President George W. Bush will receive his highest marks from the public and historians for his leadership immediately after the 9/11 attacks, particularly his well-delivered September 20, 2001, address that inspired, unified, and mobilized the nation. He adopted an innovative approach to attacking al Qaeda and the Afghan Taliban forces. President Bush prudently focused the initial military actions on al Qaeda's stronghold in Afghanistan, ignoring the entreaty of neoconservatives such as Deputy Secretary of Defense Paul Wolfowitz to simultaneously attack Iraq for "regime change." Leaders throughout the world hastened to pledge support to America in the war against terrorism. Unfortunately, much of that goodwill dissipated when America preemptively invaded Iraq.

Bush's father faced a Democrat-controlled Congress, unlike his son. However, the first President Bush recognized the importance of a truly bipartisan approach in the 1991 Gulf War against Saddam Hussein, thereby obtaining congressional cooperation across the aisle. George W. Bush could have proceeded in the war with Iraq with similar bipartisanship, rather than an intensely partisan "my way or the highway" approach. But George W. wanted to set a distinctive course for his administration, not follow George Bush's footsteps—another rebellion against being personally measured by his father's accomplishments.

President Bush assumed his Machiavellian Politico persona to challenge the patriotism of Democratic senators on the Homeland Security Act, which contributed to Republicans regaining control of the Senate in the midterm 2002 election.

However, President Bush's charge and tactics poisoned relations with Democrats, exemplified by the harsh Rove-approved TV campaign ad featuring pictures of Osama bin Laden, Saddam Hussein, and Senator Max Cleland—a triple-amputee Vietnam veteran. That "take-no-prisoners" attitude continually enlarged the partisan chasm. By September 2007 a huge 70 percent partisan gap existed in the job approval ratings of President Bush between Republicans (79 percent) and Democrats (9 percent).[72]

President George W. Bush's actions as a War President will clearly impact upon his historical ratings, particularly the preemptive war of choice in Iraq to destroy alleged weapons of mass destruction (WMDs). However, in a *Texas Monthly* March 2007 assessment of George W. Bush's legacy, Douglas Brinkley pointed out that both President James K. Polk and President William McKinley fought wars of choice—but they won their respective conflicts.

Although the Bush administration based its war in Iraq on the threat posed by Saddam Hussein's extensive deadly arsenal of WMDs, which an extensive postwar search by the CIA's Iraq Study Group found to be inaccurate, such a deception historically has not harmed a president's standing. Polk launched his war with Mexico with a false pretext and McKinley employed a phony cause for the Spanish-American War, each president winning his military campaign. Brinkley concluded: "You can have a phony pretext for war, but you've got to win."[73]

The sectarian and terrorist violence in Iraq, with no progress on enacting laws to encourage political reconciliation, raises doubts about whether President Bush can "win" the Iraq war during his 16 remaining months in office. Nevertheless, the always-resolute President Bush told a veterans group in August 2007, "As long as I'm Commander-in-Chief we will fight to win."[74] The president's addresses to the two major veterans groups in August reflected how he employed the "bully pulpit" to sell his policies: "See, in my line of work you got to keep repeating things over and over and over again for the truth to sink in, to kind of catapult the propaganda."[75] However, polls reveal that the president's repeated message on Iraq no longer registers with voters.

In addition, President George W. Bush's secret authorization in late 2001 of radical policy tools for his "new kind of war" will negatively impact upon his image in history. The disclosures of the Bush administration's torture memo, rejection of the Geneva Convention's protection of prisoners, extreme interrogation techniques, and rendition of terrorist suspects to CIA overseas "black sites" reflected in part the administration's reaction to the short-term "ticking-bomb" fear of a second terrorist attack on Americans.

The long-term effect and expansion of the use of these tactics has tainted President Bush's legacy and tarnished worldwide perceptions of the United States as a law-abiding nation committed to human rights. A 2007 BBC survey of 25 nations found that 67 percent of respondents disapproved of the U.S. handling of detainees at Guantanamo.[76] The adverse repercussions from these extreme policies will be felt for many years among allies, friends, and the Arab world.

Likewise, NSA's domestic spying on Americans without FISA Court warrants undermines the civil liberties of citizens. The actions reveal an out-of-control Executive, unchecked by either an informed Congress or an attentive court system—the Founders' mechanism to safeguard America's constitutional balance-of-power system. President Bush's unprecedented use of signing statements on 750 laws also manifests an aggressive claim of presidential power based upon the notion that the Executive can set aside any law he considers improper or unconstitutional.[77]

Taken together these policies, approved by President Bush as War President, awaken the specter of an Imperial President, reminiscent of President Richard Nixon. Nixon also considered that the challenges of his times—Vietnam and domestic turmoil—demanded a response beyond the Constitution and statutes. History has not treated the imperial pretensions and abuse of power by President Nixon kindly.

Furthermore, a vital strategic issue that arises is whether President George W. Bush's war on terror policies have made the Middle East, with its vital supplies of oil, a more secure region. President Bush laid out his vision of a democratic Middle East to counter what he labeled the ideology of "Islamo-fascism."[78] The president frames his war in Iraq in the same ideological context as the World War II battles against Nazism, fascism, and Japanese militarism, as well as the subsequent Cold War struggle against communism. President Bush boldly declared that "the American people will never be safe until the people of the Middle East know the freedom that our Creator meant for all."[79] The words reflect his Righteous Hawk persona.

Despite the rhetoric, the Bush administration's progress toward the visionary goal of a stable, democratic Middle East remains elusive. In Iraq, the August 2007 National Intelligence Estimate concluded: "Political and security trajectories in Iraq continue to be driven primarily by Shia insecurity about retaining political dominance, widespread Sunni unwillingness to accept a diminished political status, factional rivalries within the sectarian communities resulting in armed conflict, and the actions of extremists...that try to fuel sectarian violence."[80]

President George W. Bush has declined to play a major mediator role between Israel and the Palestinians for a peace settlement throughout his years in the White House. The war on terror and the embroilment in Iraq consumed the attention of President Bush. The administration's own "roadmap to peace" came to resemble, like the congressional boondoggle in Alaska, a "bridge to nowhere."

The Bush administration's ideological campaign for democracy in the region, despite clear warnings of the political strength of the Islamic Hamas party, resulted in Hamas winning the Palestinian Authority's parliamentary election in January 2006. The surprise Hamas victory upended the Bush administration's push for peace negotiations with Israel, which became further complicated when Hamas seized control of the Gaza Strip.

In addition, as President Bush leaned more toward Israel, especially during the summer 2006 fighting with Hezbollah in Lebanon, he surrendered the mantle of an honest broker. Hezbollah emerged from the standoff with Israel with greater respect and influence in Lebanon, endangering the 2005 Cedar Revolution's anti-Syria democratic coalition government, backed by President Bush.

President Bush and his national security team may receive the greatest criticism over time for destroying the strategic balance of power in the Middle East by its obsessive focus on Saddam Hussein. President Reagan pragmatically switched U.S. support from Iran to the Iraqi dictator during the eight-year war against Ayatollah Khomeini in Tehran, as did Bush's father. Reagan and the elder Bush feared the spread of the Shiite regime's revolutionary influence in the oil-rich region, a key

U.S. national interest. The Clinton administration took tentative steps to normalize relations with Iran, while simultaneously containing Saddam Hussein with air strikes, patrolling no-fly zones, and the UN oil embargo.

In contrast, the George W. Bush administration concentrated on regime change in Baghdad from its first days in office. Unfortunately, they failed to adequately weigh the broader strategic implications of removing the Baathist dictator, which were considered by his realist father in the 1991 decision against marching to Baghdad to topple Saddam Hussein. Since 60 percent of Iraq's population comprised Shiites, with Iran having provided refuge to leading Shiite clerics and Saddam's opponents, a truly democratic Iraq would likely fall under Iran's growing regional influence, a frightening prospect for Sunni regimes friendly with the United States.

President Bush now seeks to create a Sunni buffer against the growing influence of Shiite Iran. A recent $20 billion sale of sophisticated arms to Saudi Arabia and Gulf regimes aimed at cementing such a defensive alliance. Iran still proceeds with its nuclear research, despite the threatening rhetoric of the Bush administration. But air strikes against Iran, given the degree of American troop involvement in neighboring Iraq and Afghanistan, pose a serious risk to American forces in the region.

The Islamic Republic of Iran actually stands today in a stronger position in the Middle East than before George W. Bush became president. A fractured Iraq, overextended U.S. armed forces, and burgeoning revenues from the high price of oil have bolstered Iran's strategic position in the region. Therefore, President Bush's record as a War President offers little encouragement when history—and historians interpreting it—evaluate his eight years in the White House.

Ironically, the Bush administration's reversal of adamant opposition to bilateral negotiations with North Korea may have produced its major diplomatic success. Assistant Secretary of State Christopher Hill announced on September 2 that one-on-one talks had resulted in North Korea agreeing to disclose all of its nuclear activities and dismantle its nuclear program by the end of 2007.[81] Hill employed the diplomatic carrot of a U.S. normalization of relations with Democratic Peoples Republic of Korea (DPRK) in return for denuclearization.

Hallowed Pantheon

President George W. Bush's domestic record will also fit into the historical assessment of whether he will enter the hallowed pantheon of America's great presidents. Although Test by Fire focused on President Bush's foreign policy, Bush's signature "No Child Left Behind" education act, early tax cuts, and Medicare prescription drug benefits will all receive favorable but also critical attention. However, President Bush's failed vision of a major reform of Social Security and inability to rally fellow Republicans behind his comprehensive immigration reform stand out as legislative disasters, despite George W. Bush's investment of "political capital" to win passage.

And most importantly, the delayed, inept, and insensitive response to Hurricane Katrina in August 2005 casts a dark shadow over his "compassionate conservative" credentials. The dubious competence of many of the political cronies appointed to vital governmental posts, notably at the Federal Emergency Management Agency (FEMA), mars the administrative record of the Bush administration.

Another measure of George W. Bush's presidency will encompass his success in winning a second term in 2004. Length of tenure in office improves the chance of a president achieving greatness in the eyes of experts and the informed public.[82] Karl Rove in 2004 successfully "swift-boated" Senator John Kerry's image as a courageous warrior in the Vietnam War, turning Kerry's strength as a combat-tested leader against him, a favorite Rove jujitsu tactic. George W. Bush's 2004 reelection victory marked the first time in his life that he truly surpassed his father's achievements, since the elder Bush lost his bid for a second term.

But ironically, according to a November 2006 CNN Poll, the senior Bush's ratings improve when compared with the record of George W. Bush. Over three-fifths of respondents (61 percent) described the former President Bush as a better president than his son George W. Bush (25 percent).[83] The senior Bush's more internationalist approach to national security holds more appeal than his son's "forward-leaning" unilateralism.

A May 2004 survey of 415 historians found that 81 percent rated President Bush's administration a failure.[84] A Princeton University historian wrote a provocative 2006 article speculating that the George W. Bush may be remembered as the very worst president in American history.[85] The basement of worst presidents generally houses Warren G. Harding, Franklin Pierce, Andrew Johnson, James Buchanan, and sometimes Herbert Hoover.

In recent surveys of the general public, President Bush fares only a little better. A December 2006 Gallup Poll found that a 54 percent majority of respondents thought history will consider George W. Bush a below average or poor president.[86] A *Newsweek* survey in late January 2007 also found that 53 percent of respondents believed history would rate Bush as a below-average president, a slight improvement over a May 2006 survey.[87]

The author evaluates President George W. Bush's performance in office as a below-average president—but not among America's worst presidents, as some scholars have concluded. President Bush will stay-the-course in Iraq through his second term, with reductions in troops to only the pre-surge level, determined to "win" the unpopular Iraq war. Although this trait of resoluteness appealed to the American people after the horror of 9/11, today it signifies stubbornness, according to 83 percent of respondents in a January 2007 AP-AOL News Poll.[88]

President Bush's decisions about policy in Iraq and other major areas appeared as influenced more by his personal beliefs than facts, according to over two-thirds of respondents in a *Newsweek* survey.[89] But for many voters in President Bush's diminishing political base that signifies a positive trait, possibly interpreting the question as alluding to his conservative Christian beliefs.

Indeed, despite only about one-third of Americans supporting how Bush was doing his job in a July 2007 AP-Ipsos poll, Bush retained support from 56 percent of white evangelicals who attended church services each week, 53 percent of conservatives (a decline over the immigration issue), and 67 percent of Republicans (a sizeable drop).[90] George W. Bush's Righteous Hawk persona appealed to these core constituencies—but worried other Americans. As the metaphor about the blind men and the elephant symbolized in the preface, different voters hold widely divergent views of President Bush's strengths and weaknesses.

George W. Bush's presidency will remain controversial for decades. President Bush defends his administration by suggesting that his performance will compare with President Harry Truman, who left office with low job ratings but then rose in historical appraisals to the tier of great- or near-great presidents. However, historians point to Truman's bold announcement of the Marshall Plan to rebuild Europe after the destruction of World War II and the Truman Doctrine that ushered in containment of the Soviet Union, the strategy embraced by most U.S. presidents in the Cold War.

The Bush Doctrine's advocacy of preemption, after America's bitter experience in Iraq, diminishes its appeal for subsequent presidents. John Mueller, who studied public opinion during the Korean and Vietnam Wars, argued that President Bush's preemptive invasion of Iraq may have ushered in a new "Iraq Syndrome." Americans might resist another major military intervention, thus restricting the options of later presidents—like the Vietnam Syndrome.[91] Although the forty-third president hopes that history will treat him like Truman, President Bush acknowledges: "I'm not the historian. I'm the guy making history."[92] It's not clear that historians—or political scientists—will be kind to President George W. Bush and the history he made.

Notes

Preface

1. Michael Duffy and Dan Goodgame, *Marching in Place: The Status Quo Presidency of George Bush* (NY: Simon & Schuster, 1992), 131. George Bush's official portrait, which hangs in the Entrance Hall of the White House, features the oil painting "The Peacemakers" in the background.
2. John Godfrey Saxe, "The Blind Men and the Elephant." <http://www.wordfocus.com/word-act-blindmen.html> (June 14, 2006).
3. David Gergen, CNN "Reliable Sources," CNN, March 5, 2006 (Transcript: 030501CN.V50).
4. Joseph Kahn, "Agency Likely to Sue White House to Force Disclosure," *New York Times*, September 8, 2001, A10.
5. Ellen Nakashima and Dan Eggen, "White House Seeks to Restore Its Privileges," *Washington Post*, September 10, 2001, A2.
6. Dan Eggen, "Bush Authorized Domestic Spying," *Washington Post*, December 16, 2005, A1.
7. Bob Woodward, *Bush at War* (New York: Simon & Schuster, 2002), 13.
8. Jim VandeHei and Paul Blustein, "Bush's Response to the Ports Deal Faulted as Tardy," *Washington Post*, February 26, 2006, A5.
9. President Bush's job approval rating fell to 31% in the Gallup Poll conducted on May 5–7, 2006.
10. Sheryl Gay Stolberg, "An Eye for Detail and the Resolve to Push Change," *New York Times*, June 19, 2006, A15.
11. Joseph Carroll, "Bush Job Approval: 31%; Reaches New Low among Republicans, Democrats," Gallup Poll News Service, May 9, 2006.
12. Gary C. Jacobson, *A Divider, Not a Uniter: George W. Bush and the American People* (New York: Pearson Longman, 2007), 13.

Chapter One   A War President's Decisions: Seeking Insights

1. Jean-Marie Colombani, "We Are All Americans," *Le Monde*, September 12, 2001.
2. George W. Bush, "President Delivers State of the Union Address," U.S. Capitol, Washington, DC, January 29, 2002.
3. George W. Bush, "President Delivers State of the Union," U.S. Capitol, Washington, DC, January 28, 2003.
4. The strategy aimed for Rapid Dominance to weaken "the will, perception, and understanding of the adversary." The Pentagon announced the strategy several weeks before Operation Iraqi Freedom started to make Saddam Hussein's soldiers unable or willing to fight. See Harlan K. Ullman and James P. Wade, *Shock & Awe: Achieving Rapid Dominance* (Washington, DC: National Defense University Press, 1996), Chapter 2.
5. Elisabeth Bumiller, "Bush States His Case," *New York Times*, February 9, 2004, A19.
6. George W. Bush, "NBC News Transcript," Meet the Press, NBC, February 8, 2004.
7. Anne Applebaum, "Why Can't Bush Get the Words Right?" *Washington Post*, February 11, 2004, A31.
8. Laurence I. Barrett, "Junior Is His Own Bush Now," *Time* 134, no. 5 (July 31, 1989), 60.
9. Peter Baker, "Bush's Bull Session: Loud and Clear, Chief," *Washington Post*, July 18, 2006, C1.

10. Ron Suskind, *The Price of Loyalty: George W. Bush, the White House, and the Education of Paul O'Neill* (New York: Simon & Schuster, 2004), 263.

11. George W. Bush, "Press Conference of the President," The Rose Garden, White House, June 14, 2006.

12. John Brady, *Bad Boy: The Life and Politics of Lee Atwater,* (Reading, MA: Addison Wesley Publishing Company, Inc., 1997), 101; and Kevin Phillips, *American Dynasty: Aristocracy, Fortune, and the Politics of Deceit in the House of Bush* (New York: Viking Penguin, 2004), 148.

13. Brady, *Bad Boy*, 226.

14. Phillips, *American Dynasty*, 146.

15. James Moore and Wayne Slater, *Bush's Brain: How Karl Rove Made George W. Presidential* (New York: John Wiley & Sons, Inc., 2003), 137.

16. George W. Bush, *A Charge to Keep* (New York: William Morrow and Company, Inc., 1999), 26.

17. Moore and Slater, *Bush's Brain*, 149.

18. Lou Dubose, Jan Reid, and Carl M. Cannon, *Boy Genius: Karl Rove, the Brains Behind the Remarkable Political Triumph of George W. Bush* (New York: Public Affairs Reports, 2003), 72.

19. Wayne A. Rebhorn, *The Prince and Other Writings* (New York: Barnes & Noble Classics, 2003), Chapter 19, 81. Henceforth, all direct quotes from Machiavelli—using Rebhorn's translation—will be cited from Machiavelli's *The Prince* or *Discourses*, the chapter in the original text and page in Rebhorn's book.

20. Moore and Slater, *Bush's* Brain, 256.

21. Dana Milbank, *Smashmouth: Two Years in the Gutter with Al Gore and George W. Bush—Notes from the 2000 Campaign Trail* (New York: Basic Books, 2001), 197.

22. Richard L. Berke, "Aide Says Bush Will Do More to Marshal Religious Base," *New York Times*, December 12, 2001, A22.

23. George W. Bush, "President Holds Press Conference," White House, Washington, DC, November 4, 2004.

24. Michael A. Fletcher and Jim VaneHei, "Transcript of Bush Interview on Air Force One," *Washington Post*, January 16, 2005, A1.

25. Machiavelli, *The Prince*, Chapter 6, 25.

26. David Aikman, *A Man of Faith: The Spiritual Journey of George W. Bush* (Nashville: W Publishing Group, 2004), 70. Also see Stephen Mansfield, *The Faith of George W. Bush* (Lake Mary, Florida: Charisma House, 2003), 63.

27. Mansfield, *The Faith of George W. Bush*, 108.

28. David D. Kirkpatrick, "In Secretly Taped Conversations, Glimpses of the Future President," *New York Times*, February 20, 2005, A1.

29. Aikman, *A Man of Faith*, 3.

30. Brit Hume, "An Exclusive Interview with President Bush," Fox News, September 22, 2003. <http://www.foxnews.com/story/0,2933,98111,00.html> (June 21, 2006).

31. Gallup Poll, September 21–22, 2001. < http://www.pollingreport.com/BushJob1.htm> (June 21, 2006).

32. George W. Bush, "President's Remarks at National Day of Prayer and Remembrance," The National Cathedral, Washington, DC, September 14, 2001.

33. Bob Woodward, *Bush at War* (New York: Simon and Schuster, 2002), 67.

34. George W. Bush, "Address to a Joint Session of Congress and the American People," United States Capitol, Washington, DC, September 20, 2001.

35. George W. Bush, "President Pays Tribute at Pentagon Memorial," The Pentagon, Arlington, Virginia, October 11, 2001.

36. David Domke, *God Willing?: Political Fundamentalism in the White House, the "War on Terror," and the Echoing Press* (London: Pluto Press, 2004), 6.

37. Post-gazette.com, "Mission Critical: David Domke Says Bush Is Unique in Offering Himself as God's Prophet for America," < http://www.post-gazette.com/pg/pp/04298/400289.stm> (June 21, 2006).

38. George W. Bush, "Remarks Via Satellite by the President to the National Association of Evangelicals Convention," The Map Room, White House, Washington, DC, March 11, 2004.

39. Peggy Noonan, "Way Too Much God," Opinion Journal from the *Wall Street Journal* Editorial Page, January 21, 2005. < http://www.opinionjournal.com/forms/printThis.html?id=110006184> (March 21, 2006).

40. Woodward, *Bush at War*, 342.

41. George W. Bush, "Interview with President Bush on December 20, 2001," *Washington Post*, February 3, 2002, A14.

42. James Carney and John F. Dickerson, "Inside the War Room: Send in the Spooks," *Time* 158, no. 28 (December 31, 2001), 112.

43. Woodward, *Bush at War*, 137.

44. Nancy Gibbs and John F. Dickerson, "Inside the Mind of George W. Bush," *Time* 164, no. 10 (September 6, 2004), 25.

45. Gary C. Jacobson, *A Divider, Not a Uniter: George W. Bush and the American People* (New York: Pearson Longman, 2007), 83.

46. George W. Bush, "Press Conference by President Bush and Russian Federation President Putin," Brdo Castle, Brdo Pri Kranju, Slovenia, June 16, 2001.

47. John F. Burns and Dexter Filkins, "The President Makes Surprise Visit to Iraq to Press Leadership," *The New York Times*, June 14, 2006, A01.

48. Graham Allison and Philip Zelikow, *Essence of Decision: Explaining the Cuban Missile Crisis*, 2nd ed. (New York: Longman, 1999).

49. Thomas Lifson, "GWB: HBS MBA," *The American Thinker*, February 3, 2004. <http://www.americanthinker.com/articles_print.php?article_id=3378> (August 20, 2006).

50. George W. Bush, "President Discusses 2006 Agenda," Grand Ole Opry House, Nashville, Tennessee, February 1, 2006.

51. Allison and Zelikow, *Essence of Decision*, 49.

52. Jerel A. Rosati, *The Politics of United States Foreign Policy*, 3rd edition (Belmont, CA: Wadsworth/Thomson Learning, 2004), 117.

53. Allison and Zelikow, *Essence of Decision*, 23.

54. Allison and Zelikow, *Essence of Decision*, 177.

55. John M. Collins, "Military Intervention: A Checklist of Key Considerations," *Parameters: U.S. Army War College Quarterly* (Winter 1995), 53–58.

56. Seymour M. Hersh, "Selective Intelligence," *New Yorker* 79, no. 11 (May 12, 2003), 44.

57. Ron Suskind, *The One Percent Doctrine: Deep Inside America's Pursuit of Its Enemies since 9/11* (New York: Simon & Schuster, 2006), 15.

58. Michael Abramowitz, "Book Tells of Dissent in Bush's Inner Circle," *Washington Post*, September 3, 2007, A1.

59. Allison and Zelikow, *Essence of Decision*, 297.

60. Col. Lawrence Wilkerson, "Weighing the Uniqueness of the Bush Administration's National Security Decision-Making Process: Boon or Danger to American Democracy?" New American Foundation, Washington, DC, October 19, 2005. Col. Wilkerson served as former chief of staff to Secretary of State Colin Powell.

61. Suskind, *The Price of Loyalty*, 120.

62. Suskind, *The One Percent Doctrine*, 213.

63. "Authorization for Use of Military Force (S.J.Res. 23)," signed by President George W. Bush on September 18, 2001. <http://thomas.loc.gov/cgi-bin/query/z?c107:S.J.RES.23.ENR> (July 11, 2006).

64. "H.R. 3162: To Deter and Punish Terrorist Acts in the United States and Around the World, to Enhance Law Enforcement Investigator Tools, and for Other Purposes," signed by President George W. Bush on October 26, 2001. <http://thomas.loc.gov/cgi-bin/bdquery/z?d107:HR03162> (July 11, 2006).

65. Woodward, *Bush at War*. James Pfiffner relied on *Bush at War* for a professional paper, recognizing the "privileged access" Woodward received for interviews with President Bush and members of his war cabinet. Pfiffner warned readers: "He (Woodward) could not be too tough on the Bush administration without jeopardizing his access for his next book. Thus, Woodward's reporting is valuable, but must be read carefully." The author concurs with the last caveat. See James P. Pfiffner, "President George W. Bush and His War Cabinet," Conference on the Presidency, Congress, and the War on Terrorism, University of Florida, February 7, 2003, 15 (Footnote #5).

66. Sandy Berger, former National Security Advisor to President Bill Clinton, "Transcript: Wednesday's 9/11 Commission Hearings," 9/11 Commission Hearings, March 24, 2004.
67. Condoleezza Rice, National Security Advisor to President George W. Bush, "Transcript: Rice's Testimony on 9/11," 9/11 Commission Hearings, April 8, 2004.
68. Woodward, *Bush at War*, 52.
69. Suskind, *The One Percent Doctrine*, 77.
70. Suskind, *The One Percent Doctrine*, 62.
71. U.S. Supreme Court, *Hamdan v. Rumsfeld*, Decided June 29, 2006. <http://www.supremecourtus.gov/opinions/05pdf/05-184.pdf> (July 18, 2006).
72. Woodward, *Bush at War*, 2.
73. Woodward, *Bush at War*, 269 and 291.
74. Woodward, *Bush at War*, 291.
75. George W. Bush, "Remarks by the President at John Cornyn for Senate Reception," Houston, Texas, September 26, 2002.
76. Suskind, *The Price of Loyalty*, 74.
77. L. Paul Bremer III, *My Year in Iraq: The Struggle to Build a Future of Hope* (New York: Simon & Schuster, 2006), 40.
78. Michael R. Gordon, "News Analysis: Criticizing an Agent of Change as Failing to Adapt," *New York Times*, April 21, 2006, A18.
79. George W. Bush, "President Delivers State of the Union Address," White House, Washington, DC, January 29, 2002.
80. George W. Bush, "President Sworn-In to Second Term," White House, Washington, DC, January 20, 2005.
81. George W. Bush, "President Discusses the Future of Iraq," American Enterprise Institute, Washington, DC, February 26, 2003.

Chapter Two   The Fortunate Son: Star-Spangled Eyes

1. The title of this chapter comes from the 1970 lyrics of the Creedence Clearwater Revival song, "Fortunate Son." John Fogerty, who wrote and sang the lyrics, was drafted in 1966 and discharged from the Army in 1967. Fogerty's lyrics reflected his opposition to the Vietnam War, which primarily fell upon blue-collar men to fight—not the "fortunate sons," no senator's son and no millionaire's son. The lyrics included the line, "Some folks inherit star-spangled eyes," referring to the fortunate sons who could avoid going to Vietnam. <http://www.songfacts.com/detail.php?id=1916> (August 5, 2007).
2. The author differentiates between the two Bush presidents by calling the elder Bush (George H.W.), George Bush, while addressing his son as George W. Bush or George W. When he was young, the family distinguished between George and Georgie or Big George and Little George. Only Lee Atwater and other key staff called George W. Bush "Junior" during the 1988 presidential campaign. But his name is not George Bush Jr. and he dislikes being called Junior. Today, in family gatherings and bantering, they are called "41" and "43" to proudly identify each man respectively as the 41st and 43rd presidents of the United States.
3. Bill Minutaglio, *First Son: George W. Bush and the Bush Family Dynasty* (New York: Times Books, 1999), 25.
4. Minutaglio, *First Son*, 26.
5. Peter Schweizer and Rochelle Schweizer, *The Bushes: Portrait of a Dynasty* (New York: Doubleday, 2004), 98.
6. J.H. Hatfield, *Fortunate Son: George W. Bush and the Making of an American President* (New York: St. Martin's Press, 2000), 20.
7. Hatfield, *Fortunate Son*, 46.
8. George Lardner Jr. and Lois Romano, "Tragedy Created Bush Mother-Son Bond," *Washington Post*, July 26, 1999, A1.

9. George W. Bush, *A Charge to Keep* (New York: William Morrow and Company, Inc., 1999), 18.
10. Hatfield, *Fortunate Son*, 25.
11. Hatfield, *Fortunate Son*, 57.
12. Hatfield, *Fortunate Son*, 30.
13. Schweizer and Schweizer, *The Bushes*, 148.
14. Minutaglio, *First Son*, 73.
15. Bush, *Charge to Keep*, 22.
16. Schweizer and Schweizer, *The Bushes*, 150.
17. Schweizer and Schweizer, *The Bushes*, 20.
18. Schweizer and Schweizer, *The Bushes*, 154.
19. Mickey Herskowitz, *Duty, Honor, Country* (Nashville, TN: Rutledge Hill Press, 2003), 175.
20. Jane Mayer and Alexandra Robbins, "Dept. of Aptitude: How George W. Made the Grade," *New Yorker* 75 (November 8, 1999), 30.
21. Lois Romano and George Lardner, Jr., "Following His Father's Path—Step by Step," *Washington Post*, July 27, 1999, A1.
22. Minutaglio, *First Son*, 106.
23. Hanna Rosin, "Bush's Resentment of 'Elites' Informs Bid," *Washington Post*, July 23, 2000, A1.
24. George Lardner Jr. and Lois Romano, "At Height of Vietnam, Bush Picks Guard," *Washington Post*, July 28, 1999, A1.
25. Schweizer and Schweizer, *The Bushes*, 167.
26. Lois Romano and George Lardner Jr., "Bush's Life-Changing Year," *Washington Post*, July 25, 1999, A1.
27. Minutaglio, *First Son*, 104.
28. Lois Romano and George Lardner, "Following His Father's Path," A1.
29. Lawrence I. Barrett, "Junior Is His Own Bush Now," *Time* 134, no. 5 (July 31, 1989), 60.
30. Minutuglio, *First Son*, 116.
31. George Lardner Jr., "Texas Speaker Reportedly Helped Bush Get into Guard," *Washington Post*, September 21, 1999, A4; Walter V. Robinson, "1-Year Gap in Bush's Guard Duty," *The Boston Globe*, May 23, 2000; and Schweizer and Schweizer, *The Bushes*, 192.
32. Minutaglio, *First Son*, 120.
33. Lardner Jr. and Romano, "At Height of Vietnam, Bush Picks Guard."
34. Lardner Jr. and Romano, "At Height of Vietnam, Bush Picks Guard."
35. Robinson, "1-Year Gap in Bush's Guard Duty."
36. Wayne Slater, "Records of Bush's Ala. Military Duty Can't Be Found," *Dallas Morning News*, June 26, 2000, A06.
37. Robinson, "1-Year Gap in Bush's Guard Duty."
38. Ralph Blumenthal, "Bush Service Records from '72, Thought Lost, Are Discovered," *New York Times*, July 24, 2004, A7.
39. Beth Lester, "Gaps Remain in Bush Guard Service," CBSNEWS.com, May 4, 2004.
40. Romano and Lardner, "Following His Father's Path," A1.
41. Schweizer and Schweizer, *The Bushes*, 371.
42. Schweizer and Schweizer, *The Bushes*, 90.
43. Minutaglio, *First Son*, 49.
44. Lardner and Romano, "Tragedy Created Bush Mother-Son Bond," A1.
45. Barrett, "Junior Is His Own Bush Now," 60.
46. Schweizer and Schweizer, *The Bushes*, 303.
47. Minutaglio, *First Son*, 148.
48. Minutaglio, *First Son*, 157.
49. Schweizer and Schweizer, *The Bushes*, 235.
50. Minutaglio, *First Son*, 159.
51. Minutaglio, *First Son*, 164.
52. George Lardner Jr. and Lois Romano, "The Turning Point: After Coming Up Dry, Financial Rescues," *Washington Post*, July 30, 1999, A1.
53. Hatfield, *Fortunate Son*, 57.
54. Minutaglio, *First Son*, 178.

55. Minutaglio, *First Son*, 187.
56. Lois Romano and George Lardner Jr., "Young Bush, a Political Natural, Revs Up," *Washington Post*, July 29, 1999, Al.
57. Minutaglio, *First Son*, 190.
58. Minutaglio, *First Son*, 189; Hatfield, *Fortunate Son*, 63.
59. Hatfield, *Fortunate Son*, 66.
60. Minutaglio, *First Son*, 165.
61. Minutaglio, *First Son*, 170.
62. Minutaglio, *First Son*, 203.
63. Lardner and Romano, "The Turning Point," A1.
64. Hatfield, *Fortunate Son*, 70.
65. Craig Unger, *House of Bush, House of Saud: The Secret Relationship between the World's Two Most Powerful Dynasties* (New York: Scribner, 2004), 128.
66. Minutaglio, *First Son*, 246.
67. Lardner and Romano, "The Turning Point," A1.
68. Minutaglio, *First Son*, 206.
69. Barrett, "Junior Is His Own Bush Now," 62.
70. Hatfield, *Fortunate Son*, 88.
71. John Brady, *Bad Boy: The Life and Politics of Lee Atwater* (Reading, MA: Addison Wesley Publishing Company, 1997), 218. Before Atwater died in 1991 of a brain tumor, he apologized in a January 1991 *Life* magazine story for his racist comments. Brady, *Bad Boy*, 316.
72. Hatfield, *Fortunate Son*, 84.
73. Brady, *Bad Boy*, 157.
74. Hatfield, *Fortunate Son*, 77.
75. Schweizer and Schweizer, *The Bushes*, 336.
76. Lois Romano and George Lardner Jr., "Bush's Life-Changing Year."
77. Schweizer and Schweizer, *The Bushes*, 304.
78. Schweizer and Schweizer, *The Bushes*, 331.
79. Romano and Lardner, "Bush's Life-Changing Year," A1.
80. Romano and Lardner, "Bush's Life-Changing Year," A1.
81. Minutaglio, *The First Son*, 201.
82. Hanna Rosin, "Applying Personal Faith to Public Policy," *Washington Post*, July 24, 2000, A1.
83. Billy Graham, "Reverend Billy Graham Still Crusading at 86," Interview with Brian Williams, NBC Nightly News, November 22, 2004.
84. Stephen Mansfield, *The Faith of George W. Bush* (Lake Mary, FL: Charisma House, 2003), 63.
85. David Aikman, *A Man of Faith: The Spiritual Journey of George W. Bush* (Nashville, TN: W Publishing Group, 2004), 70.
86. Aikman, *A Man of Faith*, 82.
87. Minutaglio, *The First Son*, 239.
88. Lois Romano and George Lardner Jr., "Bush's Move Up to the Majors," *Washington Post*, July 31, 1999, A1.
89. Hatfield, *Fortunate Son*, 90.
90. Minutaglio, *The First Son*, 236.
91. Hatfield, *Fortunate Son*, 95.
92. Barrett, "Junior Is His Own Bush Now," 60.
93. Hatfield, *Fortunate Son*, 94.
94. Hatfield, *Fortunate Son*, 117.
95. Hatfield, *Fortunate Son*, 118.

Chapter Three   Lone Star Challenger:
A Taste of Power

1. James Moore and Wayne Slater, *Bush's Brain: How Karl Rove Made George W. Bush Presidential* (New York: John Wiley & Sons, Inc., 2003), 118.

2. Moore and Slater, *Bush's Brain*, 132.
3. Moore and Slater, *Bush's Brain*, 135.
4. Lou Dubose, Jan Reid, and Carl M. Cannon, *Boy Genius: Karl Rove, the Brains behind the Remarkable Political Triumph of George W. Bush* (New York: Public Affairs Reports, 2003), 20.
5. Moore and Slater, *Bush's Brain*, 146.
6. Wayne A. Rebhorn, *The Prince and Other Writings* (New York: Barnes & Noble Classics, 2003), Chapter 15, 66.
7. Dubose, Reid, and Cannon, *Boy Genius*, 29.
8. Robert Bryce, "The Fab Four: Meet the People Maneuvering behind the Scenes to Put George W. Bush in the White House," June 16, 1999, Salon.com. <http://www.salon.com/news/feature/1999/06/16/advisors/> (June 16, 2005).
9. Moore and Slater, *Bush's Brain*, 149.
10. Nicholas Lemann, "The Controller," *New Yorker* 79, no. 11 (May 12, 2003), 68.
11. Moore and Slater, *Bush's Brain*, 38.
12. Dubose, Reid, and Cannon, *Boy Genius*, 34.
13. Moore and Slater, *Bush's Brain*, 56.
14. Dubose, Reid, and Cannon, *Boy Genius*, 39.
15. Louis Dubose, "Bush's Hit Man: Karl Rove and the Politics of Destruction," *The Nation* 272, no. 9 (March 5, 2001), 11.
16. Moore and Slater, *Bush's Brain*, 70.
17. Moore and Slater, *Bush's Brain*, 76.
18. Dubois, Reid and Cannon, *Boy Genius*, 46.
19. Moore and Slater, *Bush's Brain*, 176.
20. Dubois, Reid, and Cannon, *Boy Genius*, 64.
21. Lemann, "The Controller," 68.
22. Joshua Green, "Karl Rove in a Corner," *Atlantic Monthly* 294, no. 4 (November 2004), 102.
23. Green, "Karl Rove in a Corner," 101.
24. Rebhorn, *The Prince*, Chapter 3, 13.
25. Tom Pauken, "The Rise and Fall of the Texas Republican Party: The Rove Machine," *Chronicles Magazine*, November 2004. <http://www.chroniclesmagazine.org/Chronicles/November 2004/1104Pauken.html> (July 12, 2006).
26. Elisabeth Bumiller, "C.I.A. Leak Case Recalls Texas Incident in '92 Race," *New York Times*, August 6, 2005, A8.
27. Louis Dubose, "Bush's Hit Man: Karl Rove and the Politics of Destruction," *Nation* 272, no. 9 (March 5, 2001), 11.
28. Green, "Karl Rove in a Corner," 96.
29. Karen Tumulty, "The Rove Warrior," *Time* (December 27, 2004), 60. The Texas statewide elective offices include: U.S. Senate (2), Governor, Lieutenant Governor, Attorney General, Comptroller, Commissioner of General Land Office, Commissioner of Agriculture, Railroad Commission (3), Supreme Court (9), and Court of Criminal Appeals (9). The election of judges in Texas would emerge as a controversial issue in 2005 when Republican Congressman Tom Delay was indicted in a campaign contribution scandal.
30. Sam Howe Verhovek, "Is There Room on a Republican Ticket for Another Bush?" *New York Times Magazine*, September 13, 1998, 52.
31. George W. Bush, *A Charge to Keep* (New York: William Morrow and Company, Inc., 1999), 3.
32. Frank Bruni, *Ambling into History: The Unlikely Odyssey of George W. Bush* (New York: Perennial, 2003), 148.
33. Mickey Herskowitz, *Duty, Honor, Country* (Nashville, TN: Rutledge Hill Press, 2003), 188.
34. Minutaglio, *First Son*, 229.
35. Bush, *A Charge to Keep*, 242.
36. Bush, 182.
37. Bush, 182.
38. Richard Ben Cramer, *What It Takes: The Way to the White House* (New York: Random House, 1992), 17. "Junior was the Roman candle of the family, bright, hot, a sparkler—and likeliest to burn the fingers."
39. Bruni, *Ambling into History*, 140.

40. Schweizer and Schweizer, *The Bushes*, 544.
41. Minutaglio, *First Son*, 285.
42. Minutaglio, *First Son*, 238.
43. Dana Milbank, "Dispelling Doubts with the Rangers," *Washington Post*, July 25, 2000, A1.
44. Minutaglio, *First Son*, 291.
45. Barrett, "Junior Is His Own Bush Now," 60.
46. Barrett, "Junior Is His Own Bush Now," 60.
47. Minutaglio, *First Son*, 279.
48. Minutaglio, *First Son*, 273.
49. Minutaglio, *First Son*, 277.
50. Minutaglio, *First Son*, 277.
51. Hatfield, *Fortunate Son*, 238.
52. Hugh Heclo, "The Political Ethos of George W. Bush," in Fred I. Greenstein ed., *The George W. Bush Presidency: An Early Assessment* (Baltimore, MD: The Johns Hopkins Press, 2003), 37.
53. Hatfield, *Fortunate Son*, 237.
54. Robert Dreyfuss, "George W.'s Compassion," *American Prospect* (September 1999), 36.
55. Schweitzer and Schweitzer, *The Bushes*, 423.
56. Hatfield, *Fortunate Son*, 134.
57. Hatfield, *Fortunate Son*, 128.
58. Hatfield, *Fortunate Son*, 129.
59. Hatfield, *Fortunate Son*, 138.
60. Moore and Slater, *Bush's Brain*, 210.
61. Lois Romano and George Lardner Jr., "Bush's Move Up to the Majors," A1.
62. Bush, *A Charge to Keep*, 133.
63. Hatfield, *Fortunate Son*, 141.
64. Herskowitz, *Duty, Honor, Country*, 209.
65. Schweizer and Schweizer, *The Bushes*, 440.
66. Bush, *A Charge to Keep*, 44.
67. Bush, *A Charge to Keep*, 97.
68. Bush, *A Charge to Keep*, 96.
69. Fred I. Greenstein, "The Leadership Style of George W. Bush," in Fred I. Greenstein ed., *The George W. Bush Presidency*, 5.
70. Minutaglio, *First Son*, 307.
71. Bush, *A Charge to Keep*, 103.
72. Karen Hughes, *Ten Minutes from Normal* (New York: Viking Penguin, 2004), 85.
73. Bush, 119. The Bush campaign initially commissioned sportswriter Mickey Herskowitz of the *Houston Chronicle* to ghostwrite Bush's campaign biography but later fired him, allegedly for being late with his draft. He claimed the Bush team would not give him details, only thousands of Bush speeches, "actually five speeches the governor has given 200 times." Dana Milbank, *Smashmouth: Two Years in the Gutter with Al Gore and George W. Bush—Notes from the 2000 Campaign Trail* (New York: Basic Books, 2001), 54.
74. Sandalow concluded that the "governor of Texas is a constitutionally weak position, with no cabinet, no power to make judicial appointments and no legislative function other than the authority to veto bills." Mark Sandalow, "For Bush, the Record Tells All," *San Francisco Chronicle*, June 29, 1999, A1.
75. Minutaglio, *First Son*, 298.
76. Hatfield, *Fortunate Son*, 147.
77. John C. Fortier and Norman J. Ornstein, "President Bush: Legislative Strategist," in Fred I. Greenstein ed., *The George W. Bush Presidency*, 142.
78. Bush, 115.
79. Edward Walsh, "Bush's Style Succeeded Even as Tax Plan Failed," *Washington Post*, November 25, 1999, A1.
80. Hatfield, *Fortunate Son*, 165.
81. Hatfield, *Fortunate Son*, 162.
82. Paul Pauken, "The Governor as Cheerleader," *Dallas Business Journal*, June 15, 2001. <http://dallas.bizjournals.com/dallas/stories/2001/06/18/editorial3.html> (July 18, 2006).

83. Minutaglio, *First Son*, 303.
84. Hatfield, *Fortunate Son*, 165.
85. Jackie Calmes, "Texas Tax Fight Yields Clues on How Bush Would Lead," *Wall Street Journal*, December 14, 1999, 24.
86. Calmes, "Texas Tax Fight Yields Clues on How Bush Would Lead," 24.
87. Hatfield, *Fortunate Son*, 169.
88. Calmes, "Texas Tax Fight Yields Clues on How Bush Would Lead," 24.
89. Minutaglio, *First Son*, 306.
90. Bush, 129.
91. Minutaglio, *First Son*, 312.
92. Dreyfuss, "George W.'s Compassion," 36.
93. Hatfield, *Fortunate Son*, 246.

Chapter Four   White House Quest: Selling the Son

1. Moore and Slater, *Bush's Brain*, 106.
2. Calmes, "Texas Tax Fight Yields Clues on How Bush Would Lead," A24.
3. Dubose, Reid, and Cannon, *Boy Genius*, 125.
4. Dubose, Reid, and Cannon, *Boy Genius*, 117.
5. Hughes, *Ten Minutes from Normal*, 114.
6. Richard L. Berke, "Training for a Presidential Race," *New York Times*, March 15, 1999, A16.
7. Dana Milbank, *Smashmouth: Two Years in the Gutter with Al Gore and George W. Bush—Notes from the 2000 Campaign Trail* (New York: Basic Books, 2001), 74.
8. Dubose, Reid, and Cannon, *Boy Genius*, 119.
9. Stuart Stevens, *The Big Enchilada: Campaign Adventures with the Cockeyed Optimists from Texas Who Won the Biggest Prize in Politics* (New York: The Free Press, 2001), 26.
10. George W. Bush, "Duty of Hope," Indianapolis, Indiana, July 22, 1999. <georgewbush.com> (August 4, 2000).
11. Tim Weiner, "Criticism Appears to Doom Republican Budget Tactic," *New York Times*, October 1, 1999, A20.
12. Dreyfuss, "George W.'s Compassion," 36.
13. Harris Poll, July 17–21, 1998, "White House 2000: Republicans." <http://www.pollingreport.com/wh2rep.htm> (July 7, 2006).
14. Republican Leadership Council Poll, February 1–4, 1999, conducted by Greg Strimple and Associates, "White House 2000: Republicans." <http://www.pollingreport.com/wh2rep.htm> (July 7, 2006).
15. ABC News Poll, August 19–22, 1999, "White House 2000: Republicans." <http://www.pollingreport.com/wh2rep.htm> (July 7, 2006).
16. Howard Fineman, "Here Comes the Son," *Newsweek* 133, no. 25 (June 21, 1999), 28–30.
17. Milbank, *Smashmouth*, 153.
18. Paul Waldman, "Political Discussion in Primary States," in Kathleen Hall Jamieson and Matthew Miller, Special Editors, *The Annals of The American Academy of Political and Social Science* 572 (November 2000), 34.
19. Milbank, *Smashmouth*, 63.
20. Janine Yagielski and Kathleen Hayden, "Bush Wins Iowa GOP Straw Poll," <CNN.com/ALLPOLITICS> (August 15, 1999).
21. Yagielski and Hayden "Bush Wins Iowa GOP Straw Poll."
22. Federal Election Commission, "Receipts of 1999–2000 Presidential Campaigns through July 31, 2000." Washington, DC, <http://www.fec.gov/finance/precm8.htm> (July 7, 2006).
23. Milbank, *Smashmouth*, 91.

24. Elizabeth Dole, "Elizabeth Dole Withdraws," *Green Papers News*, October 20, 1999. <http://www.thegreenpapers.com/News/19991020-0.html> (July 7, 2006).
25. Stevens, *The Big Enchilada*, 83.
26. Stevens, *The Big Enchilada*, 85.
27. Richard L. Berke, "Gore and Bush Strategists Analyze Their Campaigns," *New York Times*, February 12, 2001, A19.
28. Stevens, *The Big Enchilada*, 89.
29. Bruni, *Ambling into History*, 59.
30. Milbank, *Smashmouth*, 66.
31. Milbank, "Dispelling Doubts with the Rangers," 103.
32. Hughes, *Ten Minutes from Normal*, 129.
33. Milbank, *Smashmouth*, 108.
34. Stevens, *The Big Enchilada*, 122.
35. Stevens, *The Big Enchilada*, 135.
36. Waldman, "Political Discussion in Primary States," 38.
37. Milbank, *Smashmouth*, 197.
38. Bruni, *Ambling into History*, 83.
39. Milbank, *Smashmouth*, 190.
40. Richard H. Davis, "The Anatomy of a Smear Campaign," *Boston Globe*, March 21, 2004, C12.
41. Moore and Slater, *Bush's Brain*, 258.
42. Moore and Slater, *Bush's Brain*, 25.
43. Wayne Slater, "Rivals Again Fault Bush in McCain Flap," *Dallas Morning News*, December 2, 1999, 39A.
44. Diana Owen, "Media Mayhem: Performance of the Press in Election 2000," in Larry J. Sabato ed., *Overtime! The Election 2000 Thriller* (New York: Longman Publishers, 2002), 132.
45. Milbank, *Smashmouth*, 245.
46. Larry J. Sabato and Joshua J. Scott, "The Long Road to a Cliffhanger: Primaries and Conventions," in Larry J. Sabato ed., *Overtime! The Election 2000 Thriller* (New York: Longman Publishers, 2002), 25.
47. Milbank, *Smashmouth*, 14.
48. Milbank, *Smashmouth*, 18.
49. NBC News/*Wall Street Journal* Poll, "White House 2000: Comparing the Candidates," July 27–28, 2000. <http://www.pollingreport.com/wh2gen1.htm> (July 10, 2006).
50. Sabato and Scott, "The Long Road to a Cliffhanger," 32.
51. Milbank, *Smashmouth*, 294.
52. Bruni, *Ambling into History*, 185.
53. Governor George W. Bush, "Republican Party Convention Acceptance Speech," August 3, 2000.
54. Gallup/CNN/*USA Today* Poll, "White House 2000: Trial Heats," August 11–12, 2000. <http://www.pollingreport.com/wh2gen1.htm> (July 11, 2006).
55. Milbank, *Smashmouth*, 298.
56. Katharine Q. Seelye, "Marital Status Is Shaping Women's Leanings, Surveys Find," *New York Times*, September 20, 2000, A23.
57. Kevin Sack, "Oprah Show Lets Gore Reach Out To Women," *New York Times*, September 12, 2000, A22.
58. CNN, "Gore Appears on 'Oprah' as Bush Courts Florida Seniors," September 11, 2000. <cnn.com/2000/ALLPOLITICS> (July 20, 2006).
59. Alison Mitchell, "Full of Banter, Bush Goes on the 'Oprah' Circuit," *New York Times*, September 20, 2000, A22.
60. David Skinner, "Matters of the Heart," September 20, 2000. <www.salon.com> (July 21, 2006).
61. Gallup/CNN/*USA Today* Poll, "White House 2000: Trial Heats," October 4–6, 2000. <http://www.pollingreport.com/wh2gen1.htm> (July 23, 2006).
62. Stevens, *The Big Enchilada*, 157.
63. Hughes, *Ten Minutes from Normal*, 163.
64. George W. Bush, "First Presidential Debate," University of Massachusetts in Boston, Boston, Massachusetts, October 4, 2000.

65. George W. Bush, "Second Presidential Debate," Wake Forest University, Wake Forest, North Carolina, October 11, 2000.

66. Jill Lawrence, "Debate Showcases Personalities," *USA Today*, October 18, 2000, 5A.

67. George W. Bush, "Third Presidential Debate," Washington University, St. Louis, Missouri, October 17, 2000.

68. ABC News Poll, "White House 2000: Presidential Debates," October 3, 2000. <http://www.pollingreport.com/wh2gen1.htm> (July 25, 2006).

69. Sabato, 58.

70. ABC News Poll, "White House 2000: Presidential Debates," October 11, 2000. <www.polingreport.com> (July 26, 2006).

71. ABC News Poll, "White House 2000: Presidential Debates," October 17, 2000. <www.polingreport.com> (July 26, 2006).

72. Gallup/CNN/*USA Today* Poll, "White House 2000: Presidential Debates," October 17, 2000. <www.polingreport.com> (July 26, 2006).

73. Gallup/CNN/*USA Today* Poll, "White House 2000: Presidential Debates," October 18–20, 2000. <http://www.polingreport.com/wh2gen1.htm> (July 26, 2006).

74. Milbank, *Smashmouth*, 347.

75. Moore and Slater, *Bush's Brain*, 280.

76. Bruni, *Ambling into History*, 195.

77. Hughes, *Ten Minutes from Normal*, 166.

78. Berke, "Gore and Bush Strategists Analyze Their Campaigns," A19.

79. David M. Brodsky and Robert H. Swansbrough, "Tennessee: A Native Son Scorned," in Robert P. Steed and Laurence W. Moreland eds., *The 2000 Presidential Election in the South* (New York: Praeger Publishers, 2002), 181–197.

80. Berke, "Gore and Bush Strategists Analyze Their Campaigns," A19.

81. Voter News Service Presidential Election Exit Poll, November 7, 2000. <http://www.msnbc.com/m/d2k/g/polls.asp?office=P&state=N1> (July 26, 2006).

82. Berke, "Gore and Bush Strategists Analyze Their Campaigns," A19.

Chapter Five   The Early Months: Clear-Eyed Realism

1. The list of Bush foreign policy advisers included Richard Armitage, Reagan's assistant secretary of defense; Robert Blackwell, George H.W. Bush National Security Council; Stephen J. Hadley, Bush assistant secretary of defense; Richard Perle, Reagan assistant secretary of defense; Condoleezza Rice, Bush National Security Council; Paul Wolfowitz, Bush undersecretary of defense; Dov Zakheim, Reagan deputy undersecretary of defense; and Robert Zoellick, Bush deputy chief of staff. John Lancaster and Terry M. Neal, "Heavyweight 'Vulcans' Help Bush Forge a Foreign Policy," *Washington Post*, November 19, 1999, A2.

2. William Safire, "Bush Speaks Out," *New York Times*, April 15, 1999, A31.

3. Carl M. Cannon, "The Book on W," *National Journal* 31, no. 32 (August 7, 1999), 2277.

4. Robert H. Swansbrough, "A Kohutian Analysis of President Bush's Personality and Style in the Persian Gulf Crisis," *Political Psychology: Journal of the International Society of Political Psychology* 15, no. 2 (June 1994), 249.

5. Ivo H. Daalder and James M. Lindsay, *America Unbound: The Bush Revolution in Foreign Policy* (Washington, DC: Brookings Institution Press, 2003), 51.

6. James Mann, *Rise of the Vulcans* (New York: Viking, 2004), 254.

7. Daalder and Lindsay, *America Unbound*, 24.

8. Mann, *Rise of the Vulcans*, 250.

9. Daalder and Lindsay, *America Unbound*, 59.

10. Daalder and Lindsay, *America Unbound*, 27.

11. Mann, *Rise of the Vulcans*, 253. The members included Condoleezza Rice, Paul Wolfowitz, Stephen Hadley, and Richard Perle.

12. Colin L. Powell, *My American Journey* (New York: Random House, 1995), 465.

13. George Bush and Brent Scowcroft, *A World Transformed* (New York: Alfred A. Knopf, 1998), 464; Powell, *My American Journey*, 521.

14. Mann, *Rise of the Vulcans*, 191.
15. Bob Woodward, *The Commanders* (New York: Simon & Schuster, 1991), 261.
16. Mann, *Rise of the Vulcans*, 265.
17. Mann, *Rise of the Vulcans*, 51.
18. Mann, *Rise of the Vulcans*, 136.
19. Powell, *My American Journey*, 303.
20. Powell, *My American Journey*, 148.
21. Powell, *My American Journey*, 405.
22. Powell, *My American Journey*, 148.
23. NBC News Transcript, "Meet the Press with Tim Russert," NBC News, February 8, 2004.
24. Daalder and Lindsay, *America Unbound*, 56.
25. Bush and Scowcroft, *A World Transformed*, 94.
26. Bush and Scowcroft, *A World Transformed*, 89.
27. George Lardner Jr., "Clinton to Be 'Forceful' in China, Aide Says," *Washington Post*, June 15, 1995, A19.
28. "Washington in Brief," *Washington Post*, July 23, 1998.
29. James Bennet, "Despite Furor over China, Clinton Defends Trade Status," *New York Times*, June 4, 1998, A10.
30. President Bill Clinton, "Interview of the President by David Sanger, Todd Purdum, Marc Lacey, Robin Toner and Jane Perlez of the *New York Times*," White House, November 30, 2000.
31. John Pomfret, "A Buildup of Irritation in Relations," *Washington Post*, April 3, 2001, A1.
32. Governor George W. Bush, "A Distinctly American Internationalism," Ronald Reagan Library, California, November 19, 1999.
33. Condoleezza Rice, "Promoting the National Interest," *Foreign Affairs* 79, no. 1 (January/February 2000), 55.
34. Americans in the World: Public Opinion on International Affairs, "US Relations with China," Program on International Policy Attitudes. <http://www.americans-world.org/digest/regional_issues/china/china5,cfm> (August 1, 2006).
35. Steven Mufson and Mike Allen, "U.S. Voices Regret over Chinese Pilot," *Washington Post*, April 5, 2001, A1.
36. Mufson and Allen, "U.S. Voices Regret over Chinese Pilot," A1.
37. Joseph W. Prueher, "Text: Letter from Amb. Prueher to China's Minister of Foreign Affairs," April 11, 2001. <http://www.usconsulate.org.hk/uscn/wh/2001/041103.htm> (August 4, 2006).
38. Daalder and Lindsay, *America Unbound*, 69.
39. Condoleezza Rice, NBC "Nightline" with Ted Koppel, April 11, 2001.
40. Mann, *Rise of the Vulcans*, 284.
41. David E. Sanger, "Bush Is Offering Taiwan Some Arms but Not the Best," *New York Times*, April 24, 2001, A1.
42. ABC, "100 Days Interview with George W. Bush," ABC "Good Morning America," April 25, 2001.
43. Steve Mufson, "Clash with China Strengthens Hardliners," *Washington Post*, April 23, 2001, A9.
44. Paul Wolfowitz, "Deputy Secretary Wolfowitz Statement on Berets," U.S. Department of Defense, May 1, 2001.
45. George Gedda, "Powell Says China Seeks Stronger Ties and to Avoid Tension over Taiwan," Associated Press, July 29, 2001.
46. Safire, "Bush Speaks Out," A31.
47. Frank Bruni, "Bush Vows Money and Support for Military," *New York Times*, September 24, 1999, A22.
48. George W. Bush, "A Period of Consequences," The Citadel, South Carolina, September 23, 1999. <georgewbush.com> (October 2000).
49. George W. Bush, "A Distinctly American Internationalism," Ronald Reagan Presidential Library, Simi Valley, California, November 19, 1999. <www.georgewbush.com> (August 6, 2006).

50. George W. Bush, "New Leadership on National Security," Washington, DC, May 23, 2000.
51. President Bill Clinton, "Remarks on National Security," Georgetown University, September 1, 2000.
52. Donald Rumsfeld, "Transcript of Rumsfeld in Munich with Europe's Defense Ministers," CNN, February 3, 2001.
53. Colin L. Powell, "This Week with Sam Donaldson," ABC "This Week," February 4, 2001.
54. George W. Bush, "White House News Conference," White House, Washington, DC, March 29, 2001.
55. Patrick E. Tyler, "Putin Invites West to Work on a Defense for Missiles," *New York Times*, February 21, 2001, A5.
56. George W. Bush, "Remarks by the President to Students and Faculty at National Defense University," Washington, DC, May 1, 2001.
57. Robert Burns, "Bush to Cut Nuclear Forces While Accelerating Missile Defense Effort," Associated Press, May 1, 2001.
58. William Drozdiak, "NATO Deals Blow to U.S. Missile Defense Plan," *Washington Post*, May 29, 2001, A15.
59. George W. Bush, "Press Conference with Spanish President Jose Maria Aznar," Madrid, Spain, June 12, 2001.
60. Sam Nunn, "When Bush Meets Putin," *Washington Post*, June 12, 2001, A25.
61. William Drozdiak and Dana Milbank, "Bush Tries to Sell NATO On Missile Defense Plan," *Washington Post*, June 14, 2001, A1.
62. George W. Bush, "Press Conference by President Bush and Russian Federation President Putin," Brdo Castle, Brdo Pri Kranju, Slovenia, June 16, 2001.
63. Rice, "Promoting the National Interest," 57.
64. Mann, *Rise of the Vulcans*, 288.
65. Mike Allen, "Bush, Putin Agree to Arms Dialogue; Reductions, Missile Shield Are Linked," *Washington Post*, July 23, 2001, A1.
66. David E. Sanger, "A Day after Seeing Putin, a Harder-Line Bush Emerges," *New York Times*, July 24, 2001, A8.
67. David E. Sanger, "Bush's European Theater," *New York Times*, July 25, 2001, A6.
68. Evan Thomas and Roy Gutman, "See George. See George Learn Foreign Policy," *Newsweek* 137 (June 18, 2001), 20.
69. Kim Dae-jung, "Nobel Lecture," Oslo, Norway, December 10, 2000.
70. Glenn Kessler, "South Korea Offers to Supply Energy if North Gives Up Arms," *Washington Post*, July 16, 2005, A16.
71. Howard Diamond, "N. Korea Launches Staged Rocket that Overflies Japanese Territory," *Arms Control Today*, Arms Control Association, August/September 1998. <http://www.armscontrol.org/act/1998_08-09/nk1as98.asp> (August 8, 2006).
72. Steve Mufson, "Bush to Pick Up Clinton Talks on N. Korean Missiles," *Washington Post*, March 7, 2001, A20.
73. Mann, *Rise of the Vulcans*, 279.
74. George W. Bush, "Remarks by President Bush and President Kim Dae-Jung of Korea," White House, Washington, DC, March 7, 2001.
75. Colin L. Powell, "Remarks by Secretary of State Colin Powell to the Pool," White House, Washington, DC, March 7, 2001.
76. Mufson, "Bush to Pick Up Clinton Talks on N. Korean Missiles," A20.
77. Rice, "Promoting the National Interest," 22.
78. U.S. Senate, "Senate Resolution 98 (Byrd-Hagel Resolution)," 105th Congress, 1st Session, July 25, 1997.
79. Eric Pianin and Amy Goldstein, "Bush Drops a Call for Emissions Cuts," *Washington Post*, March 14, 2002, A1.
80. Eric Planin and William Drozdiak, "Bush's Reversal Could Affect Global Warming Agreement," *Washington Post*, March 16, 2001, A3.
81. George W. Bush, "Text of a Letter from the President to Senators Hagel, Helms, Craig, and Roberts," White House, Washington, DC, March 13, 2001.
82. George W. Bush, "Press Conference with Spanish President Jose Maria Aznar," Madrid, Spain, June 12, 2001.

83. George W. Bush, "Press Conference by President Bush, Prime Minister Goran Persson of Sweden," Goteborg, Sweden, June 14, 2001.

84. Peggy Noonan, "A Chat in the Oval Office," *Wall Street Journal*, June 25, 2001, A18.

85. Andrew C. Revkin, "178 Nations Reach a Climate Accord," *New York Times*, July 24, 2001, A1.

86. Thom Shanker, "White House Says the U.S. Is Not a Loner, Just Choosy," *New York Times*, July 31, 2001, A1.

87. Sanger, "Bush's European Theater," A6.

88. Donald A. Mahley, "Transcript: Mahley News Conference on Biological Weapons Protocol," Press Conference with Ambassador Donald A. Mahley, Special Negotiator for Chemical and Biological Arms Control Issues, Geneva Switzerland, July 25, 2001.

89. Colum Lynch, "Nations Reach Pact on Trade of Small Arms," *Washington Post*, July 22, 2001, A17.

90. Shanker, "White House Says the U.S. Is Not a Loner, Just Choosy," A1.

91. Condoleezza Rice, "Transcript of Condoleezza Rice on Face the Nation," CBS Face the Nation, July 29, 2001.

92. Colin L. Powell, "Secretary Powell in Hanoi, Vietnam," U.S. Department of State, July 26, 2001.

93. George W. Bush, "News Conference," White House, Washington, DC, March 29, 2001.

94. Jane Perlez, "Taking a Breather on the Mideast," *New York Times*, July 5, 2001, A6.

Chapter Six   Ignored Warnings:
A Call to Destiny

1. Bill Adair and Stephen Hegarty, "The Drama in Sarasota," *St. Petersburg Times*, September 8, 2002, 18.

2. Woodward, *Bush at War*, 15. Other accounts credit NSC Adviser Condoleezza Rice with notifying President Bush of the first attack. See Elisabeth Bumiller with David E. Sanger, "A Somber Bush Says Terrorism Cannot Prevail," *New York Times*, September 12, 2001, A1. The first terrorist attack involved American Airlines Flight 11.

3. Dan Balz and Bob Woodward, "America's Chaotic Road to War," *Washington Post*, January 27, 2002, A1.

4. Bumiller and Sanger, "A Somber Bush Says Terrorism Cannot Prevail." Also Mike Allen and Hanna Rosin, "President Pledges 'Terrorism Will Not Stand.'" *Washington Post* Final Edition, September 11, 2001, A3. This was United Flight 175. Filmmaker Michael Moore featured those six or so minutes of a passive President Bush at the onset of the terrorist crisis in the documentary *Fahrenheit 9/11*, ridiculing President Bush's failure to immediately respond to the terrorist attacks. Several years later, just four days before the 2004 presidential election, the Arab TV station Al-Jazeera broadcast a videotape of Osama bin Laden in which the al Qaeda leader mocked President George W. Bush for continuing to listen to "a little girl's talk about her goat and its butting" after the hijacked airliners had struck the World Trade Center's twin towers.

5. George W. Bush, "Remarks by the President after Two Planes Crash into World Trade Center," Emma Booker Elementary School, Sarasota, Florida, September 11, 2001.

6. Bumiller and Sanger, "A Somber Bush Says Terrorism Cannot Prevail," A1. Later the White House web site toned down Bush's hot rhetoric in the Barksdale statement to read: "Make no mistake: The United States will hunt down and punish those responsible for these cowardly acts."

7. Dick Cheney, "Tim Russert Interview with Vice President Dick Cheney," NBC's Meet the Press, Camp David, September 16, 2001.

8. Balz and Woodward, "America's Chaotic Road to War," A1.

9. David E. Sanger and Don Van Natta Jr., "In Four Days, a National Crisis Changes Bush's Presidency," *New York Times*, September 16, 2001, section 1, page 1.

10. Cheney, "Tim Russert Interview with Vice President Dick Cheney."

11. Woodward, *Bush at War*, 270.

12. Graham Allison and Philip Zelikow, *Essence of Decision: Explaining the Cuban Missile Crisis*, 2nd edition (New York: Longman, 1999).
13. Richard A. Clarke, *Against All Enemies: Inside America's War on Terror* (New York: Free Press, 2004), 5.
14. Woodward, *Bush at War*, 26.
15. Bush, "Remarks by the President after Two Planes Crash into World Trade Center."
16. George W. Bush, "Remarks by the President upon Arrival at Barksdale Air Force Base," Barksdale Air Force Base, Louisiana, September 11, 2001.
17. Woodward, *Bush at War*, 30.
18. Hughes, *Ten Minutes from Normal*, 243.
19. George W. Bush, "Statement by the President in His Address to the Nation," White House, Washington, DC, September 11, 2001.
20. "Post-ABC Poll: Terrorist Attacks," September 11, 2001. <http://www.washingtonpost.com/wp-srv/politics/polls/vault/stories/date091201.htm> (April 2, 2007).
21. CNN/*USA Today*/Gallup Poll, September 11, 2001. <http://www.pollingreport/com/terror10.htm> (April 2, 2007).
22. George W. Bush, "Remarks by the President in Photo Opportunity with the National Security Team," The Cabinet Room, Washington, DC, September 12, 2001.
23. Graham Allison, "Could Worse Be Yet to Come?" *Economist* 361, no. 8246 (November 3, 2001), 19.
24. Anonymous [Michael Scheuer], *Imperial Hubris: Why the West Is Losing the War on Terror* (Washington, DC: Brassey's, Inc., 2004), xvii. Michael Scheuer, described in the book as a senior U.S. intelligence official, wrote *Imperial Hubris* under the pseudonym Anonymous since the CIA would not allow him to use his real name while still serving in the agency.
25. Anonymous, *Imperial Hubris*, 61.
26. Anonymous, *Imperial Hubris*, 245.
27. James Risen, "Evolving Nature of Al Qaeda Is Misunderstood, Critic Says," *New York Times*, November 8, 2004, A18.
28. Jeffrey Record, "Bounding the Global War on Terrorism," Strategic Studies Institute, U.S. Army War College, December 2003, v.
29. Record, "Bounding the Global War on Terrorism," 16.
30. Woodward, *Bush at War*, 30.
31. Woodward, *Bush at War*, 81 and 98.
32. Woodward, *Bush at War*, 49 and 33.
33. Woodward, *Bush at War*, 102.
34. Gary Berntsen and Ralph Pezzullo, *Jawbreaker: The Attack on Bin Laden and Al-Qaeda: A Personal Account by the CIA's Key Field Commander* (New York: Crown Publishers, 2005), 62.
35. Woodward, *Bush at War*, 63.
36. Woodward, *Bush at War*, 32 and 43.
37. General Tommy Franks, *American Soldier* (New York: Regan Books, 2004), 251.
38. Henry A. Crumpton, "Intelligence and War: Afghanistan, 2001–2002," in Jennifer E. Sims and Burton Gerber eds., *Transforming U.S. Intelligence* (Washington, DC: Georgetown University Press, 2005), 163.
39. Woodward, *Bush at War*, 102.
40. Woodward, *Bush at War*, 48 and 65.
41. Woodward, *Bush at War*, 81.
42. Woodward, *Bush at War*, 145.
43. Woodward, *Bush at War*, 203.
44. Anonymous, *Imperial Hubris*, 24.
45. Anonymous, *Imperial Hubris*, 25.
46. Clarke, *Against All Enemies*, 245.
47. Clarke, *Against All Enemies*, 274.
48. Franks, *American Soldier*, 324.
49. Franks, *American Soldier*, 211.
50. Gary C. Schoen, *First In: An Insider's Account of How the CIA Spearheaded the War on Terrorism in Afghanistan* (New York: Ballantine Books, 2005), 28 and 36.

51. Berntsen and Pezzullo, *Jawbreaker*, 56.
52. Berntsen and Pezzullo, *Jawbreaker*, 99.
53. Berntsen and Pezzullo, *Jawbreaker*, 160.
54. Franks, *American Soldier*, 311 and 312.
55. Woodward, *Bush at War*, 195.
56. Doug MacEachin and Janne E. Nolan, "The US and Soviet Proxy War in Afghanistan, 1989–1992: Prisoners of Our Preconceptions?" Working Group Report, No IV, Institute for the Study of Diplomacy, Georgetown University, November 15, 2005, 8 and 10.
57. Woodward, *Bush at War*, 317.
58. Anonymous, *Imperial Hubris*, xvi.
59. Seymour M. Hersh, "The Other War: Why Bush's Afghanistan Problem Won't Go Away," *New Yorker* 80, no. 8 (April 12, 2004), 41.
60. Seymour M. Hersh, *Chain of Command: The Road from 9/11 to Abu Ghraib* (New York: HarperCollins Publishers Inc., 2004), 126.
61. Associated Press, "Opium Crop on Rise in Afghan Provinces," *New York Times*, November 29, 2006, A18.
62. Donald Rumsfeld, "Transcript: Interview with Donald Rumsfeld," CNN Live with Larry King, December 18, 2002. <http://transcripts.cnn.com/TRANSCRIPTS/0212/18/lkl.00.html> (August 3, 2006).
63. Anonymous, *Imperial Hubris*, 181.
64. Sandy Berger, "Testimony of Sandy Berger, National Security Adviser to President Bill Clinton," Transcript 9/11 Commission Hearings, March 24, 2004.
65. Clarke, *Against All Enemies*, 26.
66. George Tenet, "Testimony of George Tenet, Director of the Central Intelligence Agency," Transcript 9/11 Commission Hearings, March 24, 2004.
67. Colin Powell, Transcript of 9/11 Commission Hearings, March 23, 2004.
68. 9/11 Commission, *The 9/11 Commission Report: Final Report of the National Commission on Terrorist Attacks upon the United States* (New York: W.W. Norton & Company, 2004), 119.
69. Berger, "Testimony of Sandy Berger, National Security Adviser to President Bill Clinton."
70. Berger, "Testimony of Sandy Berger, National Security Adviser to President Bill Clinton."
71. Condoleezza Rice, "9/11: For the Record," *Washington Post*, March 22, 2004, A21.
72. *9/11 Commission Report*, 254.
73. *9/11 Commission Report*, 259.
74. Woodward, *Bush at War*, 35.
75. Woodward, *Bush at War*, 36.
76. Condoleezza Rice, "9/11: For the Record," A21.
77. Richard Clarke, Transcript of 9/11 Commission Hearings, March 24, 2004.
78. Richard Ben-Veniste, Transcript of 9/11 Commission Hearings, March 24, 2004.
79. Woodward, *Bush at War*, 97.
80. Berntsen and Pezzullo, *Jawbreaker*, 314.
81. Franks, *American Soldier*, 261.
82. Donald Rumsfeld, Transcript of 9/11 Commission Hearings, March 23, 2004.
83. Franks, *American Soldier*, 255–257.
84. Woodward, *Bush at War*, 152.
85. Woodward, *Bush at War*, 178.
86. Franks, *American Soldier*, 301.
87. Franks, *American Soldier*, 299.
88. Suskind, *The One Percent Doctrine*, 77.
89. Woodward, *Bush at War*, 166.
90. Berntsen and Pezzullo, *Jawbreaker*, 75.
91. Schoen, *First In*, 33.
92. Woodward, *Bush at War*, 157.
93. Woodward, *Bush at War*, 158.
94. Schoen, *First In*, 29.
95. Woodward, *Bush at War*, 168.
96. Woodward, *Bush at War*, 38.
97. Woodward, *Bush at War*, 44.

98. Woodward, *Bush at War*, 259.
99. Woodward, *Bush at War*, 176.
100. Woodward, *Bush at War*, 246.
101. Woodward, *Bush at War*, 95.
102. Woodward, *Bush at War*, 189.
103. George W. Bush, "President Freezes Terrorists' Assets," The Rose Garden, White House, Washington, DC, September 24, 2001.
104. Woodward, *Bush at War*, 131.
105. Woodward, *Bush at War*, 279.
106. Woodward, *Bush at War*, 24.
107. Woodward, *Bush at War*, 251.
108. Woodward, *Bush at War*, 215.
109. Franks, *American Soldier*, 280.
110. Franks, *American Soldier*, 290.
111. Anonymous, *Imperial Hubris*, 52.
112. Irving L. Janis, *Groupthink: Psychological Studies of Policy Decisions and Fiascoes*, 2nd edition (Boston: Houghton Mifflin, 1982).

Chapter Seven   New Kind of War: Breaking the Rules

1. George W. Bush, "Radio Address of the President to the Nation," White House, Washington, DC, September 15, 2001.
2. George W. Bush, "Press Conference by the President," White House, Washington, DC, October 26, 2006.
3. George W. Bush, "President Signs Anti-Terrorism Bill," White House, Washington, DC, October 26, 2001.
4. The House approved the antiterrorism package on October 24 (357–66) and the Senate on October 25 (98–1).
5. Nancy Kassop, "The War Power and Its Limits," *Presidential Studies Quarterly* 33, no. 3 (September 2003), 515.
6. Elizabeth A. Palmer, "Terrorism Bill's Sparse Paper Trail May Cause Legal Vulnerabilities," *CQ Weekly* 59, no. 41 (October 27, 2001), 2533.
7. John Lancaster, "Hill Is Due to Take Up Anti-Terror Legislation; Bill Prompts Worries Of Threat to Rights," *Washington Post*, October 9, 2001, A3.
8. Kassop, "The War Power and Its Limits," 515.
9. Derek H. Davis, "The Dark Side to a Just War: The USA PATRIOT Act and Counterterrorism's Potential Threat to Religious Freedom," *Journal of Church and State* 44, no. 1 (Winter 2002), 5.
10. Suskind, *The One Percent Doctrine*, 20.
11. Dana Priest, "CIA Holds Terror Suspects in Secret Prisons; Debate is Growing within Agency about Legality and Morality of Overseas System Set Up after 9/11," *Washington Post*, November 2, 2005, A1.
12. George Tenet, *At the Center of the Storm: My Years at the CIA* (New York: HarperCollins Publishers, 2007), 242.
13. Suskind, *The One Percent Doctrine*, 56.
14. Suskind, *The One Percent Doctrine*, 62.
15. Suskind, *The One Percent Doctrine*, 79.
16. John Barry, Michael Hirsh, and Michael Isikoff, "The Roots of Torture," *Newsweek* 143, no. 21 (May 24, 2004), 26.
17. John Yoo and Robert J. Delahunty, "Memorandum for William J. Haynes II, General Counsel, Department of Defense," January 9, 2002, 2. <http://www.slate.com/features/whatistorture/LegalMemos.html> (October 29, 2006).
18. Alberto R. Gonzales, "Decision Re Application of the Geneva Convention on Prisoners of War to the Conflict with Al Qaeda and the Taliban," January 25, 2001, 2. <http://www.slate.com/features/whatistorture/LegalMemos.html> (October 29, 2006).

19. Colin L. Powell, "Draft Decision Memorandum for the President on the Applicability of the Geneva Convention to the conflict in Afghanistan," January 26, 2002, 2. <http://www.slate.com/features/whatistorture/LegalMemos.html> (October 29, 2006).

20. John Ashcroft, "Letter to the President," February 1, 2002, 2. <http://www.slate.com/features/whatistorture/LegalMemos.html> (October 29, 2006).

21. William H. Taft IV, "Comments on Your (Counsel to the President) Paper on the Geneva Conventions," February 2, 2002. <http://www.slate.com/features/whatistorture/LegalMemos.html> (October 29, 2006).

22. George W. Bush, "Humane Treatment of al Qaeda and Taliban Detainees," February 7, 2002. <http://www.slate.com/features/whatistorture/LegalMemos.html> (October 29, 2006).

23. Dana Priest, "CIA's Assurances on Transferred Suspects Doubted; Prisoners Say Countries Break No-Torture Pledges," *Washington Post*, March 17, 2005, A1.

24. Michael Scheuer, "Interview on May 2006." *Alleged Secret Detentions and Unlawful Inter-state Transfers Involving Council of Europe Member States*. Rapporteur: Dick Marty (Switzerland), Committee on Legal Affairs and Human Rights, Parliamentary Assembly, Council of Europe, June 7, 2006. Hereafter called Marty Report. <http://assembly.coe.int/CommitteeDocs/2006/20060606_Ejdoc162006PartII-FINAL.pdf> (December 6, 2006).

25. Marty Report, 2006, 10.

26. Federal Bureau of Investigation, "Terrorism in the United States 1997," Department of Justice, Washington, DC, 1997, 14. <http://www.fbi.gov/publications/terror/terr97.pdf> (December 8, 2006).

27. Condoleezza Rice, "Remarks upon Her Departure for Europe," Andrews Air Force Base, December 5, 2005.

28. Jane Mayer, "Outsourcing Torture: The Secret History of America's 'Extraordinary Rendition' Program," *New Yorker* 81, no. 1 (February 14, 2005), 106.

29. Marty Report, 2006, 10.

30. Priest, "CIA's Assurances on Transferred Suspects Doubted," A1.

31. George Tenet, "Statement of DCI George J. Tenet before the SSCI on 'The Worldwide Threat in 2000: Global Realities of Our National Security," February 2, 2000. <https://www.cia.gov/news-information/cia-the-war-on-terrorism/pub_statements_terrorism.html> (January 2007).

32. George Tenet, "Transcript: Wednesday's 9/11 Commission Hearings," March 24, 2004.

33. George Tenet, "Testimony of George Tenet, CIA Director," National Commission on Terrorist Attacks upon the United States, Tenth Public Hearing, April 14, 2004.

34. Foreign Affairs Reform and Restructuring Act of 1998, H.R. 1757, 105th Congress, Chapter 3, Subchapter B, Sec. 1241 (Public Law 105–277).

35. See H.R. 952 and H. Con. Res. 101.

36. Priest, "CIA Holds Terror Suspects in Secret Prisons," A1.

37. Dick Cheney, "Interview with Vice President Cheney at Camp David," NBC, "Meet the Press," September 16, 2001.

38. Priest, "CIA's Assurances on Transferred Suspects Doubted," A1.

39. Douglas Jehl and David Johnston, "Rule Change Lets C.I.A. Freely Send Suspects Abroad to Jails," *New York Times*, March 6, 2005, A1.

40. Dana Priest, "Wrongful Imprisonment: Anatomy of a CIA Mistake; German Citizen Released after Months in 'Rendition,'" *Washington Post*, December 4, 2005, A1. The Marty Report to the Council of Europe describes almost identically the processing of rendered suspects based upon interviews and accounts of 17 men rendered by the CIA. Marty Report, 2006, 21.

41. George W. Bush, "Press Conference of the President," White House, Washington, DC, April 28, 2005.

42. Alan Cowell, "U.S. 'Thumbs Its Nose' at Rights, Amnesty Says," *New York Times*, May 26, 2005, A1.

43. Josh White, "New Rules of Interrogation Forbids Use of Harsh Tactics," *Washington Post*, September 7, 2006, A1.

44. Dan Eggen, "Chaney's Remarks Fuel Torture Debate," *Washington Post*, October 27, 2006, A9.

45. Walter Pincus, "Waterboarding Historically Controversial," *Washington Post*, October 5, 2006, A17 and Jane Mayer, "The Black Sites," *New Yorker* 83, no. 22 (August 13, 2007), 56.

46. William Douglas and Jonathan S. Landay, "Bush Sets CIA Rules on Queries of Terrorists," McClatchy Newspapers, *Chattanooga Times Free Press*, July 21, 2007, A1.
47. Mayer, "The Black Sites," 48.
48. Karen DeYoung, "Bush Approves New CIA Methods," *Washington Post*, July 21, 2007, A1.
49. Mayer, "The Black Sites," 56.
50. Priest, "CIA Holds Terror Suspects in Secret Prisons," A1.
51. Marty Report, 2006, 16–19. Marty also alleged detention centers existed in Bulgaria, Kosovo, Macedonia, and Ukraine.
52. James Risen, *State of War: The Secret History of the CIA and the Bush Administration* (New York: Free Press, 2006), 29.
53. Priest, "CIA Holds Terror Suspects in Secret Prisons," A1.
54. Marty Report, 2006, 6.
55. Associated Press, "Europeans Approve Report on C.I.A.," *New York Times*, February 14, 2007.
56. Marty Report, 2006, 4.
57. Dan Bilefsky, "European Inquiry Says C.I.A. Flew 1,000 Flights in Secret," *New York Times*, April 26, 2006, A12. Associated Press, "Pattern of CIA Flights Is Cited; EU Inquiry Finds Some Terrorism Suspects Were Transferred to Countries Where They Could Face Torture," *Los Angeles Times*, April 27, 2006, A22.
58. Justin Stares and Philip Sherwell, "EU Concealed Deal with US to Allow 'Rendition' Flights," *London Telegraph*, November 12, 2005. <http://www.telegraph.co.uk/core/Content/displayPrintable.jhtml;jsessionid=3J4G4XCUUFGULQFIQMFSFFWAVCBQ0IV0?xml=/news/2005/12/11/wrendition11.xml&site=5&page=0> (January 28, 2007).
59. Marty Report, 2006, 12.
60. Marty Report, 2006, 15 and 24–47.
61. Stephen Grey, *Ghost Plane: The True Story of the CIA Torture Program* (New York: St. Martin's Press, 2006), 128 and 124. Grey's book includes a chronology of CIA renditions from 1987. Also see Trevor Paglen and A.C. Thompson, *Torture Taxi: On the Trail of the CIA's Rendition Flights* (Hoboken, NJ: Melville House Publishing, 2006).
62. Grey, *Ghost Plane*, 151.
63. George W. Bush, "President Discusses Creation of Military Commissions to Try Suspected Terrorists," White House, Washington, DC, September 6, 2006.
64. Bush, "President Discusses Creation of Military Commissions to Try Suspected Terrorists."
65. John Donnelly and Rick Klein, "Bush Admits to CIA Jails; Top Suspects Are Relocated," *Boston Globe*, September 7, 2006, A1.
66. Priest, "Wrongful Imprisonment," A1.
67. Craig Whitlock, "Germans Charge 13 CIA Operatives in Germany Kidnapping," *Washington Post*, February 1, 2007, A1.
68. Ian Fisher and Elisabetta Povoledo, "Italy Seeks Indictments of C.I.A. Operatives in Egyptian's Abduction," *New York Times*, December 6, 2006, A12.
69. Craig Whitlock, "Testimony Helps Detail CIA's Post-9/11 Reach; Europeans Told of Plans for Abductions," *Washington Post*, December 16, 2006, A1.
70. Doug Struck, "Tortured Man Gets Apology from Canada," *Washington Post*, January 27, 2007, A14.
71. Whitlock, "Testimony Helps Detail CIA's Post-9/11 Reach," A1.
72. James Risen and Eric Lichtblau, "Bush Lets U.S. Spy on Callers without Courts," *New York Times*, December 16, 2005, A1.
73. George W. Bush, "President's Radio Address," White House, Washington, DC, December 17, 2005.
74. Alberto Gonzales, "Press Briefing by Attorney General Alberto Gonzales and General Michael Hayden, Principal Deputy Director for National Intelligence," White House, Washington, DC, December 19, 2005.
75. *Hamdi v Rumsfeld*, 542 U.S. 507 (2004), June 28, 2004, 29.
76. Michael Hayden, "Press Briefing by Attorney General Alberto Gonzales and General Michael Hayden, Principal Deputy Director for National Intelligence," White House, Washington, DC, December 19, 2005.

77. Alberto Gonzales, "Prepared Remarks for Attorney General Alberto R. Gonzales at the Georgetown University Law Center," Washington, DC, January 24, 2006.

78. Alberto Gonzales, "Letter to Senator Arlen Specter, Chairman, Committee on the Judiciary," February 28, 2006.

79. George W. Bush, "President Discusses War on Terror and Operation Iraqi Freedom," Renaissance Cleveland Hotel, Cleveland, Ohio, March 20, 2006.

80. Scott Shane and Eric Lichtblau, "Cheney Pushed U.S. to Widen Eavesdropping," *New York Times*, May 14, 2006, A1.

81. Barton Gellman and Dafna Linzer, "Pushing the Limits Of Wartime Powers," *Washington Post*, December 18, 2005, A1.

82. William Branigin, "Cheney Says Eavesdropping Program Might Have Prevented 9/11," *Washington Post*, January 4, 2006, A1.

83. Dick Cheney, "Transcript: Vice President Cheney's Commencement Address," U.S. Naval Academy, May 26, 2006.

84. Elizabeth B. Bazan and Jennifer K. Elsea, "Presidential Authority to Conduct Warrantless Electronic Surveillance to Gather Foreign Intelligence Information," Congressional Reference Service, January 5, 2006, CRS-23–25.

85. Bazen and Elsea, "Presidential Authority to Conduct Warrantless Electronic Surveillance to Gather Foreign Intelligence Information," CRS-27.

86. Bazen and Elsea, "Presidential Authority to Conduct Warrantless Electronic Surveillance to Gather Foreign Intelligence Information," CRS-43.

87. Peter Baker and Charles Babington, "Bush Addresses Uproar over Spying," *Washington Post*, December 20, 2005, A1.

88. Dan Eggen and Charles Lane, "On Hill, Anger and Calls for Hearings Greet News of Stateside Surveillance," *Washington Post*, December 17, 2005, A1.

89. *ACLU v NSA*, Case No. 06-CV-10204, U.S. District Court, Eastern District of Michigan, Southern Division, August 17, 2006, 23.

90. *ACLU v NSA*, 40.

91. Michael Abramowitz and Spencer S. Hsu, "Cheney Rejects Idea of Iraq," *Washington Post*, November 18, 2006, A4.

92. Suskind, *One Percent Doctrine*, 114.

93. Seymour M. Hersh, *Chain of Command: The Road from 9/11 to Abu Ghraib* (New York: HarperCollins Publishers, Inc., 2004), 14.

94. R. Jeffrey Smith, "Report Details Missteps in Data Collection," *Washington Post*, March 10, 2007, A1.

95. Suskind, *One Percent Doctrine*, 219.

96. Dana Priest and Barton Gellman, "U.S. Decries Abuse but Defends Interrogations," *Washington Post*, December 26, 2002, A1.

97. Seymour Hersh, "The Gray Zone," *New Yorker* 80, no. 13 (May 24, 2004), 39.

98. Hersh, *Chain of Command*, 17.

99. John C. Yoo, "Letter to Albert Gonzales, Counsel to the President," August 1, 2002, 1. <http://www.gwu.edu/~nsarchiv/NSAEBB/NSAEBB127/> (November 1, 2006).

100. Jay S. Bybee, "Memorandum for Alberto R. Gonzales, Counsel to the President," August 1, 2002, 1. <http://www.gwu.edu/~nsarchiv/NSAEBB/NSAEBB127/> (November 1, 2006).

101. Bybee, "Memorandum for Alberto R. Gonzales, Counsel to the President," 31.

102. Donald Rumsfeld, "Approval of Counter-Resistance Techniques," December 2, 2002, 1. <http://www.gwu.edu/~nsarchiv/NSAEBB/NSAEBB127/> (November 1, 2006).

103. Author not indicated, "Assessment of Legal, Historical, Policy, and Operational Considerations," March 6, 2003, 24.

104. Jane Mayer, "The Memo," *New Yorker* 82, no. 1 (February 27, 2006), 32.

105. Mayer, "The Memo," 36.

106. Mayer, "The Memo," 40.

107. Hersh, "The Gray Zone," 41.

108. CNN, "Ex-CIA Chief: Cheney 'VP for Torture,'" CNN.Com, November 18, 2005. <http://www.cnn.com/2005/WORLD/europe/11/18/turner.cheney/> (December 3, 2006).

109. CNN, "Powell Aide: Torture 'Guidance' from VP," CNN.com, November 20, 2005. <http://www.cnn.com/2005/US/11/20/torture/index.html> (December 3, 2006).

110. Dana Wilbank, "Colonel Finally Saw Whites of Their Eyes," *Washington Post*, October 20, 2005, A4.
111. Michael Abramowitz, "Bush's Tactic of Refusing Laws Is Probed," *Washington Post*, July 24, 2006, A5.
112. Jane Mayer, "The Hidden Power: The Legal Mind behind the White House's War on Terror," *New Yorker* 82, no. 20 (July 3, 2006), 44.
113. Mayer, "The Hidden Power," 52.
114. Richard W. Stevenson and Adam Liptak, "Cheney Defends Eavesdropping without Warrants," *New York Times*, December 21, 2005, A36.
115. Risen, *State of War*, 24.
116. Risen, *State of War*, 27.
117. George W. Bush, "President Bush Welcomes Prime Minister of Hungary," White House, Washington, DC, June 22, 2004.

Chapter Eight   March to War: Vision or Vengeance?

1. George W. Bush, "Remarks by the President at John Cornyn for Senate Reception," Houston, Texas, September 26, 2002. "After all, this is a guy that tried to kill my dad at one time." The assassination attempt in Kuwait could have also killed Bush's wife Laura, mother Barbara, and two of his brothers accompanying the elder Bush. Michael Isikoff and David Corn, *Hubris: The Inside Story of Spin, Scandal, and the Selling of the Iraq War* (New York: Crown Publishers, 2006), 116.
2. Lawrence Freedman and Efraim Karsh, *The Gulf Conflict 1990–1991: Diplomacy and War in the New World Order* (Princeton, NJ: Princeton University Press, 1993), 409.
3. Anthony Zinni, "Straight Talk from General Anthony Zinni," Lecture at UCLA's Ronald W. Burkle Center for International Relations, Los Angeles, California, May 11, 2004.
4. *Gallup Poll Monthly*, August 1990, 6.
5. Robert H. Swansbrough, "A Kohutian Analysis of President Bush's Personality and Style in the Persian Gulf Crisis," *Political Psychology* 15, no. 2 (June 1994), 263.
6. Tom Mathews, "The Road to War," *Newsweek* 117, no. 4 (January 28, 1991), 64.
7. *Gallup Poll*, July 31, 1990, 149.
8. Bush and Scowcroft, *A World Transformed*, 464.
9. George H.W. Bush, "Interview with former President George H.W. Bush by Mark McEwin in Florida Keys," CBS, "The Early Show," October 23, 2001.
10. Brent Scowcroft, CBS, "Face the Nation," August 4, 2002.
11. Woodward, *Bush at War*, 328.
12. George H.W. Bush, "Bush Sr. Defends Record on Hussein," Reuters, *Washington Post*, October 22, 2002, A22.
13. Glenn Kessler, "U.S. Decision on Iraq Has Puzzling Past," *Washington Post*, January 12, 2003, A1. Also see Freedman and Karsh, *The Gulf Conflict 1990–1991*, 413.
14. John Mueller, *Policy and Opinion in the Gulf War* (Chicago: University of Chicago Press, 1994), 270.
15. Mueller, *Policy and Opinion in the Gulf War*, 271.
16. Richard Perle, "Richard Perle: The Making of a Neo-Conservative," Transcript from PBS Think Tank with Ben Wattenberg, November 14, 2002.
17. Tenet, *At the Center of the Storm*, ix.
18. Paul D. Wolfowitz, "Deputy Secretary of Defense Wolfowitz Interview with *Atlantic Monthly*," January 2, 2002, with James Fallows for March issue of *Atlantic Monthly*. Department of Defense transcript.
19. Mann, *Rise of the Vulcans*, 190.
20. Freedman and Karsh, *The Gulf Conflict 1990–1991*, 412.
21. Paul Wolfowitz, "Victory Came Too Easily; Review of Rick Atkinson, *Crusade: The Untold Story of the Gulf War*," *The National Interest* 35 (Spring 1994), 91.
22. Zalmay M. Khalilzad and Paul Wolfowitz, "Overthrow Him," *The Weekly Standard*, December 1, 1997, 14.

23. Paul D. Wolfowitz, "Clinton's First Year," *Foreign Affairs* 73, no. 1 (January–February 1994), 28.
24. Wolfowitz, "Deputy Secretary of Defense Wolfowitz Interview with *Atlantic Monthly*."
25. Stephen J. Solarz and Paul Wolfowitz, "How to Overthrow Saddam," Letters to the Editor, *Foreign Affairs* 78, no. 2 (March 1999), 160.
26. Daniel Byman, Kenneth Pollack, and Gideon Rose, "The Rollback Fantasy," *Foreign Affairs* 78, no. 1 (January 1999), 24.
27. Thomas E. Ricks, *Fiasco: The American Military Adventure in Iraq* (New York: The Penguin Press, 2006), 22.
28. Special to the *New York Times*, "Excerpts from Pentagon's Feb. 18 draft of the Defense Planning Guidance for the Fiscal Years 1994–1999," *New York Times*, March 8, 1992, 14.
29. William Kristol and Robert Kagan, "Toward a Neo-Reaganite Foreign Policy," *Foreign Affairs* 75, no. 4 (July–August 1996), 20.
30. Corey Robin, "Grand Designs: How 9/11 Unified Conservatives in Pursuit of Empire," *Washington Post*, May 2, 2004, B1.
31. Project for the New American Century, "Letter to President Clinton," January 26, 1998. <http://www.newamericancentury.org/iraqclintonletter.htm> (January 4, 2007).
32. Ricks, *Fiasco*, 19.
33. Daalder and Lindsay, *America Unbound*, 47.
34. Stefan Halper and Jonathan Clarke, *America Alone: The Neo-Conservatives and the Global Order* (New York: Cambridge University Press, 2004), 139.
35. Halper and Clarke, *America Alone*, 138.
36. Halper and Clarke, *America Alone*, 11.
37. George Packer, *The Assassins' Gate* (New York: Farrar, Straus and Giroux, 2005), 13.
38. Packer, *The Assassins' Gate*, 38.
39. William Kristol, "Interview: William Kristol," PBS *Frontline*, January 14, 2003.
40. William Kristol, "Testimony of William Kristol to the Senate Foreign Relations Committee," U.S. Senate, Washington, DC, February 7, 2002.
41. Jeffrey M. Jones, "Americans Felt Uneasy toward Arabs Even before September 11," *Gallup Poll Monthly* 452 (September 2001), 53.
42. Colin Powell, "Testimony before U.S. Senate Foreign Relations Committee," U.S. Senate, Washington, DC, January 17, 2001.
43. Suskind, *The Price of Loyalty*, 75.
44. Woodward, *Bush at War*, 49.
45. *Time* Special Report, "America Is in a Military Mood," *Time* (September 13, 2001). Telephone survey of 1,082 Americans by Harris Interactive. <www.time.com/time/nation/printout/0,8816,174941,00.html> (February 2, 2007).
46. Frank Newport, "Americans Remain Strongly in Favor of Military Retaliation," *Gallup Poll Monthly* 432 (September 2001), 31.
47. *Washington Post*-ABC News Poll, "America at War," December 21, 2001. Survey conducted during December 18–19, 2001. <www.washingtonpost.com/wp/srv/politics/polls/vault/stories/data122101.htm> (February 2, 2007).
48. Clarke, *Against All Enemies*, 30.
49. Richard A. Clarke, "Interview by Leslie Stahl," CBS News, Transcripts of "60 Minutes," March 21, 2004.
50. Clarke, Against *All Enemies*, 32.
51. Clarke, "Interview by Leslie Stahl."
52. Leslie Stahl, "Interview with Steve Hadley," CBS News, Transcript of "60 Minutes," March 21, 2004.
53. Woodward, *Bush at War*, 60.
54. Woodward, *Bush at War*, 83.
55. Woodward, *Bush at War*, 84.
56. Woodward, *Bush at War*, 84.
57. Kessler, "U.S. Decision on Iraq Has Puzzling Past," A1.
58. Woodward, *Bush at War*, 84.
59. Elaine Sciolino and Patrick E. Tyler, "Some Pentagon Officials and Advisers Seek to Oust Iraq's Leader in War's Next Phase," *New York Times*, October 12, 2001, B6.

60. George W. Bush, "Prime Time News Conference," White House, Washington, DC, October 11, 2001.
61. George W. Bush, "President Delivers State of the Union Address," United States Capitol, Washington, DC, January 29, 2002.
62. Tom Squitieri and Susan Page, "Rumsfeld: Al-Qaeda-Saddam Link Is Weak," *USA Today*, October 5, 2004, 14A. See Table of *USA Today*/CNN/Gallup Poll October 1–3.
63. Michael R. Gordon, "Cheney Says Next Goal in U.S. War on Terror Is to Block Access to Arms," *New York Times*, March 16, 2002, A8.
64. Neil MacFarquhar, "Baghdad-Kuwait Accord—Support Is Rebuff to Bush's Efforts," *New York Times*, March 29, 2002, A1.
65. George W. Bush, "Press Conference by President Bush and Prime Minister Tony Blair," Crawford, Texas, April 6, 2002.
66. George W. Bush, "President Bush Delivers Graduation Speech at West Point," United States Military Academy, West Point, New York, June 1, 2002. The president's policy of preemption was formalized in his September 2002 National Security Policy.
67. George W. Bush, "President, Vice President Discuss the Middle East," White House, Washington, DC, March 21, 2002.
68. Isikoff and Corn, *Hubris*, 29. Also see Bob, Woodward, *Plan of Attack* (New York: Simon & Schuster, 2004), 168.
69. Elisabeth Bumiller, "Bush Aides Set Strategy to Sell Policy on Iraq," *Washington Post*, September 7, 2002, A1.
70. Brent Scowcroft, "Interview on *Face the Nation*," CBS Transcripts, August 4, 2002.
71. Brent Scowcroft, "Don't Attack Saddam," *Wall Street Journal*, August 15, 2002, A12.
72. James A. Baker III, "The Right Way to Change a Regime," *New York Times*, August 25, 2002, A9.
73. Richard Cheney, "Address to the Veterans of Foreign Wars," Nashville, Tennessee, August 26, 2002.
74. Tenet, *At the Center of the Storm*, 315.
75. Mike Allen, "War Cabinet Argues for Iraq Attack," *Washington Post*, September 9, 2002, A1.
76. Glenn Kessler and Peter Slevin, "Cheney Is Fulcrum of Foreign Policy," *Washington Post*, October 13, 2002, A1.
77. O'Neill, *The Price of Loyalty*, 120.
78. Peter Baker, "The President as Average Joe," *Washington Post*, April 2, 2006, A4.
79. George W. Bush, "President's Remarks at the United Nations General Assembly," New York, September 12, 2002.
80. United Nations, "Press Release SC/7564," UN Security Council, August 11, 2002.
81. Julia Preston with Todd S. Purdum, "Bush's Push on Iraq at U.N.," *New York Times*, September 22, 2002, A1.
82. George W. Bush, "Remarks by the President at Doug Forrester for Senate Event," Trenton, New Jersey, September 23, 2002.
83. Richard L. Berke, "Bush Adviser Suggests War as Campaign Theme," *New York Times*, January 19, 2002, A15.
84. Mike Allen, "Bush's Words Can Go to the Blunt Edge of Trouble," *Washington Post*, September 29, 2002, A22.
85. David E. Sanger, "Bush Sees 'Urgent Duty' to Pre-Empt Attack by Iraq," *New York Times*, October 8, 2002, A1.
86. George W. Bush, "President Bush Outlines Iraqi Threat," Cincinnati Museum Center, Cincinnati, Ohio, October 7, 2002.
87. Woodward, *Bush at War*, 106. Rumsfeld observed about the possibility of a WMD attack against the United States, "It's an energizer for the American people."
88. The joint resolution's text authorized the president "to use the Armed Forces of the United States as he determines to be necessary and appropriate in order to (1) defend the national security of the United States against the continuing threat posed by Iraq; and (2) enforce all relevant United Nations Security Council Resolutions regarding Iraq."
89. Mary Dalrymple, "Byrd's Beloved Chamber Deaf to His Pleas for Delayed Vote," *Congressional Quarterly* 60, no. 39 (October 12, 2002), 2674.

90. Miles A. Pomper, "Congressional Support May Not Count for Much with U.N. Security Council," *Congressional Quarterly* 60, no. 39 (October 12, 2002), 2676.

91. Paul Brace and Barbara Hinkley, *Follow the Leader: Opinion Polls and the Modern Presidents* (New York: Basic Books, 1992), 77

92. Karen De Young and Colum Lynch, "U.S. Proposal May Break Impasse at U.N. over Iraq," *Washington Post*, October 18, 2002, A32.

93. CNN, "Bush to U.N.: Be more than a 'debating society,'" October 22, 2002.

94. Steven R. Weisman, "Bush Team Urges Bold Inspections of Iraq's Arsenal," *New York Times*, October 21, 2002, A1.

95. Colum Lynch, "No 'Smoking Guns' So Far, U.N. Is Told," *Washington Post*, January 10, 2003, A1.

96. Paul D. Wolfowitz, "Address on Iraqi Disarmament," Council on Foreign Relations, New York, January 23, 2003.

97. Condoleezza Rice, "Why We Know Iraq Is Lying," *New York Times*, January 23, 2003.

98. News Services, "No 'Genuine Acceptance' of Disarmament, Blix Says," *Washington Post*, January 28, 2003, A14.

99. Glenn Frankel and Keith B. Richburg, "8 Leaders in Europe Back Bush on Iraq," *Washington Post*, January 31, 2003, A16.

100. BBC, "Outrage at 'Old Europe' Remarks," BBC World News, January 23, 2003. <http://news.bbc.co.uk/2/hi/europe/2687403.stm> (February 8, 2007).

101. George W. Bush, "President Delivers 'State of the Union,'" The U.S. Capitol, Washington, DC, January 28, 2003.

102. George W. Bush, "President Calls for Strengthened and Reformed Medicare Plan," Grand Rapids, Michigan, January 29, 2003.

103. David W. Moore, "Powell's U.N. Appearance Important to Public," *The Gallup Poll Tuesday Briefing* (February 4, 2003), 88.

104. Isikoff and Corn, *Hubris*, 174.

105. *Washington Post*-ABC News Poll, "Powell's U.N. Address," February 6, 2003.

106. George W. Bush, "The President Discusses the Future of Iraq," American Enterprise Institute, Washington, DC, February 26, 2003.

107. John Keegan, *The Iraq War* (New York: Alfred A. Knopf, 2004), 115.

108. Tenet, *At the Center of the Storm*, 305.

109. Packer, *The Assassins' Gate*, 45.

110. Woodward, *Bush at War*, 13. Term used by Powell and his deputy Richard Armitage.

111. Text of the Downing Street Memo as originally reported in *Sunday Times*, May 1, 2005. <http://www.downingstreetmemo.com/memotext.html> (February 8, 2007). Also see Douglas Jehl, "British Memo on U.S. Plans for Iraq War Fuels Critics," *New York Times*, May 20, 2005, A10.

112. Tenet, *At the Center of the Storm*, 310.

113. Don Van Natta Jr., "Leaders: Bush Was Set on Path to War, Memo by British Adviser Says," *New York Times*, March 27, 2006, A1. Sir David Manning became Britain's ambassador to the United States on September 2, 2003.

114. Adam Nagourney and Janet Elder, "Support for Bush Surges at Home, but Split Remains," *New York Times*, March 22, 2003, A1.

115. Isikoff and Corn, *Hubris*, 30.

116. Nagourney and Elder, "Support for Bush Surges at Home, but Split Remains," A1.

117. Bush and Scowcroft, 414.

Chapter Nine   Bush's War: Break It…and It's Yours

1. Michael R. Gordan and General Bernard E. Trainor, *COBRA II: The Inside Story of the Invasion and Occupation of Iraq* (New York: Pantheon Books, 2006), xxxi.

2. George W. Bush, October 7, 2002.

3. Franks, *American Soldier*, 362.

4. Seymour M. Hersh, "Offense and Defense: The Battle between Donald Rumsfeld and the Pentagon," *New Yorker* 79, no. 7 (April 7, 2003), 43.

5. Gordon and Trainor, *COBRA II*, 461.

6. Franks, *American Soldier*, 382.

7. Donald Rumsfeld, "The '21st Century Transformation' of U.S. Armed Forces," National Defense University, Fort McNair, Washington, DC, January 31, 2002.

8. Joyce Battle and Thomas Blanton, editors, "Top Secret Polo Step," The National Security Archive, Washington, DC, February 14, 2007. <http://www.gwu.edu/~nsarchiv/NSAEBB/NSAEBB214/index.htm> (March 21, 2007).

9. Commission on Presidential Debates, "Debate Transcript: The Second Gore-Bush Presidential Debate," October 11, 2000. <http://www.debates.org/pages/trans2000b.html> (February 12, 2007).

10. Donald H. Rumsfeld, "Beyond 'Nation-Building,'" *Washington Post*, September 25, 2003, A33.

11. Gordon and Trainor, *COBRA II*, 9.

12. Franks, *American Soldier*, 348.

13. Gordan and Trainor, *COBRA II*, 4.

14. Hersh, "Offense AND DEFENSE," 43.

15. Ricks, *Fiasco*, 13.

16. Barbara Slavin and Dave Moniz, "War in Iraq's Aftermath Hits Troops Hard," *USA TODAY*, July 21, 2003. <http://www.usatoday.com/news/world/iraq/2003-07-21-war-aftermath_x.htm> (March 25, 2007).

17. CINC USCENTCOM, "Desert Crossing Seminar: After Action Report (unclassified)," June 28–30, 1999.

18. Ricks, *Fiasco*, 34.

19. Gordon and Trainor, *COBRA II*, 103.

20. Fred Kaplan, "The Army, Faced with Its Limits," *New York Times*, January 1, 2006, section 4, page 4.

21. James Dobbins et al., *America's Role in Nation-Building: From Germany to Iraq* (Santa Monica, CA: RAND Corporation, 2003), 153 and 197.

22. Edward P. Djerejian and Frank G. Wisner, Cochairs, "Guiding Principles for U.S. Post-Conflict Policy in Iraq," Report of an Independent Working Group Cosponsored by the Council on Foreign Relations and the James A. Baker III Institute for Public Policy of Rice University (New York: Council on Foreign Relations, Inc., 2003), 1.

23. Djerejian and Wisner, "Guiding Principles for U.S. Post-Conflict Policy in Iraq," 9.

24. Djerejian and Wisner, "Guiding Principles for U.S. Post-Conflict Policy in Iraq," 5.

25. Eric Schmitt, "Pentagon Contradicts General on Iraq Occupation Force's Size," *New York Times*, February 28, 2003, A1.

26. Jim Rutenberg, "General Defends Rumsfeld, With a Caveat," *New York Times*, April 17, 2006, A17.

27. Gordon and Trainor, *COBRA II*, 486.

28. Mike Allen and Jonathan Weisman, "Congress Wants to Know Cost of War," *Washington Post*, September 22, 2002, A24.

29. Elisabeth Bumiller, "Threats and Responses: The Cost; White House Cuts Estimate of Cost of War with Iraq," *New York Times*, December 31, 2002, A1.

30. Bob Deans, "As Fourth Anniversary of War Nears, Costs Rise," Cox News Services, *Chattanooga Times Free Press*, March 18, 2007, A1.

31. Keegan, *The Iraq War*, 142.

32. Tommy Franks, "Progress Report," OnLine NewsHour, PBS, March 22, 2003. <http://www.pbs.org/newshour/bb/military/jan-june03/progress_3-22.html> (February 15, 2003).

33. Harlan K. Ullman and James P. Wade, "Shock & Awe: Achieving Rapid Dominance," National Defense University Press, December 1996.

34. Ricks, *Fiasco*, 117.

35. Franks, *American Soldier*, 400.

36. Keegan, *The Iraq War*, 186.

37. Michael R. Gordon, "New Analysis: Criticizing an Agent of Change as Failing to Adapt," *New York Times*, April 21, 2006, A18.

38. Isikoff and Corn, *Hubris*, 213.

39. Andrew Kohut, "America's Image in the World: Findings from the Pew Global Attitudes Project," Testimony of Andrew Kohut, President, Pew Research Center, before the Subcommittee on International Organizations, Human Rights and Oversight, Committee on Foreign Affairs, U.S. House of Representatives, March 14, 2007.

40. Bob Woodward, *State of Denial* (New York: Simon & Schuster, 2006), 111.

41. Woodward, *Plan of Attack*, 283.

42. Woodward, *Plan of Attack*, 150.

43. Ricks, *Fiasco*, 103.

44. U.S. Department of State, "Objectives," Future of Iraq Project, November 1, 2002. <http://www.gwu.edu/~nsarchiv/NSAEBB/NSAEBB163/index.htm> (February 15, 2007).

45. Conrad C. Crane and W. Andrew Terrill, "Reconstructing Iraq: Challenges and Missions for Military Forces in a Post-Conflict Scenario," U.S. Army War College, Strategic Studies Institute, January 29, 2003. <http://www.strategicstudiesinstitute.army.mil/pdffiles/PUB182.pdf> (February 13, 2007).

46. U.S. Senate, "Prewar Intelligence Assessments about Postwar Iraq," Report of the Select Committee on Intelligence, U.S. Senate, May 20, 2007, 6.

47. Isikoff and Corn, *Hubris*, 199.

48. .Jay Garner, "Truth, War & Consequence: Interview Gen. Jay Garner," PBS Frontline, October 8, 2001. <http://www.pbs.org/wghh/pages/frontline/shows/truth/interviews/garner.html> (February 19, 2007).

49. Ricks, *Hubris*, 103.

50. Kevin Woods, James Lacey, and Williamson Murray, "Saddam's Delusions: The View from the Inside," *Foreign Affairs* 85, no. 3 (May–June 2006), 3.

51. Garner, "Truth, War & Consequence."

52. David Leigh, "General Sacked by Bush Says He Wanted Early Elections," *Guardian*, March 18, 2004. <http://www.guardian.co.uk/print/0,4882387-103550,00.html> (February 18, 2007).

53. Ambassador L. Paul Bremer, *My Year in Iraq: The Struggle to Build a Future of Hope* (New York: Simon & Schuster, 2006), 4 and 13.

54. Bremer, *My Year in Iraq*, 40.

55. Ricks, *Fiasco*, 159.

56. Thomas E. Ricks, "In Iraq, Military Forgot Lessons of Vietnam," *Washington Post*, July 23, 2006, A1.

57. Thomas E. Ricks and Ann Scott Tyson, "Abizaid Says Withdrawal Would Mean More Unrest," *Washington Post*, November 16, 2006, A22.

58. Tony Blair, "President Bush and Prime Minister Tony Blair of the United Kingdom Participate in Joint Press Availability," White House, East Room, May 25, 2006.

59. Bremer, "Excerpts of Bremer Speech Aired on US-Run al-Iraqiya Television." <http://www.usatoday.com/news/washington/2007–02-05-iraq-contracts_x.htm?csp=34> (February 19, 2007).

60. Ricks, *Fiasco*, 161.

61. Gordon and Trainor, *COBRA II*, 162.

62. Michael R. Gordon and Bernard E. Trainor, "After Invasion, Point Man for Iraq Was Shunted Aside," *New York Times*, March 13, 2006, A8.

63. Gordon and Trainor, *COBRA II*, 483.

64. Anthony Zinni, "Remarks at CID Board of Directors Dinner," Center for Defense Information, May 12, 2004. <http://www.cdi.org/program/document.cfm?DocumentID=2208&from_page=../index.cfm> (August 2, 2007).

65. John Lee Anderson, "Out on the Street: The United States' De-Baathification Program Fueled the Insurgency," *New Yorker* 80, no. 35 (November 15, 2004), 73.

66. Bremer, *My Year in Iraq*, 48.

67. Bremer, 170.

68. Bremer, 171.

69. Robert Schlesinger and Bryan Bender, "Plan Suggests Shift on Rumsfeld," *Boston Globe*, October 9, 2003, A45.

70. Bremer, *My Year in Iraq*, 395.

71. Ken Adelman, "Cakewalk in Iraq," *Washington Post*, February 13, 2002, A27.

72. Dick Cheney, "Vice President Dick Cheney Discusses a Possible War with Iraq," NBC Meet the Press with Tim Russert, March 16, 2003.

73. George W. Bush, "President Bush Announces Major Combat Operations in Iraq Have Ended," USS *Abraham Lincoln* at sea off the coast of San Diego, California, May 1, 2003.

74. Associated Press, "Rumsfeld Blames Iraq Problems on 'Pockets of Dead-Enders," *USA Today*, June 18, 2003. <http://www.usatoday.com/news/world/iraq/2003-06-18-rumsfeld_x.htm> (February 26, 2007).

75. Peter Slevin, "Rising U.S. Death Toll in Iraq Spurs Concern," *Washington Post*, June 20, 2003, A16.

76. Ricks, "In Iraq, Military Forgot Lessons of Vietnam," A1.

77. Todd S. Purdum, *Time of Our Choosing: America's War in Iraq* (New York: Times Books, 2003), 278.

78. Reuters, "Bremer Says U.S. Was Surprised by Insurgency," *Washington Post*, January 7, 2006, A4.

79. Bremer, *My Year in Iraq*, 106.

80. George W. Bush, "President Bush Names Randall Tobias to be Global AIDS Coordinator," White House, Washington, DC, July 2, 2003.

81. Warren P. Strobel and Jonathan S. Landay, "Intelligence Agencies Warned about Growing Local Insurgency in Late 2003," Knight Ridder Newspapers, *Chattanooga Times Free Press*, February 28, 2006, A3.

82. Strobel and Landay, "Intelligence Agencies Warned about Growing Local Insurgency in Late 2003," A3.

83. CNN, "Iraq Insurgency in 'Last Throes,' Cheney says," CNN.Com, June 20, 2005. <http://www.cnn.com/2005/US/05/30/cheney.iraq/> (February 26, 2007).

84. Thomas E. Ricks, "Cheney Stands by His 'Last Throes' Remark," *Washington Post*, June 20, 2006, A13.

85. Libby Quaid, "Powell Forces Rice to Defend Iraq Planning," Associated Press, April 30, 2006. <http://abcnews.go.com/Politics/wireStory?id=1908265> (July 12, 2006).

86. Paul R. Pillar, "Intelligence, Policy, and the War on Iraq," *Foreign Affairs* 85, no. 2 (March–April 2006), 16.

87. Associated Press, "Tenet Regrets WMD 'Slam Dunk' Comment," April 28, 2005. <http://www.sfgate.com/cgi-bin/article.cgi?file=/n/a/2005/04/28/national/a061248D00.DTL> (July 12, 2006).

88. Paul Wolfowitz, "Deputy Secretary Wolfowitz Interview with Sam Tanenhaus, *Vanity Fair*, July 2003," DoD News, May 9, 2003. <http://www.defenselink.mil/transcripts/2003/tr20030509-depsecdef0223.html> (March 13, 2007).

89. Colin Powell, "U.S. Secretary of State Colin Powell Addresses the U.N. Security Council," Washington, DC, February 5, 2003. <http://www.whitehouse.gov/news/releases/2003/02/20030205-1.html> (March 12, 2007).

90. The October NIE stated the UAVs could threaten "if brought close to, or into, the United States, the US Homeland." However, the Air Force concluded that the small size of the UAVs "strongly suggested" a primary role of reconnaissance, rather than a platform to deliver chemical or biological weapons. Central Intelligence Agency, "Key Judgments (from October 2002 NIE)—Iraq's Continuing Programs for Weapons of Mass Destruction," National Intelligence Estimate, October 2002. <http://www.cianet.org/wps/dod102> (March 15, 2007).

91. George W. Bush, "President Delivers State of the Union," U.S. Capitol, Washington, DC, January 28, 2003.

92. News Services, "No 'Genuine Acceptance' Of Disarmament, Blix Says," *Washington Post*, January 28, 2003, A14.

93. Federal News Service, "In a Chief Inspector's Words: 'A Substantial Measure of Disarmament,'" *New York Times*, March 8, 2003, A8.

94. Dick Cheney, "Interview of Vice President Dick Cheney with Tim Russert," NBC "Meet the Press," March 16, 2003.

95. Dick Cheney, "Interview of Vice President Dick Cheney with Tim Russert," NBC "Meet the Press," September 14, 2003.

96. Barton Gellman and Walter Pincus, "Depiction of Threat Outgrew Supporting Evidence," *Washington Post*, August 10, 2003, A1.

97. Isikoff and Corn, *Hubris*, 137.

98. October 2002 National Intelligence Estimate. See footnote 94.

99. Gellman and Pincus, "Depiction of Threat Outgrew Supporting Evidence," A1.

100. CBS, "The Man Who Knew," CBS News, February 4, 2004. <http://www.cbsnews.com/stories/2003/10/14/6011/printables577975.shtml> (March 13, 2007).

101. Gellman and Pincus, "Depiction of Threat Outgrew Supporting Evidence," A1.

102. Dana Priest and Walter Pincus, "Search in Iraq Finds No Banned Weapons," *Washington Post*, October 3, 2003, A1.

103. Richard W. Stevenson and Thom Shanker, "Ex-Arms Monitor Urges an Inquiry on Iraqi Threat," *New York Times*, January 29, 2004, A1.

104. James Risen, "Ex-Inspector Says C.I.A. Missed Disarray in Iraqi Arms Program," *New York Times*, January 26, 2004, A1.

105. Douglas Jehl, "U.S. Report Finds Iraq Was Minimal Weapons Threat in '03," *New York Times*, October 6, 2004, A1.

106. George J. Tenet, "In the Words of the C.I.A. Director: 'Why Haven't We Found the Weapons?'" *New York Times*, February 6, 2004, A12.

107. George W. Bush, "President's Remarks at the United Nations General Assembly," New York, September 12, 2002.

108. U.S. Senate, "Report on the U.S. Intelligence Community's Prewar Intelligence Assessments on Iraq," Select Committee on Intelligence, July 7, 2004. <http://www.globalsecurity.org/intell/library/congress/2004_rpt/iraq-wmd-intell_toc.htm> (March 11, 2007).

109. Presidential Commission on the Intelligence Capabilities of the United States Regarding Weapons of Mass Destruction, Report to the President, March 31, 2005, 9.

110. Presidential Commission, 558.

111. Presidential Commission, 10.

112. Presidential Commission, 561.

113. Pillar, "Intelligence, Policy, and the War on Iraq," 18.

114. Information received from Dr. Loch Johnson, a University of Georgia expert on U.S. intelligence matters.

115. Isikoff and Corn, *Hubris*, 5.

116. Tenet, "At the Center of the Storm," 342.

117. Michael Duffy, "So Much for the WMD," *Time* 163, no. 6 (February 9, 2004). <http://www.time.com/time/printout/o,8816,586175,00.html> (March 14, 2007).

118. James P. Pfiffner, "Did President Bush Mislead the Country in His Arguments for War with Iraq?" *Presidential Studies Quarterly* 34, no. 1 (March 2004), 26.

119. Dana Milbank, "Bush Disavows Hussein-Sept. 11 Link," *Washington Post*, September 18, 2003, A18.

120. Pfiffner, Did President Bush Mislead the Country in His Arguments for War with Iraq?" 28.

121. Seymour Hersh, "Selective Intelligence," *New Yorker* 79, no. 11 (May 12, 2003), 45.

122. Hersh, "Selective Intelligence," 44.

123. Isikoff and Corn, *Hubris*, 415.

124. Walter Pincus, "Report Details Errors before War," *Washington Post*, September 9, 2006, A12.

125. Julian Borger, "Special Investigation: The Spies Who Pushed for War," *Guardian*, July 17, 2003. <http://www.guardian.co.uk/print/0,4714031-103550,00.html> (March 14, 2007).

126. U.S. Department of Defense, "Review of Pre-Iraqi War Activities of the Office of the Under Secretary of Defense for Policy: Executive Summary," Department of Defense Office of Inspector General, Report No. 07-ISTE1,-04 (Project No. D2006-DIYT01–0077 000), February 9, 2007. <http://www.dodig.mil/IGInformation/archives/Unclass%20%20Executive%20Summary.pdf> (February 10, 2007).

127. Tenet, "At the Center of the Storm," 419.

128. Gordon and Trainor, *COBRA II*, 316.

129. Tenet, "At the Center of the Storm," 398.

130. Tenet, "At the Center of the Storm," 428.

131. Michael G. Mullen, "Advance Questions for Admiral Michael G. Mullen USN Nominee for the position of Chairman of the Joint Chiefs of Staff," Senate Armed Services Committee Hearing, U.S. Senate, July 31, 2007. <http://armed-services.senate.gov/statement/2007/July/Mullen%2007-31-07.pdf> (August 4, 2007).

132. Woodward, *State of Denial*, 109.

133. Dan Balz and Jon Cohen, "Majority in Poll Favor Deadline for Iraq Pullout," *Washington Post*, February 27, 2007, A1.
134. CBS, "The Man Who Knew."

Chapter Ten   Axis of Evil:
An Inverted Threat Matrix

1. George W. Bush, "President Delivers State of the Union Address," The United States Capitol, Washington, DC, January 29, 2002.
2. David Frum, *The Right Man: The Surprise Presidency of George W. Bush* (New York: Random House, 2003), 238.
3. Woodward, *Plan of Attack*, 95.
4. Maura Reynolds, "'Axis of Evil' Phrase Caused Real Damage, Experts Opine," *Los Angeles Times, Chattanooga Times Free Press*, January 22, 2003.
5. Ali M. Ansari, *Confronting Iran: The Failure of American Foreign Policy and the Next Great Crisis in the Middle East* (New York: Basic Books, 2006).
6. Jimmy Carter, "Tehran, Iran Toasts of the President and the Shah at a State Dinner," December 31, 1977. <http://www.parstimes.com/history/carter_toast_tehran.html> (May 30, 2007).
7. Anthony Lake, "Confronting Backlash States," *Foreign Affairs* 73, no. 2 (March–April 1994), 45.
8. Kenneth Katzman, "The Iran Sanctions Act (ISA)," Congressional Reference Service, January 25, 2007.
9. Lucien J. Dhooge, "Meddling with the Mullahs: An Analysis of the Iran and Libya Sanctions Act of 1996," *Denver Journal of International Law and Policy* 27, no. 1 (Fall 1998). <http://findarticles.com/p/articles/mi_hb3262/is_199809/ai_n7962764> (May 22, 2007).
10. Mohammad Khatami, "Transcript of interview with Iranian President Mohammad Khatami," CNN.com, January 7, 1998. <http://www.cnn.com/WORLD/9801/07/iran/interview.html> (May 22, 2007).
11. Barbara Crossette, "Albright, in Overture to Iran, Seeks a 'Road Map' to Amity," *New York Times*, June 18, 1998, A1.
12. Madeleine K. Albright, "American-Iranian Relations," Remarks before the American-Iranian Council, Washington, DC, March 17, 2000.
13. Scott Macleod, Azadeh Moaveni and Douglas Waller, "Clinton and Khatami Find Relations Balmy?" *Time* 156, no. 12 (September 18, 2000). <http://www.time.com/time/printout/0,8816,997984,00.html> (May 22, 2007).
14. Christopher S. Wren, "Albright Sits Face to Face With Iranian," *New York Times*, September 16, 2000, A 6.
15. Rice, "Promoting the National Interest," 61.
16. CNN, "Khobar Towers Indictments Returned," CNN.com, June 22, 2001. <http://archives.cnn.com/2001/LAW/06/21/ashcroft.khobar/> (May 24, 2007).
17. Kenneth Katzman, "The Iran-Libya Sanctions Act (ILSA)," CRS Report for Congress, Congressional Research Service, October 11, 2006, Table I, CRS-4.
18. Associated Press, "Cheney Pushed for More Trade with Iran," Fox News.com, October 9, 2004. <http://foxnews.com/story/0,2933,134836,00.html> (May 24, 2007).
19. Lisa Myers, "Halliburton Operates in Iran Despite Sanctions," MSNBC.com, March 8, 2005. <http://www.msnbc.msn.com/id/7119752/> (May 24, 2007).
20. Mohsen M. Milani, "Iran's Policy towards Afghanistan," *The Middle East Journal* 60, no. 2 (Spring 2006), 246.
21. Milani, "Iran's Policy towards Afghanistan," 245.
22. Peter W. Galbraith, *The End of Iraq: How American Incompetence Created a War without End* (New York: Simon & Schuster, 2006), 79.
23. James Dobbins, "Time to Deal with Iran," *Washington Post*, May 6, 2004, A 35.
24. Milani, "Iran's Policy towards Afghanistan," 255.

25. Dobbins, "Time to Deal with Iran," A35.

26. James Bennet, "Israel Seizes Ship It Says Was Arming Palestinians," *New York Times*, January 5, 2002, A1.

27. David E. Sanger, "Bush Aides Say Tough Tone Put Foes on Notice," *New York Times*, January 31, 2002, A1.

28. Neil MacFarquhar, "Bush's Comments Bolster Old Guard in Tehran," *New York Times*, January 8, 2002, A 11.

29. David Frum and Richard Perle, *An End to Evil: How to Win the War on Terror* (New York: Random House, 2003), 110.

30. U.S. Senate, "Prewar Intelligence Assessments about Postwar Iraq," Select Committee on Intelligence, 110th Congress, 1st Session, Appendix A, 13. <http://intelligence.senate.gov/prewar.pdf> (May 26, 2007).

31. Nicholas D. Kristof, "Diplomacy at Its Worst," *New York Times*, April 29, 2007, 4–13.

32. Nicholas D. Kristof, "Iran's Proposal for a 'Grand Bargain,'" April 28, 2007. <http://kristof.blogs.nytimes.com/2007/04/28/irans-proposal-for-a-grand-bargain/> (May 1, 2007).

33. Flynt Leverett, "Dealing with Tehran: Assessing U.S. Diplomatic Options toward Iran," A Century Foundation Report, Century Foundation, 2006, 11.

34. Leverett, "Dealing with Tehran," 15.

35. Karl Vick, "Bush's Support for Reformers Backfires in Iran," *Washington Post*, August 3, 2002, A12.

36. George W. Bush, "Statement by the President," White House, Washington, DC, July 12, 2002.

37. Ansari, *Confronting Iran*, 191.

38. Vick, "Bush's Support for Reformers Backfires in Iran," A12.

39. Mustafa Kibaroglu, "Good for the Shah, Banned for the Mullahs," *The Middle East Journal* 60, no. 2 (Spring 2006), 209.

40. Karl Vick and Dafna Linzer, "Iran Declares Nuclear Advance," *Washington Post*, April 12, 2006, A1.

41. George Jahn, "Iran Threatens U.S. with 'Harm and Pain,'" Associated Press, *Washington Post*, March 8, 2006.

42. Lydia Saad, "Iran Threat Poses Leadership Crisis for Americans," Gallup Poll News Service, February 15, 2006.

43. *New York Times*/ CBS News Poll, March 7–11, 2007.

44. U.S. Department of Defense, "National Security Strategy," U.S. Department of Defense, March 2006, 20. <http://www.whitehouse.gov/nsc/nss/2006/> (June 7, 2007).

45. John D. Negroponte, "Annual Threat Assessment of the Director of National Intelligence for the Senate Select Committee on Intelligence," National Intelligence Council, February 2, 2006, 11.

46. Robin Hughes, "US Eyes Potential Long-Range Threat from Iran," *Jane's Defence Weekly*, May 9, 2007. <www.janes.com/security/international_security/news/jdw/jdw0705009_1_n.shtml> (June 14, 2007).

47. Steven R. Weisman, "Cheney Warns of 'Consequences' for Iran on Nuclear Issue," *New York Times*, March 8, 2006, A14.

48. Seymour Hersh, "The Next Act," *New Yorker* 82, no. 39 (November 27, 2006), 100.

49. Hersh, "The Next Act," 101.

50. Hersh, "The Next Act," 96.

51. Richard Cheney, "Transcript: Vice President Cheney on 'Fox News Sunday,'" Fox News, January 14, 2007. <http://www.foxnews.com/story/0,2933,243632,00.html> (May 29, 2007).

52. Seymour Hersh, "The Redirection," *New Yorker* 83, no. 2 (March 5, 2007), 57.

53. Peter Baker, Dafna Linzer, and Thomas E. Ricks, "U.S. Is Studying Military Strike Options on Iran," *Washington Post*, April 9, 2006, A1.

54. Molly Moore and Thomas E. Ricks, "Iranian Leader Warns U.S. of Reprisal," *Washington Post*, April 26, 2006, A1.

55. Elaine Sciolino, "U.S. Britain and France Draft U.N. Resolution on Iran's Nuclear Ambitions," *New York Times*, May 3, 2006, A12.

56. Nedla Pickler, "U.S. Tries to Dampen Talk of Iran Strike," Associated Press, *New York Times*, April 10, 2006.

57. Peter Baker, "Bush Dismisses Talk of Using Force against Iran," *Washington Post*, April 11, 2006, A2.

58. William Branigin, "U.S. Not Planning for War With Iran, Gates Says," *Washington Post*, February 2, 2007. <http://www.washingtonpost.com/wp-dyn/content/article/2007/02/02/AR2007020200539.html> (May 29, 2007).

59. Robin Wright, "In Gulf, Cheney Pointedly Warns Iran," *Washington Post*, May 12, 2007, A1.

60. Karen DeYoung and Glenn Kessler, "Policy Successes—or U-Turns," *Washington Post*, March 11, 2007, A18.

61. James A. Baker III and Lee H. Hamilton, Cochairs, *The Iraq Study Group Report: The Way Forward—A New Approach* (New York: Vintage Books, 2006), 44.

62. *Iraq Study Group Report*, 51.

63. Norman Podhoretz, "The Case for Bombing Iran," *Commentary* 123, no. 6 (June 2007), 20.

64. Glenn Kessler, "Cheney Backs Diplomacy on Iran Program, Rice Affirms," *Washington Post*, June 2, 2007, A8.

65. Helene Cooper, "Rice Plays Down Hawkish Talk about Iran," *New York Times*, June 2, 2007, A5.

66. Reuters, "Fact Box: North Korea's Missile Arsenal," *Washington Post*, July 4, 2006.

67. U.S. Department of Defense, "2000 Report to Congress: Military Situation on the Korean Peninsula," Secretary of Defense, U.S. Department of Defense, September 12, 2000. <http://www.defenselink.mil/news/Sep2000/korea09122000.html> (June 7, 2007).

68. Ben Arnoldy, "How Serious Is North Korea's Nuclear Threat?" *Christian Science Monitor*, October 5, 2006. <http://www.csmonitor.com/2006/1005/p25s01-woap.html> (June 4, 2007).

69. Selig Seidenman Harrison, *Korean Endgame: A Strategy for Reunification and U.S. Disengagement* (Princeton: Princeton University Press, 2003), 117.

70. U.S. Department of Defense, "Principle Wars in which the United States Participated U.S. Military Personnel Serving and Casualties." <http://siadapp.dmdc.osd.mil/personnel/CASUALTY/WCPRINCIPAL.pdf> (June 3, 2007).

71. Don Oberdorfer, "U.S. Decides to Withdraw A-Weapons from S. Korea," *Washington Post*, October 19, 1991, A1.

72. George H.W. Bush, "'The Peace Dividend I Seek Is Not Measured in Dollars,'" *Washington Post*, September 28, 1991, A1.

73. Tim Weiner, "C.I.A. Head Surveys World's Hot Spots," *New York Times*, January 26, 1994, A5.

74. David E. Sanger, "North Korea Says It Has a Program on Nuclear Arms," *New York Times*, October 17, 2002, A1.

75. Bill Clinton, *My Life* (New York: Alfred A. Knopf, 2004), 603.

76. Jimmy Carter, "Solving the Korean Stalemate, One Step at a Time," The Carter Center, October 11, 2006. Wendy R. Sherman, former Counselor of the State Department and North Korea Policy Coordinator in the Clinton administration, opined that the 1994 Agreed Framework "probably would not have happened" without Carter's meeting with Kim Il Jung. Wendy R. Sherman, "North Korea: Past Progress and Next Steps," Address to U.S. Institute of Peace, March 6, 2001.

77. R. Jeffrey Smith, "N. Korea, U.S. Pledge Closer Ties," *Washington Post*, August 13, 1994, A1.

78. Kim Jong Il's official title is chairman of the North Korean National Defense Commission.

79. Bill Clinton, "Excerpts from President Clinton's Session with Reporters," *New York Times*, October 22, 1994, A6.

80. Michael R. Gordon, "U.S.-North Korea Accord Has a 10-Year Timetable," *New York Times*, October 21, 1994, A8.

81. David Albright and Holly Higgins, "Light Water Reactors and Nuclear Weapons in North Korea," Institute for Science and International Security, October 27, 1999.

82. Gordon, "U.S.-North Korea Accord Has a 10-Year Timetable," A8.

83. Mark E. Manyin and Ryun Jun, "U.S. Assistance to North Korea," Congressional Research Service, Library of Congress, March 17, 2003, CRS-9.

84. Manyin and Jun, "U.S. Assistance to North Korea," CRS-1.

85. Manyin and Jun, "U.S. Assistance to North Korea," CRS-17.

86. James Risen, "C.I.A. Sees a North Korean Missile Threat," *New York Times*, February 3, 1999, A6.

87. William Perry, "Testimony before the Senate Foreign Relations Committee, Subcommittee on East Asian and Pacific Affairs," U.S. Senate, Washington, DC, October 12, 1999.

88. Victor D. Cha and David C. Kang, "The Korea Crisis," *Foreign Policy* 142 (May–June 2003), 24.

89. Steve Mufson, "Bush to Pick Up Clinton Talks on N. Korean Missiles," *Washington Post*, March 7, 2001, A20.

90. George W. Bush, "Remarks by President Bush and President Kim Dae-Jung of South Korea," White House, Washington, DC, March 7, 2001.

91. Colin Powell, "Remarks by Secretary of State Colin Powell to the Pool," White House, Washington, DC, March 7, 2001.

92. Colin Powell, "Secretary of State Colin Powell Discusses International Affairs," CNN Interview with Andrea Koppel, May 14, 2001.

93. Bush, "President Delivers State of the Union Address," January 29, 2002.

94. Michael Hirsh, Melinda Liu, and George Wehrfritz, "'We Are a Nuclear Power,'" *Newsweek*, October 23, 2006, 28. <http://www.msnbc.msn.com/id/15265432/site/newsweek/> (June 6, 2007).

95. Woodward, *Bush at War*, 340.

96. George W. Bush, "President Focuses on U.S. Economy, Iraq & N. Korea," Crawford, Texas, January 2, 2003.

97. Sanger, "North Korea Says It Has a Program on Nuclear Arms," A1.

98. George W. Bush, "President Visits Crawford Coffee Shop," Crawford, Texas, December 31, 2002.

99. John Bolton, "A Dictatorship at the Crossroads," Address to the East Asia Institute, Seoul, South Korea, July 31, 2003. <http://rpc.senate.gov/_files/FOREIGNdf073103.pdf> (June 7, 2007).

100. David E. Sanger and Eric Schmitt, "Cheney's Power No Longer Goes Unquestioned," *New York Times*, September 10, 2006, section 1, page 1.

101. Glenn Kessler, "North Korea Labels Bush a 'Dictator,'" *Washington Post*, May 1, 2005, A22.

102. George W. Bush, "President Bush Participates in Press Availability with Canadian Prime Minister Stephen Harper," White House, Washington, DC, July 6, 2006.

103. Cha and Kang, "The Korea Crisis," 23.

104. Michael A. Fletcher, "Bush Rejects Solo Talks with North Korea," *Washington Post*, July 8, 2006, A2.

105. David E. Sanger, "Bush's Shift: Being Patient with Foes," *New York Times*, July 10, 2006, A9.

106. Frank Newport, "Americans Favor Diplomacy with North Korea, Not Military Action," Gallup Poll News Service, July 13, 2006.

107. David E. Sanger, "North Korea Says It Tested a Nuclear Device Underground," *New York Times*, October 9, 2006, A1.

108. George W. Bush, "President Bush's Statement on North Korea Nuclear Test," White House, Washington, DC, October 9, 2006.

109. Bill Powell, "A New Nuclear World," *Time* 168, no. 15 (October 9, 2006). <http://www.time.com/time/world/article/0,8599,1544026,00.html> (July 30, 2007).

110. Thom Shanker and Warren Hoge, "Rice Asserts U.S. Plans No Attack on North Korea," *New York Times*, October 11, 2006, A1.

111. Warren Hoge, "Security Council Supports Sanctions on North Korea," *New York Times*, October 15, 2006, section 1, page 1.

112. U.S. Department of State, "North Korea—Denuclearization Action Plan," U.S. Department of State, Washington, DC, February 13, 2007.

113. Christopher Hill, "U.S. Envoy Christopher Hill Discusses North Korea Nukes Deal," PBS Online NewsHour, PBS Transcript, February 15, 2007. <http://www.pbs.org/newshour/bb/asia/jan-june07/hill-02-15.html> (June 10, 2007).

114. Edward Cody, "Tentative Nuclear Deal Struck with North Korea," *Washington Post*, February 13, 2007, A1.

115. Glenn Kessler, "Conservatives Assail North Korea Accord," *Washington Post*, February 15, 2007, A1.
116. PBS Online NewsHour, February 15, 2007.
117. Kwang-Tae Kim, "IAEA Says North Korea Has Shut Reactor," Associated Press, *Washington Post*, July 16, 2007.
118. Tenet, *At the Center of the Storm*, 319.
119. Jeffrey Record, "Bounding the Global War on Terrorism," Strategic Studies Institute, U.S. Army War College, December 2003.
120. Douglas Jehl, "British Memo on U.S. Plans for Iraq War Fuels Critics," *New York Times*, May 20, 2005, A10.
121. DeYoung and Kessler, "Policy Successes—or U-Turns," A18.
122. CNN, "Cheney: Realistic over N. Korea deal," CNN.com, February 22, 2007. <http://www.cnn.com/2007/POLITICS/02/22/cheney.australia/index.html> (June 10, 2007).

Chapter Eleven   Ending Tyranny: Bush's Democracy Agenda

1. George W. Bush, "President Discusses the Future of Iraq," Address to American Enterprise Institute, Washington Hilton Hotel, Washington, DC, February 26, 2003.
2. George W. Bush, "President Bush Discusses Freedom in Iraq and Middle East," White House, Washington, DC, November 6, 2003.
3. George W. Bush, "President Sworn-In to Second Term," 2005 Inaugural Address, U.S. Capitol, Washington, DC, January 20, 2005.
4. Condoleezza Rice, "Interview on The NewsHour with Jim Lehrer," PBS, Washington, DC, July 28, 2005.
5. Greg Miller, "Democracy in Iraq Doubtful, State Dept. Report Says," *Los Angeles Times*, March 14, 2003, A14.
6. Wayne White, "Testimony Delivered to Ad Hoc Senate Hearing on Pre-War Iraq Intelligence & Related Matters," Washington, DC, Middle East Institute, June 26, 2006. <http://www.mideasti.org/articles/doc535.html> (June 20, 2007).
7. Larry Diamond, *Squandered Victory: The American Occupation and the Bungled Effort to Bring Democracy to Iraq* (New York: Times Books, 2005), 29.
8. Larry Diamond, "What Went Wrong in Iraq," *Foreign Affairs* 83, no. 5 (September–October 2004), 10.
9. Dexter Filkins, "Where Plan A Left Ahmad Chalabi," *New York Times Magazine*, November 5, 2006, 6–46.
10. L. Paul Bremer III, "Iraq's Path to Sovereignty," *Washington Post*, September 8, 2003, A21.
11. David Ignatius, "Bush's Lost Iraqi Election," *Washington Post*, August 30, 2007, A21.
12. Seymour M. Hersh, "Get Out the Vote," *New Yorker* 81, no. 21 (July 25, 2005), 53.
13. Ignatius, "Bush's Lost Iraqi Election," A21.
14. Edward Wong, "Iraqi Officials Declare Charter Has Been Passed," *New York Times*, October 26, 2005, A1.
15. The CIA World FactBook gives the title of the new legislative branch as Council of Representatives, although some newspapers call it the National Assembly. Central Intelligence Agency, "Iraq-Legislative Branch," CIA World FactBook, June 14, 2007. <https://www.cia.gov/library/publicans/the-world-factbook/geos/iz.html> (June 19, 2007).
16. Tenet, *At the Center of the Storm*, 446.
17. Aram Rostom, "ABC: Chalabi's Defeat Presents Quandry," MSNBC, December 22, 2005. <http://www.msnbc.msn.com/id/10575121> (June 20, 2007).
18. Filkins, Where Plan A Left Ahmad Chalabi," 6–46.
19. Barbara Starr and Dana Bash, "Head of U.S. Command: Iraq Civil War Possible," CNN.com, August 3, 2006. <http://www.cnn.com/2006/POLITICS/08/03/iraq.hearing> (June 24, 2007).

20. Michael R. Gordon, "Military Charts Movement of Conflict in Iraq toward Chaos," *New York Times*, November 1, 2006, A12.

21. George W. Bush, "Press Conference by the President," White House, Washington, DC, November 8, 2006.

22. Michael D. Maples, "The Current Situation in Iraq and Afghanistan," Lieutenant General U.S. Army, Director, Defense Intelligence Agency, Statement for the Record, U.S. Senate Armed Services Committee, November 15, 2006.

23. Michael R. Gordon, "Bush Advisor's Memo Cites Doubts about Iraqi Leader," *New York Times*, November 29, 2006, A1.

24. Thomas E. Ricks and Peter Baker, "Tipping Point for War's Supporters?" *Washington Post*, October 29, 2006, A1.

25. George W. Bush, "President Bush Receives Report from the Iraq Study Group," White House, Washington, DC, December 6, 2006.

26. Baker, III and Hamilton, Cochairs, *The Iraq Study Group Report*, xiii.

27. George W. Bush, "President's Address to the Nation," The Library, White House, January 10, 2007.

28. Stanley A. Renshon, *In His Father's Shadow: The Transformations of George W. Bush* (New York: Palgrave, 2004), 75.

29. Jon Cohen, "Poll: Most Americans Opposed to Bush's Iraq Plan," ABC/*Washington Post* Poll, *Washington Post*, January 11, 2007.

30. John Ward Anderson, "Iraqi Premier Denies U.S. Assertion He Agreed to Timelines," *Washington Post*, October 26, 2006, A15.

31. George W. Bush, "President Bush Rejects Artificial Deadline, Vetoes Iraq War Supplemental," White House, Washington, DC, May 1, 2007.

32. Dalia Sussman, "Poll Shows View of Iraq War Is Most Negative since Start," *New York Times*, May 25, 2007, A16.

33. Michael Abramowitz and Jonathan Weisman, "President Unbowed as Benchmarks Are Unmet," *Washington Post*, July 13, 2007, A1.

34. Galbraith, *The End of Iraq*, 191. Galbraith explored the solution of creating three separate states.

35. Joseph R. Biden Jr. and Leslie H. Gelb, "Unity through Autonomy in Iraq," *New York Times*, May 1, 2006, A19.

36. Karen DeYoung and Thomas E. Ricks, "Exit Strategies: Would Iran Take Over Iraq? Would Al-Qaeda?" *Washington Post*, July 17, 2007, A1.

37. *Newsweek*, "Should We Leave Iraq?" *Newsweek* Poll (July 23, 2007), 28.

38. Richard N. Haass, "The New Middle East," *Foreign Affairs* 85, no. 6 (November–December 2006), 4.

39. Pew Research Center, "Global Unease with Major World Powers," Pew Global Attitudes Project, June 27, 2007, 3. <http://pewglobal.org/reports/pdf/256.pdf> (28 June 2007).

40. Deborah Sontag, "Clinton Watches as Palestinians Drop Call for Israel's Destruction," *New York Times*, December 15, 1998, A1.

41. Madeleine Albright, *Madam Secretary* (New York: Miramax Books, 2003), 486.

42. Albright, *Madam Secretary*, 496.

43. Suskind, *The Price of Loyalty*, 71.

44. Suskind, *The Price of Loyalty*, 72.

45. Ron Hutcheson, "Trip to Israel Explains Bush's Loyalty," McClatchy Newspapers, *Chattanooga Times Free Press*, August 6, 2006, A8.

46. Bush and Scowcroft, *A World Transformed*, 379.

47. Hutcheson, "Trip to Israel Explains Bush's Loyalty," A8.

48. George W. Bush, "Press Conference by the President," White House, Washington, DC, March 29, 2001.

49. Robert G. Kaiser and David B. Ottaway, "Saudi Leader's Anger Revealed Shaking Ties," *Washington Post*, February 10, 2002, A1.

50. George W. Bush, "Remarks by the President and Secretary Rumsfeld in Announcement of Chairman and Vice-Chairman of the Joint Chiefs of Staff," Crawford, Texas, August 24, 2001.

51. Kaiser and Ottaway, "Saudi Leader's Anger Revealed Shaking Ties," A1.

52. Unger, *House of Bush*, 243.

53. George W. Bush, "President Bush Speaks to United Nations," UN General Assembly, New York, November 10, 2001.

54. Al-bab.com, Beirut Declaration, March 28, 2002. <http://www.al-bab.com/arab/docs/league/communique02.htm> (July 6, 2007).

55. Michael Holmes and Christiane Amanpour, "Israel Declares Arafat 'Enemy,'" CNN.com, March 29, 2002. <http://archives.cnn.com/2002/WORLD/meast/03/28/mideast/index.html> (July 9, 2007)

56. Alan Sipress, "U.S. Officials Mostly Silent," *Washington Post*, March 30, 2002, A1.

57. D.T. Max, "The Making of the Speech," *New York Times*, October 7, 2001, 6–32.

58. George W. Bush, "President Bush Calls for New Palestinian Leadership," White House, Washington, DC, June 24, 2002.

59. James Bennet with Elisabeth Bumiller, "Israelis Approve Plan to End Siege and Free Arafat," *New York Times*, April 29, 2002, A1.

60. Hutcheson, "Trip to Israel Explains Bush's Loyalty," A8.

61. U.S. Department of State, "Roadmap to Solution of Israeli-Palestinian Conflict," U.S. Department of State, April 30, 2003.

62. George W. Bush, "President Discusses Middle East Peace with Prime Minister Sharon," White House, Washington, DC, July 29, 2003.

63. International Court of Justice, "Legal Consequences of the Construction of a Wall in the Occupied Palestinian Territory," Advisory Opinion, International Court of Justice, Press Release 2004/28, July 9, 2004.

64. Ariel Sharon, "Ariel Sharon Describes 'Disengagement Plan," Speech at Herzliya conference, December 18, 2003. <http://www.jewishvirtuallibrary.org/jsource/Peace/Sharon_1203.html> (July 9, 2007).

65. Barry Rubin, "Israel's New Strategy," *Foreign Affairs* 85, no. 4 (July–August 2006), 112.

66. George W. Bush, "President Bush Commends Israeli Prime Minister Sharon's Plan," White House, Washington, DC, April 14, 2004.

67. Council on Foreign Relations, "Backgrounder: Hamas," Council on Foreign Relations, New York, June 8, 2007. <http://www.cfr.org/publication/8968/> (July 5, 2007).

68. Michael Herzog, "Can Hamas Be Tamed?" *Foreign Affairs* 85, no. 2 (March–April 2006), 85.

69. Glenn Kessler, "U.S. Policy Seen as Big Loser in Palestinian Vote," *Washington Post*, January 28, 2006, A16.

70. Glenn Kessler, "Vote Complicates Area's Diplomacy," *Washington Post*, January 26, 2006, A19.

71. Scott Wilson, "Hamas Makes Strong Showing in Vote," *Washington Post*, January 26, 2006, A1.

72. Steven R. Weisman, "Rice Admits U.S. Underestimated Hamas Strength," *New York Times*, January 30, 2006, A1.

73. George W. Bush, "President Bush Holds a White House Press Conference," White House, Washington, DC, January 26, 2006.

74. Barry Schweid, "Rice Says U.S. Position on Hamas Unchanged," Associated Press, *Washington Post*, January 26, 2006.

75. Steve Erlanger, "Hamas Leader Sees No Change Toward Israelis," *New York Times*, January 29, 2006, section 1, page 1.

76. Scott Wilson, "With Hamas Takeover, Tough Calls for Israel," *Washington Post*, June 30, 2007, A1.

77. Wiesman, "Rice Admits U.S. Underestimated Hamas Strength," A1.

78. Michael Hirsh, "The Gaza Effect," *Newsweek*, (June 25, 2007), 22.

79. Kevin Sullivan, "Rice Rules Out Aiding Hamas-Led Government," *Washington Post*, January 30, 2006, A10.

80. Glenn Kessler, "Push for Democracy Loses Some Energy," *Washington Post*, February 25, 2006, A13.

81. Isabel Kershner, "In Nod to Fatah, Israel Removes Militiamen from Wanted List," *New York Times*, July 16, 2007, A4.

82. Peter Baker and Robin Wright, "Bush Renews Mideast Efforts," *Washington Post*, July 17, 2007, A1.

83. Helene Cooper, "As Her Star Wanes, Rice Tries to Reshape Legacy," *New York Times*, September 1, 2007, A1.

84. Thomas Friedman, "Help Wanted: Peacemaker," *Chattanooga Times Free Press*, July 19, 2007, B6.

85. Robin Wright and Thomas E. Ricks, "Bush Supports Israel's Move against Hezbollah," *Washington Post*, July 19, 2006, A10.

86. George W. Bush, "President Discusses American and European Alliance in Belgium," Brussels, Belgium, February 21, 2005.

87. Robin Wright, "U.S. Turns Up Heat on Syria to Leave Lebanon," *Washington Post*, March 3, 2005, A20.

88. Scott Wilson, "Israeli War Plan Had No Exit Strategy," *Washington Post*, October 21, 2006, A1.

89. Nahum Barnea, "Israel vs. Hezbollah," *Foreign Policy* 157 (November–December 2006), 24.

90. David S. Cloud and Helene Cooper, "Weapons: U.S. Speeds Up Bomb Delivery for the Israelis," *New York Times*, July 22, 2006, A1.

91. Peter Baker and Colum Lynch, "Bush Declines to Call for Israeli Cease-Fire," *Washington Post*, July 15, 2006, A16.

92. Bob Deans and Margaret Coker, "Diplomacy Key Objective for Rice on Mideast Trip," Cox News Service, *Chattanooga Times Free Press*, July 22, 2006, A1.

93. Robin Wright, "In Lebanon's Crisis, A Chance for U.S. to Broaden the Stakes," *Washington Post*, July 26, 2006, A12.

94. Associated Press, "Hezbollah Leader Regrets Actions that Led to War," *Chattanooga Times Free Press*, August 28, 2006, A3.

95. Paul Salem, "The Future of Lebanon," *Foreign Affairs* 85, no. 6 (November–December 2006), 13.

96. Scott Wilson, "Official Panel Accuses Israeli Leaders of Multiple Failures in Lebanon War," *Washington Post*, May 1, 2007, A12.

97. Michael A. Fletcher, "Hezbollah the Loser in Battle, Bush Says," *Washington Post*, August 15, 2006, A8.

98. George W. Bush, "President Bush and President Musharraf of Pakistan Participate in Press Availability," White House, Washington, DC, September 22, 2006.

99. David E. Sanger and Mark Mazzetti. "Cheney Warns Pakistan to Act on Terror," *New York Times*, February 26, 2007, A1.

100. Michael Abramowitz, "Intelligence Puts Rationale for War on Shakier Ground," *Washington Post*, July 18, 2007, A5.

101. Rohan Sullivan, "Poll: Support for Musharraf Plummets," Associated Press, August 1, 2007. <http://www.boston.com/news/world/asia/articles/2007/08/01/poll_support_for_mush arraf_plummets/> (August 12, 2007).

102. Richard Wike, "Pakistanis Increasingly Reject Terrorism…and the U.S.," Pew Research Center Publications, August 8, 2007. <http://pewresearch.org/pubs/561/pakistan-terrorism> (August 13, 2007).

103. Taimoor Shah and Carlotta Gall, "Afghan Rebels Find Aid in Pakistan, Musharraf Admits," *New York Times*, August 13, 2007, A6.

104. Wike, "Pakistanis Increasingly Reject Terrorism…and the U.S."

105. Mark Mazzetti, "U.S. Is Prodding Pakistan Leader to Share Power," *New York Times*, August 16, 2007, A1.

106. Carlotta Gall, "Even Musharraf's Allies Question His Re-election Goal," *New York Times*, August 17, 2007, A3.

107. Karen DeYoung and Joby Warrick, "Tougher Stance on Pakistan Took Months," *Washington Post*, August 5, 2007, A1.

108. George W. Bush, "President and Prime Minister Blair Discussed Iraq, Middle East," White House, Washington, DC, November 12, 2004.

109. David Brooks, "Heroes and History," *New York Times*, July 17, 2007, A21.

Chapter Twelve   Tested by Fire:
Mixed Legacy

1. Steven Thomma, "Americans Want U.S. to Move On," McClatchy Newspapers, *Chattanooga Times Free Press*, September 2, 2007, A13.

2. George W. Bush, "President Outlines War Effort," Virginia Military Institute, Lexington, Virginia, April 17, 2002.

3. David Rohde and David E. Sanger, "Losing the Advantage," *New York Times*, August 12, 2007, A1.

4. Rohde and Sanger, "Losing the Advantage," A1.

5. Rohde and Sanger, "Losing the Advantage," A1.

6. Michael A. Fletcher, "Bush, NATO Chief Seek Ways to Bolster Afghanistan Mission," *Washington Post*, May 20, 2007, A20.

7. Carlotta Gall, "Opium Harvest at Record Level in Afghanistan," *New York Times*, September 3, 2006, section 1, page 1.

8. Karen DeYoung, "Afghanistan Opium Crops Sets Record," *Washington Post*, December 2, 2006, A1.

9. CNN, "CNN Late Edition with Wolf Blitzer, Interviews with Robert Gates, Benazir Bhutto, Hamid Karzai," CNN Transcript, August 5, 2007. <http://transcripts.cnn.com/TRANSCRIPTS/0708/05/le.01.html> (August 10, 2007).

10. David Rohde, "Afghan Police Are Set Back as Taliban Adapt," *New York Times*, September 2, 2007, section 1, page 1.

11. Joseph Carroll, "Slim Majority Supports Anti-Terrorism Action in Afghanistan, Pakistan," Gallup Poll News Service, August 8, 2007.

12. CNN Transcript, August 5, 2007.

13. Karin Brulliard and Saad Sarhan, "Sadr Aides Say 6 Allies in Cabinet Will Resign," *Washington Post*, April 16, 2007, A11.

14. Megan Greenwell, "Sunnis Quit Cabinet Posts," *Washington Post*, August 2, 2007, A15.

15. David S. Cloud, "Gates Offers Blunt Review of Progress in Iraq," *New York Times*, August 3, 2007, A10.

16. George W. Bush, "President Bush Discusses American Competitiveness Initiative during Press Conference," White House, Washington, DC, August 9, 2007.

17. George W. Bush, "President Bush Discusses War on Terror in South Carolina," Charleston Air Force Base, Charleston, South Carolina, July 24, 2007.

18. *New York Times*/CBS News Poll, September 4–5, 2007. <http://www.nytimes.com/packages/ pdf/national/09102007_poll_results.pdf> (September 10, 2007).

19. Peter Baker, "9/11 Linked to Iraq, in Politics if Not in Fact," *Washington Post*, September 12, 2007, A1.

20. Anthony H. Cordesman, "Iraq's Sunni Insurgents: Looking beyond Al Qa'ida," Center for Strategic and International Studies, Washington, DC, July 16, 2007, 2. <http://www.csis.org/media/csis/pubs/070716_sunni_insurgents.pdf> (August 12, 2007).

21. Cordesman, "Iraq's Sunni Insurgents: Looking beyond Al Qa'ida," 8.

22. Walter Pincus, "NIE Cites 'Uneven' Security Gains, Faults Iraqi Leaders," *Washington Post*, August 24, 2007, A10.

23. Karen DeYoung and Thomas E. Ricks, "As British Leave, Basra Deteriorates," *Washington Post*, August 7, 2007, A1.

24. DeYoung and Ricks, As British Leave, Basra Deteriorates," A1.

25. Megan Greenwell, "Riots at Iraqi Religious Festival Leave 28 Dead," *Washington Post*, August 29, 2007, A13.

26. National Intelligence Estimate, "Prospects for Iraq's Stability: A Challenging Road Ahead," Director of National Intelligence, January 2007. <http://media.washingtonpost.com/wpsrv/nation/documents/idraq_dni_20070202_release.pdf> (February 2, 2007).

27. Daniel B. Schneider and Damien Cave, "Security Council Approves U.N. Mandate in Iraq to Seek Reconciliation," *New York Times*, August 11, 2007, A6

28. Zalmay Khalilzad, "Why the United Nations Belongs in Iraq," *New York Times*, July 20, 2007, A23.

29. Kate Zernike, "Democrats Try to Increase Leverage over Iraq Policy," *New York Times*, January 27, 2001, A8.

30. John O'Neil, "In Senate, Allies of Bush Attempt to Halt Iraq Vote," *New York Times*, January 30, 2007, A1.

31. Michael Abramowitz, "President Says His Iraq Policy Was Failing," *Washington Post*, January 17, 2007, A14.

32. Evan Thomas and Thomas Wolffe, "Bush's Bubble: Can He Widen His Circle?" *Newsweek*, December 19, 2005, 35.

33. Peter Baker, "President Confronts Dissent on Troop Levels," *Washington Post*, December 21, 2006, A1.

34. Frank Newport, "Public Trusts Iraq Study Group More than Bush on Iraq," Gallup Poll News Service, December 12, 2006.

35. Jim Rutenberg, "In Book, Bush Peeks Ahead to His Legacy," *New York Times*, September 2, 2007, section 1, page 1.

36. Thomas and Wolffe, "Bush's Bubble," 34.

37. Jim Rutenberg, "Ex-Aide Details a Loss of Faith in the President," *New York Times*, April 1, 2007, section 1, page 1.

38. Thom Shanker, "General Opposes Adding to U.S. Forces in Iraq, Emphasizing International Solutions for Region," *New York Times*, December 20, 2006, A12.

39. Michael R. Gordon, "Will It Work on the Battlefield?" *New York Times*, December 7, 2006, A1.

40. Robin Wright and Ann Scott Tyson, "Joint Chiefs Advise Change in War Strategy," *Washington Post*, December 14, 2006, A1.

41. Ann Scott Tyson, "General Says Army Will Need to Grow," *Washington Post*, December 15, 2006, A1.

42. Baker, "President Confronts Dissent on Troop Levels," December 20, 2006, A1.

43. Gellman and Becker, "The Unseen Path to Cruelty," *Washington Post*, June 25, 2007, A1.

44. Barton Gellman and Jo Becker, "A Different Understanding with the President," *Washington Post*, June 24, 2007, A1.

45. Gellman and Becker, "A Different Understanding with the President," A1.

46. Jo Becker and Barton Gellman, "A Strong Push from Backstage," *Washington Post*, June 26, 2007, A1.

47. Rutenberg, "Ex-Aide Details a Loss of Faith in the President," section 1, page 1.

48. Robin Wright, "Iranian Unit to Be Labeled 'Terrorist,'" *Washington Post*, August 15, 2007, A1.

49. Warren P. Strobel and Nancy A. Youssef, "Worry of U.S. War with Iran Grows," McClatchy Newspapers, *Chattanooga Times Free Press*, August 19, 2007, A5.

50. *New York Times/* CBS News Poll, September 4–8, 2007.

51. Dick Cheney, "Wolf Blitzer Interview with Vice President Dick Cheney," CNN, "The Situation Room," January 24, 2007.

52. *New York Times*, CBS News Poll, March 7–11, 2007.

53. Gellman and Becker, "A Different Understanding with the President," A1.

54. David S. Broder, "Cheney Unbound," *Washington Post*, June 28, 2007, A25. See four-part "Angler" series on Vice President Cheney. <http://blog.washingtonpost.com/cheney/> (August 20, 2007).

55. George W. Bush, "President's Address to the Nation," The Library, White House, Washington, DC, January 10, 2007.

56. Walter Pincus, "NIE Cites 'Uneven' Security Gains, Faults Iraqi Leaders," *Washington Post*, August 24, 2007, A10.

57. Pincus, "NIE Cites 'Uneven' Security Gains, Faults Iraqi Leaders," A10.

58. U.S. Government Accountability Office, "Securing, Stabilizing, and Rebuilding Iraq: Iraqi Government Has Not Met Most Legislative, Security, and Economic Benchmarks," Report to Congressional Committees, U.S. Government Accountability Office, September 2007, 2.

59. Karen DeYoung and Ann Scott Tyson, "Military Officials in Iraq Fault GAO Report," *Washington Post*, September 5, 2007, A1.

60. General James L. Jones, "The Report of the Independent Commission on the Security Forces of Iraq," Independent Commission on the Security Forces of Iraq, September 6, 2007, 12. <http://www.c-span.org/pdf/jonesreport090607.pdf> (September 14, 2007).

61. Jones, "The Report of the Independent Commission on the Security Forces of Iraq," 20.

62. *Washington Post*, "*Washington Post*-ABC News Poll," September 4–7, 2007, *Washington Post*, September 9, 2007. <http://www.washingtonpost.com/wp-srv/politics/polls/postpoll_090907.html> (September 9, 2007).

63. *New York Times*, "*New York Times*/CBS News Poll," September 4–8, 2007, *New York Times*, September 10, 2007. <http://www.nytimes.com/packages/pdf/national/09102007_pollresults.pdf> (September 10, 2007).

64. General David H. Petraeus, "Report to Congress on the Situation in Iraq," September 10–11, 2007, 8. <http://graphics8.nytimes.com/packages/pdf/world/20070911_policy/Petraeus_Testimony.pdf> (September 2007).

65. Petraeus, "Report to Congress on the Situation in Iraq," 2.
66. Ambassador Ryan Crocker, "Crocker and Petraeus Testify before the Senate Foreign Relations Committee on Iraq," CQ Transcripts, *Washington Post*, September 11, 2007. <http://media.washingtonpost.com/wp-srv/politics/documents/transcript_senate_hearing_on_iraq_091107.html> (September 12, 2007).
67. George W. Bush, "Address by the President to the Nation on the Way Forward in Iraq," Oval Office, White House, Washington, DC, September 13, 2007.
68. Steven Lee Myers and David S. Cloud, "Bush Fights Back on Iraq Debate," *New York Times*, September 1, 2007, A1.
69. BBC, "Global Poll: Majority Wants Troops Out of Iraq within a Year," BBC World Service Poll, September 6, 2007. <http://www.worldpublicopinion.org/pipa/pdf/sep07/BBCIraq_Sep07_rpt.pdf> (September 7, 2007).
70. Woodward, *Bush at War*, 205.
71. Jeffrey E. Cohen, "*The Polls:* Presidential Greatness as Seen in the Mass Public: An Extension and Application of the Simonton Model," *Presidential Studies Quarterly* 33, no. 4 (December 2003), 918.
72. Frank Newport, "Bush Approval Continues to Hold Steady in Low 30s," Gallup Poll News Service, September 14, 2007.
73. Douglas Brinkley and others, "The Test of Time," *Texas Monthly* (March 2007), 116.
74. George W. Bush, "President Bush Attends Veterans of Foreign Wars National Convention, Discusses War on Terror," Kansas City, Kansas, August 22, 2007.
75. George W. Bush, "President Participates in Social Security Conversation in New York," Greece, New York, May 24, 2005.
76. Kevin Sullivan, "Views of U.S. Drop Sharply in Worldwide Opinion Poll," *Washington Post*, January 23, 2007, A14.
77. Charlie Savage, "Bush Challenges Hundreds of Laws," *Boston Globe*, April 30, 2006. <http://www.boston.com/news/nation/articles/2006/04/30/bush_challenges_hundreds_of_laws> (August 23, 2007).
78. George W. Bush, "President Bush and Secretary of State Rice Discuss the Middle East Crisis," Crawford, Texas, August 7, 2006.
79. George W. Bush, "President Bush Attends Veterans of Foreign Wars National Convention, Discusses War on Terror."
80. National Intelligence Estimate, "Prospects for Iraq's Stability: Some Security Progress but Political Reconciliation Elusive," National Intelligence Council, August 2007, 1.
81. John Ward Anderson, "N. Korea Agrees to Nuclear Deadline," *Washington Post*, September 3, 2007, A10.
82. Cohen, "*The Polls*," 922.
83. CNN, "CNN Poll," November 17–19, 2006.
84. Robert S. McElvaine, "Historians vs. George W. Bush," May 17, 2004. <http://hnn.us/articles/5019.html> (November 20, 2006).
85. Sean Wilentz, "The Worst President in History?" *Rolling Stone* 999 (May 4, 2006). <http://www.rollingstone.com/news/story/9961300/the_worst_president_in_history/print> (November 20, 2006).
86. Lydia Saad, "Majority Predicts History Will Judge Bush Harshly," Gallup Poll News Service, December 13, 2006.
87. Brian Braiker, "*Newsweek* Poll: Bush Hits New Low," Web Exclusive, *Newsweek*, January 27, 2007. <http://www.msnbc.com/id/16840614/site/newsweek/print/1/displaymode/1098/> (January 26, 2007).
88. AP-AOL News Poll, "Unpopular Path," *Chattanooga Times Free Press*, January 23, 2007, A4.
89. *Newsweek* Poll, January 24–25, 2007. <http://www.pollingreport.com/bush.htm> (August 25, 2007).
90. Associated Press, "Poll Seeks to Categorize Bush Backers," *Chattanooga Times Free Press*, August 8, 2007, A7.
91. John Mueller, "The Iraq Syndrome," *Foreign Affairs* 84, no. 6 (November–December 2005), 44–54.
92. Nancy Gibbs and John F. Dickerson, "I've Gained Strength," Interview with President Bush, *Time* 164, no. 10 (September 6, 2004), 38.

Bibliography

ABC. "100 Days Interview with George W. Bush." ABC, "Good Morning America," April 25, 2001.

ABC News Poll. "White House 2000: Republicans." August 19–22, 1999. <http://www.pollingreport.com/wh2rep.htm> (July 7, 2006).

———. "White House 2000: Presidential Debates." October 3, 2000. <http://www.pollingreport.com/wh2gen1.htm> (July 25, 2006).

———. "White House 2000: Presidential Debates." October 11, 2000. <www.polingreport.com> (July 26, 2006).

———. "White House 2000: Presidential Debates." October 17, 2000. <www.polingreport.com> (July 26, 2006).

Abramowitz, Michael. "Bush's Tactic of Refusing Laws Is Probed." *Washington Post*, July 24, 2006, A5.

———. "President Says His Iraq Policy Was Failing." *Washington Post*, January 17, 2007, A14.

———. "Intelligence Puts Rationale for War on Shakier Ground." *Washington Post*, July 18, 2007, A5.

———. "Book Tells of Dissent in Bush's Inner Circle." *Washington Post*, September 3, 2007, A1.

Abramowitz, Michael, and Jonathan Weisman. "President Unbowed as Benchmarks Are Unmet." *Washington Post*, July 13, 2007, A1.

Abramowitz, Michael, and Spencer S. Hsu. "Cheney Rejects Idea of Iraq." *Washington Post*, November 18, 2006, A4.

ACLU v NSA. Case No. 06-CV-10204. U.S. District Court, Eastern District of Michigan, Southern Division, August 17, 2006.

Adair, Bill, and Stephen Hegarty. "The Drama in Sarasota." *St. Petersburg Times,* September 8, 2002, 18.

Adelman, Ken. "Cakewalk in Iraq." *Washington Post*, February 13, 2002, A27.

Aikman, David. *A Man of Faith: The Spiritual Journey of George W. Bush.* Nashville, TN: W Publishing Group, 2004.

Al-bab.com. "Beirut Declaration." March 28, 2002. <http://www.al-bab.com/arab/docs/league/communique02.htm> (July 6, 2007).

Albright, David, and Holly Higgins. "Light Water Reactors and Nuclear Weapons in North Korea." Institute for Science and International Security, October 27, 1999.

Albright, Madeleine K. "American-Iranian Relations." Remarks before the American-Iranian Council, Washington, DC, March 17, 2000.

———. *Madam Secretary*. New York: Miramax Books, 2003.

Allen, Mike. "Bush, Putin Agree to Arms Dialogue." *Washington Post*, July 23, 2001, A1.

———. "War Cabinet Argues for Iraq Attack." *Washington Post*, September 9, 2002, A1.

———. "Bush's Words Can Go to the Blunt Edge of Trouble." *Washington Post*, September 29, 2002, A22.

Allen. Mike, and Hanna Rosin. "President Pledges 'Terrorism Will Not Stand.'" *Washington Post*, Final Edition, September 11, 2001, A3.

Allen Mike, and Jonathan Weisman. "Congress Wants to Know Cost of War." *Washington Post*, September 22, 2002, A24.

Allison, Graham. "Could Worse Be Yet to Come?" *Economist* 361, no. 8246 (November 3, 2001): 19.

Allison, Graham, and Philip Zelikow. *Essence of Decision: Explaining the Cuban Missile Crisis*, 2nd ed. New York: Longman, 1999.

American Library Association. "Resolution on the USA Patriot Act and Related Measures that Infringe on the Rights of Library Users." January 29, 2003. <http://www.ala.org/ala/washoff/WOissues/civilliberties/theusapatriotact/alaresolution.htm> (December 22, 2006).

Anderson, John Ward. "Iraqi Premier Denies U.S. Assertion He Agreed to Timeline." *Washington Post*, October 26, 2006, A15.

————. "N. Korea Agrees to Nuclear Deadline." *Washington Post*, September 3, 2007, A10.

Anderson, Jon Lee. "Out on the Street: The United States' De-Baathification Program Fueled the Insurgency." *New Yorker* 80, no. 35 (November 15, 2004): 72–79.

Anonymous. "Assessment of Legal, Historical, Policy, and Operational Considerations." March 6, 2003.

Ansari, Ali M. *Confronting Iran: The Failure of American Foreign Policy and the Next Great Crisis in the Middle East.* New York: Basic Books, 2006.

AP-AOL News Poll. "Unpopular Path." *Chattanooga Times Free Press*, January 23, 2007, A4.

Applebaum, Anne. "Why Can't Bush Get the Words Right?" *Washington Post*, February 11, 2004, A31.

Arnoldy, Ben. "How Serious Is North Korea's Nuclear Threat?" *Christian Science Monitor*, October 5, 2006. <http://www.csmonitor.com/2006/1005/p25s01-woap.html> (June 4, 2007).

Ashcroft, John. "Letter to the President." February 1, 2002, 2. <http://www.slate.com/features/whatistorture/LegalMemos.html> (October 29, 2006).

Associated Press. "Rumsfeld Blames Iraq Problems on 'Pockets of Dead-Enders.'" *USA Today*, June 18, 2003. <http://www.usatoday.com/news/world/iraq/2003-06-18-rumsfeld_x.htm> (February 26, 2007).

————. "Cheney Pushed for More Trade with Iran." Fox News.com, October 9, 2004. <http://foxnews.com/story/0,2933,134836,00.html> (May 24, 2007).

————. "Pattern of CIA Flights Is Cited." *Los Angeles Times*, April 27, 2006, A22.

————. "Tenet Regrets WMD 'Slam Dunk' Comment." April 28, 2005. <http://www.sfgate.com/cgi-bin/article.cgi?file=/n/a/2005/04/28/national/a061248D00.DTL> (July 12, 2006).

————. "Hezbollah Leader Regrets Actions that Led to War." *Chattanooga Times Free Press*, August 28, 2006, A3.

————. "Opium Crop on Rise in Afghan Provinces." *New York Times*, November 29, 2006, A18.

————. "Europeans Approve Report on C.I.A." *New York Times*, February 14, 2007.

————. "Poll Seeks to Categorize Bush Backers." *Chattanooga Times Free Press*, August 8, 2007, A7.

Baker III, James A. "The Right Way to Change a Regime." *New York Times*, August 25, 2002, A9.

Baker III, James A., and Lee Hamilton, co-chairs. *The Iraq Study Group Report: The Way Forward—A New Approach.* New York: Vintage Books, 2006.

Baker, Peter. "The President as Average Joe." *Washington Post*, April 2, 2006, A4.

————. "Bush Dismisses Talk of Using Force Against Iran." *Washington Post*, April 11, 2006, A2.

————. "Bush's Bull Session: Loud and Clear, Chief." *Washington Post*, July 18, 2006, C1.

————. "President Confronts Dissent on Troop Levels." *Washington Post*, December 21, 2006, A1.

————. "9/11 Linked to Iraq, in Politics if Not in Fact." *Washington Post*, September 12, 2007, A1.

Baker, Peter, and Charles Babington. "Bush Addresses Uproar over Spying." *Washington Post*, December 20, 2005, A1.

Baker, Peter, and Colum Lynch. "Bush Declines to Call for Israeli Cease-Fire." *Washington Post*, July 15, 2006, A16.

Baker Peter, and Robin Wright. "Bush Renews Mideast Efforts." *Washington Post*, July 17, 2007, A1.

Baker, Peter, Dafna Linzer, and Thomas E. Ricks. "U.S. Is Studying Military Strike Options on Iran." *Washington Post*, April 9, 2006, A1.

Balz, Dan, and Bob Woodward. "America's Chaotic Road to War." *Washington Post*, January 27, 2002, A1.

Balz, Dan, and Jon Cohen. "Majority in Poll Favor Deadline for Iraq Pullout." *Washington Post*, February 27, 2007, A1.

Barnea, Nahum. "Israel vs. Hezbollah." *Foreign Policy* 157 (November–December 2006): 22–28.

Barrett, Laurence I. "Junior Is His Own Bush Now." *Time* 134, no. 5 (July 31, 1989): 60–62.

Barry, John, Michael Hirsh, and Michael Isikoff. "Special Report: The Roots of Torture." *Newsweek* 143, no. 21(May 24, 2004): 26–34.

Battle, Joyce, and Thomas Blanton, eds. "Top Secret Polo Step." The National Security Archive, Washington, DC, February 14, 2007. <http://www.gwu.edu/~nsarchiv/NSAEBB/NSAEBB214/index.htm> (March 21, 2007).

Bazan, Elizabeth B., and Jennifer K. Elsea. "Presidential Authority to Conduct Warrantless Electronic Surveillance to Gather Foreign Intelligence Information." Congressional Reference Service, January 5, 2006, CRS 23–25.

BBC. "Outrage at 'Old Europe' Remarks." BBC World News, January 23, 2003. <http://news.bbc.co.uk/2/hi/europe/2687403.stm> (February 8, 2007).

———. "Global Poll: Majority Wants Troops Out of Iraq within a Year." BBC World Service Poll, September 6, 2007. <http://www.worldpublicopinion.org/pipa/pdf/sep07/BBCIraq_Sep07_rpt.pdf> (September 7, 2007).

Becker, Jo, and Barton Gellman. "A Strong Push from Backstage." *Washington Post*, June 26, 2007, A1.

Bennet, James. "Despite Furor Over China, Clinton Defends Trade Status." *New York Times*, June 4, 1998, A10.

———. "Israel Seizes Ship It Says Was Arming Palestinians." *New York Times*, January 5, 2002, A1.

Bennet, James, with Elisabeth Bumiller. "Israelis Approve Plan to End Siege and Free Arafat." *New York Times*, April 29, 2002, A1.

Berger, Sandy. "Testimony of Sandy Berger, National Security Adviser to President Bill Clinton." Transcript 9/11 Commission Hearings, March 24, 2004.

Berke, Richard L. "Training for a Presidential Race." *New York Times*, March 15, 1999, A16.

———. "Gore and Bush Strategists Analyze Their Campaigns." *New York Times*, February 12, 2001, A19.

———. "Aide Says Bush Will Do More to Marshal Religious Base." *New York Times*, December 12, 2001, A22.

———. "Bush Adviser Suggests War as Campaign Theme." *New York Times*, January 19, 2002, A15.

Berntsen, Gary, and Ralph Pezzullo. *Jawbreaker: The Attack on Bin Laden and Al-Qaeda: A Personal Account by the CIA's Key Field Commander.* New York: Crown Publishers, 2005.

Biden Jr., Joseph R., and Leslie H. Gelb. "Unity through Autonomy in Iraq." *New York Times*, May 1, 2006, A19.

Bilefsky, Dan. "European Inquiry Says C.I.A. Flew 1,000 Flights in Secret." *New York Times*, April 26, 2006, A12.

Blair, Tony. "President Bush and Prime Minister Tony Blair of the United Kingdom Participate in Joint Press Availability." White House, East Room, May 25, 2006.

Blumenthal, Ralph. "Bush Service Records from '72, Thought Lost, Are Discovered." *New York Times,* July 24, 2004, A7.

Bolton, John. "A Dictatorship at the Crossroads." Address to the East Asia Institute, Seoul, South Korea, July 31, 2003. <http://rpc.senate.gov/_files/FOREIGNdf073103.pdf> (June 7, 2007).

Borger, Julian. "Special Investigation: The Spies Who Pushed for War." *Guardian*, July 17, 2003. <http://www.guardian.co.uk/print/0,4714031-103550,00.html> (March 14, 2007).

Brace, Paul, and Barbara Hinkley. *Follow the Leader: Opinion Polls and the Modern Presidents.* New York: Basic Books, 1992.

Brady, John. *Bad Boy: The Life and Politics of Lee Atwater.* Reading, MA: Addison Wesley Publishing Company, Inc., 1997.

Braiker, Brian. "*Newsweek* Poll: Bush Hits New Low," Web Exclusive, *Newsweek*, January 27, 2007. <http://www.msnbc.com/id/16840614/site/newsweek/print/1/displaymode/1098/> (January 26, 2007).

Branigin, William. "Cheney Says Eavesdropping Program Might Have Prevented 9/11." *Washington Post*, January 4, 2006, A1.

———. "U.S. Not Planning for War With Iran, Gates Says." *Washington Post*, February 2, 2007. <http://www.washingtonpost.com/wp-dyn/content/article/2007/02/02/AR2007020200539.html> (May 29, 2007).

Bremer, Paul. "Excerpts of Bremer Speech Aired on US-Run al-Iraqiya Television." BBC News, April 23, 2004. <http://www.usatoday.com/news/washington/2007-02-05-iraq-contracts_x.htm?csp=34> (February 19, 2007).

Bremer III, L. Paul. "Iraq's Path to Sovereignty." *Washington Post*, September 8, 2003, A21.

Bremer III, Ambassador L. Paul. *My Year in Iraq: The Struggle to Build a Future of Hope*. New York: Simon & Schuster, 2006.

Brinkley, Douglas and others. "The Test of Time." *Texas Monthly* (March 2007): 114–126.

Broder, David S. "Cheney Unbound." *Washington Post*, June 28, 2007, A25. See four-part "Angler" series on Vice President Cheney. <http://blog.washingtonpost.com/cheney/> (August 20, 2007).

Brodsky, David M., and Robert H. Swansbrough. "Tennessee: A Native Son Scorned." Chapter 13 in *The 2000 Presidential Election in the South*, edited by Robert P. Steed and Laurence W. Moreland, NY: Praeger Publishers, 2002.

Brooks, David. "Heroes and History." *New York Times*, July 17, 2007, A21.

Brulliard, Karin, and Saad Sarhan. "Sadr Aides Say 6 Allies In Cabinet Will Resign." *Washington Post*, April 16, 2007, A11.

Bruni, Frank. *Ambling into History: The Unlikely Odyssey of George W. Bush*. New York: Perennial, 2003.

————. "Bush Vows Money and Support for Military." *New York Times*, September 24, 1999, A22.

Bryce, Robert. "The Fab Four: Meet the People Maneuvering behind the Scenes to Put George W. Bush in the White House." <http://www.salon.com/news/feature/1999/06/16/advisors/> (June 16, 2005).

Bumiller, Elisabeth. "Bush Aides Set Strategy to Sell Policy on Iraq." *Washington Post*, September 7, 2002, A1.

————. "Threats and Responses: The Cost." *New York Times*, December 31, 2002, A1.

————. "Bush States His Case." *New York Times*, February 9, 2004, A19.

————. "C.I.A. Leak Case Recalls Texas Incident in '92 Race." *New York Times*, August 6, 2005, A8.

Bumiller, Elisabeth, and David E. Sanger. "A Somber Bush Says Terrorism Cannot Prevail." *New York Times*, September 12, 2001, A1.

Burns, John F., and Dexter Filkins. "The President Makes Surprise Visit to Iraq to Press Leadership." *The New York Times*, June 14, 2006, A1.

Burns, Robert. "Bush to Cut Nuclear Forces while Accelerating Missile Defense Effort." Associated Press, May 1, 2001.

Bush, George, and Brent Scowcroft. *A World Transformed*. New York: Alfred A. Knopf, 1998.

Bush, George H.W. "'The Peace Dividend I Seek Is Not Measured in Dollars.'" *Washington Post*, September 28, 1991, A1.

————. "Interview with former President George H.W. Bush by Mark McEwin in Florida Keys." CBS, "The Early Show," October 23, 2001.

————. "Bush Sr. Defends Record on Hussein." Reuters, *Washington Post*, October 22, 2002, A22.

Bush, George W. *A Charge to Keep*. New York: William Morrow and Company, Inc., 1999.

————. "Duty of Hope." Indianapolis, Indiana, July 22, 1999. <georgewbush.com>

————. "A Period of Consequences." The Citadel, South Carolina, September 23, 1999. <georgewbush.com> (September 2000).

————. "New Leadership on National Security." Washington, DC, May 23, 2000.

————. "Republican Party Convention Acceptance Speech." August 3, 2000.

————. "First Presidential Debate." University of Massachusetts in Boston, Boston, Massachusetts, October 4, 2000.

————. "Second Presidential Debate." Wake Forest University, Wake Forest, North Carolina, October 11, 2000.

————. "Third Presidential Debate." Washington University, St. Louis, Missouri, October 17, 2000.

————. "Remarks by President Bush and President Kim Dae-Jung of Korea." White House, Washington, DC, March 7, 2001.

————. "Text of a Letter from the President to Senators Hagel, Helms, Craig, and Roberts." White House, Washington, DC, March 13, 2001.

————. "White House News Conference." White House, Washington, DC, March 29, 2001.

———. "Remarks by the President to Students and Faculty at National Defense University." Washington, DC, May 1, 2001.

———. "Press Conference with Spanish President Jose Maria Aznar," Madrid, Spain, June 12, 2001.

———. "Press Conference by President Bush, Prime Minister Goran Persson of Sweden." Goteborg, Sweden, June 14, 2001.

———. "Press Conference by President Bush and Russian Federation President Putin." Brdo Castle, Brdo Pri Kranju, Slovenia, June 16, 2001.

———. "Remarks by the President and Secretary Rumsfeld in Announcement of Chairman and Vice-Chairman of the Joint Chiefs of Staff." Crawford, Texas, August 24, 2001.

———. "Remarks by the President after Two Planes Crash into World Trade Center." Emma Booker Elementary School, Sarasota, Florida, September 11, 2001.

———. "Remarks by the President upon Arrival at Barksdale Air Force Base." Barksdale Air Force Base, Louisiana, September 11, 2001.

———. "Statement by the President in His Address to the Nation." White House, Washington, DC, September 11, 2001.

———. "Remarks by the President in Photo Opportunity with the National Security Team." The Cabinet Room, Washington, DC, September 12, 2001.

———. "President's Remarks at National Day of Prayer and Remembrance." National Cathedral, Washington, DC, September 14, 2001.

———. "Radio Address of the President to the Nation." White House, Washington, DC, September 15, 2001.

———. "Address to a Joint Session of Congress and the American People." U.S. Capitol, Washington, DC, September 20, 2001.

———. "President Freezes Terrorists' Assets." The Rose Garden, White House, Washington, DC, September 24, 2001.

———. "President Pays Tribute at Pentagon Memorial." The Pentagon, Arlington, Virginia, October 11, 2001.

———. "Prime Time News Conference." White House, Washington, DC, October 11, 2001.

———. "President Signs Anti-Terrorism Bill." White House, Washington, DC, October 26, 2001.

———. "President Bush Speaks to United Nations." UN General Assembly, New York, November 10, 2001.

———. "President Delivers State of the Union Address." U.S. Capitol, Washington, DC, January 29, 2002.

———. "Interview with President Bush on December 20, 2001." *Washington Post*, February 3, 2002, A14.

———. "Humane Treatment of al Qaeda and Taliban Detainees." February 7, 2002. <http://www.slate.com/features/whatistorture/LegalMemos.html> (October 29, 2006).

———. "President, Vice President Discuss the Middle East." White House, Washington, DC, March 21, 2002.

———. "President Outlines War Effort." Virginia Military Institute, Lexington, Virginia, April 17, 2002.

———. "President Bush Delivers Graduation Speech at West Point." United States Military Academy, West Point, New York, June 1, 2002.

———. "President Bush Calls for New Palestinian Leadership." White House, Washington, DC, June 24, 2002.

———. "Statement by the President." White House, Washington, DC, July 12, 2002.

———. "President's Remarks at the United Nations General Assembly." New York, September 12, 2002.

———. "Remarks by the President at Doug Forrester for Senate Event." Trenton, New Jersey, September 23, 2002.

———. "Remarks by the President at John Cornyn for Senate Reception." Houston, Texas, September 26, 2002.

———. "President Bush Outlines Iraqi Threat." Cincinnati Museum Center, Cincinnati, Ohio, October 7, 2002.

———. "President Visits Crawford Coffee Shop." Crawford, Texas, December 31, 2002.

Bush, George W. "President Focuses on U.S. Economy, Iraq & N. Korea." Crawford, Texas, January 2, 2003.

———. "President Delivers 'State of the Union.'" U.S. Capitol, Washington, DC, January 28, 2003.

———. "President Calls for Strengthened and Reformed Medicare Plan." Grand Rapids, Michigan, January 29, 2003.

———. "President Discusses the Future of Iraq." American Enterprise Institute, Washington, DC, February 26, 2003.

———. "President Bush Announces Major Combat Operation in Iraq Have Ended." *USS Abraham Lincoln* at Sea off the Coast of San Diego, California, May 1, 2003.

———. "President Bush Names Randall Tobias to be Global AIDS Coordinator." White House, Washington, DC, July 2, 2003.

———. "President Discusses Middle East Peace with Prime Minister Sharon." White House, Washington, DC, July 29, 2003.

———. "President Bush Discusses Freedom in Iraq and Middle East." White House, Washington, DC, November 6, 2003.

———. "NBC News Transcript." NBC, Meet the Press, February 8, 2004.

———. "Remarks Via Satellite by the President to the National Association of Evangelicals Convention." The Map Room, White House, Washington, DC, March 11, 2004.

———. "President Bush Commends Israeli Prime Minister Sharon's Plan." White House, Washington, DC, April 14, 2004.

———. "President Bush Welcomes Prime Minister of Hungary." White House, Washington, DC, June 22, 2004.

———. "President Holds Press Conference." White House, Washington, DC, November 4, 2004.

———. "President and Prime Minister Blair Discussed Iraq, Middle East." White House, Washington, DC, November 12, 2004.

———. "President Sworn-In to Second Term." White House, Washington, DC, January 20, 2005.

———. "President Discusses American and European Alliance in Belgium." Brussels, Belgium, February 21, 2005.

———. "Press Conference of the President." White House, Washington, DC, April 28, 2005.

———. "President Participates in Social Security Conversation in New York." Greece, New York, May 24, 2005.

———. "President's Radio Address." White House, Washington, DC, December 17, 2005.

———. "President Bush Holds a White House Press Conference." White House, Washington, DC, January 26, 2006.

———. "President Discusses 2006 Agenda." Grand Ole Opry House, Nashville, Tennessee, February 1, 2006.

———. "President Discusses War on Terror and Operation Iraqi Freedom." Renaissance Cleveland Hotel, Cleveland, Ohio, March 20, 2006.

———. "Press Conference of the President." The Rose Garden, White House, June 14, 2006.

———. "President Bush Participates in Press Availability with Canadian Prime Minister Stephen Harper." White House, Washington, DC, July 6, 2006.

———. "President Bush and Secretary of State Rice Discuss the Middle East Crisis." Crawford, Texas, August 7, 2006.

———. "President Discusses Creation of Military Commissions to Try Suspected Terrorists." White House, Washington, DC, September 6, 2006.

———. "President Bush and President Musharraf of Pakistan Participate in Press Availability." White House, Washington, DC, September 22, 2006.

———. "President Bush's Statement on North Korea Nuclear Test." White House, Washington, DC, October 9, 2006.

———. "Press Conference by the President." The East Room, White House, Washington, DC, October 25, 2006.

———. "Press Conference by the President." White House, Washington, DC, November 8, 2006.

———. "President Bush Receives Report from the Iraq Study Group." White House, Washington, DC, December 6, 2006.

———. "President's Address to the Nation." The Library, White House, Washington, DC, January 10, 2007.

———. "President Bush Rejects Artificial Deadline, Vetoes Iraq War Supplemental." White House, Washington, DC, May 1, 2007.

———. "President Bush Discusses War on Terror in South Carolina." Charleston Air Force Base, Charleston, South Carolina, July 24, 2007.

———. "President Bush Discusses American Competitiveness Initiative during Press Conference." White House, Washington, DC, August 9, 2007.

———. "President Bush Attends Veterans of Foreign Wars National Convention, Discusses War on Terror." Kansas City, Kansas, August 22, 2007.

———. "Address by the President to the Nation on the Way Forward in Iraq." Oval Office, White House, Washington, DC, September 13, 2007.

Bush, Governor George W. "A Distinctly American Internationalism." Ronald Reagan Library, California, November 19, 1999.

Bybee, Jay S. "Memorandum for Alberto R. Gonzales, Counsel to the President." August 1, 2002. <http://www.gwu.edu/~nsarchiv/NSAEBB/NSAEBB127/> (November 1, 2006).

Byman, Daniel, Kenneth Pollack, and Gideon Rose. "The Rollback Fantasy." *Foreign Affairs* 78, no. 1 (January 1999): 24.

Calmes, Jackie. "Texas Tax Fight Yields Clues on How Bush Would Lead." *Wall Street Journal*, December 14, 1999, 24.

Campbell, Colin, Bert A. Rockman, and Andrew Rudalevige, eds. *The George W. Bush Legacy.* Washington, DC: CQ Press, 2008.

Cannon, Carl M. "The Book on W." *National Journal* 31, no. 32 (August 7, 1999): 2272–2279.

Cannon, Carl M., and Alexis Simendinger. "The Evolution of Karl Rove." *National Journal* 34, no. 17 (April 27, 2002): 1210–1216.

Carney, James, and John F. Dickerson. "Inside the War Room: Send in the Spooks." *Time* 158, no. 28 (December 31, 2001): 112–121.

Carroll, Joseph. "Bush Job Approval: 31%." Gallup Poll News Service, May 9, 2006.

———. "Slim Majority Supports Anti-Terrorism Action in Afghanistan, Pakistan." Gallup Poll News Service, August 8, 2007.

Carter, Jimmy. "Tehran, Iran Toasts of the President and the Shah at a State Dinner." December 31, 1977. <http://www.parstimes.com/history/carter_toast_tehran.html> (May 30, 2007).

———. "Solving the Korean Stalemate, One Step at a Time." The Carter Center, October 11, 2006.

CBS. "The Man Who Knew." CBS News, February 4, 2004. <http://www.cbsnews.com/stories/2003/10/14/6011/printables577975.shtml> (March 13, 2007).

CENTCOM. "Desert Crossing Seminar: After Action Report (unclassified)." CINC USCENTCOM, June 28–30, 1999.

Central Intelligence Agency. "Key Judgments—Iraq's Continuing Programs for Weapons of Mass Destruction." National Intelligence Estimate, October 2002. <http://www.cianet.org/wps/dod102> (March 15, 2007).

———. "Iraq-Legislative Branch," CIA World FactBook, June 14, 2007. <https://www.cia.gov/library/publicans/the-world-factbook/geos/iz.html> (June 19, 2007).

Cha, Victor D., and David C. Kang. "The Korea Crisis." *Foreign Policy* 142 (May–June 2003): 20–28.

Cheney, Dick. "Tim Russert Interview with Vice President Dick Cheney." NBC, Meet the Press, Camp David, September 16, 2001.

———. "Address to the Veterans of Foreign Wars." Nashville, Tennessee, August 26, 2002.

———. "Vice President Dick Cheney Discusses a Possible War with Iraq." NBC, Meet the Press with Tim Russert, March 16, 2003.

———. "Interview of Vice President Dick Cheney with Tim Russert." NBC, Meet the Press, September 14, 2003.

———. "Transcript: Vice President Cheney's Commencement Address." U.S. Naval Academy, May 26, 2006.

Cheney, Dick. "Transcript: Vice President Cheney on 'Fox News Sunday.'" Fox News, January 14, 2007. <http://www.foxnews.com/story/0,2933,243632,00.html> (May 29, 2007).

———. "Wolf Blitzer Interview with Vice President Dick Cheney." CNN, "The Situation Room," January 24, 2007.

Clarke, Richard A. *Against All Enemies: Inside America's War on Terror.* New York: Free Press, 2004.

———. "Interview by Leslie Stahl." CBS News, Transcripts of "60 Minutes," March 21, 2004.

———. "Transcript of 9/11 Commission Hearings," 9/11 Commission Hearing, March 24, 2004.

Clinton, Bill. "Excerpts from President Clinton's Session with Reporters." *New York Times*, October 22, 1994, A6.

———. "Remarks on National Security." Georgetown University, September 1, 2000.

———. "Interview of the President by David Sanger, Todd Purdum, Marc Lacey, Robin Toner and Jane Perlez of the *New York Times*," White House, November 30, 2000.

———. *My Life.* New York: Alfred A. Knopf, 2004.

Cloud, David S. "Gates Offers Blunt Review of Progress in Iraq." *New York Times*, August 3, 2007, A10.

Cloud, David S., and Helene Cooper. "Weapons: U.S. Speeds Up Bomb Delivery for the Israelis." *New York Times*, July 22, 2006, A1.

CNN. "Gore Appears on 'Oprah' as Bush Courts Florida Seniors." September 11, 2000. <cnn.com/2000/ALLPOLITICS> (July 20, 2006).

———. "Khobar Towers Indictments Returned." CNN.com, June 22, 2001. <http://archives.cnn.com/2001/LAW/06/21/ashcroft.khobar/> (May 24, 2007).

———. CNN/*USA Today*/Gallup Poll, September 11, 2001. <http://www.pollingreport/com/terror10.htm> (April 2, 2007).

———. "Bush to U.N.: Be More than a 'Debating Society.'" CNN, October 22, 2002.

———. "Iraq Insurgency in 'Last Throes,' Cheney Says." CNN.Com, June 20, 2005. <http://www.cnn.com/2005/US/05/30/cheney.iraq/> (February 26, 2007).

———. "CNN Poll." November 17–19, 2006.

———. "Ex-CIA Chief: Cheney 'VP for Torture.'" CNN.Com, November 18, 2005. <http://www.cnn.com/2005/WORLD/europe/11/18/turner.cheney/> (December 3, 2006).

———. "Powell aide: Torture 'Guidance' from VP." CNN.com, November 20, 2005. <http://www.cnn.com/2005/US/11/20/torture/index.html> (December 3, 2006).

———. "Cheney: Realistic over N. Korea deal." CNN.com, February 22, 2007. <http://www.cnn.com/2007/POLITICS/02/22/cheney.australia/index.html> (June 10, 2007).

———. "CNN Late Edition with Wolf Blitzer: Interviews With Robert Gates, Benazir Bhutto, Hamid Karzai." CNN Transcript, August 5, 2007. <http://transcripts.cnn.com/TRANSCRIPTS/0708/05/le.01.html> (August 10, 2007).

Cody, Edward. "Tentative Nuclear Deal Struck with North Korea." *Washington Post*, February 13, 2007, A1.

Cohen, Jeffrey E. "The Polls: Presidential Greatness as Seen in the Mass Public: An Extension and Application of the Simonton Model." *Presidential Studies Quarterly* 33, no. 4 (December 2003): 913–924.

Cohen, Jon. "Poll: Most Americans Opposed to Bush's Iraq Plan." ABC/ *Washington Post* Poll, *Washington Post*, January 11, 2007.

Collins, John M. "Military Intervention: A Checklist of Key Considerations." *Parameters: U.S. Army War College Quarterly* (Winter 1995): 53–58.

Colombani, Jean-Marie. "We Are All Americans." *Le Monde* September 12, 2001.

Commission on Presidential Debates. "Debate Transcript: The Second Gore-Bush Presidential Debate." October 11, 2000. <http://www.debates.org/pages/trans2000b.html> (February 12, 2007).

Cooper, Helene. "Rice Plays Down Hawkish Talk about Iran." *New York Times*, June 2, 2007, A5.

———. "As Her Star Wanes, Rice Tries to Reshape Legacy." *New York Times*, September 1, 2007, A1.

Cordesman, Anthony H. "Iraq's Sunni Insurgents: Looking beyond Al Qa'ida." Center for Strategic and International Studies, Washington, DC, July 16, 2007, 2. <http://www.csis.org/media/csis/pubs/070716_sunni_insurgents.pdf> (August 12, 2007).

Council on Foreign Relations. "Backgrounder: Hamas." Council on Foreign Relations, New York, June 8, 2007. <http://www.cfr.org/publication/8968/> (July 5, 2007).

Cowell, Alan. "U.S. 'Thumbs Its Nose' at Rights, Amnesty Says." *New York Times*, May 26, 2005, A1.

Cramer, Richard Ben. *What It Takes: The Way to the White House.* New York: Random House, 1992.

Crane, Conrad C., and W. Andrew Terrill. "Reconstructing Iraq: Challenges and Missions for Military Forces in a Post-Conflict Scenario." U.S. Army War College, Strategic Studies Institute, January 29, 2003. <http://www.strategicstudiesinstitute.army.mil/pdffiles/PUB182.pdf> (February 13, 2007).

Crocker, Ambassador Ryan. "Crocker and Petraeus Testify before the Senate Foreign Relations Committee on Iraq." CQ Transcripts, *Washington Post*, September 11, 2007. <http://media.washingtonpost.com/wp-srv/politics/documents/transcript_senate_hearing_on_iraq_091107.html> (September 12, 2007).

Crossette, Barbara. "Albright, in Overture to Iran, Seeks a 'Road Map' to Amity." *New York Times*, June 18, 1998, A1.

Crumpton, Henry A. "Intelligence and War: Afghanistan, 2001–2002." Chapter 10 in *Transforming U.S. Intelligence*, edited by Jennifer E. Sims and Burton Gerber. Washington DC: Georgetown University Press, 2005.

Daalder, Ivo H., and James M. Lindsay. *America Unbound: The Bush Revolution in Foreign Policy.* Washington, DC: Brookings Institution Press, 2003.

Dae-jung, Kim. "Nobel Lecture." Oslo, Norway, December 10, 2000.

Dalrymple, Mary. "Byrd's Beloved Chamber Deaf to His Pleas for Delayed Vote." *Congressional Quarterly* 60, no. 39 (October 12, 2002): 2674.

Davis, Derek H. "The Dark Side to a Just War: The USA PATRIOT Act and Counterterrorism's Potential Threat to Religious Freedom." *Journal of Church and State* 44, no. 1 (Winter 2002): 5–18.

Davis, Richard H. "The Anatomy of a Smear Campaign." *Boston Globe*, March 21, 2004, C12.

Deans, Bob. "As Fourth Anniversary of War Nears, Costs Rise." Cox News Services, *Chattanooga Times Free Press*, March 18, 2007, A1.

Deans, Bob, and Margaret Coker. "Diplomacy Key Objective for Rice on Mideast Trip." Cox News Service, *Chattanooga Times Free Press*, July 22, 2006, A1.

DeYoung, Karen. "Afghanistan Opium Crops Sets Record." *Washington Post*, December 2, 2006, A1.

————. "Bush Approves New CIA Methods." *Washington Post*, July 21, 2007, A1.

DeYoung, Karen, and Ann Scott Tyson. "Military Officials in Iraq Fault GAO Report." *Washington Post*, September 5, 2007, A1.

DeYoung Karen, and Colum Lynch. "U.S. Proposal May Break Impasse at U.N. over Iraq." *Washington Post*, October 18, 2002, A32.

DeYoung, Karen, and Glenn Kessler. "Policy Successes—or U-Turns." *Washington Post*, March 11, 2007, A18.

DeYoung, Karen, and Joby Warrick. "Tougher Stance on Pakistan Took Months." *Washington Post*, August 5, 2007, A1.

DeYoung, Karen, and Thomas E. Ricks. "Exit Strategies: Would Iran Take over Iraq? Would Al-Qaeda?" *Washington Post*, July 17, 2007, A1.

————. "As British Leave, Basra Deteriorates." *Washington Post*, August 7, 2007, A1.

Dhooge, Lucien J. "Meddling with the Mullahs: An Analysis of the Iran and Libya Sanctions Act of 1996." *Denver Journal of International Law and Policy* 27, no. 1 (Fall 1998): 1–74. <http://findarticles.com/p/articles/mi_hb3262/is_199809/ai_n7962764> (May 22, 2007).

Diamond, Howard. "N. Korea Launches Staged Rocket that Overflies Japanese Territory." *Arms Control Today*, Arms Control Association, August/September 1998. <http://www.armscontrol.org/act/1998_08-09/nk1as98.asp> (August 8, 2006).

Diamond, Larry. "What Went Wrong in Iraq." *Foreign Affairs* 83, no. 5 (September–October 2004): 34–56.

————. *Squandered Victory: The American Occupation and the Bungled Effort to Bring Democracy to Iraq.* New York: Times Books, 2005.

Djerejian, Edward P., and Frank G. Wisner. *Guiding Principles for U.S. Post-Conflict Policy in Iraq,* Report of an Independent Working Group Cosponsored by the Council on Foreign

Relations and The James A Baker III Institute for Public Policy Rice University. New York: Council on Foreign Relations, 2003.

Dobbins, James. "Time to Deal with Iran." *Washington Post*, May 6, 2004, A 35.

———. "Iraq: Winning the Unwinnable War." *Foreign Affairs* 84, no. 1 (January–February 2005): 16–25.

Dobbins, James, John G. McGinn, Keith Crane, Seth G. Jones, Rollie Lal, Andrew Rathmell, Rachel Swanger, and Anga Timilsina. *America's Role in Nation-Building: From Germany to Iraq.* Santa Monica, CA: RAND Corporation, 2003.

Dole, Elizabeth. "Elizabeth Dole Withdraws." *Green Papers News*, October 20, 1999. <http://www.thegreenpapers.com/News/19991020-0.html> (July 7, 2006).

Domke, David. *God Willing? Political Fundamentalism in the White House, the "War on Terror," and the Echoing Press.* London: Pluto Press, 2004.

Donnelly, John, and Rick Klein. "Bush Admits to CIA Jails." *Boston Globe*, September 7, 2006, A1.

Doran, Michael Scott. "Palestine, Iraq, and American Strategy." *Foreign Affairs* 82, no. 1 (January–February 2003): 19–33.

Douglas, William, and Jonathan S. Landay. "Bush Sets CIA Rules on Queries of Terrorists." McClatchy Newspapers, *Chattanooga Times Free Press*, July 21, 2007, A1.

Dreyfuss, Robert. "George W.'s Compassion." *American Prospect* (September 1999): 36–42.

Drozdiak, William. "NATO Deals Blow to U.S. Missile Defense Plan." *Washington Post*, May 29, 2001, A15.

Drozdiak William, and Dana Milbank. "Bush Tries to Sell NATO on Missile Defense Plan." *Washington Post*, June 14, 2001, A1.

Dubose, Lou, Jan Reid, and Carl M. Cannon. *Boy Genius: Karl Rove, the Brains behind the Remarkable Political Triumph of George W. Bush.* New York: Public Affairs Reports, 2003.

Dubose, Louis. "Bush's Hit Man: Karl Rove and the Politics of Destruction." *The Nation* 272, no. 9 (March 5, 2001): 11–14.

Duffy, Michael. "So Much for the WMD." *Time* 163, no. 6 (February 9, 2004). <http://www.time.com/time/printout/o,8816,586175,00.html> (March 14, 2007).

Duffy, Michael, and Dan Goodgame. *Marching in Place: The Status Quo Presidency of George Bush.* New York: Simon & Schuster, 1992.

Eggen, Dan. "Bush Authorized Domestic Spying." *Washington Post*, December 16, 2005, A1.

———. "Cheney's Remarks Fuel Torture Debate." *Washington Post*, October 27, 2006, A9.

———. "Judge Invalidates Patriot Act Provisions." *Washington Post*, September 7, 2007, A1.

Eggen, Dan, and Charles Lane, "On Hill, Anger and Calls for Hearings Greet News of Stateside Surveillance." *Washington Post*, December 17, 2005, A1.

Eggen, Dan, and Paul Kane. "Gonzales Hospital Episode Detailed." *Washington Post*, May 16, 2007, A1.

Erlanger, Steve. "Hamas Leader Sees No Change toward Israelis." *New York Times*, January 29, 2006, 1-1.

Fallows, James. "Blind into Baghdad." *Atlantic Monthly*, 293 no. 1 (January–February 2004): 52–74.

———. "Bush's Lost Year." *Atlantic Monthly* 294, no. 3 (October 2004): 68–84.

Federal Bureau of Investigation. "Terrorism in the United States 1997." Department of Justice, Washington, DC, 1997. <http://www.fbi.gov/publications/terror/terr97.pdf> (December 8, 2006).

Federal Election Commission, "Receipts of 1999–2000 Presidential Campaigns through July 31, 2000." Washington, DC <http://www.fec.gov/finance/precm8.htm> (July 7, 2006).

Federal News Service. "In a Chief Inspector's Words: 'A Substantial Measure of Disarmament.'" *New York Times*, March 8, 2003, A8.

Filkins, Dexter. "Where Plan A Left Ahmad Chalabi." *New York Times Magazine* (November 6, 2006): 46–83, 85.

Fineman, Howard. "Here Comes the Son." *Newsweek* 133, no. 25 (June 21, 1999): 28–30.

Fisher, Ian, and Elisabetta Povoledo. "Italy Seeks Indictments of C.I.A. Operatives in Egyptian's Abduction." *New York Times*, December 6, 2006, A12.

Fletcher, Michael A. "Hezbollah the Loser in Battle, Bush Says." *Washington Post*, August 15, 2006, A8.

———. "Bush Rejects Solo Talks with North Korea." *Washington Post*, July 8, 2006, A2.

———. "Bush, NATO Chief Seek Ways to Bolster Afghanistan Mission." *Washington Post*, May 20, 2007, A20.

Fletcher, Michael A., and Jim VaneHei. "Transcript of Bush Interview on Air Force One." *Washington Post*, January 16, 2005, A1.

Fortier John C., and Norman J. Ornstein. "President Bush: Legislative Strategist." Chapter 6 in *The George W. Bush Presidency: An Early Assessment*, edited by Fred I. Greenstein. Baltimore, MD: The Johns Hopkins Press, 2003.

Frankel, Glenn, and Keith B. Richburg. "8 Leaders in Europe Back Bush on Iraq." *Washington Post*, January 31, 2003, A16.

Franks, Tommy. "Progress Report." PBS, OnLine NewsHour, March 22, 2003. <http://www.pbs.org/newshour/bb/military/jan-june03/progress_3-22.html> (February 15, 2003).

Franks, General Tommy, with Malcolm McConnell. *American Soldier*. New York: Regan Books, 2004.

Freedman, Lawrence, and Efraim Karsh. *The Gulf Conflict 1990–1991: Diplomacy and War in the New World Order*. Princeton, NJ: Princeton University Press, 1993.

Friedman, Thomas. "Help Wanted: Peacemaker." *Chattanooga Times Free Press*, July 19, 2007, B6.

Frum, David. *The Right Man: The Surprise Presidency of George W. Bush*. New York: Random House, 2003.

Frum, David, and Richard Perle. *An End to Evil: How to Win the War on Terror*. New York: Random House, 2003.

Galbraith, Peter W. *The End of Iraq: How American Incompetence Created a War without End*. New York: Simon & Schuster, 2006.

Gall, Carlotta. "Opium Harvest at Record Level in Afghanistan." *New York Times*, September 3, 2006, section 1, page 1.

———. "Even Musharraf's Allies Question His Re-election Goal." *New York Times*, August 17, 2007, A3.

Gallup/CNN/*USA Today* Poll. "White House 2000: Trial Heats." August 11–12, 2000. <http://www.pollingreport.com/wh2gen1.htm> (July 11, 2006).

Gallup Poll, "White House 2000: Trial Heats." October 4–6, 2000. <http://www.pollingreport.com/wh2gen1.htm> (July 23, 2006).

———. "White House 2000: Presidential Debates." October 17, 2000. <www.polingreport.com> (July 26, 2006).

———. "White House 2000: Presidential Debates." October 18–20, 2000. <http://www.polingreport.com/wh2gen1.htm> (July 26, 2006).

———. September 21–22, 2001. <http://www.pollingreport.com/BushJob1.htm> (June 21, 2006).

Garner, Jay. "Truth, War & Consequence: Interview Gen. Jay Garner." PBS Frontline, October 8, 2001. <http://www.pbs.org/wghh/pages/frontline/shows/truth/interviews/garner.html> (February 19, 2007).

Gedda, George. "Powell Says China Seeks Stronger Ties and to Avoid Tension over Taiwan." Associated Press, July 29, 2001.

Gellman, Barton, and Dafna Linzer. "Pushing the Limits of Wartime Powers." *Washington Post*, December 18, 2005, A1.

Gellman, Barton, and Jo Becker. "A Different Understanding with the President." *Washington Post*, June 24, 2007, A1.

Gellman, Barton, and Walter Pincus. "Depiction of Threat Outgrew Supporting Evidence." *Washington Post*, August 10, 2003, A1.

Gergen, David. "Reliable Sources." CNN, March 5, 2006 (Transcript: 030501CN.V50).

Gibbs, Nancy, and John F. Dickerson. "Inside the Mind of George W. Bush." *Time* 164, no. 10 (September 6, 2004): 24–32.

———. "I've Gained Strength." Interview with President Bush, *Time* 164, no. 10 (September 6, 2004): 38.

Gonzales, Alberto R. "Decision Re Application of the Geneva Convention on Prisoners of War to the Conflict with Al Qaeda and the Taliban." January 25, 2001. <http://www.slate.com/features/whatistorture/LegalMemos.html> (October 29, 2006).

———. "Press Briefing by Attorney General Alberto Gonzales and General Michael Hayden, Principal Deputy Director for National Intelligence." White House, Washington, DC, December 19, 2005.

Gibbs, Nancy, and John F. Dickerson. "Prepared Remarks for Attorney General Alberto R. Gonzales at the Georgetown University Law Center." Washington, DC, January 24, 2006.

———. "Letter to Senator Arlen Specter, Chairman, Committee on the Judiciary." February 28, 2006.

Gordon, Michael R. "U.S.-North Korea Accord Has a 10-Year Timetable." *New York Times*, October 21, 1994, A8.

———. "Cheney Says Next Goal in U.S. War on Terror Is to Block Access to Arms." *New York Times*, March 16, 2002, A8.

———. "News Analysis: Criticizing an Agent of Change as Failing to Adapt." *New York Times*, April 21, 2006, A18.

———. "Military Charts Movement of Conflict in Iraq toward Chaos." *New York Times*, November 1, 2006, A12.

———. "Bush Advisor's Memo Cites Doubts about Iraqi Leader." *New York Times*, November 29, 2006, A1.

———. "Will It Work on the Battlefield?" *New York Times*, December 7, 2006, A1.

Gordon, Michael R., and General Bernard E. Trainor. *COBRA II: The Inside Story of the Invasion and Occupation of Iraq.* New York: Pantheon Books, 2006.

———. "After Invasion, Point Man for Iraq Was Shunted Aside." *New York Times*, March 13, 2006, A8.

Graham, Billy. "Reverend Billy Graham Still Crusading at 86." Interview with Brian Williams, NBC Nightly News, November 22, 2004.

Green, Joshua. "Karl Rove in a Corner." *Atlantic Monthly* 294, no. 4 (November 2004): 102.

Greenstein, Fred I. "The Leadership Style of George W. Bush" Chapter 1 in *The George W. Bush Presidency: An Early Assessment*, edited by Fred I. Greenstein. Baltimore, MD: The Johns Hopkins Press, 2003.

Greenwell, Megan. "Sunnis Quit Cabinet Posts." *Washington Post*, August 2, 2007, A15.

———. "Riots at Iraqi Religious Festival Leave 28 Dead." *Washington Post*, August 29, 2007, A13.

Grey, Stephen. *Ghost Plane: The True Story of the CIA Torture Program.* New York: St. Martin's Press, 2006.

Haass, Richard N. "The New Middle East." *Foreign Affairs* 85, no. 6 (November–December 2006): 2–11.

Halper, Stefan, and Jonathan Clarke. *America Alone: The Neo-Conservatives and the Global Order.* New York: Cambridge University Press, 2004.

Harris Poll, "White House 2000: Republicans." July 17–21, 1998. <http://www.pollingreport.com/wh2rep.htm> (July 7, 2006).

Harrison, Selig Seidenman. *Korean Endgame: A Strategy for Reunification and U.S. Disengagement.* Princeton: Princeton University Press, 2003.

Hatfield, J.H. *Fortunate Son: George W. Bush and the Making of an American President.* New York: St. Martin's Press, 2000.

Hayden, Michael. "Press Briefing by Attorney General Alberto Gonzales and General Michael Hayden, Principal Deputy Director for National Intelligence." White House, Washington, DC, December 19, 2005.

Heclo, Hugh. "The Political Ethos of George W. Bush." Chapter 2 in *The George W. Bush Presidency: An Early Assessment*, edited by Fred I. Greenstein. Baltimore, MD: The Johns Hopkins Press, 2003.

Hersh, Seymour M. "Offense and Defense: The Battle between Donald Rumsfeld and the Pentagon." *New Yorker* 79, no. 7 (April 7, 2003): 43–53.

———. "Selective Intelligence." *New Yorker* 79, no. 11 (May 12, 2003): 44–51.

———. *Chain of Command: The Road from 9/11 to Abu Ghraib.* New York: HarperCollins Publishers Inc., 2004.

————. "The Other War: Why Bush's Afghanistan Problem Won't Go Away." *New Yorker* 80, no. 8 (April 12, 2004): 40–47.

————. "The Gray Zone: How a Secret Pentagon Program Came to Abu Ghraib." *New Yorker* 80, no. 13 (May 24, 2004): 38–44.

————. "Get Out the Vote." *New Yorker* 81, no. 21 (July 25, 2006): 52–57.

————. "The Next Act." *New Yorker* 82, no. 39 (November 27, 2006): 94–107.

————. "The Redirection." *New Yorker* 83, no. 2 (March 5, 2007): 54–60.

Herskowitz, Mickey. *Duty, Honor, Country*. Nashville, TN: Rutledge Hill Press, 2003.

Herzog, Michael. "Can Hamas Be Tamed?" *Foreign Affairs* 85, no. 2 (March–April 2006): 83–94.

Hill, Christopher. "U.S. Envoy Christopher Hill Discusses North Korea Nukes Deal." PBS Online NewsHour, PBS Transcript, February 15, 2007. <http://www.pbs.org/newshour/bb/asia/jan-june07/hill-02–15.html> (June 10, 2007).

Hirsh, Michael. "The Gaza Effect." *Newsweek*, June 25, 2007, 22.

Hirsh, Michael, Melinda Liu, and George Wehrfritz. "'We Are a Nuclear Power.'" *Newsweek* (October 23, 2006): 28–40. <http://www.msnbc.msn.com/id/15265432/site/newsweek/> (June 2007).

Hoge, Warren. "Security Council Supports Sanctions on North Korea." *New York Times*, October 15, 2006, section 1, page 1.

Holmes, Michael, and Christiane Amanpour. "Israel Declares Arafat 'Enemy.'" CNN.com, March 29, 2002. <http://archives.cnn.com/2002/WORLD/meast/03/28/mideast/index.html> (July 9, 2007).

Hughes, Karen. *Ten Minutes from Normal*. New York: Viking Penguin, 2004.

Hughes, Robin. "US Eyes Potential Long-Range Threat from Iran." *Jane's Defence Weekly*, May 9, 2007. <www.janes.com/security/international_security/news/jdw/jdw0705009_1_n.shtml> (June 14, 2007).

Hume, Brit. "An Exclusive Interview with President Bush." Fox News, September 22, 2003. <http://www.foxnews.com/story/0,2933,98111,00.html> (June 21, 2006).

Hutcheson, Ron. "Trip to Israel Explains Bush's Loyalty." McClatchy Newspapers, *Chattanooga Times Free Press*, August 6, 2006, A8.

Ignatius, David. "Bush's Lost Iraqi Election." *Washington Post*, August 30, 2007, A21.

International Court of Justice. "Legal Consequences of the Construction of a Wall in the Occupied Palestinian Territory." Advisory Opinion, International Court of Justice, Press Release 2004/28, July 9, 2004.

Isikoff, Michael, and David Corn. *Hubris: The Inside Story of Spin, Scandal, and the Selling of the Iraq War*. New York: Crown Publishers, 2006.

Jacobson, Gary C. *A Divider, Not a Uniter: George W. Bush and the American People*. New York: Pearson Longman, 2007.

Jahn, George. "Iran Threatens U.S. with 'Harm and Pain.'" Associated Press, *Washington Post*, March 8, 2006.

Janis, Irving L. *Groupthink: Psychological Studies of Policy Decisions and Fiascoes*, 2nd ed. Boston: Houghton Mifflin, 1982.

Jehl, Douglas. "U.S. Report Finds Iraq Was Minimal Weapons Threat in '03." *New York Times*, October 6, 2004, A1.

————. "British Memo on U.S. Plans for Iraq War Fuels Critics." *New York Times*, May 20, 2005, A10.

Jehl, Douglas, and David Johnston. "Rule Change Lets C.I.A. Freely Send Suspects Abroad to Jails." *New York Times*, March 6, 2006, A1.

Johnston, David. "President Intervened in Dispute over Eavesdropping." *New York Times*, May 16, 2007, A1.

Jones, General James L. "The Report of the Independent Commission on the Security Forces of Iraq." Independent Commission on the Security Forces of Iraq, September 6, 2007, 12. <http://www.c-span.org/pdf/jonesreport090607.pdf> (September 14, 2007).

Jones, Jeffrey M. "Americans Felt Uneasy toward Arabs Even before September 11." *Gallup Poll Monthly* 452 (September 2001): 53.

Kahn, Joseph. "Agency Likely to Sue White House to Force Disclosure." *New York Times*, September 8, 2001, A10.

Kaiser, Robert G., and David B. Ottaway. "Saudi Leader's Anger Revealed Shaking Ties." *Washington Post*, February 10, 2002, A1.

Kaplan, Fred. "The Army, Faced with Its Limits." *New York Times*, January 1, 2006, section 4, page 4.

Kassop, Nancy. "The War Power and Its Limits." *Presidential Studies Quarterly* 33, no. 3 (September 2003): 509–529.

Katzman, Kenneth. "The Iran-Libya Sanctions Act (ILSA)." CRS Report for Congress, Congressional Research Service, October 11, 2006, Table I, CRS-4.

———. "The Iran Sanctions Act (ISA)." Congressional Reference Service, January 25, 2007.

Keegan, John. *The Iraq War.* New York: Alfred A. Knopf, 2004.

Kershner, Isabel. "In Nod to Fatah, Israel Removes Militiamen from Wanted List." *New York Times*, July 16, 2007, A4.

Kessler, Glenn. "U.S. Decision On Iraq Has Puzzling Past." *Washington Post*, January 12, 2003, A1.

———. "North Korea Labels Bush a 'Dictator.'" *Washington Post*, May 1, 2005, A22.

———. "South Korea Offers to Supply Energy if North Gives Up Arms." *Washington Post*, July 16, 2005, A16.

———. "U.S. Policy Seen as Big Loser in Palestinian Vote." *Washington Post*, January 28, 2006, A16.

———. "Vote Complicates Area's Diplomacy." *Washington Post*, January 26, 2006, A19.

———. "Conservatives Assail North Korea Accord." *Washington Post*, February 15, 2007, A1.

———. "Push for Democracy Loses Some Energy." *Washington Post*, February 25, 2006, A13.

———. "Cheney Backs Diplomacy on Iran Program, Rice Affirms." *Washington Post*, June 2, 2007, A8.

Kessler, Glenn, and Peter Slevin. "Cheney Is Fulcrum of Foreign Policy." *Washington Post*, October 13, 2002, A1.

Khalilzad, Zalmay. "Why the United Nations Belongs in Iraq." *New York Times*, July 20, 2007, A23.

Khalilzad Zalmay M., and Paul Wolfowitz. "Overthrow Him." *The Weekly Standard*, December 1, 1997.

Khatami, Mohammad. "Transcript of Interview with Iranian President Mohammad Khatami." CNN.com, January 7, 1998. <http://www.cnn.com/WORLD/9801/07/iran/interview.html> (May 22, 2007).

Kibaroglu, Mustafa. "Good for the Shah, Banned for the Mullahs: The West and Iran's Quest for Nuclear Power." *Middle East Journal* 60, no. 2 (Spring 2006): 207–232.

Kim, Kwang-Tae. "IAEA Says North Korea Has Shut Reactor." Associated Press, *Washington Post*, July 16, 2007.

Kirkpatrick, David D. "In Secretly Taped Conversations, Glimpses of the Future President." *New York Times*, February 20, 2005, A1.

Kohut, Andrew. "America's Image in the World: Findings from the Pew Global Attitudes Project." Testimony of Andrew Kohut, President, Pew Research Center, before the Subcommittee on International Organizations, Human Rights and Oversight, Committee on Foreign Affairs, U.S. House of Representatives, March 14, 2007.

Kristof, Nicholas D. "Iran's Proposal for a 'Grand Bargain." April 28, 2007. <http://kristof. blogs.nytimes.com/2007/04/28/irans-proposal-for-a-grand-bargain/> (May 1, 2007).

———. "Diplomacy at Its Worst." *New York Times*, April 29, 2007, 4–13.

Kristol, William. "Testimony of William Kristol to the Senate Foreign Relations Committee." U.S. Senate, Washington, DC, February 7, 2002.

———. "Interview: William Kristol," PBS. "Frontline," January 14, 2003.

Kristol, William, and Robert Kagan. "Toward a Neo-Reaganite Foreign Policy." *Foreign Affairs* 75, no. 4 (July–August 1996): 18–33.

Lake, Anthony. "Confronting Backlash States." *Foreign Affairs* 73, no. 2 (March–April 1994): 45–55.

Lancaster, John. "Hill Is Due to Take Up Anti-Terror Legislation." *Washington Post*, October 9, 2001, A3.

Lancaster, John, and Terry M. Neal. "Heavyweight 'Vulcans' Help Bush Forge a Foreign Policy." *Washington Post*, November 19, 1999, A2.

Lang, W. Patrick. "Drinking the Kool-Aid." *Middle East Policy* 11, no. 2 (Summer 2004): 39–60.

Lardner Jr., George. "Clinton to Be 'Forceful' in China, Aide Says." *Washington Post*, June 15, 1995, A19.

———. "Texas Speaker Reportedly Helped Bush Get into Guard." *Washington Post*, September 21, 1999, A4.

Lardner Jr., George, and Lois Romano. "Tragedy Created Bush Mother-Son Bond." *Washington Post*, July 26, 1999, A1.

———. "At Height of Vietnam, Bush Picks Guard." *Washington Post*, July 28, 1999, A1.

———. "Bush Name Helps Fuel Oil Dealings." *Washington Post*, July 30, 1999, A1.

Lawrence, Jill. "Debate Showcases Personalities." *USA Today*, October 18, 2000, 5A.

Leigh, David. "General Sacked by Bush Says He Wanted Early Elections." *Guardian*, March 18, 2004. <http://www.guardian.co.uk/print/0,4882387-103550,00.html> (February 18, 2007).

Lemann, Nicholas. "The Controller." *New Yorker* 79, no. 11 (May 12, 2003): 68–83.

Lester, Beth. "Gaps Remain in Bush Guard Service." CBSNEWS.com, May 4, 2004.

Leverett, Flynt. "Dealing with Tehran: Assessing U.S. Diplomatic Options toward Iran." Century Foundation Report. New York: The Century Foundation, 2006.

Lifson, Thomas. "GWB: HBS MBA." *The American Thinker*, February 3, 2004. <http://www.americanthinker.com/articles_print.php?article_id=3378> (August 20, 2006).

Lynch, Colum. "Nations Reach Pact on Trade of Small Arms." *Washington Post*, July 22, 2001, A17.

———. "No 'Smoking Guns' So Far, U.N. Is Told." *Washington Post*, January 10, 2003, A1.

MacEachin, Doug, and Janne E. Nolan. "The US and Soviet Proxy War in Afghanistan, 1989–1992: Prisoners of Our Preconceptions?" Working Group Report, No IV, Institute for the Study of Diplomacy, Georgetown University, November 15, 2005.

MacFarquhar, Neil. "Bush's Comments Bolster Old Guard in Tehran." *New York Times*, January 8, 2002, A 11.

Macleod, Scott, Azadeh Moaveni, and Douglas Waller. "Clinton and Khatami Find Relations Balmy?" *Time* 156, no. 12 (September 18, 2000). <http://www.time.com/time/printout/0,8816,997984,00.html> (May 22, 2007).

Mahley, Donald A. "Transcript: Mahley News Conference on Biological Weapons Protocol." Press Conference with Ambassador Donald A. Mahley, Special Negotiator for Chemical and Biological Arms Control Issues, Geneva Switzerland, July 25, 2001.

Mann, James. *Rise of the Vulcans*. New York: Viking, 2004.

Mansfield, Stephen. *The Faith of George W. Bush*. Lake Mary, Florida: Charisma House, 2003.

Manyin, Mark E. and Ryun Jun. "U.S. Assistance to North Korea." Congressional Research Service, Library of Congress, March 17, 2003, CRS-9.

Maples, Michael D. "The Current Situation in Iraq and Afghanistan." Lieutenant General U.S. Army, Director, Defense Intelligence Agency, Statement for the Record, U.S. Senate Armed Services Committee, November 15, 2006.

Mathews, Tom. "The Road to War." *Newsweek* 117, no. 4 (January 28, 1991): 55–66.

Max, D.T. "The Making of the Speech." *New York Times*, October 7, 2001, 6–32.

Mayer, Jane. "Outsourcing Torture." *New Yorker* 81, no. 1 (February 14 and 21, 2005): 106–123.

———. "The Hidden Power: The Legal Mind behind the White House's War on Terror." *New Yorker* 82, no. 20 (July 3, 2006): 44–55.

———. "The Memo." *New Yorker* 82, no. 1 (February 27, 2006): 32–41.

———. "The Black Sites." *New Yorker* 83, no. 22 (August 13, 2007): 46–57.

Mayer, Jane, and Alexandra Robbins. "Dept. of Aptitude: How George W. Made the Grade." *New Yorker* 75 no. 33 (November 8, 1999): 30–32.

Mazzetti, Mark. "U.S. Is Prodding Pakistan Leader to Share Power." *New York Times*, August 16, 2007, A1.

McElvaine, Robert S. "Historians vs. George W. Bush." May 17, 2004. <http://hnn.us/articles/5019.html> (20 November 2006).

Milani, Mohsen M. "Iran's Policy towards Afghanistan." *Middle East Journal* 60, no. 2 (Spring 2006): 235–256.

Milbank, Dana. "Dispelling Doubts with the Rangers." *Washington Post*, July 25, 2000, A1.

Milbank, Dana. *Smashmouth: Two Years in the Gutter with Al Gore and George W. Bush— Notes from the 2000 Campaign Trail.* New York: Basic Books, 2001.

———. "Bush Disavows Hussein-Sept. 11 Link." *Washington Post*, September 18, 2003, A18.

Miller, Greg. "Democracy in Iraq Doubtful, State Dept. Report Says." *Los Angeles Times*, March 14, 2003, A14.

Minutaglio, Bill. *First Son: George W. Bush and the Bush Family Dynasty.* New York: Times Books, 1999.

Mitchell, Alison. "Full of Banter, Bush Goes on the 'Oprah' Circuit." *New York Times*, September 20, 2000, A22.

Moore, David W. "Powell's U.N. Appearance Important to Public." *The Gallup Poll Tuesday Briefing*, February 4, 2003, 88.

Moore, James, and Wayne Slater. *Bush's Brain: How Karl Rove Made George W. Presidential.* New York: John Wiley & Sons, Inc., 2003.

Moore, Molly, and Thomas E. Ricks. "Iranian Leader Warns U.S. of Reprisal." *Washington Post*, April 26, 2006, A1.

Mueller, John. *Policy and Opinion in the Gulf War.* Chicago: University of Chicago Press, 1994.

———. "The Iraq Syndrome." *Foreign Affairs* 84, no. 6 (November–December 2005): 44–54.

Mufson, Steve. "Bush to Pick Up Clinton Talks on N. Korean Missiles." *Washington Post*, March 7, 2001, A20.

———. "Clash with China Strengthens Hardliners." *Washington Post*, April 23, 2001, A9.

Mufson, Steven, and Mike Allen. "U.S. Voices Regret over Chinese Pilot." *Washington Post*, April 5, 2001, A1.

Mullen, Michael G. "Advance Questions for Admiral Michael G. Mullen USN Nominee for the Position of Chairman of the Joint Chiefs of Staff." Senate Armed Services Committee Hearing, U.S. Senate, July 31, 2007. <http://armed-services.senate.gov/statement/2007/July/ Mullen%2007-31-07.pdf> (August 4, 2007).

Myers, Lisa. "Halliburton Operates in Iran Despite Sanctions." MSNBC.com, March 8, 2005. <http://www.msnbc.msn.com/id/7119752/> (May 24, 2007).

Myers, Steven Lee, and David S. Cloud. "Bush Fights Back on Iraq Debate." *New York Times*, September 1, 2007, A1.

Nagourney, Adam, and Janet Elder. "Support for Bush Surges at Home, but Split Remains." *New York Times*, March 22, 2003, A1.

Nakashima, Ellen, and Dan Eggen. "White House Seeks to Restore Its Privileges." *Washington Post*, September 10, 2001, A2.

National Intelligence Estimate. "Prospects for Iraq's Stability: A Challenging Road Ahead." Director of National Intelligence, January 2007. <http://media.washingtonpost.com/wpsrv/ nation/documents/idraq_dni_20070202_release.pdf> (February 2, 2007).

NBC News/*Wall Street Journal* Poll. "White House 2000: Comparing the Candidates." July 27–28, 2000. <http://www.pollingreport.com/wh2gen1.htm> (July 10, 2006).

NBC. "Meet the Press with Tim Russert," NBC News Transcript, February 8, 2004.

9/11 Commission. *The 9/11 Commission Report: Final Report of the National Commission on Terrorist Attacks upon the United States.* New York: W.W. Norton & Company, 2004.

Negroponte, John D. "Annual Threat Assessment of the Director of National Intelligence for the Senate Select Committee on Intelligence." National Intelligence Council, February 2, 2006.

New York Times. "Excerpts from Pentagon's Feb. 18 draft of the Defense Planning Guidance for the Fiscal Years 1994–1999." Special to the *New York Times*, March 8, 1992, 14.

New York Times/CBS News Poll. March 7–11, 2007.

———. September 4–8, 2007. <http://www.nytimes.com/packages/pdf/national/09102007_ poll_results.pdf> (September 10, 2007).

Newport, Frank. "Americans Remain Strongly in Favor of Military Retaliation." *Gallup Poll Monthly* 432 (September 2001): 31.

———. "Americans Favor Diplomacy with North Korea, Not Military Action." Gallup Poll News Service, July 13, 2006.

———. "Public Trusts Iraq Study Group More Than Bush on Iraq." Gallup Poll News Service, December 12, 2006.

————. "Bush Approval Continues to Hold Steady in Low 30s." Gallup Poll News Service, September 14, 2007.

News Services. "No 'Genuine Acceptance' of Disarmament, Blix Says." *Washington Post*, January 28, 2003, A14.

Newsweek. "*Newsweek* Poll." January 24–25, 2007. <http://www.pollingreport.com/bush.htm> (August 25, 2007).

————. "Should We Leave Iraq?" *Newsweek* Poll, July 23, 2007, 28.

Noonan, Peggy. "A Chat in the Oval Office." *Wall Street Journal*, June 25, 2001, A18.

————. "Way Too Much God." Opinion Journal from the *Wall Street Journal* Editorial Page, January 21, 2005.

Nunn, Sam. "When Bush Meets Putin." *Washington Post*, June 12, 2001, A25.

Oberdorfer, Don. "U.S. Decides to Withdraw A-Weapons from S. Korea." *Washington Post*, October 19, 1991, A1.

O'Neil, John. "In Senate, Allies of Bush Attempt to Halt Iraq Vote." *New York Times*, January 30, 2007, A1.

Owen, Diana. "Media Mayhem: Performance of the Press in Election 2000." Chapter 6 in *Overtime! The Election 2000 Thriller*, edited by Larry J. Sabato. New York: Longman Publishers, 2002.

Packer, George. *The Assassins' Gate.* New York: Farrar, Straus and Giroux, 2005.

Paglen, Trevor, and A.C. Thompson. *Torture Taxi: On the Trail of the CIA's Rendition Flights.* Hoboken, NJ: Melville House Publishing, 2006.

Palmer, Elizabeth A. "Terrorism Bill's Sparse Paper Trail May Cause Legal Vulnerabilities." *Congressional Quarterly Weekly* 59, no. 41 (October 27, 2001): 2533–2535.

Pauken, Tom. "The Rise and Fall of the Texas Republican Party: The Rove Machine." *Chronicles Magazine,* November 2004. <http://www.chroniclesmagazine.org/Chronicles/November 2004/1104Pauken.html> (July 12, 2006).

Pauken, Paul. "The Governor as Cheerleader." *Dallas Business Journal,* June 15, 2001. <http://dallas.bizjournals.com/dallas/stories/2001/06/18/editorial3.html> (July 18, 2006).

Perle, Richard. "Richard Perle: The Making of a Neo-Conservative." Transcript from PBS Think Tank with Ben Wattenberg, November 14, 2002.

Perlez, Jane. "Taking a Breather on the Mideast." *New York Times*, July 5, 2001, A6.

Perry, William. "Testimony before the Senate Foreign Relations Committee, Subcommittee on East Asian and Pacific Affairs." U.S. Senate, Washington, DC, October 12, 1999.

Petraeus, General David H. "Report to Congress on the Situation in Iraq." September 10–11, 2007, 2. <http://graphics8.nytimes.com/packages/pdf/world/20070911_policy/Petraeus_Testimony.pdf> (September 11, 2007).

Pew Research Center. "Global Unease with Major World Powers." Pew Global Attitudes Project, June 27, 2007, 3. <http://pewglobal.org/reports/pdf/256.pdf> (June 28, 2007).

Pfiffner, James P. "President George W. Bush and His War Cabinet." Conference on the Presidency, Congress, and the War on Terrorism, University of Florida, February 7, 2003.

————. "Did President Bush Mislead the Country in His Arguments for War with Iraq." *Presidential Studies Quarterly* 43, no. 1 (March 2004): 25–46.

Phillips, Kevin. *American Dynasty: Aristocracy, Fortune, and the Politics of Deceit in the House of Bush.* New York: Viking Penguin, 2004.

Pianin, Eric, and Amy Goldstein. "Bush Drops a Call for Emissions Cuts." *Washington Post*, March 14, 2002, A1.

Pickler, Nedla. "U.S. Tries to Dampen Talk of Iran Strike." Associated Press, *New York Times*, April 10, 2006.

Pincus, Walter. "Report Details Errors before War." *Washington Post*, September 9, 2006, A12.

————. "Waterboarding Historically Controversial." *Washington Post*, October 5, 2006, A17.

————. "NIE Cites 'Uneven' Security Gains, Faults Iraqi Leaders." *Washington Post*, August 24, 2007, A10.

Planin, Eric, and William Drozdiak. "Bush's Reversal Could Affect Global Warming Agreement." *Washington Post*, March 16, 2001, A3.

Pillar, Paul R. "Intelligence, Policy and the War on Iraq." *Foreign Affairs* 85, no. 2 (March–April 2006): 15–27.

Podhoretz, Norman. "The Case for Bombing Iran." *Commentary* 123, no. 6 (June 2007): 17–23.

Pomfret, John. "A Buildup of Irritation in Relations." *Washington Post*, April 3, 2001, A1.

Pomper, Miles A. "Congressional Support May Not Count for Much with U.N. Security Council." *Congressional Quarterly* 60, no. 39 (October 12, 2002): 2676–2677.

Post-gazette.com. "Mission Critical: David Domke Says Bush Is Unique in Offering Himself as God's Prophet for America." <http://www.post-gazette.com/pg/pp/04298/400289.stm> (June 21, 2006).

Powell, Bill. "A New Nuclear World." *Time* 168, no. 15 (October 9, 2006). <http://www.time.com/time/world/article/0,8599,1544026,00.html> (July 30, 2007).

Powell, Colin L. *My American Journey.* New York: Random House, 1995.

———. "Testimony before U.S. Senate Foreign Relations Committee." U.S. Senate, Washington, DC, January 17, 2001.

———. "This Week with Sam Donaldson." ABC, "This Week," February 4, 2001.

———. "Remarks by Secretary of State Colin Powell to the Pool." White House, Washington, DC, March 7, 2001.

———. "Secretary of State Colin Powell Discusses International Affairs." CNN, Interview with Andrea Koppel, May 14, 2001.

———. "Secretary Powell in Hanoi, Vietnam." U.S. Department of State, July 26, 2001.

———. "Draft Decision Memorandum for the President on the Applicability of the Geneva Convention to the Conflict in Afghanistan." January 26, 2002. <http://www.slate.com/features/whatistorture/LegalMemos.html> (October 29, 2006).

———. "U.S. Secretary of State Colin Powell Addresses the U.N. Security Council." Washington, DC, February 5, 2003. <http://www.whitehouse.gov/news/releases/2003/02/20030205-1.html> (March 12, 2007).

———. "Transcript of 9/11 Commission Hearings." 9/11 Commission, March 23, 2004.

Presidential Commission. "Report to the President." Presidential Commission on the Intelligence Capabilities of the United States Regarding Weapons of Mass Destruction, March 31, 2005.

Preston, Julia, with Todd S. Purdum. "Bush's Push on Iraq at U.N." *New York Times*, September 22, 2002, A1.

Priest, Dana. "CIA's Assurances on Transferred Suspects Doubted." *Washington Post*, March 17, 2005, A1.

———. "CIA Holds Terror Suspects in Secret Prisons." *Washington Post*, November 2, 2005, A1.

———. "Wrongful Imprisonment: Anatomy of a CIA Mistake; German Citizen Released after Months in 'Rendition.'" *Washington Post*, December 4, 2005, A1.

———. "Covert CIA Program Withstands New Furor." *Washington Post*, December 30, 2005, A1.

Priest, Dana, and Barton Gellman. "U.S. Decries Abuse but Defends Interrogations." *Washington Post*, December 26, 2002, A1.

Priest, Dana, and Walter Pincus. "Search in Iraq Finds No Banned Weapons." *Washington Post*, October 3, 2003, A1.

Project for the New American Century. "Letter to President Clinton." January 26, 1998. <http://www.newamericancentury.org/iraqclintonletter.htm> (January 4, 2007).

Program on International Policy Attitudes. "US Relations with China." Program Americans in the World: Public Opinion on International Affairs. <http://www.americans-world.org/digest/regional_issues/china/china5,cfm> (August 1, 2006).

Prueher, Joseph W. "Text: Letter from Amb. Prueher to China's Minister of Foreign Affairs." April 11, 2001. <http://www.usconsulate.org.hk/uscn/wh/2001/041103.htm> (August 4, 2006).

Purdum, Todd S. *Time of Our Choosing: America's War in Iraq.* New York: Times Books, 2003.

Quaid, Libby. "Powell Forces Rice to Defend Iraq Planning." Associated Press, April 30, 2006. <http://abcnews.go.com/Politics/wireStory?id=1908265> (July 12, 2006).

Rebhorn, Wayne A. *The Prince and Other Writings.* New York: Barnes & Noble Classics, 2003.

Record, Jeffrey. "Bounding the Global War on Terrorism." Strategic Studies Institute, U.S. Army War College, December 2003.

Republican Leadership Council Poll. February 1–4, 1999. Conducted by Greg Strimple & Associates, "White House 2000: Republicans." <http://www.pollingreport.com/wh2rep.htm> (July 7, 2006).

Renshon, Stanley A. *In His Father's Shadow: The Transformations of George W. Bush*. New York: Palgrave, 2004.

Reynolds, Maura. "'Axis of Evil' Phrase Caused Real Damage, Experts Opine." Article from the *Los Angeles Times, Chattanooga Times Free Press*, January 22, 2003.

Reuters. "Bremer Says U.S. Was Surprised by Insurgency." *Washington Post*, January 7, 2006, A4.

———. "Fact Box: North Korea's Missile Arsenal." *Washington Post*, July 4, 2006.

Revkin, Andrew C. "178 Nations Reach a Climate Accord." *New York Times*, July 24, 2001, A1.

Rice, Condoleezza. "Promoting the National Interest." *Foreign Affairs* 79, no. 1 (January–February 2000): 45–62.

———. "Nightline with Ted Koppel." NBC, April 11, 2001.

———. "Transcript of Condoleezza Rice on Face the Nation." CBS, "Face the Nation," July 29, 2001.

———. "Why We Know Iraq Is Lying." *New York Times*, January 23, 2003.

———. "9/11: For the Record." *Washington Post*, March 22, 2004, A21.

———. "Interview on The NewsHour with Jim Lehrer." PBS, "NewsHour," Washington, DC, July 28, 2005.

———. "Remarks upon Her Departure for Europe." Andrews Air Force Base, December 5, 2005.

Ricks, Thomas E. *Fiasco: The American Military Adventure in Iraq*. New York: The Penguin Press, 2006.

———. "Cheney Stands by His 'Last Throes' Remark." *Washington Post*, June 20, 2006, A13.

———. "In Iraq, Military Forgot Lessons of Vietnam." *Washington Post*, July 23, 2006, A1.

Ricks, Thomas E., and Ann Scott Tyson. "Abizaid Says Withdrawal Would Mean More Unrest." *Washington Post*, November 16, 2006, A22.

Ricks, Thomas E., and Peter Baker. "Tipping Point for War's Supporters?" *Washington Post*, October 29, 2006, A1.

Risen, James. "C.I.A. Sees a North Korean Missile Threat." *New York Times*, February 3, 1999, A6.

———. "Ex-Inspector Says C.I.A. Missed Disarray in Iraqi Arms Program." *New York Times*, January 26, 2004, A1.

———. "Evolving Nature of Al Qaeda Is Misunderstood, Critic Says." *New York Times*, November 8, 2004, A18.

———. *State of War: The Secret History of the CIA and the Bush Administration*. New York: Free Press, 2006.

Risen, James, and Eric Lichtblau. "Bush Lets U.S. Spy on Callers without Courts." *New York Times*, December 16, 2005, A1.

Robin, Corey. "Grand Designs: How 9/11 Unified Conservatives in Pursuit of Empire." *Washington Post*, May 2, 2004, B1.

Robinson, Walter V. "1-Year Gap in Bush's Guard Duty." *The Boston Globe*, May 23, 2000.

Rohde, David. "Afghan Police Are Set Back as Taliban Adapt." *New York Times*, September 2, 2007, 1–1.

Rohde, David, and David E. Sanger. "Losing the Advantage," *New York Times*, August 12, 2007, A1.

Romano, Lois, and George Lardner Jr., "Bush's Life-Changing Year," *Washington Post*, July 25, 1999, A1.

———. "Young Bush, a Political Natural, Revs Up." *Washington Post*, July 29, 1999, A1.

———. "Bush's Move Up to the Majors." *Washington Post*, July 31, 1999, A1.

Rosati, Jerel A. *The Politics of United States Foreign Policy*, 3rd edition. Belmont, CA: Wadsworth/Thomson Learning, 2004.

Rosen, Jeffrey. "Magazine Review." *New York Times*, September 9, 2007, 6–40.

Rosin, Hanna. "Bush's Resentment of 'Elites' Informs Bid." *Washington Post*, July 23, 2000, A1.

———. "Applying Personal Faith to Public Policy." *Washington Post*, July 24, 2000, A1.

Rostom, Aram. "ABC: Chalabi's Defeat Presents Quandry." MSNBC, December 22, 2005. <http://www.msnbc.msn.com/id/10575121> (June 20, 2007).

Rubin, Barry. "Israel's New Strategy." *Foreign Affairs* 85, no. 4 (July–August 2006): 111–125.

Rumsfeld, Donald. "Transcript of Rumsfeld in Munich with Europe's Defense Ministers." CNN, February 3, 2001.

Rumsfeld, Donald. "The '21st Century Transformation' of U.S. Armed Forces." National Defense University, Fort McNair, Washington, DC, January 31, 2002.

———. "Approval of Counter-Resistance Techniques." December 2, 2002. <http://www.gwu.edu/~nsarchiv/NSAEBB/NSAEBB127/> (November 1, 2006).

———. "Transcript: Interview with Donald Rumsfeld." CNN Live with Larry King, December 18, 2002. <http://transcripts.cnn.com/TRANSCRIPTS/0212/18/lkl.00.html> (August 3, 2006).

———. "Beyond 'Nation-Building.'" *Washington Post*, September 25, 2003, A33.

Rumsfeld, Donald. "Transcript of 9/11 Commission Hearings." 9/11 Commission Hearings, March 23, 2004.

Rutenberg, Jim. "General Defends Rumsfeld, with a Caveat." *New York Times*, April 17, 2006, A17.

———. "Ex-Aide Details A Loss of Faith in the President." *New York Times*, April 1, 2007, 1–1.

———. "In Book, Bush Peeks Ahead to His Legacy." *New York Times*, September 2, 2007.

Saad, Lydia. "Iran Threat Poses Leadership Crisis for Americans." Gallup Poll News Service, February 15, 2006.

———. "Majority Predicts History Will Judge Bush Harshly." Gallup Poll News Service, December 13, 2006.

Sack, Kevin. "Oprah Show Lets Gore Reach Out to Women." *New York Times*, September 12, 2000, A22.

Safire, William. "Bush Speaks Out." *New York Times*, April 15, 1999, A31.

Salem, Paul. "The Future of Lebanon." *Foreign Affairs* 85, no. 6 (November–December 2006): 13–22.

Sandalow, Mark. "For Bush, the Record Tells All." *San Francisco Chronicle*, June 29, 1999, A1.

Sanger, David E. "Bush Is Offering Taiwan Some Arms but Not the Best." *New York Times*, April 24, 2001, A1.

———. "A Day after Seeing Putin, A Harder-Line Bush Emerges." *New York Times*, July 24, 2001, A8.

———. "Bush's European Theater." *New York Times*, July 25, 2001, A6.

———. "Bush Aides Say Tough Tone Put Foes on Notice." *New York Times*, January 31, 2002, A1.

———. "Bush Sees 'Urgent Duty' to Pre-empt Attack by Iraq." *New York Times*, October 8, 2002, A1.

———. "North Korea Says It Has a Program on Nuclear Arms." *New York Times*, October 17, 2002, A1.

———. "Bush's Shift: Being Patient with Foes." *New York Times*, July 10, 2006, A9.

———. "North Korea Says It Tested a Nuclear Device Underground." *New York Times*, October 9, 2006, A1.

Sanger, David E., and Don Van Natta Jr. "In Four Days, A National Crisis Changes Bush's Presidency." *New York Times*, September 16, 2001, section 1, page 1.

Sanger David E., and Eric Schmitt. "Cheney's Power No Longer Goes Unquestioned." *New York Times*, September 10, 2006, section 1, page 1.

Sanger, David E., and Mark Mazzetti. "Cheney Warns Pakistan to Act on Terror." *New York Times*, February 26, 2007, A1.

Savage, Charlie. "Bush Challenges Hundreds of Laws." *Boston Globe*, April 30, 2006. <http://www.boston.com/news/nation/articles/2006/04/30/bush_challenges_hundreds_of_laws> (August 23, 2007).

Saxe, John Godfrey. "The Blind Men and the Elephant." <http://www.wordfocus.com/word-act-blindmen.html> (June 14, 2006).

Scheuer, Michael. *Imperial Hubris: Why the West Is Losing the War on Terror.* Washington, DC: Brassey's, Inc., 2004.

———. "Interview on May 2006." *Alleged Secret Detentions and Unlawful Interstate Transfers Involving Council of Europe Member States.* Rapporteur: Dick Mary (Switzerland), Committee on Legal Affairs and Human Rights, Parliamentary Assembly, Council of Europe, June 7, 2006. <http://assembly.coe.int/CommitteeDocs/2006/20060606_Ejdoc162006PartII-FINAL.pdf> (December 6, 2006).

Schlesinger, Robert, and Bryan Bender. "Plan Suggests Shift on Rumsfeld." *Boston Globe*, October 9, 2003, A45.

Schmitt, Eric. "Pentagon Contradicts General on Iraq Occupation Force's Size." *New York Times*, February 28, 2003, A1.

Schneider, Daniel B., and Damien Cave. "Security Council Approves U.N. Mandate in Iraq to Seek Reconciliation." *New York Times*, August 11, 2007, A6

Schoen, Gary C. *First In: An Insider's Account of How the CIA Spearheaded the War on Terrorism in Afghanistan.* New York: Ballantine Books, 2005.

Schweid, Barry. "Rice Says U.S. Position on Hamas Unchanged." Associated Press, *Washington Post*, January 26, 2006.

Schweizer Peter, and Rochelle Schweizer. *The Bushes: Portrait of a Dynasty.* New York: Doubleday, 2004.

Sciolino, Elaine. "U.S. Britain and France Draft U.N. Resolution on Iran's Nuclear Ambitions." *New York Times*, May 3, 2006, A12.

Sciolino, Elaine, and Patrick E. Tyler. "Some Pentagon Officials and Advisers Seek to Oust Iraq's Leader in War's Next Phase." *New York Times*, October 12, 2001, B6.

Scowcroft, Brent. "Interview." CBS, "Face the Nation," August 4, 2002.

————. "Don't Attack Saddam." *Wall Street Journal*, August 15, 2002, A12.

Seelye, Katharine Q. "Marital Status Is Shaping Women's Leanings, Surveys Find." *New York Times*, September 20, 2000, A23.

Shah, Taimoor, and Carlotta Gall. "Afghan Rebels Find Aid in Pakistan, Musharraf Admits." *New York Times*, August 13, 2007, A6.

Shane, Scott, and Eric Lichtblau. "Cheney Pushed U.S. to Widen Eavesdropping." *New York Times*, May 14, 2006, A1.

Shanker, Thom. "White House Says the U.S. Is Not a Loner, Just Choosy." *New York Times*, July 31, 2001, A1.

————. "General Opposes Adding to U.S. Forces in Iraq, Emphasizing International Solutions for Region." *New York Times*, December 20, 2006, A12.

Shanker, Thom, and Warren Hoge. "Rice Asserts U.S. Plans No Attack on North Korea." *New York Times*, October 11, 2006, A1.

Sharon, Ariel. "Ariel Sharon Describes 'Disengagement Plan." Speech at Herzliya Conference, December 18, 2003. <http://www.jewishvirtuallibrary.org/jsource/Peace/Sharon_1203.html> (July 9, 2007).

Sherman, Wendy R. "North Korea: Past Progress and Next Steps." Address to U.S. Institute of Peace, March 6, 2001.

Singer, Peter. *The President of Good & Evil: The Ethics of George W. Bush.* New York: Dutton, 2004.

Sipress, Alan. "U.S. Officials Mostly Silent." *Washington Post*, March 30, 2002, A1.

Skinner, David. "Matters of the Heart." September 20, 2000. <www.salon.com> (July 21, 2006).

Slater, Wayne. "Rivals Again Fault Bush in McCain Flap." *Dallas Morning News*, December 2, 1999, 39A.

————. "Records of Bush's Ala. Military Duty Can't Be Found." *Dallas Morning News*, June 26, 2000, A6.

Slavin, Barbara, and Dave Moniz. "War in Iraq's Aftermath Hits Troops Hard." *USA TODAY*, July 21, 2003. <http://www.usatoday.com/news/world/iraq/2003-07-21-war-aftermath_x.htm> (March 25, 2007).

Slevin, Peter. "Rising U.S. Death Toll in Iraq Spurs Concern." *Washington Post*, June 20, 2003, A16.

Smith, R. Jeffrey. "N. Korea, U.S. Pledge Closer Ties." *Washington Post*, August 13, 1994, A1.

————. "Report Details Missteps in Data Collection." *Washington Post*, March 10, 2007, A1.

Solarz, Stephen J., and Paul Wolfowitz. "How to Overthrow Saddam." Letters to the Editor, *Foreign Affairs* 78, no. 2 (March 1999): 160.

Sontag, Deborah. "Clinton Watches as Palestinians Drop Call for Israel's Destruction." *New York Times*, December 15, 1998, A1.

Squitieri, Tom, and Susan Page. "Rumsfeld: Al-Qaeda-Saddam Link is Weak." *USA Today*, October 5, 2004, 14A.

Stahl, Leslie. "Interview with Steve Hadley." CBS News, Transcript of "60 Minutes," March 21, 2004.

Stares Justin, and Philip Sherwell. "EU Concealed Deal with US to Allow 'Rendition' Flights."*London Telegraph*, November 12, 2005. <http://www.telegraph.co.uk/core/Content/displayPrintable.jhtml;jsessionid=3J4G4XCUUFGULQFIQMFSFFWAVCBQ0IV0?xml=/news/2005/12/11/wrendition11.xml&site=5&page=0> (January 28, 2007).

Starr, Barbara, and Dana Bash. "Head of U.S. Command: Iraq Civil War Possible." CNN.com, August 3, 2006. <http://www.cnn.com/2006/POLITICS/08/03/iraq.hearing> (June 24, 2007).

Stevens, Stuart. *The Big Enchilada: Campaign Adventures with the Cockeyed Optimists from Texas Who Won the Biggest Prize in* Politics. New York: The Free Press, 2001.

Stevenson, Richard W., and Adam Liptak. "Cheney Defends Eavesdropping without Warrants." *New York Times*, December 21, 2005, A36.

Stevenson, Richard W., and Thom Shanker. "Ex-Arms Monitor Urges an Inquiry on Iraqi Threat." *New York Times*, January 29, 2004, A1.

Stolberg, Sheryl Gay. "An Eye for Detail and the Resolve to Push Change." *New York Times*, June 19, 2006, A15.

Strobel, Warren P., and Jonathan S. Landay. "Intelligence Agencies Warned about Growing Local Insurgency in Late 2003." Knight Ridder Newspapers, *Chattanooga Times Free Press*, February 28, 2006, A3.

Strobel, Warren P., and Nancy A. Youssef. "Worry of U.S. War with Iran Grows." McClatchy Newspapers, *Chattanooga Times Free Press*, August 19, 2007, A5.

Struck, Doug. "Tortured Man Gets Apology from Canada." *Washington Post*, January 27, 2007, A14.

Sullivan, Kevin. "Rice Rules Out Aiding Hamas-Led Government." *Washington Post*, January 30, 2006, A10.

————. "Views of U.S. Drop Sharply in Worldwide Opinion Poll." *Washington Post*, January 23, 2007, A14.

Sullivan, Rohan. "Poll: Support for Musharraf Plummets." Associated Press, August 1, 2007. <http://www.boston.com/news/world/asia/articles/2007/08/01/poll_support_for_musharraf_plummets/> (August 12, 2007).

Suskind, Ron. *The Price of Loyalty: George W. Bush, the White House, and the Education of Paul O'Neill*. New York: Simon & Schuster, 2004.

————. *The One Percent Doctrine: Deep inside America's Pursuit of Its Enemies since 9/11*. New York: Simon & Schuster, 2006.

Sussman, Dalia. "Poll Shows View of Iraq War Is Most Negative Since Start." *New York Times*, May 25, 2007, A16.

Swansbrough, Robert H. "A Kohutian Analysis of President Bush's Personality and Style in the Persian Gulf Crisis." *Political Psychology* 15, no. 2 (June 1994): 227–276.

Taft IV, William H. "Comments on Your (Counsel to the President) Paper on the Geneva Conventions." February 2, 2002. <http://www.slate.com/features/whatistorture/LegalMemos.html> (October 29, 2006).

Tanenhaus, Sam. "Bush's Brain Trust." *Vanity Fair* 515 (July 2003): 114–118, 164–169.

Tenet, George J. "In the Words of the C.I.A. Director: 'Why Haven't We Found the Weapons?'" *New York Times*, February 6, 2004, A12.

————. "Testimony of George Tenet, Director of the Central Intelligence Agency." Transcript 9/11 Commission Hearings, March 24, 2004.

————. "Testimony of George Tenet, CIA Director." National Commission on Terrorist Attacks upon the United States," Tenth Public Hearing, April 14, 2004.

Tenet, George, with Bill Harlow. *At the Center of the Storm: My Years at the CIA*. New York: HarperCollinsPublishers, 2007.

Thomas, Evan, and Roy Gutman. "See George. See George Learn Foreign Policy." *Newsweek* 137 (June 18, 2001): 20–23.

Thomas, Evan, and Thomas Wolffe. "Bush's Bubble: Can He Widen His Circle?" *Newsweek*, December 19, 2005, 35.

Thomma, Steven. "Americans Want U.S. to Move On." McClatchy Newspapers, *Chattanooga Times Free Press*, September.ber 2, 2007, A13.

Time Special Report. "America Is in a Military Mood." *Time* (September 13, 2001). Telephone survey of 1,082 Americans by Harris Interactive. <www.time.com/time/nation/printout/0,8816,174941,00.html> (February 2, 2007).

Tumulty, Karen. "The Rove Warrior." *Time* 164 (December 27, 2004): 60–72.

Tyler, Patrick E. "Putin Invites West to Work On a Defense for Missiles." *New York Times*, February 21, 2001, A5.

Tyson, Ann Scott. "General Says Army Will Need to Grow." *Washington Post*, December 15, 2006, A1.

Ullman, Harlan K., and James P. Wade. *Shock & Awe: Achieving Rapid Dominance* Washington, DC: National Defense University Press, 1996.

Unger, Craig. *House of Bush, House of Saud: The Secret Relationship between the World's Two Most Powerful Dynasties*. New York: Scribner, 2004.

U.S. Department of Defense. "2000 Report to Congress: Military Situation on the Korean Peninsula." Secretary of Defense, U.S. Department of Defense, September 12, 2000. <http://www.defenselink.mil/news/Sep2000/korea09122000.html> (June 7, 2007).

———. "Principle Wars in Which the United States Participated U.S. Military Personnel Serving and Casualties." <http://siadapp.dmdc.osd.mil/personnel/CASUALTY/WCPRINCIPAL.pdf> (June 3, 2007).

———. "National Security Strategy." U.S. Department of Defense, March 2006. <http://www.whitehouse.gov/nsc/nss/2006/> (June 7, 2007).

———. "Review of Pre-Iraqi War Activities of the Office of the Under Secretary of Defense for Policy: Executive Summary." Office of Inspector General, Department of Defense, Report No. 07-ISTE1,-04 (Project Yo. D2006-DIYT01–0077 000), February 9, 2007. <http://www.dodig.mil/IGInformation/archives/Unclass%20%20Executive%20Summary.pdf> (February 10, 2007).

U.S. Department of State. "Objectives." Future of Iraq Project, U.S. Department of State, November 1, 2002. <http://www.gwu.edu/~nsarchiv/NSAEBB/NSAEBB163/index.htm> (February 15, 2007).

———. "Roadmap to Solution of Israeli-Palestinian Conflict." U.S. Department of State, April 30, 2003.

———. "North Korea—Denuclearization Action Plan." U.S. Department of State, Washington, DC, February 13, 2007.

U.S. Government Accountability Office. "Securing, Stabilizing, and Rebuilding Iraq: Iraqi Government Has Not Met Most Legislative, Security, and Economic Benchmarks." Report to Congressional Committees, U.S. Government Accountability Office, September 2, 2007.

U.S. Senate. "Senate Resolution 98 (Byrd-Hagel Resolution)." 105th Congress, 1st Session, July 25, 1997.

———. "Report on the U.S. Intelligence Community's Prewar Intelligence Assessments on Iraq." Select Committee on Intelligence, U.S. Senate, July 7, 2004. <http://www.globalsecurity.org/intell/library/congress/2004_rpt/iraq-wmd-intell_toc.htm> (March 11, 2007).

———. "Prewar Intelligence Assessments about Postwar Iraq." U.S. Senate, Select Committee on Intelligence, 110th Congress, 1st Session, Appendix A, 13. <http://intelligence.senate.gov/prewar.pdf> (May 26, 2007).

———. "Prewar Intelligence Assessments about Postwar Iraq." Report of the Select Committee on Intelligence, U.S. Senate, May 20, 2007, 6.

U.S. Supreme Court. *Hamdan v Rumsfeld*, Decided June 29, 2006. <http://www.supremecourtus.gov/opinions/05pdf/05-184.pdf> (July 18, 2006).

United Nations. "Press Release SC/7564." UN Security Council, August 11, 2002.

VandeHei, Jim and Paul Blustein. "Bush's Response to the Ports Deal Faulted as Tardy." *Washington Post*, February 26, 2006, A5.

Van Natta Jr., Don. "Leaders: Bush Was Set on Path to War, Memo by British Adviser Says." *New York Times*, March 27, 2006, A1.

Verhovek, Sam Howe. "Is There Room on a Republican Ticket for Another Bush?" *New York Times Magazine*, September 13, 1998, 52.

Vick, Karl. "Bush's Support for Reformers Backfires in Iran." *Washington Post*, August 3, 2002, A12.

Vick, Karl, and Dafna Linzer. "Iran Declares Nuclear Advance." *Washington Post*, April 12, 2006, A1.

Voter News Service. "Presidential Election Exit Poll." November 7, 2000. <http://www.msnbc.com/m/d2k/g/polls.asp?office=P&state=N1> (July 26, 2006).

Waldman, Paul. "Political Discussion in Primary States." In *Annals of the American Academy of Political and Social Science*, 572 (November 2000), 29–32.

Walsh, Edward. "Bush's Style Succeeded Even as Tax Plan Failed." *Washington Post*, November 25, 1999, A1.

Washington Post. "Washington in Brief." *Washington Post*, July 23, 1998.

Washington Post. "*Washington Post*-ABC News Poll." September 4–7, 2007, *Washington Post*, September 9, 2007. <http://www.washingtonpost.com/wp-srv/politics/polls/postpoll_090907.html> (September 9, 2007).

Washington Post-ABC News. "Terrorist Attacks," *Washington Post*, September 11, 2001. <http://www.washingtonpost.com/wp-srv/politics/polls/vault/stories/date091201.htm> (April 2, 2007).

Washington Post-ABC News Poll. "America at War." December 21, 2001. December 18–19, 2001. <www.washingtonpost.com/wp-srv/politics/polls/vault/stories/data122101.htm> (February 2, 2007).

Washington Post-ABC News Poll. "America at War." December 21, 2001. Survey conducted December 18–19, 2001. <www.washingtonpost.com/wp-srv/politics/polls/vault/stories/data122101.htm> (February 2, 2007).

Washington Post-ABC News. "Powell's U.N. Address." *Washington Post*-ABC News Poll, February 6, 2003.

Weiner, Tim. "C.I.A. Head Surveys World's Hot Spots." *New York Times*, January 26, 1994, A5.

———. "Criticism Appears to Doom Republican Budget Tactic." *New York Times*, October 1, 1999, A20.

Weisman, Steven R. "Bush Team Urges Bold Inspections of Iraq's Arsenal." *New York Times*, October 21, 2002, A1.

———. "Rice Admits U.S. Underestimated Hamas Strength." *New York Times*, January 30, 2006, A1.

———. "Cheney Warns of 'Consequences' for Iran on Nuclear Issue." *New York Times*, March 8, 2006, A14.

White, Josh. "New Rules of Interrogation Forbids Use of Harsh Tactics." *Washington Post*, September 7, 2006, A1.

———. "Interrogation Research Is Lacking, Report Says." *Washington Post*, January 16, 2007, A15.

White, Wayne. "Testimony Delivered to Ad Hoc Senate Hearing on Pre-War Iraq Intelligence & Related Matters." Washington, DC, Middle East Institute, June 26, 2006. <http://www.mideasti.org/articles/doc535.html> (20, June 2007).

Whitlock, Craig. "Testimony Helps Detail CIA's Post-9/11 Reach." *Washington Post*, December 16, 2006, A1.

———. "Germans Charge 13 CIA Operatives in Germany Kidnapping." *Washington Post*, February 1, 2007, A1.

Wike, Richard. "Pakistanis Increasingly Reject Terrorism…and the U.S." Pew Research Center Publications, August 8, 2007. <http://pewresearch.org/pubs/561/pakistan-terrorism> (August 13, 2007).

Wilbank, Dana. "Colonel Finally Saw Whites of Their Eyes." *Washington Post*, October 20, 2005, A4.

Wilentz, Sean. "The Worst President in History?" *Rolling Stone* 999 (May 4, 2006). <http://www.rollingstone.com/news/story/9961300/the_worst_president_in_history/print> (November 20, 2006).

Wilkerson, Col. Lawrence. "Weighing the Uniqueness of the Bush Administration's National Security Decision-Making Process: Boon or Danger to American Democracy?" New American Foundation, Washington, DC, October 19, 2005.

Wilson, Scott. "Hamas Makes Strong Showing in Vote." *Washington Post*, January 26, 2006, A1.

———. "Israeli War Plan Had No Exit Strategy." *Washington Post*, October 21, 2006, A1.

———. "Official Panel Accuses Israeli Leaders of Multiple Failures in Lebanon War." *Washington Post*, May 1, 2007, A12.

———. "With Hamas Takeover, Tough Calls for Israel." *Washington Post*, June 30, 2007, A1.

Wolfowitz, Paul D. "Clinton's First Year." *Foreign Affairs* 73, no. 1 (January–February 1994): 28–44.

————. "Victory Came Too Easily: Review of Rick Atkinson, *Crusade: the Untold Story of the Gulf War.*" *National Interest* 35 (Spring 1994): 87–93.

————. "Deputy Secretary Wolfowitz Statement on Berets." U.S. Department of Defense, May 1, 2001.

————. "Deputy Secretary Wolfowitz Interview with Sam Tanenhaus, *Vanity Fair,* July 2003." DoD News, May 9, 2003. <http://www.defenselink.mil/transcripts/2003/tr20030509-depsecdef0223.html> (March 13, 2007).

————. "Address on Iraqi Disarmament." Council on Foreign Relations, New York, January 23, 2003.

Wong, Edward. "Iraqi Officials Declare Charter Has Been Passed." *New York Times,* October 26, 2005, A1.

Woods, Kevin., James Lacey, and Williamson Murray. "Saddam's Delusions: The View from the Inside." *Foreign Affairs* 85, no. 3 (May–June 2006): 2–26.

Woodward, Bob. *The Commanders.* New York: Simon & Schuster, 1991.

————. *Bush at War.* New York: Simon & Schuster, 2002.

————. *Plan of Attack.* New York: Simon & Schuster, 2004.

————. *State of Denial.* New York: Simon & Schuster, 2006.

Wren, Christopher S. "Albright Sits Face to Face with Iranian." *New York Times,* September 16, 2000, A6.

Wright, Robin. "U.S. Turns Up Heat on Syria to Leave Lebanon." *Washington Post,* March 3, 2005, A20.

————. "In Lebanon's Crisis, a Chance for U.S. to Broaden the Stakes." *Washington Post,* July 26, 2006, A12.

————. "In Gulf, Cheney Pointedly Warns Iran." *Washington Post,* May 12, 2007, A1.

————. "Iranian Unit to Be Labeled 'Terrorist.'" *Washington Post,* August 15, 2007, A1.

Wright, Robin, and Ann Scott Tyson. "Joint Chiefs Advise Change in War Strategy." *Washington Post,* December 14, 2006, A1.

Wright, Robin, and Thomas E. Ricks. "Bush Supports Israel's Move against Hezbollah." *Washington Post,* July 19, 2006, A10.

Yagielski, Janine, and Kathleen Hayden. "Bush Wins Iowa GOP Straw Poll." <CNN.com/ALLPOLITICS> (August 15, 1999).

Yoo, John C. "Letter to Albert Gonzales, Counsel to the President." August 1, 2002. <http://www.gwu.edu/~nsarchiv/NSAEBB/NSAEBB127/> (November 1, 2006).

Yoo, John, and Robert J. Delahunty. "Memorandum for William J. Haynes II, General Counsel, Department of Defense." January 9, 2002. <http://www.slate.com/features/whatistorture/LegalMemos.html> (October 29, 2006).

Zernike, Kate. "Democrats Try to Increase Leverage over Iraq Policy." *New York Times,* January 27, 2001, A8.

Zinni, Anthony. "Straight Talk from General Anthony Zinni." Lecture at UCLA's Ronald W. Burkle Center for International Relations, Los Angeles, California, May 11, 2004.

————. "Remarks at CID Board of Directors Dinner." Center for Defense Information, May 12, 2004. <http://www.cdi.org/program/document.cfm?DocumentID=2208&from_page=/index.cfm> (August 2, 2007).

Index

Abbas, Mahmoud, (President of Palestinian
    Authority), 186
  Fatah/Hamas tensions, 187
  relinquish Gaza Strip, 188
Addington, David (counsel to Vice President
    Cheney), 115, 120–1, 204
Afghanistan (Islamic Republic of Afghanistan)
  Geneva Convention restrictions, 107–8
  Taliban resurgence, 199
  war 2001, 95, 100, 102–3, 198–9
Ahmadinejad, Mahmoud (President of Iran)
  criticism of U.S. invasion of Iraq, 167
  right to nuclear conversion, 165
Alexander, Lamar (former Secretary of
    Education)
  2000 presidential GOP candidate, 57
Allawi, Ayad (Prime Minister of Iraq), 147
  CIA favored leader, 178–89
Allison, Graham, 11–14
  administration lacked terrorism strategy, 92
  axis of evil, 159
  decision-making analytical approach, 121
  government organization model, 97–101,
      118, 139, 142, 149, 155
  government politics model, 100–3, 120–1,
      144, 153–5, 175, 176, 193
  rational actor model, 91, 97, 99–101, 103,
      117, 136, 142, 154, 174, 176, 193
al Qaeda
  in Afghanistan, 93, 129, 191
  9/11 attacks, xvii, 105
  1996 terrorist bombing Khobar Towers,
      Saudi Arabia, 15
  1998 terrorist bombings U.S. Tanzania and
      Kenya embassies, 91, 94
  in Pakistan, 191
  prisoners of war, 107–8, 119–20
  terrorists, 4, 9–10, 16, 19–20, 92–3, 98, 102,
      127
  U.S. target, 96–8, 100, 103, 125
al Qaeda in Iraq, 200, 207
Arafat, Yasser (President of Palestinian
    Authority)
  death, 186
  Israeli siege and isolation, 185
  Oslo Accords, 182
  Saudi support and ultimatum Bush, 184
  Wye River Memorandum, 183
Arbusto Energy, 30–1

Armitage, Richard (Deputy Secretary of State,
    2001–2005)
  9/11 hearings, 99
  objection to Iraq occupation, 144, 179
  political career, 75–6
Ashcroft, John (U.S. Attorney General)
  CIA renditions, 112
  hospital administration conflict, 116–17
  indictments mention Iran, 162
  interrogation briefings, 122
  Patriot Act, 105, 107–8
Atwater, Lee, 7–8, 60
  national College Republicans, 38
  1988 presidential campaign, 32–3, 53
axis of evil, 3, 18–19, 82, 131, 168, 174–6, 198
  Iranian target for U.S., 163–4
  weapons of mass destruction, 159

Berger, Sandy (National Security Advisor,
    1997–2001), 98, 100
Berntsen, Gary (CIA agent), 96, 101
Bhutto, Benazir (exiled Pakistani leader), 192
bin Laden, Osama (leader of al Qaeda), 10, 103,
    200
  Afghanistan, 15–17, 100
  9/11 involvement, 92–3
  opposition to Northern Alliance, 94
Black, Cofer (Director, Counter Terrorism
    Center), 15, 94
Blair, Tony (British Prime Minister)
  de-Baathification criticism, 146
  G-8 summit, 6
  Iraq war planning, 131–2, 137
Blind Men and Elephant, xvii, xix, xvix, 213
Bolten, Joshua (White House Chief of Staff,
    2004–), xvii, 205
Bradley, Bill (former U.S. Senator, New Jersey), 61
Bremer, L. Paul III (U.S. Ambassador and
    Special Envoy to Iraq, 2003–2004)
  de-Bathification criticism, 17
  post-war Iraq plan, 178
  presidential envoy to Iraq, 145–6, 193
  pressure for more troops in Iraq, 148
Buchanan, Pat, 57, 65
Bush, Barbara (daughter), 46
Bush, Barbara (mother), 23–4, 28–9, 35
Bush Exploration, 31
Bush, George H. W. (President, 1989–1993)
  attempted assassination of, 126

China policy, 78
Middle East peace, 182
1988 presidential campaign, 23
1991 Gulf War, 123–5, 138
oil industry, 23–31: *see also* Bush-Overbey Oil
removal U.S. nuclear weapons in South Korea, 169
tested by fire, xvii
vice president, 23
Bush, George W. (President, 2001–), 3–4, 11, 54, 71–7
Afghanistan: al Qaeda presence, 209; policy, 198–9
Bush Doctrine, 93, 128, 214
China policy, 78: spy plane crisis 2001, 79–81
credibility gap, 207
decision making, 202–5: 9/11 influence, 197
domestic policy, 54–5, 105
education, 5, 25–6: Andover, 5, 25, 28; Harvard, 7, 28–9; Skull and Bones Society, 26; Yale, 5–6, 25, 28
foreign policy, 10, 19–20, 83, 84–7, 98, 127–8; forward leaning, 197–8
governor of Texas (1995–2001), 6, 9, 20, 35, 44–52
House of Representatives campaign 1978, 30–1, 53
Iran: diplomacy with Iran, 167; energy concerns, 162; policy, 164–6; potential attack on Iran, 167; strategic deficit, 164
Iraq: deception, 153; decision making, 136–8, inadequate troop presence, 147–8, 155, pragmatic policy, 176, Running Start strategy, 140; democracy agenda, 177, 179, 193, meddling in Iraqi election, 180; Gulf War influence, 130; Hussein preoccupation as nuclear threat, 174–5; new surge strategy, 181, rejection of withdrawal, 181, timetable, 181–2; NSC focus on Iraq, 129–30; policy, 16–17, 75; postwar planning, 141–2, conflicting policy proposals, 142; post 9/11 foreign policy, 159, uncertain plans, 178; preparation for Iraq war, 131, 140, axis of evil strategy, 159, preemptive war strategy in Iraq, 131–6, 139, shock and awe, 143
Leave No Child Behind Act 2001, 89, 212
Middle East policy, 188, 190, 198, 211: against Hamas, 187; Israel/Palestine coexistence, 185; pro-Israel policy, 183–6; Syrian policy, 189
missile defense system, 81–2, 92
new kind warfare, 106–10, 117, 122, 210: admission of black sites, 112; domestic spy program, 113–16; interrogation guidelines, 110–11; wartime powers, 118, 121
9/11 response, xvii, 4, 14, 89–92, 99: lack of actionable intelligence, 99–100; mission against global terrorism, 123

North Korea: distaste for Kim Jong-Il, 171; policy, 171, diplomacy, 172–3, disarmament, 173; domestic reaction, 174
oil career, 29–31
Pakistan: policy, 191
personality conflicts on national security team, 101, 103
terrorist policy: coalition of coalitions, 93; lack of priority, 98–9
Texas Air National Guard, 6, 27, 29, 32, 34
Texas Rangers, 6, 20, 35–6, 44–6
toxic Texan, 102
war on terror strategy, 11, 13–16, 102, 104
War President, 3–5, 11, 14, 20, 197–8, 202, 204, 208–12: legacy, 200, 202, 206–10, 212, abuse of presidential powers, 211, domestic legacy, 212–13; regime change in Afghanistan, 197
see also neoconservatism; Personas
Bush, Jenna, 46
Bush, John Ellis, (Jeb), 24
Bush, Laura (First Lady), 8, 30, 33–4, 57, 63
Bush, Prescott (U.S. Senator, Connecticut), 23
Bush-Overbey Oil, 34

Card, Andrew (White House Chief of Staff, 2001–2004), 84, 89–90, 102, 116–17, 130–1, 136
Central Intelligence Agency
Afghanistan strategy, 101, 103
delay following Executive Order, 100
lack of intelligence presence in Iraq, 149, 153–4
post 9/11 strategy, 94–6
Rendition Group, 110: erroneous rendition, 112–13; rendition program, 112
secret flights, 112
secret prisons, 111
Chalabi, Ahmed (exile leader of Iraqi National Congress), 17, 126, 144, 146–8, 154–5, 178, 180, 193
election status, 180
Pentagon favored leader, 178
sovereignty now campaign, 147
Cheney, Dick (Vice President, 2001–)
foreign policy, 13, 75: Iran, military power, 168, oil concern, 162, policy, 167, 205, weapons of mass destruction, 166
Gulf War 1991, 125
9/11 response, 90
secrecy, xviii
vice president, xviii, 13–14, 72
war on terror policy, 15–17, 95: cakewalk victory, 147–8; presidential wartime powers, 115–16, 118, 121, 204; proponent of coercive techniques, 110, 120; wartime strategy, 106, 132
China
U.S. diplomacy, 78–81
Clarke, Richard (Coordinator, White House Counterterrorism Security Group), 91–2, 95, 98, 129

Clinton, Bill (President, 1993–2001)
China policy, 78–9
defense policy, 81–2, 84
domestic policy, 67
foreign policy, 85–6: removal of Hussein,
127; rendition program, 108–9
Iran: dual containment, 161; product boycott,
161
Iraq: U.S. efforts to free Iraq, 127–30
Middle East peace negotiations, 183
North Korea policy, 18: nuclear disarmament,
169
Curveball (Iraqi exile intelligence source), 152–3

Dae-jung, Kim (President of South Korea), 18, 84
sunshine policy, 170
Dole, Elizabeth (former Secretary of Labor)
2000 presidential GOP candidate, 55–7
Downing Street Memorandum, 137

Election 2000, 9, 51, 55, 58, 68, 85
Bush campaign strategy, 56–7, 59, 63, 65–6
candidate images, 61–3
debates, 64–5: domestic issues, 64; foreign
issues, 64–5
Florida ballot count, 66–7
Election 2004, 4, 8, 213

Forbes, Steve
2000 presidential GOP candidate, 56–7, 60
Foreign Affairs Reform and Restructuring Act
1998, 109
Foreign Intelligence Surveillance Act, 114–16
Franks, Tommy (General, Central Command),
94–5, 97, 99–103
Iraq invasion strategy, 140

Garner, Jay M., (retired General, head of Office
of Humanitarian and Reconstruction
Assistance), 145–6
Geneva Convention on Treatment Prisoners of
War 1950, 15–16, 106–8, 118, 120
Global Islamic insurgency, 93
Global War on Terror, 92
counterterrorism campaign, 132
Gonzales, Alberto R. (Attorney General,
2005–2007)
domestic spy program, 113, 116
Geneva Conventions, 108, 121
interrogation guidelines, 107
White House Counsel (2001–2005), 16
Gore, Albert (Vice President, 1993–2001)
presidential image, 62–3
2000 presidential race, 56, 59, 61, 64, 66
Groupthink, 104, 136, 151–3, 155, 204

Haas, Richard (U.S Department of State,
director of policy planning), 87
Hamas (Palestinian Islamic movement)
Fatah tensions, 188
opposition to Iraq war, 182
Parliament election victory 2006, 20
political engagement, 187: election victory, 187
Harken Energy, 32, 47
Hayden, Michael V. (General, director of
Central Intelligence Agency, 2006–)114
Hezbollah (Lebanese Islamic militia)
drive out Israeli force, 189
terrorism, 12, 18
war with Israel 2006, 20
Hussein, Saddam (President of Iraq), 4, 16, 64,
135
attempted assassination of G.H.W. Bush, 126
dismissal of U.N. inspectors, 127
fall of regime, 143–4
Gulf War 1991, xvii, 123–5
9/11 involvement, 129
1980 attack on Iran, 160
nuclear threat, 18–19, 124, 127, 133–4, 139,
149–51: non-threatening, 175

Iran (Islamic Republic of Iran), 3
Afghanistan: relations with, 162–3
nuclear capability, 18–19, 165–6
terrorist support, 93
U.S. relations, 160–3: American embassy
hostages, 160; Bush administration,
162, 164, lucrative oil sector, 162;
cooperation against Afghanistan, 164;
end of ally relationship, 163; potential
U.S. attack, 166
see also axis of evil
Iraq, ix, 3, 18
al Qaeda presence, 200–1
citizen uprising, 143, 145
democracy: election process, 179–80
internal conflict, 201: government dysfunction,
206–7
Iraq Liberation Act 1998, 127
jihadists, 4
Kurd Gulf War uprising, xvii, 125–6
9/11 responsibility, 125
1991 U.S. occupation, 125–6
postwar violence, 193
Shiite Gulf War uprising, xvii, 126
terrorist support, 93
U.S. military invasion 2003, 4, 14, 19,
126, 129–31: escalated violence level,
148; international opposition, 135–6;
postwar analysis, 141–2, 144–7; role of
Iraqi military, 141; shock and awe, 143;
start of war, 143; U.S. response, 207
weapons of mass destruction, 3–4, 17,
19, 126, 130–5: lack of U.S. nuclear
evidence, 150–1; restructure of nuclear
program, 152
see also axis of evil
Israel
war with Hezbollah 2006, 20

Joint Authorization for Use of Military Force
2001, 114
Joint Resolution to Use Force against Iraq 2002,
134

Jung Il, Kim (founder of Democratic People's
  Republic of Korea), 18, 170
  reaction to disarmament agreement, 174

Kagan, Robert, 127–8
  benevolent global hegemony, 127
Kahn, Mohammed Fahim (General, Northern
  Alliance Force), 96
Karzai, Hamid (President of Afghanistan), 97,
  103, 141, 163, 176, 199–200
  lack of Afghanistan control territory, 199
Khatami, Mohammad (President of the Islamic
  Republic of Iran), 161–2
  condemnation of 9/11, 163
Kristol, William, 80, 127–8, 172
  benevolent global hegemony, 127

al-Maliki, Nouri (Prime Minister, Republic of
  Iraq), 10–11
  cabinet turmoil, 200
  rejection of Bush timetable, 181
  selected prime minister, 180
Massoud, Ahmed Shah (General, Northern
  Alliance), 94
McCain, John (U.S. Senator, Arizona)
  2000 presidential GOP candidate, 56–7:
    presidential race strategy, 58–9; push
    polls, 59–60
Middle East
  influence of Islam, 92
  Islamic insurgency, 92, 103
  U.S. peace settlement, 87
Mubarak, Hosni (President of Egypt), 188
Musharraf, Pervez (General and President of
  Pakistan, 1999–), 20
  partnership with U.S., 192
  U.S. support of terrorism in Afghanistan, 191

Nader, Ralph (Green Party)
  2000 presidential race, 65–6
National Security Agency, 113
  domestic surveillance program, 115–17, 210
National Security Council, 13
  creation, 12
  Iraq meeting, 129
neoconservatism, 125–8
  U.S. policy recommendations, 128, 138
North Atlantic Treaty Organization (NATO), 199
North Korea (Democratic People's Republic of
  Korea), 3, 18, 84–5
  nuclear capability, 18–19, 168, 170–2:
    disarmament, 169, 173
  war, 168
Northern Alliance, 94–5
  Iranian support, 162

Olmert, Ehud (Prime Minister of Israel), 186
  criticism of handling Hezbollah war, 190
Omar, Mullah Mohammed (Taliban Supreme
  Leader), 93
One Percent Doctrine, 15–16, 106, 117–18
  see also Cheney, Dick

O'Neill, Paul H. (Treasury Secretary,
  2001–2002), 6, 13
  Iraq NSC meeting, 129

Pachachi, Adnan (Iraqi Governing Council
  member)
  State Department favored leader, 178
Pakistan (Islamic Republic of Pakistan), 20
  Afghanistan war, 16–17, 20, 95, 100, 162
  conflict war on terror and democracy goals,
    191–4
  nuclear weaponry, 106
  polls, 143
  rendition, 110
Patriot Act 2001, 14, 118
  formation, 105
  law enforcement: black bag sneak-and-peek,
    105; harboring terrorist, 105;
    money-laundering laws, 105;
    monitor Internet traffic, 105;
    roving wiretaps, 105; spy, 105
Pentagon
  Bush National Guard records, 27
  delayed boots on ground in Afghanistan, 100,
    102, 104
  9/11 attack, xvii, 14, 90, 100
  Office of Special Plans, 12
  post Iraq war plans, 146
  secret detention policy, 120
  torture standards, 120
  treatment of prisoners of war, 118
Persian Gulf War 1991, xviii, 18–19, 123–5
  postwar defense strategy, 126
Personas, 5–11, 197
  Bombastic Bushkin, 5–6, 28, 37, 45, 148, 175
  Machiavellian Politico, 5–6, 8, 209
  Righteous Hawk, 5, 8–10, 137, 165, 175,
    194, 197, 211, 213
Petraeus, David (Commanding General, Multi-
  Nation Force—Iraq), 203
  report to Congress, 205–8
Powell, Colin L. (Secretary of State, 2001–2005)
  career, 73, 75–7
  China spy plane crisis, 79–81
  defense policy, 82
  foreign policy, 84–5: Iraq, case against
    Hussein, 149–50, disarmament, 134–6,
    inadequate troop presence, 149, isolation
    from Iraq war plan, 136, objection
    to Iraq occupation, 144; Middle East
    policy, 184; North Korea policy, 171–2
  Joint Chiefs of Staff, 12, 55
  Secretary of State, 4, 13, 18, 86
  treatment of detainees, 107
  war on terror policy, 95, 129: Geneva
    Convention reaction, 107
  in White House "icebox", xviii, 137
Putin, Vladimir (President of Russian
  Federation), 10, 82–3, 88

Quayle, Dan (former Vice President)
  2000 presidential GOP candidate, 56–7

Reagan, Ronald (President, 1981–1989), 5
  evil empire rhetoric, 159
  rendition programs, 109
  support of Hussein regime, 160
Rice, Condoleezza (Secretary of State, 2005–)
  National Security Advisor (2001–2005), 13,
    15, 71, 75, 86: foreign policy, 54, 83,
    98, 101; Iraq policy, 17, 20, 135, 162,
    205, Bush diplomatic approval, 168,
    175, 177, restructuring of Iraq, 147;
    Middle East policy: against Hamas
    leadership, 187, Syrian policy, 190; 9/11
    response, 90, 98–9; North Korea policy,
    173
  political career, 73, 85
Richards, Ann (Governor of Texas), 42, 52
  first term, 41
  reelection campaign 1994, 44, 47–8
Rove, Karl, 6–8
  Bush political consultant, 44, 46–8, 52–4,
    56–7, 63, 67, 213
  national College Republicans, 38
  9/11 response, 89
  political consultant career, 38–43, 49–50
  political tactics, 39–43, 52, 58–60
Rumsfeld, Donald (Secretary of Defense,
    2001–2006)
  controlling administrative style, 139–40
  counter-resistance techniques, 119
  defense policy, 82
  foreign policy, 101–2
  interagency leadership, 103
  leaves Department of Defense, 175
  9/11 response, 90
  Secretary of Defense, 13, 71
  Torture Memo, 119
  war on terror policy, 16, 95, 97, 100, 103,
    129: dismissal from Iraq reconstruction
    lead role, 147; Iraq agenda, 129

Saudi Arabia (Kingdom of Saudi Arabia)
  Khobar Towers terrorist attack 1996, 15
Scheuer, Michael (head of CIA Osama bin
    Laden unit), 92, 95, 97
  rendition program, 108–9
Scowcroft, Brent (National Security Adviser,
    1989–1993), 73, 78, 125, 132, 184
September 11, 2001 terrorist attacks
  Pennsylvania hijacked plane crash, 90
  Pentagon attack, 90
  World Trade Center attack, xvii, 3, 9, 13–14,
    100, 177
Sharon, Ariel (Prime Minister of Israel), 87,
    183–7, 194
  Bush ally, 183–4
  disengagement plan, 186

  isolation of Arafat, 185
South Korea (Republic of Korea)
  North Korean nuclear target, 168
  weapons of mass destruction development, 168
Spectrum 7, 31–2
Syria (Syrian Arab Republic), 93
  occupation of Lebanon, 189

Taliban (Islamic rulers of Afghanistan)
  Afghanistan presence, 101, 129, 198
  drug influence, 97, 199
  9/11 attacks, xvii, 3, 93
  prisoners of war, 108, 119–20
  terrorists, 9, 20
  U.S. target, 96–7
Tehran
  drive for nuclear power, 176
Tenet, George (CIA Director, 1997–2004)
  defense of CIA intelligence flap, 152
  leadership career, 74–5
  9/11 failure, 13
  9/11 response, 91–2, 94, 98
  war on terror policy, 16, 101: intelligence, 106,
    109; isolation from Iraq war plan, 136
Tora Bora battle, 16
Torture Convention 1984, 119

U.N. Security Council, 4, 20
  disarmament resolution, 133–4
  1991 Gulf War resolution, 132

War on Terror, 16
  black sites, 111
  interrogation, 15, 106, 110, 120
  rendition, 108–9
  torture, 106, 110–11, 119: sleep deprivation,
    106; stress factors, 106; use of phobias,
    106; water-boarding, 110, 112
White House, 5
  Bush administration secrecy, xvii
  interagency deliberations, 155
  Oval Office, 5, 9, 11
  self-delusion, 148
  White House Iraq Group, 131, 151
Wilkerson, Lawrence B. (former Chief of
    Staff to Secretary of State Colin Powell,
    2002–2005), 120
Wolfowitz, Paul D. (Deputy Secretary of
    Defense, 2001–2005)
  advocate of Iraq war, 125: Iraq agenda,
    129–30, 135; 1991 U.S. conflict with
    Iraq, 126
  political career, 76–7
  ties with Chalabi, 17

Zapata Off-Shore, 24